Essential Skills in Family Therapy

From the First Interview to Termination

THIRD EDITION

Wenu Lareo

Printed in the United States of America

Library of Congress Cataloging-in-Publication Data

Names: Patterson, JoEllen.
Title: Essential skills in family therapy : from the first interview to
termination / JoEllen Patterson and [4 others].

Revision of: Essential skills in family therapy / JoEllen Patterson . . .
[et al.] ; foreword by Douglas H. Sprenkle. 2009. 2nd ed. | Includes
bibliographical references and index.

ISBN 9798858519249 Paperback

Subjects: LCSH: Family psychotherapy. | Family psychotherapy—Practice. |
BISAC: PSYCHOLOGY / Psychotherapy / Couples & Family. | MEDICAL /
Psychiatry / General. | SOCIAL SCIENCE / Social Work. | RELIGION /
Counseling.

Also Available

*Clinician's Guide to Research Methods
in Family Therapy: Foundations of Evidence-Based Practice*
Lee Williams, JoEllen Patterson, and Todd M. Edwards

*Essential Assessment Skills
for Couple and Family Therapists*
Lee Williams, Todd M. Edwards, JoEllen Patterson,
and Larry Chamow

*The Therapist's Guide to Psychopharmacology,
Revised Edition: Working with Patients, Families,
and Physicians to Optimize Care*
JoEllen Patterson, A. Ari Albala, Margaret E. McCahill,
and Todd M. Edwards

In memory of George Sargent, PhD,
our friend, mentor, and colleague

About the Authors

JoEllen Patterson, PhD, is Professor of Marital and Family Therapy at the University of San Diego and Associate Clinical Professor in the Department of Family Medicine and Public Health, Division of Global Health, and the Department of Psychiatry at the University of California, San Diego. She is on the editorial boards of five journals focused on families and has published five books. Dr. Patterson has written books and articles on family therapy training and the integration of mental health services into primary care. In addition, she has received Fulbright Awards to work in Hong Kong, New Zealand, and Norway.

Lee Williams, PhD, is Professor of Marital and Family Therapy at the University of San Diego. He is a Clinical Fellow and Approved Supervisor in the American Association for Marriage and Family Therapy and does couple therapy with veterans at the VA San Diego Medical Center. His research and publications have focused primarily on marriage preparation, couples with religious differences, and family therapy training.

Todd M. Edwards, PhD, is Professor and Director of the Marital and Family Therapy Program at the University of San Diego. He is a Clinical Fellow and Approved Supervisor in the American Association for Marriage and Family Therapy and Voluntary Assistant Clinical Professor in the Department of Family Medicine and Public Health at the University of California, San Diego. Dr. Edwards's primary research interests are family therapy training and supervision, integrative family therapy, and friendship in adulthood.

Larry Chamow, PhD, is Clinical Professor of Marital and Family Therapy at the University of San Diego and is in full-time private practice at the Pacific Family Institute in Carlsbad, California. He is a Clinical Fellow and Approved Supervisor in the American Association for Marriage and Family Therapy. Dr. Chamow's interests and publications focus on couple therapy, supervision, the self of the therapist, and family businesses.

Claudia Grauf-Grounds, PhD, is Professor of Marriage and Family Therapy at Seattle Pacific University and served as a clinical faculty member at the University of Washington School of Medicine for over 10 years. She conducts research, publishes, and presents on family therapy training, supervision, and collaborative healthcare models that embrace spirituality. Dr. Grauf-Grounds is a Clinical Fellow and Approved Supervisor in the American Association for Marriage and Family Therapy. Honored as Supervisor of the Year by the Washington Association for Marriage and Family Therapy, she enjoys mentoring the next generation of psychotherapists, pastors, and physicians.

Preface

Almost 20 years ago, we wrote *Essential Skills in Family Therapy* for our students at the University of San Diego (USD). We hoped that other family therapy students would find the information in it useful, but we wrote the book as if it were a personal letter to our students. Our letter attempted to answer the questions our students asked most frequently and also to answer some questions we thought they wanted to ask. For example, our students commonly reported feeling inadequate during the first few months of their clinical work. Other students had concerns about loyalty. If they found value in an individual treatment model, could they still be family therapists? As they advanced in their training, their questions became more complex. For example, they wondered how to balance individual, couple, and family assessment. They considered the impact of psychotropic medications on their clients and how they could coordinate care with physicians. More recently, our students have been interested in the role of neurobiology and genetics in their work as family therapists.

A strength and a weakness of our program has been that USD does not have its own training clinic. Thus, from their first clinical days, our students see clients in community settings where the focus is on expedient, cost-effective treatments. In addition, our students work with a variety of professionals including physicians, attorneys, school counselors, teachers, and other mental health professionals. While we struggle with gently easing our students into their roles as therapists, we also recognize that the community clinics' focus on results translates into a training emphasis at USD on what works, regardless of the treatments' origins.

Together, the USD faculty has developed some core beliefs that have guided our program. Following the tenets of George Engel, we believe a biopsychosocial perspective should guide our work, while placing particular emphasis on systemic thinking. In addition, we believe our primary goal is to help individual clients and their families, and we are open to all ideas, procedures, treatments, and models that help us achieve that goal. Finally, regardless of the treatment, we believe clients are strengthened when therapists can enlist family members in caring for each other. These tenets have continued to guide our work for the last 20 years.

Essential Skills in Family Therapy reflects the USD program's focus on students, its pragmatic approach to treatment, its regard for multidisciplinary perspectives, and its respect for the influence of families on clients. Since we wrote the first two editions, these beliefs have guided us, and we've simultaneously evolved. This third edition reflects the new influences that have begun to shape our teaching and our clinical work. We've tried to mention most of the significant, new influences on our work. But we found that putting all of the new information in one book that is meant to be a concise introduction became untenable. Thus, we've written three other books for The Guilford Press that we hope augment the core ideas introduced in this volume: *The Therapist's Guide to Psychopharmacology* discusses strategies for providing cotreatment with physicians and highlights the importance of families in medication decision making and involvement in treatment. In addition, we wrote *Essential Assessment Skills for Couple and Family Therapists* and the *Clinician's Guide to Research Methods in Family Therapy*. These books build and expand upon the ideas found in *Essential Skills*, our first book.

Chapter 1 identifies concerns that new therapists frequently have, such as building confidence in their clinical work. The rest of the book is devoted to helping a beginning therapist develop a clear understanding of clinical issues and an ability to apply therapeutic skills. Chapters 2–6 follow the usual time sequence of therapy—from initial contact with clients, to comprehensive assessment, to treatment planning and intervention. Mental health skills needed by all therapists are intertwined with family therapy knowledge. Our goal here is to provide beginning therapists with the tools for thinking about clinical issues, rather than merely applying an approach propounded by their instructors.

Chapters 7–10 deal with specific clinical situations based on presenting problems and the nature of client families. We examine major issues and approaches for working with children and adolescents, older adults, couples, and families that are struggling with serious mental illness.

Chapter 11 highlights some common obstacles all therapists encounter, and provides concrete ideas on how to get unstuck when treatment is not progressing. Chapter 12 focuses on an often overlooked part of therapy: termination. In Chapter 13, we conclude the book by looking at emerging issues within family therapy. We believe beginning therapists should pay attention to these emerging themes so they can continue to grow along with the field in providing clients the best possible care.

During the past 20 years, we have been heartened to learn that students in the United States and abroad have found this book both practical and clear. Our goal has been to condense the many ideas and models that we've learned into a succinct practical guide. We hope that the third edition of *Essential Skills* reflects our purpose.

Acknowledgments

This book is a joint effort of the authors and reflects conversations we have had at the University of San Diego over the last 20 years. Our editor at The Guilford Press, Jim Nageotte, inspired us to share our best ideas. Caroline Thompson, Alicia Joseph, Julius Espiritu, Nicole Goren, and Shelby Bambino, our graduate assistants/editors/reviewers, kept us on track and attended to the many details that we might have overlooked. Our students continue to challenge us to find new ways to teach family therapy. Finally, we are most grateful to our own families and the inspiration they provide for our work.

Contents

CHAPTER 1. The Beginning Family Therapist: 1
Taking On the Challenge

Getting Started   4
Managing Anxiety and Issues of Confidence   4
Stages of Therapist Development   6
Obsessing about Clinical Work   9
Dealing with Burnout   9
Conclusion   11

CHAPTER 2. Before the Initial Interview   12

Dealing with Families' Expectations and Anxieties
about Therapy   12
Suggestions for Initial Contact with the Client   14
What Information Should Be Obtained?   16
Who Should Come to Therapy?   17
Initial Hypothesizing   21
Conclusion   22

CHAPTER 3. The Initial Interview   24

Stages of the Initial Interview   24
Developing a Connection: How to Join
with Clients   25
Handling Administrative Issues   27
Defining Client Expectations for Therapy   33
Assessing and Building Motivation   37

Establishing Credibility 40
Conclusion: The First Session and Beyond 42

CHAPTER 4.   Guidelines for Conducting Assessment   43

Initial Assessment 45
Potential Issues of Harm 47
Assessing for Substance Abuse 58
Assessing for Biological
     and Neurological Factors 60
Psychological Assessment 64
Social Assessment 66
Spiritual Assessment 72
Assessing Social Systems Outside the Family 73
Assessing Larger Systems: Context, Gender,
     and Culture 74
Conclusion 77

CHAPTER 5.   Developing a Treatment Focus   78
             and Treatment Plan

Four Obstacles to Developing a Treatment Focus 79
Building a Conceptual Map Using Theory
     and Research 81
Components of a Treatment Plan 86
Evaluating the Effectiveness of Treatment 99
Conclusion 100

CHAPTER 6.   Basic Treatment Skills and Interventions   102

The Rush to Intervention versus Developing
     a Relationship 102
Basic Counseling Skills 105
Skills Unique to the Systemic/
     Relational Therapist 114
Becoming More Sophisticated
     in Using Interventions 122
Conclusion 123

CHAPTER 7.   Working with Families and Children   125

Assessment of Children and Adolescents 126
Emerging Resources for Treating Children
     and Adolescents 128
The Family Life Cycle Revisited 130
Variations in Family Development 149
Conclusion 156

CHAPTER 8. Working with Older Adults   157
and Their Caregivers

Assessment and Treatment of Older Adults   158
Family Caregiving   165
Conclusion   175

CHAPTER 9. Working with Couples   176

Keys to Providing Solid Couple Therapy   177
Special Topics   191
When Couple Therapy Might Not Work   205
Conclusion   206

CHAPTER 10. When a Family Member Has a Mental Illness   207

Individual and Family Concepts   208
Individual Diagnosis in a Family Context   212
Depression   217
Anxiety   222
Alcoholism and Drug Abuse   226
Impulse Disorders and
  Neurodevelopmental Disorders   231
Conclusion   234

CHAPTER 11. Getting Unstuck in Therapy   235

Understanding Clients' Ambivalence
  about Change   236
Therapist–Client Agenda and Timing
  Mismatch   238
Matching Level of Directness to the Client   239
The Therapist's Reluctance to Intervene   239
Therapists' Lack of Conceptual Clarity   240
Change and Acceptance   241
Countertransference: How Therapist
  Issues Interfere   242
Dealing with Cancellations and No-Shows   245
Difficulty Getting Other Family Members
  to Therapy   247
Handling Secrets   248
Dealing with Clients We Dislike   249
How Agencies Contribute to Being Stuck   251
Supervision   254
Self-Supervision Questions   256
Getting Unstuck Using Research and Literature   256
Conclusion   261

CHAPTER 12. Termination   262

Mutual Terminations   263
Therapist Terminations   269
Client Terminations   271
Conclusion   274

CHAPTER 13. Family Therapy in the Future   275

Pertinent Issues for Beginning Clinicians   276
Healthcare Reform: Implications for You
    and Your Clients   277
Emerging Trends in Treatment   282
Benefits and Liabilities of Being a Therapist   290
The Personal and Professional Journey
    of Being a Therapist   290
Conclusion   292

APPENDIX.   Screening Instruments   293

Mood Disorders   293
Anxiety Disorders   293
Impulse Control Disorders   293
Addictive Behaviors   294
Eating Disorders   294
Trauma   294
Psychosis   294
Family Measures   295
Couple Measures   295
Somatization   295
Personality Disorders   295
Spirituality   295

References   297

Index   319

CHAPTER 1

The Beginning Family Therapist

TAKING ON THE CHALLENGE

Tom is handed the intake paperwork for his first client at his new practicum site. Both excited and anxious, he scans the information. In the section "Primary Reason for Coming to Therapy," the client has written, "Need ways to cope with my husband's drinking and his hitting the children." Tom grows more apprehensive as he wonders where to start. Should he simply listen to the woman's story as it unfolds? Or should he take a more direct approach and immediately assess for a substance abuse problem? Still another focus is the indication of child abuse. Perhaps this very serious matter takes precedence over every other issue.

Sally reviews today's back-to-back schedule and wonders if she will make it through the day. After learning yesterday that her father has cancer and is likely to die within the year, she tossed and turned all night. Exhausted but wanting to do a good job with her clients, she begins thinking about her first client family that day. The Joneses have an 8-year-old son with a multitude of problems: leukemia and attention-deficit/hyperactivity disorder (ADHD), to name two. He has been referred by the family's physician "to develop coping skills." For a fleeting moment, Sally wonders if the pain she feels about her father will affect her therapy today, but she does not have much time to reflect on this question because her first session starts in 5 minutes.

Ann winces as she recalls her group supervision session yesterday. She had thought the videotaped session of her work with Mrs. Thomas showed what excellent joining skills she had. It would be clear to her supervisor and her fellow students that Mrs. Thomas liked therapy and took Ann's suggestions very seriously. But instead of focusing on the therapist–client rapport, the group had overwhelmed Ann with assessment questions she had not even considered. How was Mrs. Thomas's divorce connected to her depression? Did Ann think her late-night alcohol use reflected a substance abuse problem? Were Mrs. Thomas's children being neglected because she had little energy or time for parenting? What should Ann's level of involvement be in helping Mrs. Thomas find a job? Ann wondered if she had the necessary qualities to even be the therapist when she had so clearly missed important assessment questions for her client.

Most beginning therapists experience a host of anxious feelings when they start clinical work (Skovholt & Rønnestad, 2003). They are aware of their inadequacies more than their strengths, and need help to learn how to acquire the skills, knowledge, and sense of competency necessary to do good clinical work.

Many therapists complete the didactic part of their training with a sense of mastery and competence. After all, by the time they enter graduate school, the life of a student is very familiar, and they are accustomed to academic achievement in their course work. Academic accomplishments, however, do not necessarily translate easily into therapeutic competence. Faculty and students are left wondering how best to impart and acquire, respectively, the skills basic to clinical work.

The gap between academic work and the implementation of techniques or the application of theories in clinical sessions can seem huge. After a year of intense academic instruction, students often begin their clinical work with unstated questions:

"What am I supposed to say to the client?"

"How do I handle situation X?"

"What should happen after I complete the intake form?"

"Can clients tell I'm new at this and feeling completely inadequate and overwhelmed?"

"How do I keep all the information from the session clear and how do I know what is most important?"

"If I don't use a powerful intervention or technique during the first couple of sessions, am I a failure?"

"I know I should have a theory for this case, but I just don't understand how to apply information from my theories class to this acting-out adolescent and her hostile mother."

What students need is a way to develop their skills as therapists as they begin their clinical work. This book provides practical "how to" guidelines on essential therapeutic skills from thorough assessment to careful treatment planning, from the nuts and bolts of specific interventions to the nuances of establishing therapeutic relationships and troubleshooting when treatment gets "stuck."

Reflecting the trend toward integrative approaches in family therapy, mental health, and the medical field, we stress a biopsychosocial view of assessment and treatment. This perspective provides the clinician with an effective and comprehensive framework for addressing the broad issues that clients can present in therapy. Thus, while family interaction remains a focus of attention herein, our goal is to prepare beginning therapists to integrate information and skills from other areas as well to best meet the needs of diverse client families.

The ability to integrate family therapy theory and interventions with individual diagnosis and treatment will be especially valuable as therapists begin their careers. While family therapy offers a unique and important perspective in clinical work, much of what goes on in treatment shares common assumptions with all therapies. Certain clinical skills—for example, assessing for suicide risk or substance abuse, making an effective referral—are intrinsic to any good therapy. This book goes beyond the boundaries of traditional family therapy to be as inclusive as possible regarding essential clinical skills.

Frequently, beginning family therapy students make treatment decisions based on their supervisors' favorite theoretical orientation or the specific theoretical approach predominant in their clinic. We believe that assessing the appropriateness of a family therapy treatment for a specific problem is an essential clinical skill. It is important to be able to recognize when a problem is outside the scope of a family therapist's practice (or skill level) and could best be treated by another mental health professional or in tandem with another healthcare professional.

Indeed, research on biological etiologies of mental illness and psychopharmacology suggests that therapists must be conversant with more than "talk therapies." A growing focus on treatment teams and multidisciplinary treatment approaches means that therapists must increasingly attend to the biological component of the biopsychosocial model and learn to collaborate with other healthcare professionals. A knowledge base in medication management and the ability to consult with physicians is one aspect of this multidisciplinary approach.

While the bulk of this book discusses specific processes and skills that are important throughout the therapeutic journey, we devote the first chapter to that most basic of concerns for the beginning therapist: understanding and managing beginners' jitters.

GETTING STARTED

"It was my first session with a client and my heart was racing. I had no idea what to do with this family, and I wasn't really sure if they knew why they were all there. I was talking with the mother, who requested the appointment, to find out how much the other family members knew about why they came in when I realized that I didn't really like this lady."

This story, shared by a practicum student, encompasses two essential and pressing issues shared by most beginning therapists. One revolves around the question "What do I do?" and the other involves managing one's own feelings and reactions to diverse clients and clinical situations.

Learning the art and science of doing therapy is a challenging task, particularly when first seeing clients. Beginning therapists frequently experience feelings of inadequacy and insecurity about their clinical abilities (e.g., Bischoff & Barton, 2002; Bischoff, Barton, Thober, & Hawley, 2002; Watkins, 2012; Woodside, Oberman, Cole, & Carruth, 2007). They fear that they will not be able to help their clients because of their inexperience. They may even fear that they will directly harm their clients or cause their conditions to deteriorate because of clinical mistakes. A few doubt their talent and ability as therapists to the extent that they seriously question whether to remain in the field.

Therapists and supervisors alike need to see confidence issues from a developmental perspective (Bischoff & Barton, 2002). Given their lack of clinical experience, it is only natural that beginning therapists question their competence. In fact, as supervisors, we worry more about beginning therapists who seem extremely confident in their abilities. These individuals underestimate the complexity and difficulty of learning to do therapy well.

MANAGING ANXIETY AND ISSUES OF CONFIDENCE

How does the beginning therapist deal with a lack of confidence, or with feeling overwhelmed and anxious? First, therapists must recognize that these feelings are completely normal. Learning to do something as complicated as therapy can be difficult, especially in the beginning. Paradoxically, the more one learns about how to do therapy, the more one realizes how much one doesn't know. This paradox can feed an individual's insecurity about being a therapist. In fact, it is not uncommon for students to question whether they have what it takes to be a therapist (Watkins, 2012). Beginning therapists may interpret feelings of being overwhelmed as a possible sign that they are not cut out to be therapists, which only serves to fuel their anxiety and insecurity. Although the intensity of these feelings and the ways of coping will vary from therapist to therapist, every beginning therapist struggles to some degree with these feelings.

Second, beginning therapists need to share their insecurities with other therapists and supervisors. Unfortunately, it is fear of being incompetent or a failure that prevents beginning therapists from sharing their struggles with others. When a therapist does take the risk and shares his or her fears with peers, others will typically disclose similar worries. This disclosure helps the beginning therapist to accept that these struggles are developmentally appropriate rather than a sign of being unsuited for the profession (Bischoff et al., 2002). Supervisors can also provide reassurance that anxiety and lack of confidence are expected and normal at this stage of development.

Third, it is crucial to realize that the therapist–client relationship is inherently therapeutic. A therapist doesn't need to *do* something for clients to have a positive experience. This is very reassuring to most beginning therapists because they generally have confidence in their relational skills. When beginning therapists are instructed as to the importance of joining and empathically listening to their clients, most therapists are relieved, feeling "I can do that!"

Fourth, beginning therapists need to recognize that their early experiences in seeing clients often involve a steep learning curve, like any other new job. In the first few months, you will be doing a number of things for the first time. It is natural to be anxious doing something the first time because you are uncertain if you are doing it right. However, you will feel more confident doing something once you have done it multiple times. For example, you will be less anxious doing an intake with a family if you have two or three intakes "under your belt." It takes time, however, to gain enough experience so that many situations become familiar.

Finally, beginning therapists should examine if distorted cognitions or unrealistic expectations are contributing to their fears or struggles with confidence. Beginning therapists can struggle with perfectionistic tendencies or critical self-talk (Hill, Sullivan, Knox, & Schlosser, 2007), which may need to be challenged. Theo was hard on himself as a beginning therapist, and even questioned if it was ethical for him to treat many of his clients given his inexperience. He frequently thought that his clients would be better served by working with more experienced therapists. However, one day Theo recognized that the experienced therapists he thought his clients should be working with were once beginning therapists too. The only pathway to becoming an experienced therapist was to go through the learning process that he was going through. It was reassuring for him to know that even famous therapists like Salvador Minuchin or Virginia Satir were inexperienced therapists at one time too. A good battery of constructive thoughts and images goes a long way toward soothing beginners' jitters.

Many beginning therapists wonder at what point they will stop struggling with issues of confidence. Experienced clinicians indicated that after 5–7 years (or about 5,000–7,000 hours) of clinical experience, they had encountered most clinical issues or problems several times. As a result, they felt very secure or confident in their abilities as therapists.

Fortunately, therapists don't need to complete 5,000–7,000 hours of work to see a notable improvement in their confidence. Even in the first year of seeing clients, beginning therapists will see their confidence increase (Bischoff & Barton, 2002). The intense feelings of anxiety and being overwhelmed that are common in the beginning generally subside after 1–3 months of seeing clients. Beginning therapists also become less fearful that they will do something to directly harm their clients, although they continue to struggle with feelings of being ineffective or unhelpful.

When therapists have reached about 500–700 hours of clinical experience, they have achieved another milestone in therapist confidence. By this point in time, therapists have experienced enough clinical successes that they are beginning to develop some initial confidence in their abilities to help clients. At this level of experience, beginning therapists generally report greater ability in conceptualizing cases. They often know what needs to be changed, yet are sometimes unsure of how to intervene to bring about that change.

Most therapists will have confidence in their overall abilities by the time they have had 1,000–1,500 hours of clinical experience. At this point, they are better at conceptualizing cases and have also developed a repertoire of effective interventions. Of course, therapists can still experience periodic doubts about their abilities, particularly when struggling with difficult cases or issues. Issues of confidence may also reemerge if therapists start working with new and unfamiliar populations. However, most therapists at this stage are no longer plagued by significant doubts about their clinical ability.

STAGES OF THERAPIST DEVELOPMENT

McCollum (1990) notes that therapists trained in individual therapy generally go through three stages of development when learning to do family therapy. In the first stage, they focus on acquiring the skills necessary to work with families. In the second stage, they learn to apply systemic theory to their clinical work, and in the third, "self of the therapist" stage, they focus on more personal issues in relationship to their clinical work, such as exploring how their family-of-origin experiences affect their work with families.

Although McCollum's observations were based on teaching experienced therapists to do family therapy, these stages also apply to individuals learning family therapy without prior clinical experience. In essence, the initial skills stage is characterized by the therapist trying to figure out what to do with clients. This focus then shifts in the theory stage to how to think. In the final stage, the therapist focuses on the use of self in being with a family.

Although each stage has a particular emphasis, all three may overlap from time to time. While developmental stages are differentiated by time and experience, other factors can bring any or all of their foci to the forefront—particular client families and clinical issues, the emphasis of a certain supervisor or training program, and the abiding interests of the therapist, among others.

Stage One: Learning Essential Skills

Before therapists start their clinical work, they often experience a mixture of feelings. Most report an excitement at finally beginning to "do" therapy, and some even express impatience to see clients. They are eager to apply what they have learned in their classes by working with people in therapy. However, the predominant emotion that most therapists report before seeing their first client is significant anxiety.

It is natural for therapists to have these worries before they see their first client and even after they begin to work. Beginning therapists report feeling overwhelmed by the experience. Many report going home after seeing clients and crying, while others report that the stress results in headaches, difficulty sleeping, stomachaches, or changes in appetite.

This early stage is a time for beginners to learn and practice basic skills. Learning to relax and be present in the therapy room with clients is a good place to start. A solid assessment and effective treatment hinge on the therapist's ability to listen and attend to the client's story, and to show the client that he or she is understood. Beginners can learn to replace their anxiety about "doing something" with relaxed curiosity and empathy. This approach leads to useful questions and inquiries, which is where therapy begins.

Stage Two: Learning to Conceptualize Cases

Beginning therapists soon recognize that the therapeutic relationship is a necessary but not always sufficient ingredient for change. They no longer are content simply to be with their clients; they realize that some clients need concrete ideas or suggestions for change. At the same time, therapists also become aware that to be effective, interventions must be rooted in a clear understanding of family dynamics. As a result, therapists soon move into a second stage, where emphasis is placed on conceptualizing what is happening in their cases.

Learning to conceptualize cases can be difficult and frustrating. In this stage, therapists frequently struggle with issues such as the following:

> "How do I know what is the most important information to attend to in a case?"
>
> "My clients keep coming in with a different problem each week. How do I figure out what to focus on?"
>
> "I know I should have a theory for this case, but I'm not sure what theory would 'work' here."
>
> "I thought I knew what we should be working on last week, but now I'm confused again."
>
> "I know I should be focusing on the process, but I feel like I'm stuck in the content."

Typically, beginning therapists are able to develop good insights and hypotheses, but will have difficulty connecting these pieces together into a coherent picture or treatment plan. Gradually, there will be moments of clarity when the pieces fit together. With the passage of time, these moments begin to last longer than the periods of haze and confusion.

Early in the second stage, many therapists find it helpful to adopt a particular theoretical orientation for conceptualizing cases (McCollum, 1990). As they gain intensive experience with one theoretical framework, they begin to recognize its limitations and may try others. As therapists explore different theories, they eventually develop their own framework, integrating the best parts of the different orientations that they have adopted.

Stage Three: The Therapist-as-Self

As therapists become more skilled at and comfortable with conceptualizing cases, they shift more of their focus to looking at themselves in therapy. There is a growing recognition that the self of the therapist can greatly influence therapy, and beginning family therapists gradually become more interested in identifying their unique contributions to the therapeutic encounter.

During this stage, therapists will often explore how the therapist-as-self is both an asset and a liability in therapy. Many of our personal experiences can become catalysts for new ideas and understanding in therapeutic work. For example, a therapist who has been able to successfully develop an adult-to-adult relationship with his or her parents may use that personal experience in working with clients who are struggling with issues of differentiation. Specific life experiences—trauma, parenthood, separation, illness—may all come into play in a way that benefits therapeutic work.

However, therapists' unresolved issues or "growth areas" can become impediments in therapy. Therefore, some therapists choose to explore their personal issues more closely at this stage, often by seeking therapy for themselves. The growth and insight derived from working on these issues can provide the perspective necessary to make constructive use of life experiences in therapy.

OBSESSING ABOUT CLINICAL WORK

Many beginning therapists report that they cannot stop thinking about therapy or their clients. In fact, thinking about clients seems to fill every waking moment and even many nonwaking moments. It is not unusual for beginning therapists to report having dreams about their clients or about doing therapy.

Learning to do anything new, particularly something as challenging as therapy, can easily consume much of one's time, attention, and energy. Furthermore, most people who choose therapy as a profession have a deep compassion and concern for people. It is often difficult not to think about clients, particularly when they are in considerable pain or distress.

Thinking (or even obsessing) about clients is something that tends to subside with time and experience. Most experienced therapists report thinking very little about their clients outside the therapy hour. One reason for this change is that the therapist gradually gains a greater sense of clinical mastery by virtue of experience. In addition, therapists learn to balance objectivity and emotional involvement with clients. In a sense, therapists learn how to construct an emotional boundary (Skovholt & Rønnestad, 2003). If the boundary becomes too diffuse, the therapist may be overwhelmed and inducted into the family system. If it is too rigid, he or she may lack the empathy necessary to adequately understand the issues and join with the family. The former problem is characteristic of beginning therapists, who, with time, learn to better regulate this boundary.

DEALING WITH BURNOUT

At first glance, one would not anticipate that someone who is just beginning a career as a family therapist would experience feelings of burnout. Yet many beginning therapists experience some degree of burnout during their clinical training. It is not uncommon for individuals struggling with burnout even to question whether they want to continue their careers as therapists. The potential for burnout among beginning therapists exists because of several factors.

First, learning to do therapy can be demanding. As noted above, beginning therapists may be constantly thinking about their clients, making it difficult to get a mental break from their clinical work. Also, worrying about one's competence as a beginning therapist can diminish some of the enjoyment of doing therapy (Edwards & Patterson, 2012).

Second, therapists have other stressors outside of their clinical work. For example, you may have other classes, comprehensive exams, or a master's or doctoral thesis to complete as part of your training program. You may need to work to pay for school or living expenses, or may have a family or partner who needs your time and energy. You may experience considerable stress from trying to successfully meet all these commitments.

Third, the courses or clinical work may raise personal issues for you as you learn to do therapy. Insights gained from clinical training inevitably lead student therapists to reexamine their own lives and families. Although this process can become the catalyst for significant personal growth, it can also place one more additional demand on the beginning therapist.

In order to avoid burnout, practicing good self-care is essential (Norcross & Guy, 2007). For example, you need to build in time for "recharging your batteries." Individuals who are faced with extreme time demands often put off taking personal time to do this. Taking time for yourself seems counterintuitive when faced with an overwhelming number of tasks to accomplish, but the time lost is often made up by being able to work with renewed energy and efficiency. Ironically, many therapists are willing to give this advice to their clients but have difficulty following it themselves.

Being willing to set limits is another important tool to avoid burnout. Beginning therapists often report setting their client schedule based largely on the convenience of their clients. In some cases, beginning therapists come in 5 days a week even though their caseload requires only 3 or 4 days. As therapists gain experience, they often will become more willing to set some limits on their availability, giving them some protected time for themselves.

You also need a strong social support network. Many of us owe our families a great deal of credit for the emotional and financial support they provided during our training. Being with family and friends outside the field will allow you to temporarily escape the demands of being a beginning therapist. Yet, you also need support from those within the field who understand the unique stressors that come with being a therapist. You will find that connecting and obtaining support from your peers within your program is invaluable (Edwards & Patterson, 2012). Both experienced and inexperienced therapists need colleagues with whom they can share clinical experiences to avoid burnout.

CONCLUSION

This chapter has identified some of the common challenges that beginning therapists encounter early in their careers. While dealing with these challenges, it's important to keep the "big picture" in mind and recall the benefits of being a therapist. Learning to do therapy can be a strong catalyst for personal growth. What one learns about helping other families can be applied to one's own life and family, making it more enriching. As a therapist, you will be privileged to witness deeply moving moments of courage and compassion on the part of your clients. It is rewarding to see individuals create more fulfilling lives, knowing that we contributed in part to this growth or change. Often the clients whom we struggle the most to help are the ones who give us the greatest sense of fulfillment when they actually do succeed in changing. As you move through the rough spots, it can be helpful to keep the following "reminders" at hand:

1. *Becoming a therapist takes time.* This is an opportunity for you to be a learner; you are not expected to be an expert. Becoming an effective therapist takes several years of training.
2. *Make sure you take care of yourself.* Use constructive means for stress reduction. Develop resources for support from other students, peers, and colleagues.
3. *Self-doubts are normal.* Be patient with yourself, focus on the positive, and pay attention to the developmental tasks of becoming a therapist.
4. *Use the skills that brought you to the field.* While you are learning lots of new theory and material, continue to pay attention to your intuition, your desire to work with others, and your natural abilities.

CHAPTER 2

Before the Initial Interview

Mrs. Escutia's voice quivers nervously over the phone line at a community counseling clinic. "I must speak to a counselor . . . please!" she exclaims. "My grandson is in trouble, he needs help. I don't know what to do anymore. I'm afraid he could . . ." The clinic intake worker jots down a few notes and quickly calls up one of the clinic's family therapy interns. "I've got a woman on the phone whose grandson just put his fist through a wall," the intake worker says. "Can you take her?" For a brief moment, the new client and the new intern share a silent space filled with questions and anxieties. The first contact is about to take place, and it can easily make or break a future collaboration where healing work can be done.

DEALING WITH FAMILIES' EXPECTATIONS AND ANXIETIES ABOUT THERAPY

The moment captured in the preceding case material provides a glimpse of one of the most critical points in the therapeutic experience: the period before therapy ever begins. It is during this fragile period that prospective clients decide if they want to risk going to therapy. While clients with previous positive therapy experiences may reinitiate treatment with a hopeful attitude, others are ambivalent in their hopes, expectations, and fears about beginning therapy.

Consider Mrs. Escutia. In her family, problems have traditionally been handled by husbands and wives, aunts and uncles, grandparents, longtime friends, and others who are close to the family hearth. Her anxiety about calling in "professional" help is matched only by her concern for her grandson, whose violent temper has pushed the entire family past its limits. With no previous experience in therapy, she wonders what a stranger in this clinic could possibly do to help—after all, everything has been tried! Will this counselor believe her? How should she present this terrible dilemma? Will anyone out there really care? Does seeking help mean she has failed?

It is not uncommon for families to be at their wit's end when they finally decide to seek treatment or are referred and call for an appointment. Chances are they're worn out, fed up, and feeling hopeless. Furthermore, individual family members may differ remarkably in their attitudes, expectations, and motivations regarding a try at therapy. They may have both overt and covert reasons for coming to therapy, and rarely are the family members' reasons the same. Much of this information may not be uncovered until the first interview or even beyond, but it is a good idea to keep the following questions in mind right from the first contact:

"What are the clients' expectations about therapy?"
"What are their anxieties about coming to therapy?"
"What motivates them to come to therapy, and who is the referral source?"
"Why do they want to come to therapy now?"

If the therapist isn't aware of the often hidden issues related to clients' motivation, expectations, and anxieties, he or she may inadvertently respond in a manner that causes clients to decide that therapy is not worth the risk, or, conversely, that leads to accepting clients who might be better served elsewhere. For example, beginning therapists may find themselves drawn into legal cases that involve divorce, custody, adoption, or numerous other types of litigation issues. Family therapists are seldom trained in the specifics of mediation or custody evaluation, and, for most of us, it is best to decline doing therapy in such situations.

Even in cases where therapy is clearly indicated and doesn't involve potential legal tangles, family members' reasons for starting treatment and levels of motivation are important to assess. In individual work, these issues may be less salient because rarely do individuals come to therapy without wanting to be there. Conjoint treatment presents a different picture. For example, in couple therapy there is often one person who is more motivated to come to therapy or at least who views therapy as an effective method for dealing with relationship problems. The partner may be resistant to treatment, have other preferred solutions for addressing marital issues, or be willing to come to therapy only if it is framed as a way to "help my partner" or "save the marriage."

With families, reasons and motivations for therapy vary further. Perhaps one powerful family member is coercing others to attend. Perhaps the safety of a "neutral" therapist and a scheduled weekly hour is necessary for a family to talk together about personal and significant issues. In addition, referral sources and previous treatment are absolutely crucial to consider when gauging family members' diverse responses to seeing a therapist. Court-ordered treatment may indicate a potentially resistant or reluctant client, though this is by no means the rule. Referrals by school counselors, ministers, physicians, or family friends will likely influence how families first approach treatment. For example, family members may not agree with a school counselor's view of "the problem" and as a result have little investment in seeking therapy. On the other hand, such a referral from a perceived professional may be just the validation the family needs to actively seek help. Similarly, the nature of previous contacts with other agencies or individuals may predispose a family to have enormous expectations for therapy, or none at all. Since these rarely articulated expectations and anxieties will alter how a therapist approaches treatment with a new family, it is essential to get a feel for them from the outset.

Clients like Mrs. Escutia will have as many questions swirling about as the therapist does when the first contact is made. Topping the list may be concerns about the therapist's ability to truly understand and care, and questions about whether he or she can actually help. Clients may find answers to these questions in how quickly their phone calls are returned or in their sense that the listener understands a brief explanation of the problem. The therapist's (or agency's) flexibility in responding to individual needs communicates answers to these questions. The degree of focus on charges and payments versus listening to the client may communicate that the client is not a priority—money is. If the client decides, via these early perceptions, that the therapist doesn't care or can't help, the initial session may never happen. On the other hand, an initial call that relays empathy and confidence can begin to create the foundation upon which a successful therapy can be built.

SUGGESTIONS FOR INITIAL CONTACT WITH THE CLIENT

Keeping in mind the myriad expectations, anxieties, and questions of potential clients, therapists can be guided through the first-time telephone conversation by using a number of pragmatic suggestions for handling initial contacts:

1. *Listen and reflect to the client what you hear.* Simply by listening and briefly reflecting what is said, you can help the prospective client feel that he or she has been heard. Effective listening can be done in 5 minutes, and the client can hang up with a new sense of hope about resolving the problem.

2. *Assess if this is a crisis situation.* The initial phone call may indicate a need for immediate crisis intervention, hospitalization, removal of family members from the home, or involvement of other agencies such as police or child protective services. Therapists should be knowledgeable about the clinic's or agency's protocol for handling crises, and about community or state laws that may apply (e.g., child abuse reporting laws).

3. *Consider scope-of-practice issues.* Do you have the knowledge and experience to diagnose and treat the presenting problem? Some agencies carefully screen the clients that beginning therapists treat. For example, a problem that is primarily biomedical, one that involves suicide risk or serious drug or alcohol use, or a purely individualized problem (such as a phobia) may not be within the scope of practice for a marriage and family therapist. You can begin clarifying your strengths and limits immediately.

4. *Respond as promptly as possible.* Return phone calls, set up the initial session, and complete an assessment as quickly as you can. These behaviors indicate that you take the client's concerns seriously and are competent to respond to his or her needs. You create a sense of credibility and assure the client that you can help early on.

5. *Consider why this particular family member made the initial contact, and keep in mind that a sense of rapport with each individual in the family is important.* Therapists often make several mistakes around this issue. It is easy to be drawn to the most "psychologically minded" or powerful client and inadvertently ignore those who are likely part of the problem as well as part of the solution. Before the first session, the family member who made the phone call is in essence the family spokesperson. However, the therapist may want contact with other family members before the first session. The goal of additional phone contacts is to make sure every family member feels welcome and knows that his or her feelings and ideas matter to the therapist.

6. *Address the "business" of therapy as quickly and efficiently as possible while not detracting from the client's need to be heard.* Basic explanations about fees and payment, how to make appointments, and policies about keeping and canceling appointments are important. Transportation issues are relevant for many families, too. Do the clients

have a car, or someone who can drive them to appointments? Must they navigate and pay for public transportation? Do they have directions to the clinic? What about family work and school schedules? Do they have childcare, if this is needed? Addressing such concerns up front can assist the therapist and family in avoiding no-shows and cancellations due to logistical problems that were never worked out. Issues such as informed consent and confidentiality may be dealt with on the telephone, or more frequently through mailed information or forms provided at the clinic just before the first session. (Chapter 3 addresses these issues in detail.) Regardless of how this information is communicated, it is important to ensure that clients are clearly informed about what is expected of them and what they can expect from therapy.

7. *Limit the first contact by sticking to basic, relevant information and issues.* This is not the time to offer interventions, advice, or suggestions. Be prepared to direct the telephone interview. Prospective clients may be interested in lengthy venting of problems; in getting detailed information about your qualifications, methods, and philosophy; or in obtaining an immediate diagnosis, or they may have other concerns that, while valid, are best saved for a first meeting. You want to make the client feel understood but also focus on the opportunity to explore the problems in more depth in your initial meeting. Typically, clients' anxiety will be significantly reduced once they know they have an appointment and a place to discuss their concerns.

WHAT INFORMATION SHOULD BE OBTAINED?

Most agencies and therapists have an intake form that gathers basic information about the client during the initial contact. The format of intakes (phone call, waiting room form, interview, etc.), the specific questions asked, and the length all vary depending on the scope and mission of the clinic. This information may be obtained by an intake receptionist or a therapist over the phone. Other possibilities include mailing the form to the client before the first session or having the client complete the form in the waiting room before the first session. Even though initial telephone contacts are time-limited and may not be as comprehensive as formal intake questionnaires, the call can still begin the processes of evaluation and joining by focusing on the following questions:

1. What is the problem and how does the client present it? Is this a crisis, a severe or moderate problem, a discrete situation, a chronic difficulty?

2. How has the family responded to the situation? How have they managed so far?
3. Has there been previous therapy?
4. Why is the family seeking treatment now?
5. What additional factors are influencing the situation (e.g., nature and frequency of various stressors—whether they are vocational, personal, physical, or otherwise)?

Figure 2.1 provides a sample intake form that reflects the information deemed most important by marriage and family therapists. The emphasis on specific information varies, depending on the training of the mental health professional. For example, most psychiatric intake forms focus on individual symptoms instead of relationships, whereas a child psychologist may include questions about a child's prenatal history and delivery. Regardless of the therapist's orientation, all intake forms should include a place for the client's brief description of the problem (in the client's own words), notes about previous treatments, and inquiries about current medications and medical problems. Whether this information is obtained during an initial phone contact or at the first session, it is crucial data that helps direct assessment and treatment.

For a more comprehensive list of possible assessment tools, therapists can examine the multitude of resources found in *The Paper Office for the Digital Age* (Zuckerman & Kolmes, 2017). The fifth edition of this excellent resource contains forms that many therapists have contributed over the years. Thus, the book covers every imaginable topic including record keeping, risk reduction, computer resources, informed consent, treatment planning, and financial records. A new therapist can learn a great deal about the therapeutic process simply by reviewing the bounty of resources gathered over the years and compiled in this book.

WHO SHOULD COME TO THERAPY?

During the initial phone contact, the therapist needs to indicate that involvement of the family is critical. While most therapists are flexible enough not to insist that everyone involved be present at every session, an early message that therapy is usually a family affair lays the groundwork for involvement by members who may be perceived as peripheral to the problem. When the presenting problem clearly involves a relationship (sibling fights or parent–child standoffs), it is a useful general rule to get all the people in the relationship to come to therapy.

Name: Telephone: Date of Birth: Place of Birth: Age:

_____   _____   _____   _____   _____

Address: Marital Status: Religion: Race: Gender:

_____   _____   _____   _____   _____

Place of Employment: Length of Employment:

_____   _____

Last Place of Employment: Length of Employment:

_____   _____

Address: Supervisor:

_____   _____

Telephone: Hours Worked: Salary:

_____   _____   _____

Education Completed: Where:

_____

Name(s) of Child/   Date of Birth: Age: School Attended:
Children:

_____   _____   _____   _____

_____   _____   _____   _____

_____   _____   _____   _____

Have you (or your spouse) ever been involved in therapy or any other type of
counseling program?   ☐ Yes   ☐ No

If yes, when? _____ Where? _____

Reasons: _____

Reasons for considering counseling at this time: _____

_____

Have you been referred to this agency before?   ☐ Yes   ☐ No   If yes, by whom? ____

_____

Reasons for the referral: _____

Are you in treatment with another counselor at this time?   ☐ Yes   ☐ No   If yes, with
whom? _____

When? _____ How long? _____

Have you ever been hospitalized for any mental health problems?   ☐ Yes   ☐ No
If yes, when? _____

Where? _____ By whom? _____

Have you ever been, or are you now being, treated for any type of chemical
dependency or abuse?   ☐ Yes   ☐ No

If yes, when? _____ Where? _____

(continued)

FIGURE 2.1. Sample intake form.

By whom? _____ Length of treatment? _____

Are you at the present time using any type of chemical substance? ☐ Yes ☐ No
If yes, please indicate what you are using (drugs and/or alcohol): _____

How frequently do you use these substances? _____

Are you presently under a physician's care for physical problems? ☐ Yes ☐ No
If yes, please list medication: _____

Name of family physician: _____ Telephone: _____

Address: _____

Have you ever been arrested and/or committed a crime? ☐ Yes ☐ No

If yes, when? _____ For what? _____

Outcome of situation: _____

What problems are you presently experiencing? _____

_____

What do you expect from therapy? _____

_____

Please list everyone in your family with whom you presently live:

_____   _____

_____   _____

_____   _____

_____   _____

Identify the primary problem(s) you are now experiencing: _____

_____

If need be, would other relatives be willing to come in to therapy
sessions? ☐ Yes ☐ No

If no, please indicate reason: _____

Person to contact in case of emergency: _____ Telephone: _____

Address: _____

_____   _____
Signature   Date

TO ALL CLIENTS:

If any concerns arise about your treatment, please discuss them with your therapist.

Intake comments: _____

_____

Preliminary treatment plans: _____

_____

FIGURE 2.1. *(continued)*

19

Beyond this basic principle, the following guidelines can help you determine, early on, the best possible format for new clients:

1. Ask the family who they want to come to therapy, and why.
2. Try and identify who in the family is impacted by the current problems. Ask if they might want to come to a session.
3. Consider generational boundaries. Is it appropriate to have all age groups in therapy?
4. Even if the problem is primarily an individual one, would other family members' presence facilitate treatment or feel supportive to the individual?
5. Would other family members hinder the therapy and be potentially damaging to it?
6. What motivation and capacity does the family have to participate in a family format?
7. Be open to changing who comes for each session depending on the problem, but try to establish a relationship with all members.

Clients naturally have an opinion about who should come to therapy, and the reasons underlying such views should be considered and addressed. For example, sometimes a spouse will request individual therapy "because I'm the one causing the problems in the marriage." The therapist can point out that a relationship problem is involved and can recommend that both partners attend. Similarly, family members may consider the "identified patient" to be the only one who needs to come to therapy. Clearly, a direct relationship exists between treatment goals and who attends therapy. Therapy goals may be limited or broadened depending on the willingness of different family members to participate in therapy. As long as the relationship between participation and goals is clarified for the family when the terms of therapy are being established, there need not be any hard-and-fast rules about who comes to each session.

In a survey of marriage and family therapists, Doherty and Simmons (1996) reported that family therapists are most likely to see, in rank order, individuals, then couples, then families—a pattern which remains over a decade later (Beaton, Dienhart, Schmidt, & Turner, 2009). Northey (2002) confirmed those findings in another survey of American Association for Marriage and Family Therapy (AAMFT) clinical members, finding "clients being seen individually 54% of the time and in couple and family sessions between 35% and 42% of the time respectively" (p. 493). Marital and family problems were seen as the

most common presenting problems. It seems that the public is beginning to conceptualize problems as being relational rather than primarily individual. Radio and television talk shows, as well as many popular magazines and movies, have emphasized the relational nature of
mental health problems, and there appears to be a greater willingness
to look at the stresses of normal relationships as well as dysfunctional
ones. Therapists may need to educate new clients about the benefits
of conjoint treatment by emphasizing the power of relationships in
influencing how people feel, think, and act. The role that social and
cultural factors play in creating relationship difficulties may also need
to be discussed. While there are many times when individual therapy is
appropriate, family therapists generally focus their treatment on relationships by having more than one person present. When a marriage
and family therapist is working individually, he or she is likely to take
a systemic view of the case, which means that the focus of the therapy
will include looking at the main players and social systems involved in
the client's life.

INITIAL HYPOTHESIZING

After the initial contact, most therapists find themselves with enough
basic information to begin forming a few hypotheses, which provide
them with areas to pursue further in the first interview. Questions
should be designed to elicit data that will either support or invalidate
the hypotheses.

In order to begin the process of clinical thinking, the therapist
needs to pay close attention to what is known and how that information might be useful. Too often we look quickly for underlying meanings of events before we have a working understanding of the presenting problem. It can be helpful to first summarize what information is
available and then pick out the key issues. What is the client telling you
that he or she thinks is important? Initially, the process of asking key
questions will prove far more fruitful than making interpretations of
the client's motives or behavior.

The process of developing hypotheses is an opportunity for creative thinking. Our guesses and speculations are based on our previous experiences with similar cases, our knowledge about individual
or family development, and our clinical hunches or intuitions. At this
stage of the process, we are not looking for answers, but finding questions. Hypotheses relate to what may be happening or what events
could have occurred. The therapist's position is not to presume to

know, but to form some hunches and then ask. The following example of a clinical situation shows how developing some hypotheses proves useful in beginning a clinical assessment.

A 9-year-old girl who has never really liked school suddenly refuses to go at all. She has become withdrawn and sullen. When asked why she doesn't want to go to school, she simply cries and refuses to answer. In order to develop some hypotheses about this case, it is first useful to note and summarize the key issues. The presenting problem is the child's refusal to go to school. Her response to being asked about the problem is to cry and withdraw. A key word in the vignette is "suddenly." That this change was abrupt is critical information for developing our hypotheses. A sudden change in her attitude and behavior can lead to speculation that something uncomfortable and possibly traumatic has occurred. Her difficulty in responding to questions about her behavior would add fuel to the notion that something frightening has happened and that she is withdrawing from it. These are some of the hypotheses for the clinician to explore. Others might be the following:

1. The girl is being intimidated by someone at school.
2. An abrupt change has occurred at home and she wants to be there.
3. She is developing a school phobia.
4. She is depressed and her school difficulties are symptomatic of her depression.
5. She has a physical problem that she is afraid to talk about.

These hypotheses provide the therapist with possible explanations for the changes in her behavior. They provide direction for further inquiry, but are not intended to be a complete list. Hypotheses help narrow our focus and rule out possibilities. Once a few hypotheses have been developed, the therapist can begin to think about what additional information might prove helpful. Being curious about a client can be a useful, nonevaluative position for the therapist's inquiry. Similarly, in consultations, supervisors and colleagues can suggest directions to take and questions to pursue. In addition, even preliminary information may suggest the need for referrals for physical examinations, psychological testing, or developmental evaluation.

CONCLUSION

Therapy begins with the first contact, before the clients ever meet with their therapist. The clients begin to form impressions about therapy and the therapist. In addition, the therapist can start gathering information for initial hypothesizing. We recently talked to a client new to therapy. She said that the warmth in the voice of the intake administrator and the warmth of the waiting room immediately made her feel safe. She was ready to begin therapy. A student therapist told us that her new clients started arguing about their son as she walked them from the waiting room to her office. She wondered what that meant. We recommend that you consider any contact the clients have with you or your agency starting with the first phone call. Handling early interactions well can set a positive tone for the rest of the therapy.

CHAPTER 3

The Initial Interview

It is 5 minutes to the hour when Sarah looks anxiously at the clock, just before the first session. For what feels like the thousandth time, she mentally rehearses exactly what she wants to say at the beginning of the session. She is worried that she will forget something important because of nervousness. She desperately wants to make a good impression. It is now 2 minutes to the hour—if only the butterflies in her stomach would disappear, she might feel ready. She looks at the door, and wishes for a brief second that she could leave. She takes a deep breath as the door to the therapy office opens.

Did you imagine this to be the client or the therapist waiting for the first session to begin? Either could be true. For therapists and clients alike, beginning therapy can elicit feelings of fear, excitement, and nervous anticipation. Each client will take you on a different journey. This chapter covers the basic issues that must be addressed in the initial interview to ensure that your journey gets off to a good start.

STAGES OF THE INITIAL INTERVIEW

Many beginning therapists find it helpful to think of the initial interview in stages. In the first stage, the therapist welcomes the clients to therapy. The goal of this stage is to do introductions and put the clients at ease. Administrative issues are addressed in the second stage. The purpose of this stage is to ensure clients have a clear understanding of the therapy process, including confidentiality, videotaping, and fees. After covering administrative issues, the therapist can transition to the goal-setting phase. Here the therapist learns what the clients hope to accomplish through therapy. Once a good understanding of client goals and expectations for therapy has been reached, the therapist can begin the assessment phase, which typically extends beyond the first interview.

The length of time devoted to each phase can vary greatly from client to client. Often the first two stages of the initial interview, welcoming the client and handling administrative issues, can be accomplished within the first 10–15 minutes. In some cases, however, clients may have a lot of questions about the therapy process, which may extend the second stage. The length of the goal-setting stage can depend on several factors. Some clients will be able to succinctly state their concerns, while others will go off on tangents or tell long stories about the presenting issues. The time devoted to goal setting will also depend on the number of clients being seen. Soliciting everyone's perspective on goals within a family will generally take longer than working with an individual. In most cases the therapist will be able to devote some time to assessment in the initial interview. However, with some clients, simply being able to establish goals for therapy is a realistic expectation.

You will need to accomplish several important tasks to make the initial interview successful. Some tasks, like goal setting, will fit nicely within a particular stage. Other tasks, however, may not fit easily within a particular stage, or may require attention across multiple stages of the initial interview. For example, at each stage of the initial interview, you should be working on building your relationship with your clients. Important assessment information may also come out at any point in the first session, even before the therapist has begun a more formal assessment phase.

DEVELOPING A CONNECTION: HOW TO JOIN WITH CLIENTS

The most crucial task in the first session is for you to successfully join with your clients. *Joining* means that clients feel a sense of connectedness with you, which usually arises when they feel you understand, respect, and care about them. Joining is both a technique (developing rapport) and an attitude. The importance of joining cannot be overstated: It is the foundation for future work. Failure to successfully join with your clients will hamper all of your efforts, from assessment to treatment. Clients will be reluctant to share sensitive information if you have not established a safe and secure relationship with them. Likewise, clients may be resistant to or defensive toward suggestions if you have not created a strong therapeutic relationship with them. Ultimately, failure to join with clients can lead to premature termination of therapy (Roos & Werbart, 2013; Sharf, Primavera, & Diener, 2010).

Joining is a process that should be carefully attended to throughout the entire initial interview. It begins in the first moments of therapy, as clients are welcomed into your office. When asked about her experience in going to a therapist, Jean shared, "It didn't feel right from the very beginning." When she introduced herself, the therapist seemed preoccupied. She was busy finishing up a task and was distracted. She didn't shake Jean's hand and didn't make eye contact. The therapist missed an opportunity to connect with the client and create a safe environment for therapy to take place.

When you begin the session, you should attempt to put your clients at ease given that they are most likely anxious about coming to therapy. Some therapists engage in brief social talk with their clients to break the ice before discussing problems. You might ask them, for example, what kind of work they do or what they like to do for fun. Besides making your clients feel comfortable talking with you, this approach demonstrates your personal interest in them. You might also share some information about yourself so that the clients can get to know you. Ideally, you will be able to identify something you have in common with your clients that will help develop a sense of connection.

Joining also takes place at other points throughout the initial interview. For example, joining can occur when you respectfully listen to and address questions your clients have about confidentiality, fees, and other issues. Likewise, giving each of your clients an opportunity to tell his or her story facilitates joining by allowing each person to feel heard and understood. Reflective listening, maintaining direct eye contact, or leaning forward can also reinforce for your clients that you are interested in them and concerned about what they are saying. Concluding the initial interview with a positive message for your clients can be another way to strengthen your connection. For example, a husband who resists coming to therapy can be complimented for caring enough about his relationship to come despite his strong reservations about therapy.

Although skills to facilitate joining can be learned, it is important to recognize that developing a relationship with another person cannot be reduced to a recipe or set of techniques. In fact, who you are is the greatest asset you bring to therapy. Your personality, attitudes, life experiences, and compassion become a part of and help create the relationship.

Although who you are is usually an asset to joining, there are times when therapist characteristics can create a barrier to developing a connection. Therapists who have prejudices or negative preconceptions about people based on race, ethnicity, sexual orientation, socioeconomic status, or religious orientation will likely have difficulty establishing a connection with clients who have these characteristics. Likewise, therapists may have a difficult time joining with a client who reminds them of someone with whom they had a painful relationship (perhaps a parent or mate). Therefore, you should be vigilant in assuring that personal issues or prejudices do not interfere with your developing a relationship with your clients.

HANDLING ADMINISTRATIVE ISSUES

One of the early tasks in an initial interview is to address administrative issues so clients understand the therapy process. It is important to recognize that therapeutic issues may be played out when going over administrative issues. One client who was adamant about not being videotaped was discovered through further assessment to have a high level of distrust toward people, which became a key area of focus in therapy. Therefore, the therapist who is attuned to the process and not just the content when handling administrative issues may discover important opportunities for assessment or even intervention.

Confidentiality and Release of Information

It is vital that you discuss confidentiality in therapy with your clients. They need to be informed not only of the confidential nature of therapy, but also of the possible exceptions to confidentiality (e.g., threat of harm to self or others, child abuse, elder/dependent abuse). It is best practice to cover confidentially both orally and in writing with your client. The consent form for treatment (discussed later in this section) should include what is and what is not kept confidential in therapy.

Therapists working with couples and families must also consider how confidentiality among family members will be handled. Some therapists, for example, will conduct individual sessions as part of a couple's treatment. Likewise, a therapist may meet individually with a child or adolescent in addition to family treatment. The therapist must address the extent to which information obtained during these individual sessions will be kept confidential or shared with other family members. Some therapists insist on a "no-secrets policy" between family members, while others allow information learned in individual sessions to remain confidential. Regardless of one's position, it is important to offer clear guidelines as to the bounds of confidentiality at the beginning of therapy.

You may want to consult with other individuals or institutions connected with particular cases, such as previous therapists, psychiatrists, physicians, teachers, lawyers, courts, or parole officers. In these cases, you will need to have clients sign a release of information form, such as the one depicted in Figure 3.1, to permit communication between you and the other parties. The signatures of all participants in therapy are required for the release of information. For example, you should obtain *both* the husband's and the wife's signatures if both have been participants in the course of therapy. If others contact you about your clients, you should not even acknowledge that they are in therapy unless you have obtained the appropriate release of information. It can be surprising that some other professionals may not adhere to the importance of having a written release in order to share information. Regardless of the position taken by another professional, it is imperative that you obtain a written release of information before discussing a case.

Therapeutic issues may arise when discussing confidentiality with clients. For example, if a husband or wife in couple therapy inquires if the court can obtain therapy records, you might suspect that one of the partners is seriously thinking of divorce.

Videotaping and Observation

Beginning family therapists are frequently instructed to record or videotape therapy sessions for supervision purposes. Most clients will agree to be videotaped if they are properly approached. You can explain why the videotaping is beneficial to both you and the client, and address issues of confidentiality regarding videotaping. You can tell your clients that you regularly consult with your supervisor, and that videotaping allows your supervisor to witness firsthand what happened in therapy. Consulting with your supervisor in this manner is helpful too because "two heads are better than one." You can add that videotaping allows you to review what happened in previous sessions and perhaps have a new insight, much like people notice something new when watching a movie for the second time. Finally, recording a session gives the therapist the option to replay part of the session for clients. Used in this manner, videotaping can help clients take an observer role in seeing how they interact, much like football teams watch game films to see how they might improve.

You should inform the client who will view the recordings, emphasizing that videotapes are considered confidential information. You also need to assure clients that recordings are not kept permanently, but are regularly erased or recorded over. Clients should be asked to sign a form giving their consent for videotaping sessions. The form should

To: _____
             (practitioner, hospital, etc.)

I have been informed that under _____ (state) law, communications between a client and his or her therapist are privileged and may not be disclosed by the therapist unless the client consents. I also have been informed that client records maintained by a therapist may not be disclosed to third parties except with the client's consent or through legal process.

I authorize _____ (name of therapist) to share information and/or records about my therapy to _____ (name of person or entity to whom the disclosure will be made).

I am permitting authorized disclosure of information about my therapy for the following purposes:

_____

_____

_____

I am permitting authorized disclosure of the following types of information (choose one):

__ All information or records related to my therapy

__ Only the following information (please specify)

_____

_____

_____

This authorization shall remain in effect until _____ (date). I understand that any cancellation or modification of this authorization must be in writing.

_____
Date

_____
Client name (printed)

_____
Client signature

_____   _____
Witnessed by   Date

FIGURE 3.1. Authorization for release of information.

outline the purpose of the videotaping, who will view the recordings, and what will happen to the recordings after therapy is completed.

Some clients may be reluctant to be videotaped. You should carefully explore what is behind their reservations. In many cases, clients are simply self-consciousness about being taped. Most of these clients will be agreeable to being videotaped if assured that their reaction is a common one and that people generally forget about being recorded after a short time. You should pay careful attention to clients who are insistent about not being videotaped given they are the exception rather than the rule. These clients often have sensitive information that they wish to protect or keep secret. For example, one client who refused to be videotaped disclosed indirectly that he had engaged in illegal activities. Some will agree to be videotaped if you will turn off the video camera when they indicate that they are ready to disclose particularly sensitive information. If a client is not open to videotaping under any circumstances, you should respect this decision in order to avoid damaging the therapeutic relationship and possibly precipitating a premature termination of therapy. Clients may eventually agree to be videotaped once they have established greater trust in you or the therapeutic process.

If therapy will include live supervision or the use of observing/ reflecting teams, discuss this with your clients. Most clients will agree to this format if the rationale and benefits are clearly explained. It is often helpful to allow clients, at their request, to meet supervisors or team members who observe the sessions from behind the one-way mirror.

Fees

Determining the client's fee can be an uncomfortable process for many therapists. It is difficult to assign a monetary value to therapy, and therapists often feel uneasy about charging fees while acting in a helping role. Therapist anxiety about fees can easily be transferred to clients and can create conflict and stress in therapy. Comfort in handling fees will increase with therapeutic experience and confidence in your ability to provide a worthwhile service.

There is a business aspect of the therapy relationship and discussing fees should be handled in a business-like manner. This discussion should be clear, straightforward, and matter-of-fact. Instead of purchasing a product, the client is purchasing a service. Some agencies offer guidelines for fee setting based on the client's income. The term "customary and usual" is used to identify the typical fee in a particular area. Customary fees will vary based on the geographic area. Most programs or clinicians establish a minimum fee and then work within a range. Some clinicians prefer to deal with fees in the beginning of the session when handling other administrative issues, while others feel it is best done toward the end of the initial interview.

In addition to setting the fee, you should discuss acceptable forms of payment, when the fee should be paid, and the fee for late cancellation or "no-show" appointments, if applicable. It is often useful to have a written agreement that discusses the fees and policies regarding fees. If a third party is responsible for payment, their terms for payment should be clearly understood by therapist and client. Often third-party payers limit the number of sessions, or the types of presenting problems or diagnoses they will reimburse. For example, many third-party payers will not reimburse for couple counseling or "problems of living" such as those listed in the "V" codes of the *Diagnostic and Statistical Manual of Mental Disorders, Fifth Edition* (DSM-5; American Psychiatric Association, 2013). If a third-party payer is involved, the therapist should verify insurance coverage at the outset of therapy. Issues that need to be addressed may include provider eligibility, annual deductibles, rate of reimbursement, limitations on the number of sessions, or types of treatments covered. Usually a DSM-5 diagnosis will need to be assigned to the insured patient.

As with other administrative issues, working out the details for payment can be part of the diagnostic process and help to clarify the family's expectations of and responsibilities for therapy. In discussing fees you might learn, for example, that a client is unable to pay the full therapy fee due to certain hardships, such as medical expenses. Alternatively, a client's unwillingness to pay the full therapy fee may reflect low motivation for therapy. Generally, free services tend not to be valued by clients. A fee, even a small one, provides some incentive to make effective use of services. Paying a fee also indicates that the therapy has value to the client.

Other Administrative Issues

Several other administrative issues need to be addressed with clients. In some cases, therapists may be required to discuss with clients their professional qualifications. For example, California law requires that all unlicensed family therapists identify themselves to their clients as trainees or interns. Many agencies and practitioners have clients read and sign an informed consent statement that generally includes a brief description of what therapy is, including the potential risks, such as being asked to examine painful issues. Informed consent statements also summarize many of the issues discussed in this chapter, such as confidentiality and payment of fees. Permission to videotape may be included in this or a separate form. Figure 3.2 is a basic informed consent form that covers some of these issues.

I understand that treatment at _____ (name of treatment facility) may involve discussing relationship, psychological, and/or emotional issues that may at times be distressing. However, I also understand that this process is intended to help me personally and with relationships. I am aware of alternative treatment options available to me.

My therapist has satisfactorily answered all of my questions about treatment at _____ (name of treatment facility). If I have further questions, I understand that my therapist will either answer them or find answers for me. I understand that I may leave therapy at any time, although I have been informed that this is best accomplished in consultation with the therapist.

I understand that at _____ (name of treatment facility):

1. Master's or doctoral students in family therapy conduct therapy under close supervision by licensed therapists.
2. Therapy sessions are routinely videotaped and/or observed by supervisors or other therapists on the treatment team. I agree to have my sessions videotaped for the purpose of supervision or consultation with the treatment team. I understand that the videotapes are erased at the end of my treatment.

I understand that what is discussed in therapy will generally remain confidential unless I give written permission to share information from my sessions by signing a release of information. However, the therapist may share information about or videotapes of my therapy with the supervisor or treatment team in the interest of providing quality care. My therapist has also informed me that there are other possible exceptions to confidentiality, which may include, but are not limited to, the following:

1. Disclosure of child abuse
2. Disclosure of elder or dependent abuse
3. Threats to harm oneself
4. Threats to harm others
5. If a court issues a subpoena
6. If you are required to be in therapy or be evaluated by a court order
7. If you claim harm to your mental or emotional state in a legal proceeding

The fee for each session will be _____, and is to be paid at the time of the therapy session. I have been informed of the cancellation policy, which states that I will pay half of the normal fee if I fail to show for the appointment or cancel a session with less than 24 hours' notice.

In the event of an emergency, I have been instructed to call the Crisis Center hotline at _____ (phone number) or go to the nearest hospital emergency room.

To be signed by all participating members.

Signed: _____ Date: _____

Signed: _____ Date: _____

Signed: _____ Date: _____

Signed: _____ Date: _____

Signed: _____ Date: _____

FIGURE 3.2. Basic informed consent form.

DEFINING CLIENT EXPECTATIONS FOR THERAPY

Another important task in the initial interview is to define clients' expectations for what therapy will accomplish and how it will be conducted. This is essential to ensure that clients' needs are compatible with what you, as the therapist, can or are willing to offer.

Defining Client Goals for Therapy

The first step in defining expectations is to ask your clients what they would like to accomplish through therapy. An effective way to introduce this subject is simply to ask questions such as "How can I be helpful to you?" or "What are you hiring me to do?" Generally, clients will initially respond by describing what they see as the primary problems or issues. Clients hope that you will be able to fix these problems. Individuals will often say what they want to eliminate ("I want Dad to stop nagging me") and have a harder time articulating what they want ("I want Dad to tell me I'm doing a good job"). If possible, encourage your clients to describe desired changes in positive language (what will be happening) rather than in negative language (what won't be happening).

It is important that each family member is given the opportunity to be heard when discussing problems and goals. This will help in joining with each individual. In addition, you may discover there is disagreement about the problem itself or who has the problem. You want to give yourself the opportunity to see the problem from different perspectives, since each person will provide some information that other family members will not. An issue that can arise during this process is one family member monopolizing the conversation. It is absolutely critical that you provide enough structure to interrupt this process in order to provide space for other family members. You don't want to anger the person who talks excessively, but if you fail to interrupt this behavior, other family members may lose faith in your ability to lead the session.

In defining goals, a number of challenges can arise. Your clients may identify multiple problem areas, with little distinction of priorities. Some couples, for example, may have a "laundry list" of complaints about each other or their relationship. In these cases, you will need to obtain your clients' perspective on the relative importance of their problems. For example, you might ask, "Of the issues you have presented, which is most important, and which is least important?"

In other cases, your clients may not have a clear idea of what the problem is or what their goals for therapy are. In these situations you may need to contract for a limited number of sessions to explore and define problem areas and goals. Another potential problem is that clients may have unrealistically high expectations or goals. One husband, for example, expressed his belief that the couple should be totally free from any conflict after therapy. Here you will need to have a conversation with your client regarding what can be realistically expected from therapy.

Setting goals may be further complicated by the unstated agenda of a client, one that he or she feels is not appropriate to disclose. A couple may come into therapy with the stated goal of working on the marriage. Later you may discover that the husband entered therapy to make sure you would take care of his wife after he informed her of his intention to leave the marriage. Sometimes, even the clients may not be totally aware of their reasons for seeking therapy. A woman was eventually able to recognize that she probably was not invested in working on the relationship with her husband. Rather, she acknowledged that her motivation to try marital counseling was primarily driven by a desire to alleviate feelings of guilt about ending the marriage.

Alternatively, individuals in couples or families may define goals that initially appear incompatible. In these situations, you may need to creatively reframe the goals in such a way as to make them compatible or link them together. For example, parents may want to see their adolescent behave in a more mature and responsible manner, while the adolescent wants greater freedom. A therapist could potentially link these goals together by discussing how both the parents and adolescent have a common desire to see the adolescent become successfully launched as an adult, also pointing out that becoming an adult carries with it certain privileges as well as responsibilities. The therapist can then work with the family to help the adolescent achieve more freedom and privileges consistent with his or her ability to manage responsibility.

Once you have a clear understanding of what your clients want or expect from therapy, you need to decide whether it is appropriate for you to take on the case. First, you must assess whether the case is within your scope of practice, that is, whether the clients are expecting help for issues that would be considered appropriate for a family therapist to treat. Offering legal or medical advice would not be within your scope of practice, but working with a couple on their relationship obviously would be. The scope of practice is defined for therapists by the laws that license or certify therapists in their state. If the case falls outside your scope of practice, you will need to refer your clients to an appropriate professional.

Second, you need to assess if the case falls within your scope of competence. In other words, do you have the necessary skills, training, or experience to effectively treat the issues? If not, you need to refer the clients to another therapist who has the appropriate skills or qualifications. For example, a referral would be necessary if your client wanted hypnosis but you did not have any training or experience with this form of treatment. In some cases, you may be able to treat clients provided you take appropriate measures during treatment to gain the necessary competence. For example, a therapist who has never worked with encopresis could do a literature review on treating this condition and seek supervision on the case.

Third, if you are working within an agency setting, you will need to evaluate if the services the clients are seeking fit within the agency's scope of practice. Some agencies specialize in addressing specific issues or problems, and may not want therapists working with clients who are seeking help for other concerns. Because clients present with multiple issues, some may fit under the agency's scope of practice while others may not. For example, Oliver works in an agency that serves children and adolescents. Oliver is working with Desmond, an 8-year-old boy whose anxiety seems to be heavily impacted by the conflict in his parents' marriage. Oliver firmly believes that Desmond's symptoms would greatly improve if the parents could resolve issues in their marriage. Oliver's supervisor encourages him to refer Desmond's parents to therapists outside the agency to work on their marriage. Seek consultation with your supervisor if these concerns arise, especially if there is any ambiguity around whether the issues fit under the agency's scope of practice.

Finally, there may be occasions where your clients' needs are best met by working on other goals first before addressing the goals with which they initially present. A couple in which a partner has a significant substance abuse issue may need an initial period of sobriety or abstinence before the couple's goals of working on their relationship can be effectively addressed. You will need to present a rationale to your clients as to why a particular sequence of treatment will ultimately be in their best interest.

Client Goals Compared to Therapist Goals

Client goals are often defined in terms of what problems or issues need to be resolved. In contrast, therapist goals generally reflect what changes clients need to make to resolve their problems. Client goals tell the therapist where they want to go, whereas therapist goals describe how the client will get there. A client goal might be stated as "I want to feel less depressed." The therapist's goal might be to help the client learn how to challenge distorted thinking using cognitive-behavioral techniques. Thus, client goals must be integrated with therapist goals to develop an effective treatment plan, which is discussed in Chapter 5.

Additional Expectations for Therapy

Many clients not only bring in expectations about *what* therapy will accomplish, but also about *how* therapy will be done. Therefore, it is often helpful to assess what clients expect therapy will be like. Some clients who have had previous therapy may assume you will do therapy in a similar manner. If the previous therapist assigned homework, your client may also expect that of you. Whenever a client has had previous therapy, it is often beneficial to explore what the experience was like, as it can strongly shape (both positively and negatively) a client's expectations regarding therapy. Many clients tend to be vague when discussing previous therapy. It may be helpful to ask specific questions about the previous therapy. What did the client find most useful? What about the process didn't work for him or her? More specific questions will generate a clearer picture of what occurred and how you might apply it to the current therapy situation. In some cases, clients may not know what they expect from therapy, or they may have unrealistic expectations. In these circumstances, the therapist may need to educate clients about the therapy process (DeFife & Hilsenroth, 2011).

Clients may hold expectations about therapy in a number of different areas. For example, clients may come in with expectations on how long therapy will be. Some may anticipate that therapy will be only one or two sessions, while others may expect the process to last a year or more. You need to assess if their expectations align with what you think is realistic.

Clients can also have expectations about who will be in therapy. For example, some parents bring a troubled child to therapy with the belief that the therapist will "fix" the child with little involvement on their part. These parents may question why they are expected to participate in family therapy. Conversely, other parents anticipate being an active participant in therapy, and may become frustrated if the therapist chooses to see the child or adolescent individually.

It is also important that the therapist and client share similar views on the purpose of therapy. Some clients come to therapy with the expectation that therapy is a place to vent, and that the therapist will simply provide a listening ear and support. Other clients come with the understanding that therapy is a place where the goal is to create change. If the therapist and client are not on the same page in this regard, then problems are likely to arise. For example, a therapist trying to promote change may become frustrated when a client does not complete homework assignments. However, the client may view therapy primarily as a safe place to vent and complain about problems in life. The therapist and client will need to discuss what therapy is about and hopefully reach a mutually agreed-upon understanding.

It is also possible that other client expectations may impede the therapeutic process. For example, one couple stated that they did not want to look at family-of-origin issues because they felt this had been unproductive in previous therapy. Yet many of the couple's concerns seemed intimately tied to difficulties with their parents. In a case like this, you would need to determine how rigid the couple is in their desire to avoid family-of-origin exploration. If they persisted in this stance, you would have to decide how flexible you are willing to be to accommodate their desire. In some instances, you may decide against continuing therapy because the expectations are too restrictive and would severely limit your ability to be effective.

ASSESSING AND BUILDING MOTIVATION

Clients come to therapy with varying degrees of motivation. Although many clients are motivated, you may discover that others have little motivation to change. For example, motivation is often a concern for clients who are forced to come to therapy. Some clients come to therapy because they have been mandated by the courts to do so because of substance abuse, juvenile delinquency, child abuse, or other issues. However, others are forced to come to therapy by family members. A spouse may be threatened with divorce if he or she does not attend therapy; adolescents may be compelled by their parents to go to therapy. The initial interview is a good time to assess and perhaps begin to build motivation for therapy.

A logical time to assess motivation is when you are defining goals for therapy. Answers to the question "What brings you to therapy?" will differentiate motivated from unmotivated clients. The former usually respond by describing the problems or growth areas they would like to see addressed. If a client responds by saying that someone asked or insisted he or she come to therapy, problems with motivation may be anticipated. Nevertheless, some of these clients can become quite committed to therapy as they experience its benefits.

You should also inquire as to who first suggested therapy or called for the appointment. Generally this person is the most motivated for therapy. A good question to ask your clients is what led them to come to therapy now, rather than sooner or later in their lives? The answer may provide clues to your clients' motivation, as well as important assessment information, such as precipitating events.

A client's overall level of motivation will be based on a number of factors, the assessment of which can guide you in choosing interventions that increase motivation. Where clients are on the Stages of Change Cycle (Prochaska, Norcross, & DiClemente, 1994), for example, may determine their motivation for change. This cycle recognizes that clients spend a great deal of time (precontemplation and contemplation stages) thinking about changing before they decide to take action and change. In addition, the cycle recognizes that maintaining changes, such as not drinking alcohol again, can be challenging. Thus, addressing relapse is part of the process leading to permanent change. The therapist must match his or her interventions to where the client is in terms of their stage of change.

Motivational interviewing (Miller & Rollnick, 2013) suggests that the therapist's job is to help the client resolve his or her ambivalence about change. Instead of using confrontation, the empathic therapist validates the client's perspective and freedom to decide. In addition, the therapist listens for the client's own self-motivational statements (e.g., "I know this is a problem that I have to address").

Pain around unmet needs often drives clients to change. Therefore, it is important that you are clear on what the unmet needs are for your clients, and how much pain or distress they experience around these unmet needs. Clients who are in little pain or do not perceive themselves as having a problem will have little motivation for change.

It can be a challenge as a therapist to work with clients who do not believe there is a problem (or that the problem is not serious), but they are being told they must come to therapy. You will need to figure out why the client is minimizing the problem, which will guide how you approach the situation. Some clients may not be aware of the seriousness of their situation. In these cases, it can helpful to explore with clients why others believe there is a problem and the possible negative consequences of not addressing it. For example, you might warn a client that a failure to heed a partner's complaints could lead to the eventual breakup of the relationship.

Sometimes clients will deny that a problem exists out of fear of consequences or injury to their self-image. For example, those who have sexually abused children will frequently deny or minimize the molestation to avoid legal consequences as well as avoiding having to admit to themselves that they are child molesters. Therefore, building motivation for therapy will need to be done in conjunction with addressing the client's denial.

If a mandated client refuses to acknowledge that a problem exists, you can suggest that there is at least one problem—he or she is being told to come to unwanted therapy. If your client agrees (which is typically the case), then you can explore what needs to happen so that the client is no longer required to come to therapy. This approach allows you to join with your client, while at the same time working on intermediate goals that address the problem.

Some clients may have poor motivation because they do not anticipate any benefit from therapy, believing that therapy is useless or the situation is hopeless. Building a positive expectation that therapy can be helpful will be vital for these clients (DeFife & Hilsenroth, 2011). A positive experience early in therapy might spark hope and increase motivation. For clients who lack confidence in their ability to change, you may need to highlight their strengths or help them challenge their negative self-talk. Noting exceptions to the problem might help build confidence and motivation.

Other factors might also reduce clients' motivation for therapy, which will need to be uncovered through careful assessment. For example, feelings of hopelessness and lack of motivation could be a symptom of major depression. Hope and energy for therapy can grow as the depression begins to lift through the use of medication or other interventions. Clients who have difficulty trusting others may initially be reluctant to invest in therapy until sufficient safety has been established. Some clients may have practical barriers that need to be resolved, such as difficulties with transportation, finances, or work schedules.

Using the above strategies does not guarantee client motivation. You may still have a poorly motivated client, particularly in court-ordered cases in which the client can avoid prosecution by participating in therapy. In these situations, you need to become comfortable with using the leverage for change provided by the courts. For example, you may need to inform the client that therapy will be discontinued and the termination reported to the courts unless satisfactory progress is maintained.

A common struggle that beginning therapists may face is when they are more motivated than their clients. At times, clients fail to show up for appointments, come late, have little to say, or do not complete their homework assignments. In these situations, the therapist may end up working much harder than the clients. This dynamic suggests that the therapist needs to step back, review the reasons for therapy, and once again evaluate the clients' motivation.

At times, clients might seem motivated "for the wrong reasons." For example, a client only quits smoking in response to a life-threatening illness. A depressed client wants to die but restrains herself because of the impact her suicide could have on her children. In couple therapy, couples may state that they are only trying to preserve their marriage "for the sake of the children." You don't need to agree with the clients' motivations. Usually, it is enough that clients, for whatever reason, will face the demanding process of change.

ESTABLISHING CREDIBILITY

Beginning therapists often fear their clients will ask, "How long have you been doing therapy?" Similarly, unmarried or childless therapists may dread questions about one's marital status or parenthood because such questions reflect a key issue that the beginning therapist must frequently deal with in the initial session: the issue of credibility.

In order for clients to have hope or an expectation of change, they must see the therapist and therapy as credible, or they may prematurely terminate therapy. Therefore, it is important for you to assess early on if any issues of credibility need to be addressed. First, do the clients see therapy as an effective way to solve problems? Or do they believe that therapy is only for "crazy people"? Second, do the clients see you, in your role as the therapist, as being competent or credible? Clients may question a therapist's ability to help them because he or she looks too young, or a parent may question a childless therapist's ability to understand and help.

If you suspect there is a credibility problem, you should attempt to pinpoint where and why credibility is lacking. For example, one beginning therapist described how a woman came into the first session saying that she wanted a gay or lesbian counselor. The therapist indicated that she was not a lesbian, and that she had very few friends who were either gay or lesbian. However, she expressed a willingness to learn more about these issues. At the end of the session, when the therapist asked how the woman felt about continuing in therapy with her, given her desire for a gay or lesbian counselor, the woman indicated she was quite comfortable about continuing with the therapist. Through further discussion, the therapist discovered that what initially had appeared to be concern about the therapist's sexual orientation was actually a fear on the client's part that she would be unfairly judged by a "straight" person. When the therapist expressed an open and accepting stance toward the woman, she was able to earn the client's trust. The more precise your understanding of why the client does not see you or the therapy as credible, the more likely your intervention will be "on target" in addressing this issue.

In cases where clients are resistant to therapy in general, you may be able to reframe the process in a way that builds its credibility. For individuals who think therapy is only for crazy people, you must work to reduce the stigma. You can compare therapy to coaching, in that even the best athletes, such as Olympians or professionals, use coaches. Therapy could also be compared to consulting work, similar in the way that businesses hire someone with special expertise to help them.

When clients question a therapist's credibility, they usually focus on the lack of professional or life experience. Often you can redefine for the client what type of experience is needed to be helpful. For example, a parent may doubt a therapist's ability to be helpful if he or she has not parented children of his or her own. In this instance, the therapist may be able to build credibility by discussing other types of experience working with children, such as being a nanny, teacher, or childcare worker. Alternatively, the therapist may state that in working with several families in therapy, he or she has learned through experience what works and doesn't work in parenting. Thus, the parents' intimate knowledge of their children plus the therapist's experience with families in general will increase the likelihood of therapy being successful. If you are concerned about your age and lack of experience, it may also be helpful to dress professionally and present in a professional manner.

In some cases, you may need to directly address with your clients how you will compensate for your lack of experience with a particular problem or population. For example, you can discuss how you will be receiving supervision from a more experienced clinician who can provide guidance. When working with clients who come from a different cultural background than you, you might express your willingness to learn from them about their culture. While some clients are open to this approach, others will feel it is not their responsibility to educate the therapist about their culture. Especially for these clients, it will be important for you to take the initiative to educate yourself through reading the literature.

If clients still harbor doubts, a frequently effective strategy is to contract with them for a set number of sessions (perhaps three). This gives you time to demonstrate your competence. You can explain to your clients that if they are still uncertain about your ability to help them after the agreed-upon number of sessions, you will gladly refer them elsewhere. Nearly all clients are willing to give you this chance, provided the number of sessions is reasonable. In these situations, you need to identify a problem that can be quickly resolved to build credibility with your clients.

It is important that you not become defensive if your credibility is being questioned. If you can deal with your clients' concerns in a nondefensive and respectful manner, this may actually build your credibility. In order to do this, you must be clear in your own mind what you do have to offer, even if you have limited clinical or life experience.

First, you need to recognize that clients value having someone compassionately and respectfully listen to their story at a difficult time in their lives. Part of the reason that clients' problems are so distressing to them is that they feel isolated, lonely, and inadequate in relation to others. The therapeutic relationship can provide a sense of connection and support for clients at a time when these essentials are in short supply. For some clients, the relationship with the therapist may be their first healthy relationship, and this aspect alone can be quite therapeutic. In simply being present with another human being, you have something important to offer your clients.

Second, you can frequently offer important insights to your clients because you do not have the kind of emotional involvement in the situation that they do. As an outside observer, you may help illuminate for your clients important aspects of themselves or their relationships that they are having a difficult time seeing.

Third, even the inexperienced therapist has access to clinical knowledge that most clients do not possess or could not easily access. Through your course work, you have learned important concepts and theories that you may use to inform your work, thereby tapping into a source of practical knowledge and wisdom beyond your years of actual clinical experience.

CONCLUSION: THE FIRST SESSION AND BEYOND

The initial interview is a critical time in the therapy process; several important tasks must be accomplished to ensure that therapy will proceed successfully. Developing a connection and establishing credibility with your clients is essential for their return for a second session. Defining goals and expectations for therapy, building motivation, and properly handling administrative issues are also crucial.

Clearly, many of the issues discussed in this chapter are important throughout therapy, not just in the first interview. You need to remain connected or joined with your clients in order to effectively confront and challenge them at all stages. Likewise, the goals or expectations for therapy may need to be revisited and redefined as therapy proceeds.

Guidelines for
Conducting Assessment

Beth reviews her notes after the first session with Mr. and Mrs. Thompson. She gathered a lot of information. Based on what she learned in her couple therapy class, she realizes that the Thompsons have many predictors of divorce. At the same time, she learned the symptoms of depression in her psychopathology class and recognizes that Mr. Thompson has had significant changes in sleeping, concentration, and energy. He seems hopeless and sad.

The Thompsons told a long story about what happened over the past year—job changes, family conflict, dependence on sleeping pills, trouble with in-laws, financial struggles. Beth wants to sort out the most important information and decides to review her assessment questions and observations with her supervisor during her next supervision. She wants to be sure she has obtained the most pertinent information and not missed important diagnostic considerations. The Thompsons shared so much information during the first session that she is grateful she can review the session with her supervisor to make sure she is prioritizing her clinical observations correctly. She prepares for her supervision by making lists of individual symptoms for both clients, their couple issues, family stressors, and resources.

Often it takes several sessions to sort out the clinical priorities of a specific case. In addition, the clients' situations and struggles constantly evolve. This chapter presents a plan for approaching assessment. Beginning therapists may easily feel overwhelmed by the amount of information that needs to be gathered in the first few interviews. Many

TABLE 4.1. General Assessment Plan

1. Conduct initial assessment.
   - Explore presenting problems.
   - Assess for attempted solutions.
   - Assess for crisis and stressful life events.

2. Rule out potential issues of harm.
   - Assess for suicide.
   - Assess for family violence and abuse.
   - Assess for sexual abuse.
   - Assess for duty-to-warn issues.

3. Rule out possible substance abuse.

4. Rule out possible biological problems.

5. Conduct general psychosocial assessment.
   - Assess affect, behavior, and cognitions.
   - Assess meaning system.
   - Assess spirituality.
   - Assess the couple and family system.
   - Assess social systems outside the family.
   - Assess families within the larger social context.

community mental health agencies require that assessment be completed in one session, which adds to the pressure.

In an attempt to clarify the assessment process and make it less daunting, we have broken it down into various components and presented them in a logical sequence. However, in reality, the various areas overlap, and assessment seldom proceeds in such a straightforward manner. When gathering assessment data, therapists need to be aware that some clients may withhold some information until trust develops; it is not uncommon for some of these areas to be explored more openly over time.

Table 4.1 shows the general outline for conducting a comprehensive assessment. Overall, assessment needs to take a biopsychosocial systems perspective, moving from more specific concerns to broader contextual information. The initial assessment typically begins by exploring with clients their problems or concerns, and the solutions that have been attempted. At this early stage, you must also assess if your clients are in crisis, or if any possible issues of harm are relevant. For example, a client who is depressed or hopeless must be assessed for suicide. You must also be alert to possible signs of abuse or violence toward others. Since alcohol and substance abuse are commonly associated with relationship problems, they can impede effective treatment if overlooked. In addition, problems may have an underlying biological component that must be ruled out. This chapter also covers the various areas that are important to consider within a general psychosocial assessment, including assessing the individual, the couple or family system, social systems outside the family, and larger social systems such as culture and gender socialization.

This chapter provides guidelines for conducting a comprehensive assessment within each of these areas. Such a thorough assessment will help you arrive at a more accurate picture of your client and thereby develop an effective treatment plan.

INITIAL ASSESSMENT

Exploring the Presenting Problems

The problems that bring clients to therapy, the presenting problems, are explored first. For example, you will want to know the nature or description of the problem—what it is, and how long it has existed. You might also inquire about who is most affected by the problem. Is it only manifested at a certain time or in a certain place? You also need to know whom the family conceptualizes as having the problem. Is the problem seen as being a relational one ("We don't know how to communicate"), or is it seen as primarily one individual's problem ("Our child is having difficulty")? When only one person is identified as having the problem, this person is often referred to as the "identified patient" (IP).

When a single IP is identified, you need to listen for and explore problems other family members may have. This has a twofold purpose. First, it helps you develop some possible hypotheses regarding family dynamics. For example, a family may initially present with a child who has problems at home or at school. With further exploration, you may discover the couple's relationship is conflictual, leading to a possible hypothesis that the child is acting out because he or she is triangulated in the couple's conflict. Second, the family is more likely to understand the justification for family therapy in lieu of individual therapy with the IP if you can successfully highlight other problems within the family system. Obviously, the more invested the family is in having an IP, the more cautiously you will need to proceed.

You should also find out who else knows about or is involved in the problem. This information can help you assess what areas of functioning have been affected by it. For example, you may learn that a child is having difficulties at school if the family discloses that a teacher knows about the problem, or you may discover that your clients are involved in the legal system. In all of these cases, you would be wise to consider getting a release of information from your clients so you can talk with others who may be knowledgeable about the problem. This can also help you assess what resources or social support the clients have. For example, a couple may mention talking to their minister or parents for advice on marital difficulties. In some cases, you may want to include some of these individuals in the treatment plan. You may solicit a teacher's help when dealing with a child's school-related problems, or parents of adult children might be invited in to deal with important family-of-origin issues.

Finally, it is often enlightening to ask the clients why they think the problem exists. Their insights in this area can help you develop hypotheses. It is not uncommon for one spouse to have good insights on what issues the other partner might need to look at, and vice versa. What is usually missing is insight regarding one's own issues or contributions to the problem. Likewise, ask the clients what others have said about why the problem exists. Again, this information can provide a valuable starting point for you to build hypotheses.

Some therapists who follow a solution-focused approach believe that a detailed knowledge of the problem is not always necessary to discover solutions or exceptions to the problem. Although this may indeed be true in many cases, therapists need to recognize that having clients tell us their stories (even if problem-saturated) can have value in other ways. For example, listening respectfully can help the client develop a connection with the therapist. In their eagerness to begin treatment, we have seen some beginning therapists prematurely cut off clients. Therapists need to be careful about pushing too quickly for solutions, or they risk appearing disrespectful of clients' need to tell their stories.

Assessing for Attempted Solutions

In addition to exploring the problems, it is frequently helpful to assess what solutions your clients have either attempted or considered. You thereby can avoid recommending solutions that have been unsuccessfully tried by your clients, which could damage your credibility. You should also explore what solutions your clients have considered but not tried, as well as solutions others have suggested. You can then explore with the clients why they didn't try particular solutions. This often provides you with good information about potential barriers to or negative consequences of change. Another reason to explore attempted solutions is that in some cases they may contribute to or exacerbate the problem (Fisch, Weakland, & Segal, 1985). A husband who withdraws to avoid conflict may actually create conflict with his partner because she interprets his withdrawal as a lack of caring. The therapist may recognize a pattern in a client's attempt to solve the problem and suggest that he or she take a completely different approach.

When assessing attempted solutions, it is extremely helpful to explore if therapy has been tried before. If so, you can explore what was helpful and not helpful about that experience, enabling you to build on past successes or avoid making similar mistakes. You may want to consider recommending books or giving homework assignments if your clients indicate that these were particularly helpful in the past. It would also be wise to explore why the clients are no longer seeing the previous therapist. Did the clients or therapist move, necessitating a change? Or, do your clients have a history of working with therapists for a short time and then dropping out of treatment? This information will help you assess the likelihood that therapy will have a positive outcome.

Assessing for Crisis and Stressful Life Events

During the initial assessment you should assess the extent to which your clients may be in crisis. Is there a specific event bringing them into therapy, or has there been a pileup of life events that has created stress? These life events could be of a personal nature (e.g., divorce, illness, death of family member) or involve external social, economic, or political events (e.g., layoffs due to recession, immigration forced by economic or social/political hardship) or both. Are the stressors of an acute or chronic nature? To what extent are the life stressors an underlying cause of the presenting problems? What resources do your clients have for coping? Is the stress imposing a burden on the clients that exceeds their coping resources? How has the stress impacted their family relationships? It is not uncommon for stress to be divisive and fracture relationships. It can be most helpful for the family to join around making the stress the problem and working to support each other. Whenever clients are in crisis, you should also consider assessing for suicide or other potential issues of harm. Chapter 6 discusses how to deal with clients in crisis.

POTENTIAL ISSUES OF HARM

A critical rule of assessment is the need to be constantly vigilant toward any possible issues of harm. Issues of potential harm include harm to self (suicide) or others (domestic violence or homicide, child abuse, or sexual abuse). Assessment of each of these issues is discussed next, along with other clinical considerations.

Suicide

Research on suicide suggests that the majority of people who kill themselves have told someone about their plan in the months preceding the suicide. This person may be a family member or friend, or a physician or therapist. Family therapists work with depressed clients on a daily basis and must always be alert for signs that a client is considering suicide.

Many new therapists bring misperceptions about suicide to their first clinical experience. Two common ones are the notion that discussing thoughts of suicide may cause an attempt on the client's part, and the tendency to discount the seriousness of suicide threats, especially when others perceive them as an attempt to get attention or some other goal. Other common misperceptions include the belief that a therapist cannot intervene effectively with a client who has decided to commit suicide or that people who commit suicide really want to die.

People who kill themselves frequently are ambivalent about dying. It is usually after a series of unrelenting losses and failures, with little or no relief or hope, that a client finally chooses suicide. Even after making the decision, many suicidal people leave open a way to be rescued. For example, writer Sylvia Plath, after several failed suicide attempts, was aware that rescue was possible from her final attempt. She turned on the gas in her stove to kill herself but knew that her maid would arrive shortly. Unfortunately, on the day of that attempt, the maid was late to work and Sylvia Plath died.

Assessing for suicide is a therapeutic skill that all beginning therapists should learn Dub. Research has suggested there are certain demographic factors and warning signals that should alert the therapist to the possibility of client suicide attempts. Table 4.2 reflects the demographics of suicide, while Table 4.3 provides a list of danger signs that indicate suicide risk. The combination of three risk factors in particular produce the highest probability of death by suicide: thwarted belongingness, perceived burdensomeness, and capability for suicide (Chu et al., 2015).

In assessing for suicide, the therapist may begin with general questions and transition to more specific questions if needed:

"Are there times when it feels that life isn't worth living?"
[If yes] "At times like that, are there ever times you actually wish to die?"

TABLE 4.2. Demographics of Suicide

Features	Trends and comments
Age	Suicide rises with age. The increase is linear in white males and peaks at about age 50 in females. There has been a recent increase in adolescent and youth suicide.
Sex	More males commit suicide. More females attempt suicide. Recent statistics show rises in suicide rates among young white females.
Ethnicity	More whites commit suicide than nonwhites. Recent statistics show an increase in young black males ages 15–35.
Childhood loss	Early loss is associated with completed suicide, later loss with attempted suicide. Early loss is also associated with scientific and artistic creativity.
Recent loss	The more irrevocable the loss, the greater the risk of suicide. Suicide is associated with an accumulation of losses throughout life.
Alcoholism	Alcohol is associated with high risk of suicide. Treatment for drinking and suicide problems has many features in common.
Mental illness	Suicide is mostly associated with depressive illness.
Physical illness	Suicide is associated with declining health and potency.
Downward economic mobility	Unemployment, frequent job changes, and a trend toward lower status and lower-paying jobs are traditionally associated with male risk, but are no longer sex-linked characteristics.
Living in the center city	Areas of high crime, alcoholism, mental illness, poverty, and family disorganization are associated with social isolation and alienation.
Marital disruption, including divorce, widowhood, and the breaking up of a love affair	The more final the change, the more serious the risk. Marriage is more of a protection against suicide for males. Women can survive the loss of a husband better than men can survive the loss of a wife.

(continued)

TABLE 4.2. *(continued)*

Features	Trends and comments
Previous suicide attempts	People who have attempted suicide are in a high-risk group. The more serious the previous attempts, the greater the rate of subsequent completed suicide.
History of attempted or completed suicide in relatives and other important figures	Family members' suicide is associated with a higher risk, as suicide tends to run in families.
A "death trend"	An accumulation of losses and death are a risk factor, and therefore a major reason for relieving the severe death anxiety in the family.

Note. Data from Hirschfeld and Russell (1997).

TABLE 4.3. Warning Signs of Suicide

Features	Manifestations and comments
1. Quiet, withdrawn, few friends	Often not recognized because the individual is not noticed and makes no obvious trouble. Associated with social and family isolation.
2. Changes in behavior	Personality changes, for example, from friendliness to withdrawal and lack of communication, sad and expressionless appearance; from a quiet demeanor to acting out and troublemaking. The important thing is the change.
3. Increased failure or role strain	Often pervasive in school, work, home, friends, and love relationships, but often manifested most clearly in school pressures.
4. a. Recent family changes	a. Illness, job loss, increased drinking by parents or other family members. Often the background of the crisis.
b. Recent loss of a family member	b. Death, divorce, separation, or someone leaving home.
5. Feelings of despair and hopelessness	Shows itself in many forms, from changes in posture and behavior to verbal expression of such feelings. Hopelessness is even more closely associated with suicide than depression.

(continued)

TABLE 4.3. *(continued)*

Features	Manifestations and comments
6. Symptomatic acts	Taking unnecessary risks, becoming involved in drinking and drug abuse, becoming inappropriately aggressive or submissive. Giving away possessions. Associated with changes in behavior.
7. Communication of suicidal thoughts or feelings	Such statements as "Life is not worth living," "I'm finished," "Done for," "I might as well be dead," or "I wish I was dead." Best understood in the context of life changes and family changes.
8. Presence of a plan	Storing up medication, buying a gun. The meaning of these acts and communication can best be understood by sensitive responding to and questioning of the suicidal person.
9. Negative or fearful attitudes toward treatment or psychiatrists	"Shows you're crazy," "It's the end of the road," "I'll end up in the crazy house," and so on. Refusal of help. Associated with conflicts over family loyalties.
10. Impasse in therapy	"Sabotaging" of the therapy, extreme resistance, becoming increasingly depressed or suicidal. Known as the "negative therapeutic reaction," it is often associated with success in therapy and threats to the status quo. Also part of a potentially positive therapeutic crisis.

Note. Data from Hirschfeld and Russell (1997).

> [If yes] "Are these just vague thoughts, or do you think about specific ways to die?"
> [If "specific ways"] "What specific ways have you thought about?"
> [If some are named] "Have you taken any step toward planning or acting to do that?" [going to buildings or a bridge where one might jump, hoarding pills, purchasing a rope, writing a suicide note, making a will]

In listening to the client's reply, the therapist should assess (1) detail or specificity in the plan (Is there mention of a method, time and date, or a planned or written suicide note?); (2) lethality and reversibility (e.g., shooting vs. cutting oneself); (3) intentionality (providing for the possibility of rescue); and (4) proximity (whether important support people know of the plan, are nearby, and express care or concern for the client). The therapist should also assess the same factors in any previous suicide attempts. Additional risk factors include psychiatric diagnosis, antisocial or borderline personality disorders, substance use, sense of urgency, poor impulse control, poor reality testing, serious medical illness, and life stress (Adler, Slootsky, Griffith, & Khin Khin, 2016). A quick way to recall risk assessment questions is through the 4 Ps: plan, previous attempts, probability that client will attempt, and protective factors that would prevent client from attempting (Dube, Kurt, Bair, Theobald, & Williams, 2010).

Examining what would prevent the individual from committing suicide is important because it helps the therapist to discover what gives the person hope. For example, a divorced, unemployed woman stated that the only reason she did not commit suicide was the pain it would cause her children. The therapist realized that the client was in so much pain that no amount of talk about caring for herself would change her mind. However, her sense of duty and love for her children combined with her religious beliefs about suicide served as strong enough deterrents to keep her alive until her living situation improved. Therapists can listen to and reinforce reasons their clients have for not killing themselves.

Discussing the suicidal ideation or suicide attempts of an individual in front of other family members involves important considerations. The therapist should determine what role family members may serve in preventing or increasing the possibility of a member attempting suicide. For example, family members sometimes threaten suicide when they perceive the possibility of rejection or abandonment by another family member (as in divorce). Intense family conflict can be the precipitating event in an adolescent's suicide attempt. On the other hand, the desire to protect young children from harm can be the only reason a parent stays alive. One client family lost a 16-year-old son in a skiing accident, causing the mother to go into a deep depression. Two years later the mother reported that the only factor that kept her from a suicide attempt was the desire to protect her 12-year-old daughter from further loss.

The possibility of suicide is often an unstated family secret of which members are aware in varying degrees. Depending on the age, maturity, and relationships of family members, an open discussion of suicide can lift a burden off the family. As mentioned, sometimes therapists believe that bringing up the topic will make the suicide more likely; in fact, open acknowledgment and conversation will often be protective. Social isolation, family history of suicide attempts, and loss of family members through death or separation are predictors of suicide that specifically involve family relations. Relationships among family members are an important consideration in any discussion of suicide.

Assessing for Violence and Abuse

Family violence and child abuse are two additional areas that should be considered during your initial evaluation. Violence can take many forms and be inflicted in many different relationships. While spousal abuse and physical abuse of children are probably the most common forms of violence that therapists see, violence against older adults is becoming increasingly common. Victims of family violence can suffer a wide range of physical and psychological problems. Battering, for example, is the most common cause of injury for women.

It is recommended that you routinely evaluate all couples for domestic violence (Riggs, Caulfield, & Street, 2000). One way to uncover domestic violence is to ask couples to describe what an argument or fight looks like. It may be necessary to ask directly if one or both individuals has ever hit, harmed, or threatened his or her partner. Some individuals may be reluctant to admit in front of their partner that there has been domestic violence out of a fear that this will lead to more violence at home after the therapy session. As a result, some clients will not admit to any domestic violence unless asked in an individual session. The clinician should suspect domestic violence if an individual has sustained injuries and does not offer a plausible explanation for them. Assessment measures such as the Conflict Tactics Scale (Straus, 1979) can also be used to screen for possible intimate partner violence.

While many warning signs may suggest that some type of violence is occurring, therapists should also pay attention to their internal responses to the clients. Frequently, students report having a nagging concern about a family member's safety, even when the session is over. Another frequent internal clue is the therapist's sense of fearfulness, intimidation, and concern for personal safety, particularly because many beginning therapists are young and female.

There is increasing evidence that there are different types of domestic violence (Greene & Bogo, 2002). In one type of violence ("patriarchal terrorism"), the perpetrator uses violence to exert control over the partner. Men are most likely to be the perpetrator in this type of domestic violence. In the second type of violence ("common couple violence"), partners intermittently become physical with one another when an argument escalates. In contrast to the first type, this type of violence is not characterized by a pervasive pattern of control, and may be initiated by either partner. Regardless of the type, it is important that the therapist takes the violence seriously and contract with the client that it will stop.

Greene and Bogo (2002) suggest four factors that may help clinicians distinguish between patriarchal terrorism and common couple violence. In contrast to common couple violence, the perpetrator in patriarchal terrorism uses a variety of control tactics besides violence, including emotional abuse, isolation, threats, and control of finances or other resources. Second, the motivation for violence is different. In patriarchal terrorism, the goal is to establish control over one's partner, which is not true for common couple violence. Third, the impact is usually more severe in patriarchal terrorism, often because the type of violence is more severe. Physical and emotional well-being, occupational functioning, and relationships with those outside the couple (e.g., friends, family) are more likely to be affected if the individual is suffering from patriarchal terrorism. Finally, the individual's subjective experience of the violence may be different. In common couple violence, individuals may not fear their partner, whereas this is almost always the case in patriarchal terrorism.

Distinguishing between these two types of domestic violence is important because it can have implications for treatment. It may be feasible, for example, to conduct conjoint couple therapy with common couple violence if appropriate safeguards are taken (e.g., a no violence contract). However, conjoint therapy would be contraindicated if either partner engages in patriarchal terrorism. Rather, treatment for the perpetrator focuses on addressing male power and control. Emotional dependence and lack of economic options are two reasons women stay in relationships where there is battering or patriarchal terrorism. This situation has led to treatment ideas that focus on finding shelter, economic options, and new connections to supportive people and resources for victims. Importantly, clinicians should remember that females can be perpetrators too (Stith, McCollum, Amanor-Boadu, & Smith, 2012). Domestic violence is a serious risk, so inexperienced therapists should check with their supervisors often as they make treatment plans.

Although society and the legal system historically have been slower to intervene in violence between two adults, they have been more attentive to cases that involve potential child abuse. This heightened responsiveness to child abuse is most likely in response to the fact that children are less powerful and able to protect themselves than adults. Frequently, domestic violence and child abuse occur in the same families. Additional predictors of abuse are families who suffer economic hardships and who are isolated from outside support systems.

Although some children will disclose directly (often privately) an incidence of physical abuse, others will not. Physical abuse should be suspected if children give evasive or unconvincing stories as to how they obtained their injuries (e.g., bruises, burns, welts, broken bones). When asked about how they discipline their children, parents may disclose examples of physical abuse, but may either not recognize it as abuse or justify the behavior (e.g., as necessary to get the child to behave).

Therapists also need to be alert to possible neglect, another form of child abuse. Children who suffer from neglect may wear clothing that is dirty, ill-fitting, or inappropriate for the weather. They may also be consistently dirty or have severe body odor. A home that is dirty or severely cluttered may be evidence of neglect. Neglect should also be suspected if children receive inadequate medical or dental care, or are left home alone without proper supervision. You should carefully assess for neglect if parents are severely depressed or using substances because this may impact their ability to provide for their children.

As with violence, sexual abuse occurs more frequently than reported. The definition of sexual abuse varies from state to state, but usually it is said to occur when an adult or older child initiates an interaction with a child for the purpose of sexually stimulating or gratifying the perpetrator. Although research varies, national surveys indicate that approximately one in five women and one in nine men report being victims of sexual abuse as children (Finkelhor, Hotaling, Lewis, & Smith, 1990). The majority of sexual abuse cases involve male perpetrators and female victims.

Perpetrators and victims of childhood sexual maltreatment usually do not voluntarily self-report; detection is often left to the therapist, who may be given indirect behaviors as clues. Due to the legal implications of both physical and sexual abuse, it is vital to handle each case with care, since specific court testimony might be needed. Limiting the number of times a child discloses his or her experience is vital for the emotional welfare of the child.

Using a biopsychosocial-systems perspective, sexual abuse assessment stems from information about a child's physical condition, behavior, and social context. If a child indicates several of the following symptoms, further interviewing needs to be done: (1) physically, a child may display sleep disturbances, encopresis or enuresis, complain of abdominal pain, or suffer from appetite disturbances with corresponding weight change; (2) behaviorally, a child may manifest a sudden, unexplained change in behavior (anxiety or depression), regressive behavior, or overly sexualized behavior or knowledge given the child's age, experience suicidal thoughts, run away, or abuse substances; (3) socially, family conditions may include a child's parentified role, inadequate parental coping skills, relationship difficulties leading to one parent seeking physical affection from the child, isolated social context, alcohol and drug use, and a history of parental sexual abuse (Edwards, 1986).

Child sexual abuse can negatively impact individuals in a number of ways, including risk of posttraumatic stress disorder, depression, suicide, and sexual promiscuity (Paolucci, Genius, & Violato, 2001). Survivors of child sexual abuse can also experience problems later on in their intimate relationships as result of the abuse, including issues with sexual functioning (Davis & Petretic-Jackson, 2000; Rumstein-McKean & Hunsley, 2001). Multiple factors such as the duration and severity of the abuse can influence the effects on the victim. The family response to the disclosure of sexual abuse can also mediate the impact of the abuse. Families that believe the child's claims of sexual abuse and take appropriate action to protect the child from further abuse can aid in the child's healing. In contrast, a family that does not believe the child or blames the child for the abuse can add to the child's victimization. In many cases, victims of child sexual abuse misplace blame on themselves for the abuse, which increases their sense of shame. If sexual abuse is uncovered, you should carefully assess what effect the abuse has had on the individual and factors that may mediate its impact.

When working with older adults or families with dependent adults, you should also be alert to the possibility of abuse or neglect. Elder or dependent adults may tell you directly about possible abuse, which can take many forms, such as physical abuse, sexual abuse, neglect, or financial abuse. Like other forms of family violence or abuse, you may need to ask directly if the individual has experienced any form of violence, abuse, or neglect, especially if you have any suspicions. Unexplained injuries such as bruising or marks, for example, should be inquired about. Caretakers can be asked how they deal with the elder or dependent individual when they are frustrated. You should also be attentive to possible signs of neglect, such as the individual not being properly groomed, or not receiving appropriate care for medical or physical needs.

Legal issues are an important concern when either violence or abuse is suspected or known. In most states, the law mandates the reporting of physical abuse, neglect, or sexual abuse of children. Reporting of elder or dependent abuse may also be mandated. Therapists may have no legal responsibility to report domestic violence unless children are being physically or emotionally harmed by the domestic violence, elder or dependent abuse applies, or a *Tarasoff* or "duty to warn" situation arises (see below). It is imperative that you know the laws of your state in this regard.

Beyond legal knowledge, one's best clinical judgment will be required in some situations. For example, in most states mandated reporters (which usually include therapists) are required to report *suspected* abuse. What constitutes enough evidence to report requires judgment that most beginning therapists are still developing. When new therapists initially suspect abuse, they should immediately involve their supervisors.

Gathering information is another skill that therapists develop over time. Particularly when abuse is suspected, the therapist must be careful in eliciting and documenting information. Ideally, the interview could be recorded, carried out with a supervisor or more experienced therapist. The therapist wants to know the who, what, how, where, and why of each situation without asking leading questions or giving responses that might influence what the victim says. The therapist also needs to assess for imminent risk. Interviewing possible child abuse victims is an art requiring specialized training and skill development. If child abuse is suspected, the family therapist will continue to interview if trained to do so, or will refer the child to a specialist, usually through child protective services available in the community.

When violence or abuse is an issue, the therapist can no longer conduct "therapy as usual." Insight into the violence will not protect the victims. Safety of the victims at home and during the therapy sessions is of paramount importance. This means that the therapist must become very practical in his or her treatment approach, finding out if the victims can escape and if they have a safe place to go. If the victims are children or older adults and are unable to protect themselves, the therapist must be even more active, becoming a representative of society by stating unequivocally that the violence must stop immediately and then notifying the proper authorities to ensure that it does.

The switch from being the client's advocate to using one's authority to stop a client's behavior can be a difficult process for beginning therapists. Most therapists choose their profession because they want to help people in a collaborative manner. Violence and abuse are two of the infrequent therapeutic situations in which therapists must take an authoritarian stance and insist that a behavior stop. Guidance from one's supervisor will help new therapists know how to respond to these challenging situations.

Duty-to-Warn Issues

Another potential safety issue therapists may encounter is a client who threatens to kill or harm another. A psychologist at a university counseling center faced one such situation when his client, Prosenjit

Poddar, threatened to kill his girlfriend. The therapist notified campus police, who questioned and released Prosenjit. Two months later, Prosenjit killed his girlfriend, Tatiana Tarasoff. The courts (*Tarasoff v. Regents of the University of California*) later ruled that the psychologist had not taken sufficient action to prevent the harm because he did not notify Tatiana Tarasoff of the threat. As a result of this case, many states require therapists to inform potential victims if a serious threat has been made against them, referred to as a duty-to-warn. You must learn the laws in your own state regarding when a "duty to warn" situation exists and what actions are required from you. In California, for example, therapists are mandated to warn identifiable potential victims and contact law enforcement to obtain legal immunity.

In identifying the seriousness of the risk, several factors should be considered. Borum and Reddy (2001) have suggested six factors that clinicians can use, which together form the acronym ACTION. The first factor is to explore "Attitudes that support or facilitate violence." For example, does the client believe that violence is justified in certain situations or circumstances? *C* refers to "Capacity." Does the client have access to the means (e.g., weapons) to carry out the threats? Does the client have access to the individual or individuals that he or she is threatening to harm? The letter *T* represents "Thresholds crossed," which encourages the therapist to find out if the client has a plan, and the extent to which he or she has begun to put a plan into action. Therapists should also assess for "*I*ntent." Does a client's comment reveal a serious intent to harm others, or is it a general comment that reflects frustration but no serious intention of harming another? *O* stands for "Others' reactions and responses." Have others, for example, encouraged or discouraged the individual with regard to acting in a hostile way? "*N*oncompliance with risk reduction" is the last factor. Risk is higher if the individual shows an unwillingness to consider alternatives to harming others. In addition to the above factors, it is important to assess if the client has a previous history of violence toward others, or has a mental illness that would predispose him or her to violence.

ASSESSING FOR SUBSTANCE ABUSE

Substance abuse is one of the major mental health problems in the United States. In fact, many healthcare payer groups single out substance abuse as a separate budget item. Although some experts assert that there is a substance abuse epidemic, abuse and addictions are commonly overlooked in therapy unless the substance problem is the presenting problem.

Therapists overlook substance abuse issues for a variety of reasons. First, the clients may not consider the abuse to be a problem itself, but rather the result of some other issue: a bad job, painful childhood, or conflictual marriage. Clients come to therapy asking for help with the presenting problem and fail to mention their substance abuse. The therapist might collude by failing to ask about use of substances, or drug and alcohol abuse might be overlooked because there is no clear definition of when a social drinker becomes a problem drinker or when the latter becomes an alcoholic. In other words, the abuser might not view his or her substance use as problematic. The family may consider the substance use a problem but be afraid to mention it.

One of the authors had a client family report that the father could not be an alcoholic because he only drank beer. Families have different definitions about what constitutes a substance abuse problem. Is dependence on caffeine an addiction? Is recreational use of marijuana a problem? When does regular substance use become a problem? Experts do not agree on these issues, and neither do families. Even if families believe that a member's substance abuse is a problem, they often collude to hide it from the therapist.

For example, a therapist had as clients a couple who defined the wife's presenting problem as the husband's drinking. The husband's presenting problem was the wife's nagging, particularly about his drinking. The therapist presented the following three theories to the couple and suggested that the goal of therapy was to decide which theory was true: (1) alcohol abuse by the husband was the problem; (2) conflict about the alcohol was the problem in the relationship; or (3) the wife's distortions about the alcohol were the problem. He then challenged the husband to quit drinking for 2 weeks to help discern "the truth." When the husband could not quit drinking, he became willing to consider the first theory.

The most common mistake new therapists make regarding substance abuse is to overlook the possibility of it. Substance abuse is frequently comorbid or exists along with other disorders such as depression or anxiety. It also is associated with violence, abuse, automobile accidents, homicides, and suicide. It is essential to know the variety of ways substance-abusing clients can present in therapy. The second step is to routinely ask about substance use in initial interviews with new clients.

There are several commonly used screening tests for assessing alcohol abuse (Kitchens, 1994; Selzer, 1971). Questions raised in these tests can be asked about substances other than alcohol. Two frequently used tests are the Michigan Alcoholism Screening Test (MAST) and the Alcohol Use Disorders Identification Test (AUDIT). The Substance

Abuse and Mental Health Services Administration (SAMSHA) of the United States government publishes many substance abuse instruments including the MAST and AUDIT. One can simply put the words *SAMSHA* and *screening* in a search engine and find numerous assessment instruments that are in the public domain. A sample instrument, AUDIT, is shown in Figure 4.1.

The CAGE (*C*utting down, *A*nnoying, *G*uilt, *E*ye-opener) questionnaire (Ewing, 1984) consists of four questions: (1) Have you ever felt you ought to cut down on your drinking? (2) Have people annoyed you by criticizing your drinking? (3) Have you ever felt bad or guilty about your drinking? and (4) Have you ever had a drink first thing in the morning to steady your nerves or get rid of a hangover (an eye-opener)? These simple questions can be memorized and integrated with a regular intake interview. The CAGE questionnaire has been tested for accuracy in several different settings. Generally, a positive response to two or more questions identifies a problem drinker.

Frequency is another key variable in the assessment of a substance problem. However, clients may underreport the amount that they use. Other behaviors that might indicate a substance problem include the amount of substance used in one setting, the reasons the client uses the substance, and what happens when the client tries to stop using the substance.

ASSESSING FOR BIOLOGICAL AND NEUROLOGICAL FACTORS

George Gershwin spent several years in psychoanalysis with an analyst who had two medical degrees. When Gershwin finally died, an autopsy found a brain tumor that explained his aberrant behavior. To avoid making the same mistake as Gershwin's analyst, family therapists must consider biological or organic factors in assessment. Unfortunately, the reality is that family therapists are trained to recognize and treat psychological and social problems, and frequently have limited knowledge of biological influences on behavior. Thus, we run the risk of misinterpreting important clues to a possible biological problem as a symptom of something we have been trained to treat—interpersonal problems. However, being mindful of this risk can help keep us from overlooking possible biological or organic factors.

An awareness of biological problems does not require that you be an expert in human physiology. However, therapists must recognize the telltale signs of an underlying biological problem and also recognize that psychological symptoms do not necessarily imply psychological causes (Taylor, 1990). You also need sensitivity to any information that

Points	Questions
2	1. Do you feel you are a normal drinker?
2	2. Have you ever awakened the morning after some drinking the night before and found that you could not remember a part of the evening before?
1	3. Does your spouse or do your parents ever worry or complain about your drinking?
2	4. Can you stop drinking without a struggle after one or two drinks?
1	5. Do you ever feel bad about your drinking?
2	6. Do friends or relatives think you are a normal drinker?
2	7. Are you always able to stop drinking when you want to?
5	8. Have you ever attended a meeting of Alcoholics Anonymous?
1	9. Have you gotten into fights when drinking?
2	10. Has drinking ever created problems with you and your spouse?
2	11. Has your spouse or other family member ever gone to anyone for help about your drinking?
2	12. Have you ever lost friends or girlfriends/boyfriends because of your drinking?
2	13. Have you ever gotten into trouble at work because of drinking?
2	14. Have you ever lost a job because of drinking?
2	15. Have you ever neglected your obligations, your family, or your work for two or more days in a row because you were drinking?
1	16. Do you ever drink before noon?
2	17. Have you ever been told you have liver trouble? Cirrhosis?
2	18. Have you ever had delirium tremens (DTs) or severe shaking, heard voices, or seen things that weren't there after heavy drinking?
5	19. Have you ever gone to anyone for help about your drinking?
5	20. Have you ever been in a hospital because of your drinking?
2	21. Have you ever been a patient in a psychiatric hospital or on a psychiatric ward of a general hospital where drinking was part of the problem?
2	22. Have you ever been seen at a psychiatric or mental health clinic or gone to a doctor, social worker, or clergyman for help with an emotional problem in which drinking had played a part?
2	23. Have you ever been arrested, even for a few hours, because of drunken behavior?
2	24. Have you ever been arrested for drunk driving or driving after drinking?

FIGURE 4.1. Alcohol Use Disorders Identification Test (AUDIT). From Saunders, Aasland, Babor, De La Fuente, and Grant (1993). Copyright 1993 by the Society for the Study of Addiction to Alcohol and Other Drugs, Carfax Publishing Ltd., Abingdon, UK. Reprinted by permission of Blackwell Publishing Ltd.; permission conveyed through Copyright Clearance Center, Inc.

seems outside the usual content of a family therapy session. Instead of dismissing the unusual content because it does not fit with one's model, a therapist needs an attitude of openness and curiosity to pursue a line of questioning wherever it may lead, including to a referral.

Therapists should be aware of several clues that might indicate biological problems, including (1) no history of similar symptoms; (2) no readily identifiable cause; (3) age 55 or older; (4) chronic physical disease; (5) premature birth and (6) drug use. Some clues in particular suggest the possibility of organic brain disease. Symptoms of a brain disease might result from a brain tumor, seizures, heart disease, or liver failure. One or more of the following cognitive deficits suggest a brain syndrome: inattention, disorientation, recent memory impairment, diminished reasoning, and sensory indiscrimination. Other clues suggesting a brain syndrome include head injury, changes in headache pattern, visual disturbances, speech deficits, abnormal body movements, and alterations in consciousness. The more clues there are, the more suspicious you should be. These clues should alert you to begin a different line of questioning, focusing on the individual and his or her symptoms. Other family members may be asked to corroborate details given by the IP or to give their own impressions. Discovery of these symptoms should lead you to make a prompt referral for medical evaluation. Document this referral in the client's record and note the reasons the referral was made.

An important diagnostic tool that family therapists should be familiar with is the mental status exam (MSE). Physicians frequently use MSEs as a rapid assessment tool to detect changes in orientation, intellectual functioning (language, memory, and calculation), thought content, judgment, mood, and behavior. MSEs are used less frequently in family therapy, perhaps because most clients who come for family treatment do not demonstrate any behaviors that would raise concerns about intellectual functioning.

While it is probably prudent to refer a client to a physician if unusual symptoms (such as those listed earlier) are noted, you can conduct an MSE immediately and obtain information that will be helpful in making a referral. When doing an MSE, the therapist should consider the client's appearance; his or her interaction with others; the client's awareness of where he or she is and what he or she is doing; appropriateness of behavior; the client's mood, use of language, attention, and concentration; short- and long-term memory; ability to perform simple calculations and answer specific questions; the presence of delusions (bizarre thoughts) with or without hallucinations; social and moral judgment; and impulsiveness (Dilsaver, 1990). A therapist can put the words *mental status exam* in a computer search engine and easily find multiple versions of the mental status exam including some short versions that might be more appropriate in therapy.

A short mnemonic to remember the elements of an MSE is JOIMAT: *j*udgment, *o*rientation, *i*ntellectual functioning, *m*emory, *a*ffect, and *t*hought processing. A family therapist may perform MSEs so infrequently that it is difficult to remember the details of the exam. However, by memorizing the mnemonic and asking oneself "What is unusual about this client and what questions should I ask to obtain more information?," you can begin investigating possible biological etiologies. For example, an elderly couple was receiving supportive family therapy in conjunction with the husband's treatment for lung cancer, which was in remission. During one session, the husband seemed confused and unable to focus. The therapist wondered if these behaviors were cognitive symptoms of depression, which is a normal response to cancer. However, the therapist referred the husband back to his physician, and a CT scan was done, with the results indicating that the cancer had spread to his brain.

In general, a family therapist might consider requesting a neuropsychological evaluation when the following problems emerge: learning problems in children or adults, memory problems, language struggles, and organizational struggles with planning or completing tasks. If a client's daily functioning changes dramatically or quickly at school or work, the therapist can consider requesting a neuropsychological evaluation. For neuropsychological evaluations, young clients and elderly clients are the most commonly referred patients. Young clients who struggle at school might have learning disabilities. Older adults might have dementia, delirium, or depression. Another common reason to refer a client is if one suspects a traumatic brain injury. A neuropsychological evaluation can help tease out the reasons for the client's struggles and suggest a direction for treatment.

In general, neuropsychiatric testing evaluates intellectual functioning, attention, decision making, memory, visual–spatial skills, language, motor functioning, and emotional functioning. Most evaluations are done by neuropsychologists with PhDs. However, school psychologists can also do evaluations, and these are less costly. For older adults, a neurologist or psychiatrist would probably complete the evaluation. Family therapists often treat families with the presenting complaint of a child's "laziness," "attitude problem," or "defiance." In fact, the child might have a known syndrome such as ADHD. A wonderful opportunity exists for family therapists to help their client families understand how a child's brain works and what the child needs to prosper and learn. A good neuropsychological exam can provide new understanding of the child's struggles. The family therapist can reframe the problem and provide insight into the child's unique learning style. In like manner, using the results of a neuropsychological evaluation, a family therapist can help a family understand the special needs of an elderly family member. These skills will be especially important as the general population continues to age.

Research from genetics and neuroscience is changing the family therapist's understanding of how problems develop. Concepts such as epigenetics, neural plasticity, and toxic stress hint at the growing understanding of how biology and environmental influences interact to create unique human beings. This research also highlights the critical importance of a nurturing environment to facilitate healthy brain development in children. At present, few specific guidelines exist to help family therapists evaluate biological forces. But in the coming years, new information from epigenetic research can guide family therapists as they assess for both psychosocial and biological influences on children, adults, and families (Lester, Conradt, & Marsit, 2016; Patterson & Vakili, 2014).

PSYCHOLOGICAL ASSESSMENT

Psychological ABCs and Psychopathology: Assessing Affect, Behavior, and Cognition

Most psychological theories focus on affect, behaviors, or cognitions. As a result, both assessment and treatment goals usually address one or more of these domains. We believe that all good clinicians attend to affect, behavior, and cognitions regardless of their theoretical orientation. A key reason to assess all three domains is that symptom descriptions for mental disorders in the *Diagnostic and Statistical Manual of Mental Disorders* usually fall into one of these categories.

Certain disorders of childhood, such as oppositional defiant disorder and conduct disorder, focus almost exclusively on behaviors, while delusional disorder focuses on patients' beliefs about themselves or their relationships, and mood disorders primarily involve changes in emotion and affect. Symptom lists for most DSM disorders address all three domains, although the focus varies by disorder. In recent years, DSM editors have tried to remove the theory-driven terminology (e.g., phrases such as "defense mechanisms") and instead use observable criteria. These changes should make it easier to do an assessment of the patient's symptoms.

During your assessment, consider whether the problems the client describes and those you observe fit more into one category than another. You can consider the "ABCs" as well as whether the symptoms cluster together in a way that matches a DSM diagnosis, although family systems theory usually describes interaction, not individual symptoms (Denton, Patterson, & Van Meir, 1997). It is not necessary to be a purist, choosing an exclusive focus on family interaction or individual diagnosis—using both frameworks can lead to the most complete assessment picture.

It is important that you have a basic understanding of DSM because it represents the common language shared by mental health clinicians. In addition, many treatment methods and psychopharmacological remedies are tied to DSM individual diagnostic categories. While you may not have memorized criteria for every possible diagnosis, you should be able to recognize depression, anxiety, substance abuse, somatization, and other common disorders. Cultivate an attitude of curiosity, and think of yourself as a keen observer of the human condition. Write down a list of the most salient symptoms your patient describes, and note your own observations along with the nature of your interaction with the client. Then ask yourself, "Do these symptoms cluster in a way that fits a DSM diagnostic category?" Consider also the possibility that your client may demonstrate more than one disorder; comorbidity is common.

Assessing for Meaning

One of the most important aspects of assessment is to understand the meaning that each client attaches to the issues presented in therapy. Meaning is derived from the various cognitions, beliefs, memories, and emotions that a client consciously or unconsciously uses to make sense of his or her daily experiences. Meaning informs how an individual views and interprets internal and external experiences, and how he or she chooses to respond to those experiences. Narrative therapy, in particular, notes how we develop stories to make meaning of our lives.

It will be difficult for you to create change without understanding how your clients make meaning out of their experiences. In one case, a woman with a chronic illness became upset whenever her husband offered any type of advice regarding her illness. She accused him of being very unsupportive of her and her illness, and was threatening to leave the relationship. He in turn was hurt and confused by this accusation because he felt he was expressing concern whenever he suggested things to her. By exploring the meaning that the woman ascribed to her husband's advice giving, the therapist discovered that she interpreted his advice as evidence that he thought her chronic illness could be cured. She feared that once he truly discovered that her illness was chronic and not curable, he would perceive her as a burden and leave.

This opened the door to discussing important issues in the relationship regarding illness, caretaking, and trust.

You can use a variety of approaches to understand how your client is making meaning out of what is happening. Usually the best approach is to ask your client directly what meaning he or she attributes to something. However, this approach is not infallible. In order to trust your client's self-report, you must have confidence that your client is being honest, is cooperative, and is sufficiently self-aware. Clients are not always willing or capable of this. For example, child molesters may be unwilling to fully disclose details or even admit to molesting a child out of shame or fear of legal consequences. In some cases, clients may have little psychological insight into their motives or reasons for doing things. To the extent that we all have some psychological processes that operate outside of our immediate awareness, client self-report has some limitations.

In addition to self-reports, meaning can sometimes be inferred based on a client's observable behavior and the context in which that behavior happens. When a husband silently withdraws after his wife criticizes him, the inference can be made that the husband was hurt by the remark. The difficulty with making inferences based on behaviors is that several alternate meanings are possible, raising the possibility that an incorrect inference will be made. This risk is evident when working with distressed couples; clients frequently attribute a more negative intent to their partner's behavior than the partner intended.

Your knowledge in specific content areas can also be an important aid in inferring the meaning behind an individual's behavior. For example, a good grounding in human development can help you understand an adolescent's behavior in the context of his or her need for independence. Likewise, understanding a client's cultural background may provide important insights when an individual's interpretations of certain behaviors or events differ from those common in the dominant culture.

SOCIAL ASSESSMENT

Assessing the Family System

One of the things that distinguishes family therapy is the importance it places on assessing the couple or family system in order to place the individual in proper context. Obviously, the theoretical lens that you use will influence your assessment approach with couples and families. A structural family therapist may see enmeshment or diffuse boundaries, whereas a Bowenian therapist may see fusion or an undifferentiated ego mass within the same family. However, they each tap into an underlying concept of closeness or distance. Thus, our approach in this section is to outline important areas of assessment to consider regardless of which theoretical orientation you choose. The specific way in which these issues are explored will depend on your personal style as well as your theoretical orientation.

Family Structure

The first step in the family assessment process is to obtain the family structure. If you are interested in multigenerational issues, the family structure assessment ideally should include at least three generations (e.g., child, parent, and grandparents). A genogram (McGoldrick, Gerson, & Petri, 2008) is a convenient way to capture the family structure visually. The family structure should reflect all the individuals who are significant in the client's life either by their presence or absence. For example, the family structure should include both biological parents even if the client has little or no contact with one of them, because the absence of a parent is often a therapeutic issue. Likewise, the family structure should not be restricted to biologically related relatives since other people, such as stepparents and live-in nannies, can have a significant influence on a client's life. Asking about multiple marriages and who lives with whom is often helpful in uncovering significant individuals who may not be biologically related.

The family structure can be an important source of clinical hypotheses. You could explore possible loyalty conflicts that may exist in a remarried family constellation, or discuss how a single parent without proper social support may be overwhelmed by parenting responsibilities. Likewise, hypotheses could also be generated based on the sibling constellation (birth order, gender, age difference of siblings). For example, a firstborn child may be more likely to be parentified.

Family Functioning

Families should also be assessed for their commitment to each other, relational bonds, and communication. In terms of commitment, you should assess how committed the parent or parents are to their children. In an intact family, are both parents equally invested in parenting? In divorced or separated families, are both parents still involved with the children? If not, why? How has the child or children made sense of this? Do the parents have favorites or certain children with whom they are more responsive than others?

One area to explore is the nature of relationship bonds between family members. Are any parent–child dyads particularly conflicted? Do the parents spend an appropriate amount of time with their children, helping with homework, playing, or taking part in other activities? Do the children receive praise from their parents, as well as verbal and physical affection? Or is the relationship primarily characterized by negativity? Do the parents rely too much on their children for their own emotional needs? Is there any evidence of physical abuse, neglect, or sexual abuse (see "Potential Issues of Harm" section, pages 47–58)?

When exploring the relationship bonds between family members, it is important that you consider other relationships within the family besides those of parent and child. Sibling relationships can be an important source of support for children. In addition, sibling conflict may indicate that the children are aligned with different parents, who in turn are in conflict with one another. Therefore, you should also assess what types of interactions the children have with one another. Do they do a lot of activities together? Are the relationships generally harmonious or tense? In multigenerational households, you should also assess the relationships between various family members across generational lines. For example, does the child have a close or distant relationship with a grandparent who also lives in the household?

You should observe how family members communicate with one another. Are family members able to speak without being interrupted? Do family members speak for one another? Are children comfortable sharing their thoughts, feelings, or fears with their parents? Do family members have difficulty talking about certain topics or issues? Likewise, are certain emotions such as anger or sadness unacceptable to have or to express? Are family members respectful when talking to one another, or are they verbally abusive? Does conflict ever escalate to the point of one or more family members being physically aggressive with each other (see "Potential Issues of Harm" section)? Do the conflicts seem to follow a repetitive pattern?

In order to determine how a family functions instrumentally, it is important to explore if one or both parents have other commitments or problems that negatively impact their parenting. For example, are the children's needs being ignored as a parent focuses energy on a new relationship or marriage? Are one or both parents focusing too much energy on work at the expense of their children? Is a mental illness or some other stressor reducing the parent's energy for managing and nurturing children?

You should also assess for possible issues of control and responsibility within the family. Consider how the parents monitor their children's activities and behavior. Also assess how discipline is handled. Are the parents consistent in enforcing the rules? Do parents give appropriate consequences when the rules are broken? Are the consequences administered in a calm and nonreactive manner, or do the parents become angry and perhaps even physically abusive (see "Potential Issues of Harm" section)? You should assess if the children have developmentally appropriate levels of responsibility and privileges. Look at the responsibilities each child has. Is a child being parentified? For example, is a child being given too much responsibility for taking care of the needs of other children or a parent? Is the child knowledgeable or concerned about issues that would only be appropriate for adults? To what extent are children given age-appropriate input into making decisions?

Family Life-Cycle Issues

You should also consider life-cycle issues when conducting an assessment, as clients often come to therapy during a life transition. Be curious: Is the family experiencing a new life stage such as the birth of the first child or launching children, or is the family dealing with an acute crisis, like the sudden death of a family member? Is the family having difficulty with this developmental transition? And is the transition occurring in the normative range, or are stressors disrupting the common trajectory? For instance, increased conflict between a parent and an adolescent may be related to the adolescent seeking greater autonomy during this normative developmental stage. Yet, a child's temper tantrums may be related to her need for attention as a result of a parent focusing on a new marriage.

Assessment of life-cycle issues is valuable in two primary ways: first, it allows you to explore and understand dysfunctional patterns throughout the system over time, not just in the present moment; and second, it helps you identify predictable (e.g., transition to parenthood) and unpredictable changes (e.g., death, onset of illness) in a system's natural growth and development. The ability to work together and accommodate these changes is central to functioning as a family. According to Nichols and Everett (1986), "Some families may present themselves for therapy at the onset of the [developmental] disruption, others may not feel that there is a problem until disruptive events have accumulated and . . . resulted in severe symptomatology" (p. 186). In Chapter 7, we explore predictable and unpredictable stressors in family development in greater detail.

Assessing the Couple System

Assessing the couple's relationship is obviously important when doing marital or couple therapy. However, it is also important for you to assess the couple relationship even if the presenting problem centers on a child. Marital or couple conflict can have a significant impact on children. For example, a parent may inappropriately turn to a child to get his or her emotional needs met if the couple relationship is not fulfilling, or a child may act out because he or she is triangulated in the parents' conflict.

A good place to start when assessing a couple is to administer a measure of marital adjustment or marital quality, such as the Dyadic Adjustment Scale (Spanier, 1976), the Couple Satisfaction Index (Funk & Rogge, 2007), or the Marital Satisfaction Inventory (Snyder, 1979). These instruments will give you an idea of the overall level of distress in the relationship. In addition, answers to specific questions may help you quickly assess areas where the couple is struggling (e.g., sex, finances, in-laws) or, conversely, the areas in which the couple is doing well.

You should also assess for possible issues of commitment. If the couple is not married, is one or both of the individuals ambivalent about continuing the relationship? If the couple is married, has either one seriously considered divorce? Brief pencil-and-paper instruments such as the Marital Instability Index (Edwards, Johnson, & Booth, 1987) or the Marital Status Inventory (Crane, Newfield, & Armstrong, 1984; Weiss & Cerrato, 1980) can be used to measure the likelihood the couple will divorce. You should also assess whether one or both individuals may be significantly involved with other people or activities that impact their commitment to a relationship. Is one individual having an affair? Do one or both partners spend a significant amount of time with friends, parents, or children at the expense of time with the partner? Likewise, does the amount of time that one or both partners spend at work or with hobbies negatively impact the relationship?

Assessing how issues of control and responsibility are handled in the relationship is also important. An excellent way to assess this is to explore how the couple makes decisions. Do they share decisions together, or does one person usually make the decision? Is physical violence or the threat of it used for control (see previous section "Potential Issues of Harm")? Gender roles can also impact how a couple shares control and responsibility. Does the couple follow a traditional or an egalitarian model? Is there agreement about the roles and responsibilities that each has in the relationship? In terms of responsibilities, is there a pattern where one partner overfunctions and the other under-functions?

The nature of the couple's interactions can also reveal much about their relationship bond. Does the couple do activities together, or do they lead independent lives? What types of activities (e.g., leisure, vacations, projects, church attendance, volunteer work) do they share? To what extent is the couple verbally or physically affectionate with one another? Does the couple have a satisfactory sexual relationship? If not, what are the concerns? Exploring the couple's courtship can be helpful in assessing relationship bonds. For example, what first attracted them to one another? What kind of things did the couple do during their courtship to bond? In some cases, a review of the courtship history may uncover concerns that may impact the couple's relationship bond (e.g., marrying to legitimize an unexpected pregnancy).

You should also assess a couple's communication and conflict resolution skills. In terms of communication, can the couple listen to one another? Can the couple express their thoughts and feelings to one another? In addition, are they able to take responsibility for their own feelings and actions, or do they frequently take a blaming stance? Having the couple discuss an issue while you observe their interaction can be an excellent approach to assessing communication skills. In addition, you will want to assess how the couple handles conflict. Do both partners avoid conflict, creating a conflict-avoidant pattern? Does the couple follow a demand–withdraw pattern where one individual pursues discussion of issues while the other is avoidant? Or do both attack, resulting in conflict that can quickly escalate? If the latter, does the couple ever get physically violent during fights (see Potential Issues of Harm, above)? Fights or conflicts often follow a predictable sequence or pattern. Identifying and interrupting this cycle or sequence can be critical to success in couple therapy. Circular questioning (see Chapter 6) can be a particularly effective tool for uncovering the pattern in a couple's fights.

You will also want to explore how children impact the couple's relationship. If the couple does not have children, do they plan to have children? Are there any factors (e.g., infertility, one partner does not want children) that are keeping them from having children at this time? If the couple has children, are they able to support one another in their roles as parents, or is parenting a source of conflict? Does the couple still take time to nurture their relationship despite the demands of parenting? Even if the couple is no longer married, you should assess the impact of children on the relationship. For example, have they been able to work out an effective coparenting relationship, or is there ongoing conflict over parenting or custody?

SPIRITUAL ASSESSMENT

One of the most crucial areas that therapists often overlook in their assessment is the client's religious or spiritual life (Bergin, 1991; Hodge, 2005; Walsh, 2010). Therapists have been reluctant to address spiritual issues for several reasons. One is that many therapists were trained during a time when the value of nonempirical work was questioned. During their training, therapists learned that if it can't be measured, it shouldn't be considered in assessment. In addition, conducting an assessment implies the possibility of treatment. Many therapists would consider themselves unable to provide spiritual solutions or treatment and would perhaps equate any spiritual treatment as a form of proselytizing.

However, argument has increased to include spiritual and religious assessment as a central dimension to culturally sensitive clinical care (Bergin, 1991; Hodgson, Lamson, & Kolobova, 2016). These and other authors encourage psychotherapists to consider spiritual issues as part of psychotherapy by noting that a spiritual perspective can strongly contribute to a client's (and therapist's) view of human nature, morality, and religious rituals and practices. In addition, they point out that therapists' lack of recognition of religious and spiritual practices is largely at odds with the beliefs of the clients they treat. The general public is more religious, and more prone to rely on religious tenets, than psychotherapists are. For example, a Gallup poll found that 50% of older adults surveyed said they wanted their doctors to pray with them as they faced death, and 75% said that physicians (and therapists) should address spiritual issues as part of their care (Connell, 1995; Tanyi, McKenzie, & Chapek, 2009).

When assessing spiritual issues, you can conceptualize your role as one of asking open-ended questions, assuming a position of curiosity about your client's beliefs, and seeking simply to understand your client's story (Griffith & Griffith, 1994). For example, you can ask yourself, "In what ways and for how long has this patient's life been changed as a result of spiritual beliefs and experiences?" The spiritual experience need not be dramatic for a genuine "conversion" in terms of a changed life to occur. You could also use several tools available to family therapists for exploring spiritual beliefs and resources such as a spiritual genogram (Hodge, 2005).

Several models for spiritual assessment have been developed in the last 25 years (Fitchett, 1993; LaRocca-Pitts, 2012). La Rocca-Pitts (2012) discusses several spiritual screeners and spiritual assessment tools. All of these instruments are brief and easy to remember. One example is HOPE but there are others that can easily be found on the Web by typing in the words *spiritual screeners*. Anandarajah and Hight's (2001) acronym HOPE assesses for sources of hope, meaning, and strength in life (H); organized religion (O); personal practices outside of religious identity (P); and end-of-life decisions and medical care as influenced by spiritual beliefs (E). Many of these models focus on understanding how spiritual beliefs or practices serve a person rather than on examining specifically what the beliefs and practices are. These models view spirituality as a multidimensional process that "does not displace the accumulated empirical knowledge of mental functioning and mental health treatment," but complements it (Bergin, 1991, p. 399). For instance, Hodgson, Lamson, and Kolobova (2016) develop several strategies for incorporating a biopsychosocial-spiritual assessment for different types of couple's therapy.

ASSESSING SOCIAL SYSTEMS OUTSIDE THE FAMILY

Although as a family therapist you will be primarily concerned with assessing the couple or family system, it is important to recognize that a thorough assessment will also extend beyond these boundaries. Family members interact with a variety of social systems outside the immediate family. For example, the extended family often plays a critical role in the immediate family's life. Schools, work environments, friendship networks, and neighborhoods are also important social systems to assess. In some cases, the courts, social service agencies, health and medical services, or other psychotherapists may be involved with one or more family members. A thorough assessment will consider the potential influence that each of these systems may have on your clients.

To begin, you should assess the degree to which individuals or systems outside the family can provide support or resources. We know from much of our work that increasing social support will be vital for improved functioning in the family system. Extended family members may be able to provide important emotional or instrumental support. Friends may also be able to provide needed help. If you find that your clients have limited support outside the family, then you may want to work with them to develop a better social support network.

It is important that you assess each family member's level of functioning outside the family. Do family difficulties impact the individual's work performance? Does a child's misbehavior occur primarily at home, or is it present at school as well? Asking questions like these will help you assess the severity and context of the problem. In some cases, you may find that a family member has a higher level of functioning in another system—for example, a child may manifest fewer problems at school than at home. In these cases, you can take a solution-focused approach and identify what factors contribute to your client's functioning or well-being in one setting.

Assessing external systems is another way of gathering important clues to individual and interpersonal dynamics within the family. In many cases, individuals relate to people outside the family in ways similar to how they relate to family members. One client openly discussed his distrust of friends and work colleagues, which in turn illuminated his pattern of interaction with his divorced wife. Carefully assessing family members' interactions with people outside the family can uncover or confirm dynamics within the family.

Finally, you should assess the potential impact that systems outside the family can have on the therapy process. Some clients, for example, are mandated to come to therapy by the courts. You will want to be clear on what the courts want to see accomplished and what the consequences are for noncompliance. Whenever you must work with another individual or system outside the family, there is always the potential for triangles or alliances to exist that may interfere with the therapy process. For example, you may need to guard against being triangulated between a school and a family over a child's behavior. In some cases, multiple therapists might be involved with various family members. Ideally, therapists will work closely with one another to avoid working at cross-purposes.

ASSESSING LARGER SYSTEMS: CONTEXT, GENDER, AND CULTURE

Family therapy has been criticized in the past for ignoring the important influence that historical, social, and economic contexts have on individuals and families (Goldner, 1985; James & McIntyre, 1983; Taggart, 1985). Feminist family therapists, for example, have discussed how gender socialization and inequity in society have important implications for how men and women experience family. Just as individually oriented therapists have been said to ignore the family context of a child's misbehavior, family therapists have been accused of ignoring the societal context of family dynamics.

Gender socialization is an important contextual system that should be included in assessment. It is not uncommon for differences in gender socialization to contribute to conflicts between men and women in intimate relationships. In one case, a husband complained that his wife was always checking up on him, which he resented and saw as controlling. The wife insisted that she was simply interested in hearing how his day went and wasn't checking up on him. She felt distressed over how he angrily withdrew, which resulted in her feeling isolated and alone. This in turn increased her need for connection with her husband. For this couple, gender socialization was contributing to their cycle of distancing and pursuing. Like many men, the husband was socialized to value independence and to be sensitive to issues of status, hierarchy, and control. As a result, he interpreted her "checking in" as "checking up" on him. The couple was able to interrupt the distance–pursuit pattern through a better understanding of how gender socialization was contributing to it.

As with any generalization, however, the therapist needs to recognize that exceptions occur with regard to common gender patterns. Some women may have stereotypical male behaviors or beliefs, while some men may have stereotypical female behaviors or beliefs. Gender patterns should be regarded as hypotheses that need to be confirmed or ruled out with further assessment, not rigidly applied to all male–female dynamics.

When gender socialization is a contributing factor to a problematic dynamic, the therapist will frequently find other factors that reinforce it. For example, the dynamics of an enmeshed family of origin may reinforce the societal message that a woman receives—to take care of others' needs at the expense of her own. In the preceding case example, having had a controlling parent reinforced the husband's fear of being controlled. Therefore, you should be aware that factors in addition to gender socialization might reinforce a problematic dynamic.

The racial or ethnic background of a family is also important to consider when doing assessment, particularly if it differs from your own. Sensitivity to culture is critical, beginning with the initial interview, so that a solid therapeutic relationship develops and the client remains engaged in therapy. Fortunately, respectful and sensitive awareness can instill more confidence in the therapeutic relationship. For example, one of the authors, a 115-pound, middle-class, non-drug-using Caucasian, recalls her first client in her first internship: a 250-pound, tattoo-bearing, heroin-addicted, economically disadvantaged Hispanic male. What developed was a wonderful working relationship, due to the client's willingness to educate the therapist and the therapist's ability to find empathic connections with the client.

Three general guidelines apply to a culturally sensitive assessment. First, you should consider a client's cultural background when interpreting the information gained through assessment. Therapists may misinterpret certain behaviors if they do not place them in the proper cultural context. In American culture, a child who fails to make eye contact with adults might be perceived to have poor self-esteem. However, in other cultures a child who makes direct eye contact with an adult would be showing disrespect. Likewise, be aware of your own cultural filter because this will affect how you perceive different clients and their actions. For example, you and your clients may have different expectations regarding appropriate family communication or the way to raise children due to your different cultural backgrounds.

Second, you should not assume that group norms for specific cultural groups will automatically apply to an individual from that group. Any assumptions about an individual's behavior based on cultural norms must be regarded as tentative until they can be confirmed through further assessment. Children from a family of recent immigrants, for example, may be more acculturated to American culture than their parents or grandparents. To some degree, each family must be taken as a "case study," since the degree to which a family accepts or displays a cultural prescription is unique to that family.

Third, you should be aware of how cultural differences may influence the therapist–client relationship, and the implications that this might have for assessment. For example, members of a minority group might be reluctant to discuss sensitive information because they fear prejudice from the majority group (Garbarino & Stott, 1989). This in turn can affect a therapist's approach to assessment. Expectations for how therapy can help also need to be explored. Many cultures expect therapists to take on an authoritative role, while others expect more mutuality.

The preceding guidelines for sensitive, cross-cultural assessment can also be applied when exploring cultures that are defined by a characteristic other than race or ethnicity. Cultural differences, for example, can be anticipated between individuals who belong to different religious backgrounds, sexual orientations, social classes, and so forth. Each of these social groups has the potential to influence an individual's sense of identity, beliefs, and manner of relating to others. Therefore, you should determine which of these potential cultures is most salient to each family member and assess for its impact on the family.

However broadly one chooses to define "culture," we need to be reminded that when a family's cultural heritage is positively accessed, a clinician acquires one further resource for change. As Minuchin and Fishman (1981) point out, "Every family has elements in their own culture which, if understood and utilized, can become levers to actualize and expand the family members' behavioral repertoire" (p. 262).

CONCLUSION

In many ways, conducting a thorough assessment is a little like putting a puzzle together. The initial assessment involves placing the corner and edge pieces together first in order to get oriented to the case. Then, you begin to put the rest of the puzzle together piece by piece until a clinical picture emerges. Important pieces of the clinical puzzle include assessing for potential issues of harm, possible substance abuse concerns, and possible biological factors. You must connect these concerns to other pieces of the puzzle, such as possible psychopathology, the way in which clients make meaning as to what is happening, and issues of spirituality. One must put these pieces together with parts of the puzzle that reveal the relationship dynamics between family members. However, the puzzle may be incomplete unless you also consider other systems outside the family. If you address each of these interconnected pieces of the puzzle, we believe that you will obtain a complete clinical picture of your clients.

CHAPTER 5

Developing a Treatment Focus
and Treatment Plan

Rosalinda, age 29, brings in her 9-year old son, Jacob, to your clinic. The school strongly suggested that she do this since Jacob is having several difficulties there—he is often late and he isn't turning in his homework. His teacher reports that he mostly spends time alone. Recently, he has had several pushing incidents on the school playground, not enough to suspend him, but very close. Rosalinda does not know what to do. She is very anxious and reports she has not been sleeping very well.

Imagine that you have met with this family twice, started to join with each of them by asking questions, playing a board game with Jacob, and asking a variety of assessment questions. You found out that Jacob was born a month prematurely and that he had witnessed domestic violence between his mother and father. The father left when he was 4 years old and has had no contact with them since. Rosalinda's boyfriend recently left her for another woman and she reports to you that Jacob only listened to him. She has two younger children at home (their father was the boyfriend) and she is working just enough to pay her bills. Jacob has struggled in school before and has a quick temper, but shows a deep care and helps out with his younger siblings. Rosalinda's mother helps with childcare when she is working but criticizes her about her parenting abilities. You notice that Jacob plays very aggressively with the toys in the therapy room and only looks at his mother when she mentions the boyfriend's name. You also notice that Rosalinda seems to only notice when bad things happen and that she grabs ahold of her necklace with a crucifix on it each time she mentions her concerns about her son. You wonder if it might make sense to bring in Jacob's grandmother or siblings to a therapy session in order to understand better how they interact.

Many beginning clinicians feel overwhelmed at this juncture of therapy process. Even though you and the client have reviewed important information together and you may even experience trust developing in the relationship, it's common for therapists to ask where to start, what to treat, what to ignore, and how to prioritize problems. Developing a treatment focus using a conceptual map and clinical reasoning will help you organize assessment information and design a treatment plan. The treatment plan defines the problems to be addressed in the therapy and identifies the interventions that will be offered to address the problems. Writing an initial treatment plan begins to formalize the treatment contract with your clients. All family therapists need to know how to conceptualize and articulate what they do, partly to demonstrate proficiency in their professional discipline and partly to satisfy funders of clinical services. There are several obstacles that can hinder a therapist's effort to define a treatment focus.

FOUR OBSTACLES TO DEVELOPING A TREATMENT FOCUS

Obstacle 1: Too Little Structure in the First Two to Three Sessions

In their classic groundbreaking book *The Family Crucible,* Napier and Whitaker (1978) state the importance of therapists winning the "battle for structure." In other words, therapists, not clients, need to establish and communicate (verbally and nonverbally) the ground rules for the process and content of therapy beginning with the first contact. For example, who is going to attend the first session? Napier and Whitaker believed it was essential for *all* family members to be present from the beginning of therapy and refused to start therapy until all were present. Such an expectation offers the family an orientation to systems thinking (Weber & Levine, 1995). However, few family therapists follow this rigid stance (Berg & Rosenblum, 1977), and instead most make the decision about who will attend on a case-by-case basis (Nichols & Everett, 1986).

Although we're uncomfortable with the "battle" metaphor, we strongly believe in the idea of therapists assuming a leadership role with their clients and guiding them through the assessment and treatment process. It is the therapist's job to provide a structure, including a time, a place, and a setting for clients to safely talk about their concerns. Basic responsibilities of the therapists include being on time for therapy sessions, maintaining a professional posture in the relationship (including dress and demeanor), following through on information you promise to offer in therapy (such as psychoeducational resources or referrals), remembering to ask about homework assignments, and taking responsibility for structuring the therapeutic time together (ending on time, reviewing treatment goals as needed, stopping an escalating argument), all of which strengthen the working relationship.

The therapist is also responsible for the format of therapy, including rules for the communication process, such as each person having a turn to talk and be heard. In very chaotic or volatile cases, the therapist may need to closely monitor the communication to assist the family in developing more effective communication skills. He or she may choose to initiate discussion of how material from the sessions will be used outside therapy. Again, the therapeutic environment needs to include an umbrella of safety; it may be useful to suggest to clients that certain topics are best discussed only in therapy, at least until the family develops more effective communication skills.

Obstacle 2: Every Session Feels Like a First Session

Our students will often say they have a session agenda but it isn't implemented because the client is in crisis each session, which results in immediate problem solving but no resolution of his or her core issues. If a client is at risk for harm to self or others, the therapist will prioritize and address these concerns. However, in most cases, many immediate concerns and worries can be designated a limited amount of time to allow the therapist to conduct a thorough assessment and define a treatment plan. Rather than addressing each problem in sequence, the treatment plan links these daily or weekly problems (e.g., a specific argument between parent and adolescent) to key themes (e.g., patterns in communication).

Each session can also feel like a first session when clients miss appointments. Appointments may be missed for a variety of reasons, including problems with transportation, inability to pay for therapy, conflicting responsibilities, and lack of motivation. Long intervals between sessions at the beginning of treatment can make it difficult to gain momentum and develop a treatment focus. We recommend discussing with clients the challenges of attending therapy, what can be done to achieve more consistent attendance, and the possible limitations on progress if consistent attendance isn't possible. Many clinical settings will have rules about no-shows and late cancellations (e.g., three no-shows results in termination of therapy). If your clinical setting doesn't have explicit expectations, you will benefit from defining your own expectations and communicating these expectations at the beginning of therapy.

Obstacle 3: Thinking You Need to Address Every Problem

Once a family therapist meets with a family to listen to their areas of concern and completes a thorough assessment, he or she can often have a long list of problems to address. Take a breath for a moment and just list the problems you have discovered with your client. At this juncture, what will be important is to prioritize the problems. The issues of safety and crisis must always be addressed first. However, after these have been attended to, the therapist and the family have some choices. Sometimes it will be helpful to verbally review the list (maybe there are four to eight issues on it) and ask the family to prioritize them with you. Generally, it is useful to develop the treatment plan that focuses the therapy on two or three issues. As you begin to use your conceptual map to understand how to intervene with the problem areas, you will often notice that the problems are interrelated.

Obstacle 4: The Therapist Lacks a Theoretical Orientation

A major task for any therapist is organizing the immense amount of data at the beginning of therapy. Working with multiple family members increases the amount and complexity of information. Therapists need a theoretical orientation to filter the information and organize their thinking about a client to develop a treatment focus. The absence of a theoretical orientation often leaves therapists feeling overwhelmed with information and filtering information through their own personal lens. Although all therapists use their personal experiences to understand problems and make treatment decisions, it shouldn't be the only lens or primary lens for developing a treatment focus. Articulating a theoretical orientation helps us provide a professional rationale for our treatment decisions. In a practical way, a coherent orientation helps us build a bridge between the presenting problem, our assessment, and what we'll do with the client to create change.

BUILDING A CONCEPTUAL MAP USING THEORY AND RESEARCH

In supervision, we have found that the menu of available theories for conceptualization and treatment confuses beginning family therapists. Historically, family therapists often identified with one particular school of family therapy. In the 1970s and 1980s, it was common for family therapists to identify themselves with a particular theoretical school, as in "I'm a structural family therapist" or "I'm a solution-focused therapist." Training programs in this era frequently taught only one or two theories, often structural and strategic family therapy. Family therapists who trained at this time would usually treat every client they saw using their preferred theoretical orientation. Theoretical purity still exists and may be very effective with some clients and in specialized settings. But therapists working on the front lines of community mental health with diverse clients and presentations need theoretical flexibility and integration. By "integration," we don't mean simply sampling techniques from different theoretical models. Rather, we're advocating for an integration of theoretical concepts (e.g., family structure, cognitions, emotions, larger social systems) that will inform treatment decisions (Mikesell, Lusterman, & McDaniel, 1995; Nichols & Everett, 1986; Pinsoff, 1995).

The biopsychosocial (BPS) model and general systems theory form the foundation for our emphasis on integration (Bertalanffy, 1968; Engel, 1977). Systems theory is the bedrock of family therapy and emphasizes the concept of wholeness, the idea that "the whole is greater than the sum of its parts." Rather than reducing entities to their parts in a reductive manner, family therapists look for patterns and processes in problem descriptions and appreciate the idea that whatever affects one part of a system (an individual) affects other parts of the system (the family). A traditional family systems view means that the family is the unit of understanding and care, no matter who comes to therapy. Even when working with individuals, family therapists understand their clients' relational and cultural contexts and recognize that there are multiple perspectives to any problem. How does systems theory inform treatment? Family therapists prioritize relationships in assessment and treatment by opening their doors to other family members and improving relationships to address the presenting concerns of our clients.

The BPS model, introduced in 1977 by George Engel at the University of Rochester, describes an expansive, layered hierarchy of systems that are in constant interaction over time. Although the model was developed to train physicians, it's compatible with systems-based family therapy by emphasizing the linkages between systems. We can't fully understand a system (or part of a system) without understanding its relevant context. Whereas Engel was trying to help physicians understand the psychosocial aspects of their medical concerns, proponents of a BPS model within family therapy aim to help family therapists understand the individual aspects of their clients' psychosocial concerns, particularly in situations where clients are coping with serious mental and/or physical illness (Shields, Wynne, McDaniel, & Gawinski, 1994).

An integrated worldview will help you organize your assessment data and eventually make treatment decisions that incorporate a range of theoretical models.

The Role of Specific Theoretical Models

Once a therapist has done a thorough assessment that is informed by a biopsychosocial-systems framework, he or she can then begin conceptualizing the case, prioritizing the problems, and choosing interventions that are consistent with the conceptualization. The conceptualization is a brief summary of the therapist's thinking or hypotheses about the presenting problem—in what part of the systems does the problem or problems exist, what explains the presence of a particular problem, and what is the relationship between the problems? Theories of psychotherapy and family therapy tend to privilege a particular part of the client's experience, such as emphasizing cognition or emotion, and focus on a particular time period, such as current functioning or historical data. For example, emotionally focused therapy targets here-and-now interactions, whereas Bowen theory emphasizes family of origin and the development of problems over time. Rather than being constrained by one theoretical approach, we prefer integrating multiple theoretical perspectives by recognizing, for example, the synergy between emotion *and* cognition; current interactions *and* the perspective of history (Hardy, 2011; Lebow, 2004; Seaburn, Landau-Stanton, & Horwitz, 1995). The integrative influence can be seen in the following case examples:

* A therapist working with a couple may identify a demand–withdraw pattern, and then work toward interrupting the pattern and creating a more secure attachment via emotionally focused therapy. She may also be curious about the earlier relationship history and family-of-origin influence on this particular pattern.

* A therapist working with an adolescent and her single mother may identify a flat hierarchy and work toward empowering the parent via structural family therapy. He may also be curious about how the single parent was parented herself in her adolescence and her current relationship with her parents.

* A therapist working with an adult male may identify problems in multiple systems, including depression and suicide ideation, recent job loss, conflict in his relationship with his 6-year-old son's mother, lack of driver's license due to legal problems, and current use of marijuana.

In addition to prioritizing and addressing the current problems above (e.g., first, depression and suicide ideation), the therapist learns that the client's mother died from cancer 2 years ago and begins to address unresolved complicated grief in collaboration with his father and grandmother.

Integration allows therapists to adapt their model and approach to the unique circumstances of the client. However, there is still a place for theoretical purity. With some clients and in some specialized settings, the implementation of a particular model may be the right decision. For example, the research literature might provide compelling evidence to use a specific model to treat a specific problem. Contemporary mental health practice now expects therapists to use evidence-based interventions.

The Role of Evidence-Based Practice

Evidence-based practice (EBP) is the integration of the best research evidence with clinical expertise and patient values (Williams, Patterson, & Edwards, 2014). EBP is about *using* research, not clinicians collecting data themselves. Attempts to bridge research and the practice of marital, couple, and family therapy have generated controversy and passionate debate. Family therapists have questioned the usefulness of research that focuses on individual therapy for treating mental health disorders, which ignores the complexity of interacting relational systems (e.g., couple/marital, parent–child, intergenerational, and larger system relationships) and families coping with multiple problems. The populations often studied in research do not accurately reflect the complexity of multiproblem families seen by family therapists and run counter to the systems-based clinical training that characterizes family therapy training. As a result, family therapists have sometimes asked, "What does research have to do with my systems-based clinical work?" Although there may not be perfect alignment with the research literature and systems-based therapy, we encourage you to consider the resources below to inform your work.

Division 12 of the American Psychological Association has a website (*www.div12.org/PsychologicalTreatments*) that lists various evidenced-based treatments for treating many adult psychological disorders. For each disorder, a brief description of the disorder is provided, along with various psychological treatments that have been evaluated. The level of research support for each treatment (e.g., strong support, modest support) is noted. A brief description of the treatments is also available. The large majority of treatments described on this site are individually oriented treatments, which is consistent with a focus on individual psychopathology. Division 53 of the American Psychological Association has a website (*www.effectivechildtherapy.com*) that focuses specifically on child and adolescent disorders. Like the other site, possible evidence-based treatments for each disorder are listed, along with the level of evidence for each. Treatments are classified as being well established, probably efficacious, possibly efficacious, or experimental based on the level of empirical support. The site also provides a brief description for many of the treatments, which include individual-, group-, and family-based treatments.

The American Psychiatric Association also has a website (*www.psych.org/practice/clinical-practice-guidelines*) that offers practice guidelines for treating various psychiatric illnesses for adults. For treating children and adolescent disorders, one can consult the American Academy of Child and Adolescent Psychiatry's site (*www.aacap.org/AACAP/Resources_for_Primary_Care/Practice_Parameters_and_Resource_Centers/Practice_Parameters.aspx*). Their practice guidelines also include recommendations for screening or assessing children and adolescents for these disorders. As one might expect, practice guidelines for these two sites place a heavy emphasis on using medications for treating psychiatric disorders.

Since 1995, the *Journal of Marital and Family Therapy* has published three issues of research reviews of family-based interventions for specific family problems, including conduct disorder and delinquency in adolescents, drug abuse, child and adolescent disorders, alcoholism, couple distress, intimate partner violence, affective disorders, and physical health problems. The couple therapy models with the most empirical support are emotionally focused couple therapy, behavioral couple therapy, and integrative models. Integrative models (functional family therapy, brief strategic family therapy, multisystemic therapy, and multidimensional family therapy) also show effectiveness for child-focused presenting problems. These models share much in common. First, they integrate theory in their attentiveness to multiple systems: the individual, the couple/marital dyad, the family, and the community. They borrow interventions from multiple systemic and nonsystemic couple and family therapy models, including structural family therapy, strategic family therapy, and cognitive-behavioral therapy. Second, they emphasize joining skills, a therapeutic alliance, and active engagement of the therapist. Therapists don't take a passive approach; they are simultaneously providing support, leadership, and direction to mobilize the family toward making desired changes. Third, they focus on structural change and the disruption of dysfunctional patterns, both within and outside the family, during and outside the sessions. Finally, they emphasize the importance of looking at peers and developing a prosocial group of friends. We return to these areas of emphasis in Chapter 6.

A thorough assessment, a conceptualization grounded in theory, familiarity with a range of therapy models, and an ability to search the evidence-based literature positions a therapist to write a comprehensive treatment plan. Most community agencies will require therapists to complete a treatment plan after the first three sessions, partly as good professional practice and partly to communicate with their funders of mental health services. With or without the requirement, a written treatment plan is a window into the therapist's thinking process and vision for treatment; it provides a structure for the therapist and client and helps communicate actions to other professionals in cases where treatment is shared or might be shared in the future.

COMPONENTS OF A TREATMENT PLAN

Community agencies and individual therapists use a variety of structures, but most treatment plans include the components identified in Table 5.1.

Below is a treatment plan for the family described at the beginning of this chapter.

Basic Information

Client's name: Jacob, age 9

Date of birth: October 12, 2008

Referral source: Rockville Elementary School

Other family members living in the home: Rosalinda, mother, age 29; sisters, Ana, age 3; Elena, age 1; boyfriend, John, lived in home 2013 to December 2016

Other agencies or people involved in care of the client: Fourth-grade schoolteacher, Ms. Ross; Grandmother, Isabela, who provides childcare for Jacob and his siblings when Rosalinda works. Rosalinda and Jacob's father, Francisco, divorced several years ago. Francisco moved away and hasn't maintained any contact.

Genogram

See Figure 5.1.

TABLE 5.1. Components of a Treatment Plan

Basic information
  Client's name
  Date of birth
  Referral source
  Other family members living in the home
  Other agencies or people involved in care of the client (e.g., psychiatrist, primary
    care physician, IEP)

Genogram
  A description of the client's family, either written as a narrative or constructed
  using genogram symbols.

Presenting problem
  How does the client/family describe the presenting problem? (Using the client's
    words, write a factual account of what brings the client to therapy; capture
    multiple perspectives if a couple or family)
  What solutions have they attempted?
  What does the client/family want to change?

History of presenting problem
  How long has the problem been present?
  How has it changed over time?
  What other changes have taken place in the family (life-cycle changes, other
    transitions)?

Biopsychosocial-systems assessment
  Individual assessment (cognitions, emotions, possible DSM diagnosis, health-
    related concerns, medication)
  Couple/family assessment (structure, patterns over time, role of extended family)
  Larger system assessment (housing, neighborhood, school)
  Contextual assessment (race, culture, ethnicity, spirituality/religion, gender,
    sexual orientation, gender identity, socioeconomic status)

Clinical hypotheses
  What are your hypotheses about the presenting problem based on your
  assessment and theory?

Problems/goals/interventions
  Prioritize problems based on goals negotiated between therapist and client and
  level of severity
  • Problem/symptom #1
    ○ Goal
    ○ Intervention/action (consistent with conceptualization and informed by
      research)
  • Problem/symptom #2
    ○ Goal
    ○ Intervention/action (consistent with conceptualization and informed by
      research)

Referrals/collaboration

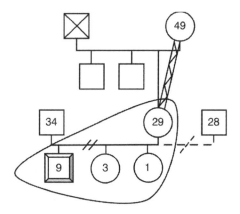

FIGURE 5.1. Jacob's genogram.

Presenting Problem

Mom and Jacob report that they are coming to therapy "so he wouldn't get suspended." The school principal warned Jacob that he will be suspended if there is one more school incident. At home, Mom says Jacob doesn't listen and occasionally "talks back," which she doesn't like. Mom says that Jacob has "always struggled in school." Jacob says school is OK, but he doesn't like it. Jacob reports school has gotten harder in fourth grade and there is more homework. Mom reports that everyone has been struggling since her boyfriend, John, moved out 3 months ago. She says she feels anxious "all the time" and isn't sleeping well. Rosalinda's mouther is providing help, but, according to Rosalinda, is "critical of everything" when she is around. To cope with the problem, Mom tries to set limits with Jacob by taking away television and computer access, but she says it doesn't work. She regretfully says she yells at him when he doesn't listen. Grandmother begs Jacob to be "the man of the family." Both Mom and Jacob want things to be better at school and to have less anger and stress in the home.

History of Presenting Problem

Intermittent anger outbursts and school struggles have been present throughout the family's life; school incidents have started recently. The family is experiencing many transitions, including loss of Mom's boyfriend; increase of Mom's work hours and presence of Grandmother; school expectations have increased.

Biopsychosocial-Systems Assessment

Individual assessment: Mom is anxious; client appears to be depressed, with outbursts of anger. Both report a sense of hopelessness. Mom and Grandmother have Type II diabetes and take Metformin; there is no other medication or substance use in the family. Client's biological father was probably an alcoholic. Both biological mom and dad struggled in school, particularly around reading.

DSM diagnosis for Jacob: Adjustment disorder with mixed disturbance of emotion and conduct; rule out specific learning disorder (moderate impairment in reading)

DSM diagnosis for Rosalinda: Generalized anxiety disorder

Couple/family assessment: *Family structure* is a fairly closed system (rigid external boundaries; diffuse internal boundaries) with household only depending on extended family member (Grandmother) for help. *Family functioning* is stressed instrumentally, with limited financial resources and very low affective engagement except for anger and critical responses; *family life cycle* has been disrupted by recent loss of Mom's boyfriend who provided financial resources and emotional care. Also, the family never processed grief related to the loss of biological father.

Larger system assessment: Housing, neighborhood, and school are stable and adequate.

Contextual assessment: Biological family is Latino in origin; boyfriend was Caucasian. Family does not identify strongly with their ethnicity. Catholic faith is very important to both Rosalinda and her mother. Also, strong gender messages ("Be a man") from Grandmother have been directed toward Jacob. Lower socioeconomic status.

Clinical Hypotheses

The assessment brings to light that this family is negotiating a significant and recent practical and emotional loss when Rosalinda's boyfriend left the family. Research suggests that boys might act out when confronted by loss (conduct problems), while women might act inwardly (increase anxiety). There is much to *normalize* here. Since the family is more isolated due to closed external boundaries, increasing social supports (therapy, community, faith-based) may be useful for this family. Also, there may be undiagnosed learning disabilities that might increase the school difficulties currently experienced.

Problems/Goals/Interventions

Problem/Symptom #1: Anger outbursts at school and home

- **Goal 1:** Decrease anger by increasing expression of other emotions such as sadness.
  - ○ **Intervention/Action 1A:** Review genogram with the family to explore emotional reactions when client's biological father and Mom's boyfriend left the family.
  - ○ **Intervention/Action 1B:** Use games and drawing to broaden the emotional identification of family member's individually and in the family, particularly the naming of sadness and fears.

- **Goal 2:** Increase positive communication among family members.
  - ○ **Intervention/Action 2A:** Use solution-focused questioning to uncover times when family members experienced positive support. Include Grandmother in some of these sessions.
- **Goal 3:** Empower mother in the family hierarchy.
  - ○ **Intervention/Action 3A:** Identify and implement additional parenting strategies to cope with Jacob's angry outbursts.
  - ○ **Intervention/Action 3B:** Help mother set appropriate boundaries with her mother when criticized as a parent.

Problem/Symptom #2: Mother's anxiety

- **Goal 1:** Decrease symptoms of anxiety as evidenced by less self-criticism and improved sleep.
  - ○ **Intervention/Action 1A:** Normalize current difficulties as predictable stressors rather than personal failures.
  - ○ **Intervention/Action 1B:** Refer Rosalinda for medication evaluation.
- **Goal 2:** Increase social support from school, community, and faith-based resources.
  - ○ **Intervention/Action 2A:** Develop a sociogram with family members to identify other family members, friends, community resources such as youth sports or after-school programs, or church connections (Catholic priest) that might be able to provide support.
  - ○ **Intervention/Action 2B:** Explore ways for family members to connect to these resources.

Medication Consultations

Some family therapists have been reluctant about using psychotropic medications as part of their treatment planning (Patterson & Magulac, 1994). In the early years of family therapy, using medication could be seen as an admission of failure. Attitudes about using medication have changed. Therapists who do not have a medical degree and thus cannot prescribe medication are participating in a joint treatment model wherein they work with a physician (usually a psychiatrist, internist, family physician, or pediatrician) in coordinating treatment (Patterson, Albala, McCahill, & Edwards, 2010). The physician prescribes and manages the psychotropic medication while the therapist provides the "talk therapy."

Family therapists need to make medication referrals with caution. Negative side effects of medication are common. In addition, patients can interpret the referral as the therapist saying "You are really crazy—too crazy for family therapy" or as the therapist abandoning the client to another provider. However, medication should not be overlooked as an option. Frequently, family therapists have no training or knowledge about psychotropic medications and have limited biological knowledge; thus, they do not consider medication as a possible intervention. In addition, therapists fear losing control of their client's treatment or view referral to another provider as a sign of failure or inadequacy. For all these reasons, family therapists might not consider making a medication referral.

While many family therapists support the idea of a BPS-systems model of assessment and treatment, the biological part is rarely emphasized or even considered. However, a true BPS model would consider both assessment of biological influences, such as genetic history, and biologically based treatment, including medication and surgery. This holistic approach argues for including a biomedical provider if the therapist does not have expertise in biological assessment.

Beyond the BPS model, other factors compel therapists to consider medication consultations. One is that their clients ask about them. Research in the last 20 years has produced powerful new psychotropic medications with fewer negative side effects. Popular articles on the success of these new drugs can be found on any newsstand. Another reason therapists might consider medication is that they may work in a setting where the biomedical model is paramount and physicians are in charge. Health maintenance organizations and preferred provider organizations encourage medication use because it is often a relatively inexpensive and effective treatment.

Speed of treatment is another reason therapists consider medication. Timeliness and cost are key criteria in many therapy settings. While some may consider it sloppy treatment, many therapists feel pressure to use a shotgun approach in which every possible treatment is given to the patient. Since medication can bring rapid symptomatic improvement, there is increasing emphasis on using medication from the start of treatment (McNeil, 2001).

Changes within the profession also account for the growing awareness of medication. The early years of family therapy were characterized by a period of marking boundaries and separating from mainstream, traditional mental health treatments. As family therapy has become an established profession, magnifying these distinctions has become less important. Instead of acknowledging only the family as the patient, most family therapists today will recognize one family member as perhaps needing a biologically based treatment while the rest of the therapy remains focused on family interaction. Although family therapists cannot prescribe or monitor medications, they have an obligation to clients to assess for or otherwise recognize various problems and pathologies that might benefit from treatment with psychotropic drugs. Knowing when and how to obtain a psychiatric consultation is an important part of our work, as the following case demonstrates.

Bill, a 39-year-old man, presented with marital problems that included constant arguing, financial problems, and a lack of mutual interests. Mary, his wife, was a 37-year-old woman who had just begun to work full time as an insurance sales agent. She complained about Bill's moodiness and lack of involvement with the family, saying, "All he wants is to be left alone." Bill had worked as a stockbroker for the previous 10 years and indicated that business had been bad and was taking up more of his time than usual. This couple was seen in marital therapy for four visits. The husband quickly identified himself as "the problem," and said he felt an inability to control the way he felt and his negative attitude. He also expressed some anger toward his wife for her lack of support, particularly since she had started working full time. The wife said that she felt she had been supporting her husband emotionally for years and needed to do something for herself. Both indicated that they felt lonely in their relationship and had little understanding of how things had deteriorated to this point of dissatisfaction. Further exploration of their individual issues indicated that the husband displayed several depressive symptoms, including a poor appetite, an erratic sleep pattern, a lack of energy, and irritability. He said he had been feeling "down" for the past several years and really couldn't remember when it seemed to have started. Family history indicated that he felt traumatized and partially responsible for his brother's accidental death when Bill was 14.

The duration and magnitude of Bill's depressive symptoms indicated that an evaluation for antidepressant medication was warranted. Since the marriage was presented as the primary problem, it was anticipated that either Bill or his wife might be reluctant to consider medication. They didn't come to marital therapy expecting to see a physician in addition to a couple therapist. They both had some preconceived beliefs about the uses of psychotropic drugs. Some discussion of their experiences with medications and education about psychotropic drugs was necessary. It was also important for the therapist to present Bill's need for a medication evaluation as being in the couple's best interest. Referrals are most effective if they are presented as beneficial to the client. In this case, Bill was receptive to seeing a psychiatrist for a medical evaluation. His wife's primary concern was that medication was "a crutch and addicting." It was suggested that she see the psychiatrist with her husband in order to find answers to any questions and concerns. Both agreed to go to the initial appointment.

Finally, family therapists cannot ignore the burgeoning research indicating a biological role for at least some mental disorders, such as schizophrenia, bipolar disorder, and other diseases thought previously to originate in dysfunctional family patterns. Recognizing a biological etiology naturally leads to a biological treatment, frequently medication.

With increasing public awareness about medication, the family therapist needs to learn more about psychotropic drugs. Perhaps one of the best ways to learn is through on-the-job training—experience is a powerful influence in demonstrating the efficacy of medication for certain problems. Establishing a professional relationship with a psychiatrist or primary care physician who is willing to use a joint treatment model is an ideal way to learn about medication. If possible, we try to personally know the physicians we are sending our patients to for medical evaluations so that we can be sure of both their competence and interpersonal skills. Other possibilities include participating in a continuing education course or reading one of the many books on psychotropic medications for nonphysicians. A brief "primer" on commonly used medications is provided in Table 5.2.

Psychological Testing Consultations

Another consultation possibility is to refer a client for psychological testing to obtain a more standardized report on observations the therapist has already made or a more in-depth description of some aspect of a client's life. When making a testing referral, the therapist should be as specific as possible about what he or she would like to learn. Therapists should be familiar with the variety of tests available and know what to ask for. Whereas one would use a physician for a medication consultation, psychologists are the mental health professionals with specialty training in tests and measures. Usually a report is written based on the tests the psychologist administers. Major types of tests include intelligence tests, projective tests, self-report instruments that describe some aspect of the client's emotional life, and behavioral checklists.

Testing is most commonly used in psychiatric hospitals, school settings, forensic work, and other institutional settings where standardized information beyond the therapist's clinical observations is sought. For example, parents and teachers may request testing when they have a concern about a child's behaviors or abilities. Legal experts may request testing when they are concerned about their client's mental stability or cognitive capacities. A typical psychological report would include the following information: reason for testing and referral source, brief history and description of the client, tests administered, test results, and recommendations.

TABLE 5.2. Psychotropic Drug Primer

	Drugs for depression[a]
SSRIs and SNRIs	Selective serotonin reuptake inhibitors (SSRIs) are generally recommended for first-line treatment of major depression. There is no convincing evidence that any one SSRI is more effective than any other. Fluoxetine has been shown to be effective and is the only SSRI approved by the FDA for treatment of major depressive disorder in children. Fluoxetine and escitalopram are both approved for treatment of major depressive disorder in adolescents. Serotonin and norepinephrine reuptake inhibitors (SNRIs) are also considered first-line options for treatment of major depression. It is not clear that they offer any advantage in efficacy over SSRIs, and they cause more adverse effects.
Bupropion	Bupropion can be used as an alternative to an SSRI for depressed patients who do not have severe anxiety or a primary anxiety disorder. Bupropion may improve hypoactive sexual desire disorder and antidepressant-induced sexual dysfunction. It is not sedating and has not been associated with weight gain, sexual dysfunction, or an increased risk of bleeding.
Mirtazapine	Mirtazapine may be useful when insomnia is prominent, and its appetite-stimulating and weight-gain-promoting properties may be helpful in depressed patients with marked anorexia.
Other drugs	*Trazodone,* which is also sedating, is seldom used as monotherapy, but is commonly used in low doses as an adjunct to an SSRI in patients with insomnia.
	Nefazodone, which is structurally similar to trazodone, has been withdrawn from the market in some countries because of rare severe hepatotoxicity.
	Vilazodone is an SSRI and partial serotonin 1a receptor agonist; it appears to be an effective antidepressant, but there is no acceptable evidence for claims that it acts more rapidly than SSRIs.
	Vortioxetine, which inhibits reuptake of serotonin and acts as an agonist or antagonist at various serotonin receptors, is FDA-approved for treatment of major depressive disorder.
	Tricyclic antidepressants (TCAs) and *monoamine oxidase inhibitors (MAOIs)* remain valuable alternatives for patients with moderate to severe treatment-resistant depression.

(continued)

TABLE 5.2. *(continued)*

Other drugs *(continued)*	*MAOIs* are contraindicated for use with serotonergic drugs (SSRIs) or other drugs that increase monoamines (noradrenergic, dopaminergic), and their use requires strict adherence to a low tyramine diet to avoid life-threatening drug interactions.
Second-line treatment	When patients show little to no response to an adequate trial of an SSRI (4–8 weeks), many expert clinicians switch to another SSRI or try an antidepressant from a different class. Combining two antidepressants from different classes, such as bupropion and an SSRI, or adding another drug for augmentation are additional alternatives. Augmentation with second-generation antipsychotic drugs has been effective, but it can cause weight gain, metabolic adverse effects, and akathisia. Extended release quetiapine, aripiprazole, and brexpiprazole are FDA-approved for adjunctive treatment of major depressive disorder. A fixed-dose combination of olanzapine and fluoxetine (Symbyax) is FDA-approved for treatment-resistant depression. Augmentation with liothyronine has been reported to be effective, but thyroid function must be monitored. Augmentation with low doses of lithium has been reported to be effective with both TCAs and newer antidepressants
Nondrug therapy	Psychotherapy, particularly cognitive-behavioral therapy (CBT) and interpersonal therapy, is an effective treatment for mild to moderately severe, nonpsychotic depression. Electroconvulsive therapy (ECT) is highly effective for severe depression, depression with psychosis, bipolar depression, and depression refractory to medications. Transcranial magnetic stimulation (TMS) and vagus nerve stimulation (VNS) are FDA-approved for treatment-resistant depression. TMS, unlike ECT, does not require anesthesia and does not appear to have cognitive side effects. Studies of TMS have demonstrated response and remission rates similar to those with antidepressants; it may be a reasonable treatment option when patients are unable to tolerate or do not respond to antidepressants. Deep brain stimulation has been effective in a small number of patients with treatment-resistant depression, but was not found to be superior compared to sham treatment in clinical trials

(continued)

TABLE 5.2. *(continued)*

	Drugs for anxiety[b]
Benzodiazepines	Includes diazepam (Valium), alprazolam (Xanax), lorazepam (Ativan), oxazepam (Serax), and clonazepam (Klonopin). Benzodiazepines have a high risk of pharmacological dependence and should be limited to short-term or intermittent use. "Alprazolam may cause rebound anxiety between doses and has been associated with a withdrawal syndrome, including seizures" (p. 40).
Buspirone	BuSpar, a nonbenzodiazepine antianxiety drug, does not cause sedation or functional impairment, or have high potential for abuse. Takes 1–2 weeks for results.
Propranolol	Inderal and other beta-blockers are useful in preventing performance anxiety or "stage fright" by suppressing peripheral autonomic symptoms of anxiety.
Antidepressants	Some antidepressants may be used for symptom relief of anxiety disorders. Clomipramine (Anafranil), fluvoxamine (Luvox), fluoxetine (Prozac), sertraline (Zoloft), and paroxetine (Paxil) are the drugs of choice for obsessive–compulsive disorder. For highly anxious patients with obsessive–compulsive disorder, adding a benzodiazepine or antipsychotic drug may be beneficial. SSRIs and MAOIs including paroxetine (Paxil), sertraline (Zoloft), and venlafaxine (Effexor), are the most effective treatments for social anxiety disorder. Posttraumatic stress disorder is most frequently treated with an SSRI; however, MAOIs and TCAs may also be beneficial.
	Drugs for bipolar disorder[c]
Treatment of mania	Second-generation antipsychotics, lithium, and valproate are effective for treatment of acute manic episodes. Both lithium and valproate may take days to weeks to have a full therapeutic effect; treatment of an acute manic episode with these agents generally requires addition of an antipsychotic drug.
Treatment of depression	The second-generation antipsychotics quetiapine and lurasidone and the combination of olanzapine and fluoxetine have been shown to be effective in treating bipolar depression. Antidepressant drugs such as SSRIs or bupropion can be effective for treatment of bipolar depression, but they can precipitate mania and generally should be used only as an adjunct to mood-stabilizing drugs such as lithium. Lithium

(continued)

TABLE 5.2. *(continued)*

Treatment of depression *(continued)*	has been shown to have protective effects against suicide and self-harm when used for treatment of bipolar depression. Lamotrigine may be modestly effective for this indication, but its usefulness in treating an acute episode is limited by the amount of time required for safe titration to an effective dose.
Maintenance	Lithium remains the drug of choice for maintenance treatment of bipolar disorder, especially for prevention of manic episodes. The anticonvulsant lamotrigine is effective for prevention of recurrent depressive episodes. Antiepileptic drugs such as valproate and carbamazepine are also widely used for maintenance treatment, but they are generally less effective than lithium. Maintenance therapy with lithium alone or in combination with valproate, carbamazepine, or lamotrigine decreases the risk of recurrent manic and depressive episodes. Second-generation antipsychotics may also be effective in preventing recurrences of manic and depressive episodes, especially when taken in combination with lithium.

Drugs for obsessive–compulsive disorder

Included under "Drugs for anxiety."

Drugs for psychotic disorders[b]

Atypical (second generation)	Atypical (second-generation) antipsychotics are now more widely used than first-generation, conventional antipsychotics. Although efficacy advantages have not (except for clozapine) been unequivocally demonstrated, they are better tolerated and have less serious side effects. Clozapine (Clozaril) is effective in patients with schizophrenia who are resistant to other treatment and better reduces the risk of suicide than first-generation antipsychotics. Other atypical antipsychotics include aripiprazole (Abilify), olanzapine (Zyprexa), quetiapine (Seroquel), risperidone (Risperdal), and ziprasidone (Geodon). The more recently FDA-approved antipsychotic drugs asenapine, iloperidone, and lurasidone may be effective for some patients but their safety and efficacy is yet to be determined.
First generation	First-generation antipsychotics are generally more effective in treating the "positive symptoms" (hallucinations, delusions) than "negative symptoms" (social withdrawal, apathy).

(continued)

TABLE 5.2. *(continued)*

First generation *(continued)*	Conventional antipsychotic drugs include such medications as chlorpromazine (Thorazine), fluphenazine (Prolixin), perphenazine (Trilafon), haloperidol (Haldol), thioridazine (Mellaril), thiothixene (Navane), and trifluoperazine (Stelazine). The first-generation antipsychotic loxapine (Loxitane) has been approved by the FDA for oral inhalation for acute treatment of agitation associated with bipolar disorder or schizophrenia.
Adverse effects	*First generation:* All first-generation antipsychotic drugs have been associated with sexual dysfunction, hyperprolactinemia, neuroleptic malignant syndrome and tardive dyskinesia (involuntary movements of lips, tongue, fingers, toes, or trunk). Prescribing lower doses can minimize these risks. Other side effects include dry mouth, constipation, drowsiness, postural hypotension, and extrapyramidal effects (rigidity, akinesia, tremor). *Second generation:* Patients are at risk for hyperglycemia, diabetes, and weight gain. Other possible side effects include hyperlipidemia, postural hypotension, insomnia, constipation, somnolence, akathesia, anxiety, and headache. Less likely to cause extrapyramidal effects, tardive dykinesia, and neuroleptic malignant syndrome than first-generation antipsychotics. Increased risk of death among elderly patients with dementia (similar effects are seen with first-generation antipsychotics as well).

[a]Adapted with special permission from *The Medical Letter on Drugs and Therapeutics,* July 4, 2016; Vol. 58, 85–90. *www.medicalletter.org*
[b]Adapted with special permission from *Drugs for Psychiatric Disorders* (2013). Copyright 2013 by *The Medical Letter.*
[c]Adapted with special permission from *The Medical Letter on Drugs and Therapeutics,* August 15, 2016; Vol. 58, 103–107. *www.medicalletter.org*

When would a family therapist ask for psychological testing? Besides the legal and academic reasons just mentioned, the therapist might consider testing in the following situations:

1. A client is not processing information or following the conversation (e.g., signs of possible cognitive problems).
2. The client displays aberrant, inappropriate behavior.
3. A mental status exam reveals problems.
4. A client shows signs of a major mental disorder.
5. Corroborative information is needed for legal purposes.
6. A student is referred to therapy for learning, emotional, and/or behavioral problems.

There are also reasons not to do testing. Clients can experience psychological testing as intrusive and tedious, or they may see little reason to participate. Referral to a consultant also brings in another professional and an additional therapeutic relationship. The therapist or the client may be concerned about privacy and confidentiality, and want as little formal documentation as possible. Psychological testing can be expensive, and clients or third-party payers may be reluctant to bear the added expense.

If testing is done, the family therapist, the clients, and the recommending agency frequently find the results to be helpful, but this is not always the case. Family therapists need basic tools to evaluate the quality of the report. Probably the most common criticism of test results is that they are too vague or abstract. Having read the results, the therapist might respond, "So what?" The report will only have value when it offers information pertinent to the direction of treatment.

To improve the chances of receiving a relevant report, a family therapist can become familiar with what tests are available and the qualities of a good report. One way to identify a helpful test is to take some (e.g., the Minnesota Multiphasic Personality Inventory [MMPI] or a family therapy instrument like the Dyadic Adjustment Scale) and consider whether the information is useful. Another helpful thing to do is to read a number of testing reports; quality reports will stand out. Family therapists frequently learn about two or three psychologists in their community who do excellent evaluations of children, adults, or specific areas such as memory. Asking these examiners to do evaluations of some of the therapist's own clients will begin the collaborative relationship.

EVALUATING THE EFFECTIVENESS OF TREATMENT

Once you implement a treatment plan, it's important to regularly evaluate its effectiveness: How are your clients progressing and what is contributing to their progress (or lack of progress)? Are they getting better, worse, or staying about the same? Can you predict how they'll be doing near the end of therapy? As you will read in the next chapter, the research has been consistent and clear: the elements of successful psychotherapy include client motivation, the ability of a therapist to cultivate hope, a strong alliance between therapist and client, a client's expectations that therapy will be helpful, and an alliance with the family (e.g., common understanding, caring, respect for familial bonds) (Chenail et al., 2012).

The evaluation of our clinical work has been called practice-based evidence (Dattilio, Piercy, & Davis, 2014; Swisher, 2010). In contrast to treatment-focused research that is concerned with the effectiveness of specific clinical interventions, practice-based evidence is concerned with monitoring a client's progress in therapy and using client feedback to inform therapy. Client-focused feedback will allow you to quickly and immediately evaluate the progress of your clinical work, help you understand the change process of your clients, and potentially alter your treatment approach to increase the likelihood of successful outcomes.

Miller, Duncan, Sorrell, and Brown's (2005) Partners for Change Outcome Management System (PCOMS) includes two brief scales (four items each) that a client completes and reviews with the therapist during the session to assess therapy process and progress. The Session Rating Scale (SRS) is a four-item pencil-and-paper scale designed to assess key dimensions of effective therapeutic relationships or therapy alliance (Duncan & Miller, 2008). Metaphorically, it takes the temperature of the session. At the end of the session, you can ask a client to complete the SRS to evaluate the session, with a particular focus on your effectiveness: Did the client feel heard, understood, and respected? Did you focus on areas the client wanted to work on and talk about? Was your approach a good fit for the client? Finally, did the overall session feel right or was something missing? You can review the results with the client at the end of the session, or review it between sessions and discuss the data at the next session.

The Outcome Rating Scale (ORS; Miller, Duncan, Brown, Sparks, & Claud, 2003) is a four-item scale designed to assess areas of life functioning known to change as a result of therapeutic intervention. At the beginning of the session, a client is asked to quietly complete the ORS, which gives a snapshot of how the client is doing on a scale of 1 to 10 at that moment in time in three areas over the past week: individually, interpersonally (family), and socially (work, school, friendships). In addition, the client is asked to evaluate how he or she is doing overall (general well-being). The scale is scored immediately. Once a score is determined, the score can be easily placed on a graph to track progress from session to session. When the therapist and client are able to see which of the three areas receives the lowest scores, it can sometimes help determine areas that need immediate attention.

CONCLUSION

Developing a treatment focus allows the beginning therapist to move from being a good listener to becoming a professional. By using an initial treatment plan, you will be able to conceptualize and explain how therapy will address the painful presenting problems brought to you. Suggestions on who needs to be in therapy, how long the therapy may last, and what methods you will use can be articulated and offered to the family. Networking with other professionals or community groups may also benefit clinical care.

The family therapist balances the relational, therapeutic, and ethical concerns of practice. It is a taxing role, yet very rewarding. Creativity and professional knowledge combine to help persons in the healing process. The basic treatment skills discussed in this chapter must be coordinated with the art of matching these skills to particular clients with particular problems, keeping in mind the kind of therapist you are, and consistently evaluating the effectiveness of your work. This is a lifelong and challenging component of being a family therapist.

CHAPTER 6

Basic Treatment Skills and Interventions

Karen and Rick stare at each other in frustration. Karen begins, "You don't help with the kids. I can't even . . ." Rick interrupts, "You're too sensitive. What about the time I took the kids all afternoon . . . ?" Karen rolls her eyes. Sammy, age 9, interrupts, "Don't yell. I can't stand it when you yell." There is an awkward silence in the therapy room.

What skills are necessary to be an effective therapist with this family? In this chapter, we first review the elements crucial to relating to your clients. Effective therapists display common qualities no matter what theory or intervention they use. Next, we discuss basic counseling skills that are the foundation of solid therapeutic work. Finally, we emphasize that marriage and family therapists hold a unique repertoire of skills related to their systems perspective. These skills need to be selected intentionally, and several guidelines will be offered emphasizing the therapist's role and responsibility in this selection.

THE RUSH TO INTERVENTION VERSUS DEVELOPING A RELATIONSHIP

Research on the effectiveness of therapy has identified one variable as critical in predicting a positive outcome. While therapists focus on compelling theoretical models or powerful techniques, research suggests that the therapist–client relationship is the most important variable, and, more specifically, the client's perception of the therapist and the relationship (Baldwin, Wampold, & Imel, 2007; Grunebaum, 1988; Miller, Duncan, & Hubble, 1997). Acknowledging the powerful impact of the therapeutic relationship is both a sobering and a humbling experience.

Beginning family therapists who are overwhelmed by their clients' problems and their own sense of inadequacy are often impatient to "do something" in the therapy session. Family therapy students are especially vulnerable to the "do-something syndrome" because their training has usually involved watching numerous master therapists perform brilliant therapeutic techniques on videos. After watching several of these videos and hearing about the success of their classmates, students are left wondering why nothing dramatic is happening in their sessions, and the pressure for something to happen intensifies.

This "do-something syndrome" is unfortunate because students fail to recognize their most powerful therapeutic tool—themselves. Often in supervision we suggest that students sit back, relax, and simply try to get to know and understand the client and his or her story. The point is that before technique and theory can be effective, there must be a relationship. Building it is the first and perhaps central task of the therapy, even for therapists who use a model in which the therapeutic relationship is not a focus.

Showing interest and communicating real empathy are examples of how beginning therapists can use themselves effectively in therapy and begin to build a relationship. Empathy—the ability to enter into a client's subjective world and to use one's own life experiences, thoughts, and feelings in relating to the client's pain—creates a powerful bond between the therapist and client and often builds an intimate relationship. Because of this profound connection, therapists must take the responsibility to conduct themselves appropriately with their clients. They need not understand the experience of their client to be empathic. The pain belongs to the client, not the therapist. The therapist shares the burden in relieving the difficulties, not in carrying them.

In our experience, there is also some truth to the idea of "fit" between client and therapist. Some therapists will be a good match with particular clients and some will not. A lack of fit might signal the therapist to offer a referral to someone else, or to suggest that the client shop for another therapist. In either case, the capacity of the therapist to empathize with the client is a relational quality basic to building the therapeutic alliance.

When one is working with a couple or family, empathy becomes more complicated. The therapist may relate strongly to one member and not to another. These emotional dynamics affect the connections within the clinical session and can be positive or negative contributors to treatment. Allowing for multiple empathic attachments within the clinical relationship taxes the therapist emotionally.

Some beginning therapists think that separating family members and seeing them individually will help the family, but this strategy is often a way of protecting one's own emotional energy and reducing one's own anxiety. Learning how to create appropriate emotional boundaries with a client is essential for solid work. The ability to stay outside the system while maintaining some emotional attachment to its members is a delicate balancing act for the therapist. Supervision can provide feedback about this balancing, including a number of signs that indicate lack of it, such as going over the session time limit, responding to frequent client phone calls without setting clearer and more stringent guidelines for crisis calls, becoming preoccupied by the client so much that it interferes with other areas of life (insomnia, or thinking about a client all the time), or feeling like you're the only one who can help the client (the savior complex).

Good therapists provide a nonthreatening and trusting climate in which their clients are invited to be honest and to change. Therapists need to communicate a warm and accepting stance even in the midst of looking directly at difficult problems that are impacting clients. For example, a client may warily watch his therapist's reaction when she discloses that her father may have molested her when she was a child. Ready for blaming or shaming reactions, clients closely monitor how trustworthy and safe the therapist will be.

Trust is primary (Rogers, 1972). Clients often have been accused of being "bad" or "wrong" for feeling, thinking, or acting in certain ways. A basic and open acceptance of each person must be in place in order to develop a therapeutic alliance. Clients need to experience the therapist as coming alongside of them and assisting them, not recoiling from them.

Clients also need to know that the therapist will be honest and appropriately self-disclosing when needed. For example, if the therapist is functioning outside of his or her comfort zone about a particular issue, sometimes it may be necessary to let the client know this. Beginning marriage and family therapists often feel this way when they start to provide therapy. Rather than "faking it," being clear about one's status as a trainee, about being supervised, and about working as a team with the client can engender more trust. Of course, trainees need to remember that they too have training and expertise from their education, previous clinical exposure, and their own life experience to bring to the therapeutic relationship.

As in assessment, curiosity contributes to developing a positive relationship with clients. Especially when working with persons with different life experiences than one's own—such as differences in age or culture—taking a learning posture will often be helpful. It is difficult to stereotype when one takes this position, as a case example illustrates. A Laotian family came into therapy because their 12-year-old had run away, that is, stayed overnight with a friend her parents didn't know, without telling them. One of the authors asked the parents how 12-year-olds spend time with their friends in Laos when they were growing up, since the therapist didn't know their culture very well. They commented that 12-year-olds spend time with their friends only at school and spend time only with their families outside of school. Families would also get together with other families, and then their children would play together. The therapist asked these parents if they had discussed any legitimate way for their daughter to spend time with her peers other than at school or at their home. After looking at each other, they answered that they had not. The daughter then shyly commented that sneaking out was the only way she could be with her friends. The therapist and family then created some new ways for the 12-year-old to spend time with friends (besides school and family gatherings) that the parents and adolescent could accept. Listening and being curious about your clients' stories doesn't end after the first session. Probing to elicit information about them and their perspectives will promote a safe, healing context for understanding and change.

BASIC COUNSELING SKILLS

The following section highlights several core skills useful for family therapists, although not unique to our profession; they encompass skills used by many types of psychotherapies.

Using (and Not Using) Self-Disclosure

One aspect of structuring is to ensure that the relationship with the client is one-sided: the content of the therapy is about the client, therapeutic goals are about the client, and self-disclosure is done by the client. Instead of seeking mutuality in the relationship, the therapist cares for the client and focuses on his or her problems. However, therapists may choose to make certain self-disclosures in a therapeutic context.

Therapists' disclosure of personal information will vary according to each one's personal style. Personal style in self-disclosure may be indicated by how intimately therapists decorate their office (e.g., with photographs of spouse and children) and how directly they answer a client's questions about their own family life.

A therapist should consider some of the following guidelines in determining level of self-disclosure:

1. The therapeutic relationship, like any relationship, takes some time to develop. It is more appropriate to talk more personally about yourself after you've known someone for a longer time.
2. Most therapists self-disclose more freely with children and adolescents. These clients tend to equate self-disclosure with a measure of trust. They will ask more personal questions than adults and appear to be curious about the therapist.
3. Therapist credibility may be enhanced by self-disclosure of information about one's educational or professional credentials.
4. A therapist should keep in mind that self-disclosure may impact each client differently. Some clients will be more comfortable with a professional distance in which self-disclosure is kept to a minimum, while others will prefer to know something about the therapist before they feel comfortable opening up about themselves.
5. A therapist should disclose only personal information that has been thought about and processed, and avoid current issues that are creating personal turmoil.

The therapist must consider the impact of self-disclosure on the client. Providing information about oneself such as educational background or professional training can be very helpful in joining with a client and increasing confidence in the therapeutic process. Sometimes clients will ask personal questions, perhaps about marital status or whether you have children, and this can also be helpful in joining and in creating rapport. A therapist can offer personal reactions or feelings to a situation, such as being concerned about a client's well-being, as a leading statement to help generate a reaction from the client. A therapist may offer a story about his or her life or something that happened to someone else in order to stimulate the client's thinking or provide an alternative perspective on an issue. However, the therapist may also get caught up in his or her own reactions to a client and share feelings inappropriately, which might indicate that the therapist has lost direction in the therapeutic process.

It's helpful for the therapist to understand his or her own intentions in self-disclosing personal information and reactions, and attempt to anticipate the impact on the client. A couple on the brink of divorce doesn't need to know that their therapist is currently in the process of divorcing him- or herself. In another case, it may be helpful for the therapist to normalize a couple's difficulty in coping with new parenthood by discussing personal experiences. Clearly, the degree to which a therapist's role encompasses sharing is driven by a combination of personal preference, theoretical orientation, and client considerations.

Although this discussion has been devoted to the therapist's responsibilities, remember that clients carry some responsibility as well—for their behavior and for making their own decisions. The therapist's role is to guide clients, not to make decisions for them. If a client decides to enter into a relationship that may be personally destructive, that decision needs to be respected by the therapist. He or she may offer alternatives or look at the client's motivation in entering into the relationship, but, ultimately, it is the client's choice. The client has to live with it. Finally, clients are responsible for bringing their concerns to therapy and maintaining some respect for the process. The therapy will likely be more productive if the client comes prepared to talk about issues of current concern.

Using Questions

From the first phone call, the therapist must use good questions in order to discover needed clinical information. Especially in the early and middle parts of the therapeutic relationship, questions keep the therapy focused on the client's perceptions and needs. They can also help create change by helping the client to think differently about an issue.

In an effort to clarify the kinds of questions that can be used and the impact of specific types, Tomm (1988) describes four categories of questions used in uncovering and understanding possibilities for treatment. He labeled them lineal, circular, strategic, and reflexive questions. Each category of questions is seen as having a purpose or intent.

Lineal questions are investigative, deductive, and content-loaded, involving a "just the facts, ma'am" perspective. Information gathered by these questions is thought to explain the problem. For example, questioning about why a child is truant and coming home late may be answered with "He doesn't like it; he hates the teachers; he hates the kids; he didn't like school last year, either; he needs an attitude adjustment." Often lineal questions point to something or someone who is wrong and needs to be fixed.

Circular questions are exploratory and stem from a posture of curiosity on the therapist's part. Instead of singling out who or what needs changing, information from these questions highlights interconnections within the family and to larger systems. Underlying the questions is the assumption that everything is connected to everything else. A therapist might ask, "What, if anything, is different about the days when your son doesn't cut school?" or "Who in the family first finds out that your son has cut school? What happens after?" Circular questions help to expose patterns in the relationships.

O'Brian and Bruggen (1985) have classified circular questions into four different categories. One type of question has a family member comment on the relationship or interaction between two other family members. For example, the therapist may ask the mother, "How do your son and husband get along?" Or the therapist may ask a child, "What does your mother do when your father comes home and has been drinking?" Another type of circular question may have individuals rank-order family members' responses to an actual or hypothetical situation. A therapist might ask, "Who is most upset about the divorce? Who next?" Or he might ask more generally, "Who will be most relieved when this problem is resolved? Who will be next most relieved?" A third type examines differences that occur over time. Questions can relate to a specific event that happened in the past or is anticipated to happen in the future. For example, a mother might be asked how her child's behavior has changed since the divorce, or a father might be asked how his marriage will change once the children leave home. A fourth type of circular question is used to solicit information indirectly about an individual who is unwilling to answer questions or is not present. A wife may be asked by the therapist, "If your husband were here today, what would he say are the biggest problems in your marriage?"

Strategic questions, or influencing questions, are challenging in nature. They pose new possibilities, often in a particular direction. A therapist might ask, for example, "What would it take to have you and your ex-husband take a united parental stand with your child on this matter?" or "What might happen if you and your child's father temporarily ignored your child's behavior of leaving school early?" In both questions the therapist attempts to interrupt the current interactional sequence by having the parents align their behavioral reactions to their child. The question is purposive and often corrective. Changing the way the family currently responds to a problem is primary when asking strategic questions.

Reflexive questions facilitate change in the family without moving the family in any particular direction. Therapists, through their questions, attempt to mobilize new response possibilities from the family. The therapist assumes clients have and can access internal resources for change. Examples of reflexive questions are "What if your son had some strong feelings that he couldn't share with you, how could you let him know that you wanted to hear them?" or "If your son started attending school regularly again, how would your lives be different?" In both examples, a fairly neutral stance is taken by the therapist, with a hope that the client can find new responses that are different and better than previous responses. Rather than focusing on any precise behavior change, the door is opened to alternatives. Reflexive questions facilitate change without directing it.

In all these types of questions, nonverbal as well as verbal skills communicate the posture and perspective of the therapist. For example, a question like "What is your reaction?" can be asked in a demanding or a requesting way. Keeping nonverbal communication and verbal questions congruent allows more effective communication. In any case, the skill of questioning contributes to our ability to act as agents of change in the lives of the families we serve.

Normalizing

Normalizing requires some knowledge of what's common for many families to experience. It means that the therapist understands the symptoms presented by a client as part of common behavior connected with particular developmental phases in an individual's or a family's life. Framing a 14-year-old's moodiness as "a common part of adolescence" often helps relieve a family's concern. Normalizing a couple's distress over decreasing romantic interest while they have two preschool-age children can help them accept and understand rather than fear the changes in their relationship. Often a therapist notices an immediate calming in the client system when something has been normalized. Sometimes the family will respond by offering up stories that validate the normality of the symptoms (e.g., when Uncle John had the same problem).

Providing psychoeducational resources such as developmentally sensitive books or self-help groups and readings can be helpful for normalizing problems. We have included in this text discussions about normative reactions to life-cycle and other developmental issues. Self-help groups also provide a strong normalizing experience for clients, especially those who are more socially isolated. For some, committing to a very short-term treatment contract (three to five sessions) helps to reassure the family that their concerns are interpreted as normal, and sets the appropriate clinical tone for the family. After brief therapy, one can reevaluate if the problem has been adequately addressed after labeling symptoms as normal. Many good developmental texts are available to clinicians to assist in normalizing.

Reframing

During a parent–teacher conference, Micah's fourth-grade teacher tells his mother that he can be a bit loud in class, he sometimes speaks out without raising his hand, and he can act like a know-it-all. She also says that on the playground Micah is a leader, a good athlete, and a positive role model. Micah's disruptive behavior in the classroom may be much more appropriate and positive on the playground. When the context of the behavior changes, the frame changes and the behavior is perceived differently. A reframe is changing the frame in which a person perceives events in order to change the meaning (Bandler & Grinder, 1982).

In reframing, the behavior remains the same but the frame or perception of the behavior is changed. A house that is filled with personal mementos can be perceived as representing a fulfilling life or it can be viewed as cluttered. In therapy, we use reframing as a technique to put a different, often positive spin or frame on a negative behavior. A child's stubborn, headstrong behavior could also be seen as an ability to be assertive or stand up for him- or herself. Reframing relies on the therapist's creative ability to reinterpret symptoms in therapy.

Providing Support

As our society becomes more and more transient, providing a stable, consistent, and nurturing relationship in a client's life often resembles throwing a life jacket to a drowning person. The key way that therapists provide this nurturance is through attentive and active listening to the client's story. As the therapist begins to reflect back, understand, and grant permission to explore any and all feelings or thoughts, clients experience reassurance, a solid foundation from which to build new possibilities. "Just being there" makes a difference.

Yet support, however valuable, doesn't guarantee change. Support is more stabilizing in function than change-inducing. Providing a reassuring place to be might not address the problem presented by the client. Clients coming to therapy are often experiencing tremendous pain. The pain signals something significant and must be respected. Support can help to alleviate some of the pain but often won't remedy it. Change resulting from a supportive stance can be dramatic but often requires a long-term relationship before results are seen.

Confronting

To facilitate change, at some point during the therapy clinicians may need to sensitively ask clients if they really want to change. This may or may not be done directly. Some therapies based on strategic models spend little time providing verbal support (although they do provide nonverbal support) and jump right into the domain of confrontation by using strategic or reflexive questions. For example, the first question from the therapist might be "What would need to happen during our first session today to help with the problem you called about?" A change posture is expected and therapy may be terminated if change doesn't occur. Confrontation, although delivered with caring words, may begin immediately.

For many therapists and some clients, beginning therapy with a more confrontive posture isn't fitting. These therapists and clients must discover the appropriate time to move into more change-focused activities. Of course, this might be done sooner than one thinks. For example, as soon as a therapist develops an appropriate treatment plan, he or she necessarily moves into the confrontive domain since the treatment plan identifies specific areas to change. Likewise, as soon as the therapist wonders if involving other family members might help the situation, he or she is confronting the status quo. When a therapist tries to evaluate if therapy is helping, he or she moves into doing something different. Confrontation comes in many forms and is essential to change.

Systemically oriented therapists know something about the difficulty we have in facilitating change. We know that clients tend to maintain homeostasis—the familiar way of handling a problem. Change takes energy and is often difficult to achieve. Directly or indirectly, the therapist must confront old ways of doing things and seek new possibilities in order for change to occur.

Pacing

The pace at which a therapy session moves involves how slowly or rapidly the client reveals information. The therapist's interventions can alter the pace by creating opportunities for further exploration of a particular issue, changing the focus to another topic, adding depth or breadth to the discussion, or exploring the emotions related to the issue. All of these interventions will impact what clients reveal and will lead them in a particular direction. Most interventions will be focused on either pacing or leading the client or family. In its simplest form, pacing involves following the client. Mirroring a client's behavior enables the therapist to move at the client's pace. Techniques such as reflecting, active listening, and tracking also provide useful vehicles for pacing. Pacing a client is an essential aspect of the joining process and is critical in developing rapport and building a trustful, working relationship.

Leading is an attempt by the therapist to select a direction for exploration and lead the client there. Joining with the client must precede moving to a leading stance. If a young man is talking about his concerns about going to college, the therapist might first place the client's concerns by listening to him. The therapist can then lead him by asking questions regarding his feelings about college and his thoughts about his ability to be successful. The introduction of the new focus expands the breadth and depth of the discussion and leads the client in a particular direction.

The therapist should monitor the pace of the session. If too much material is revealed too rapidly, there might not be sufficient time to follow up on critical events or issues, or the family's emotional response to a particular concern may be obscured. Slowing down the pace of the session often proves helpful in allowing clients to follow their own belief or feeling about an issue. If the pace is too slow, clients or therapists can become complacent and bored with the session. The therapist may need to intervene to move the session along by asking thought-provoking questions or focusing on present, here-and-now behavior. Most sessions will alternate between some pacing of the concerns and some leading to assist in developing alternative directions to be explored.

Several factors should be considered in determining the pace of therapy. If the family is highly motivated to change, then the pace of the therapy can be more rapid. High levels of resistance will likely mean that the pace will be slower. The length of treatment is also a factor. Brief therapy may limit the depth of exploration. The client's level of anxiety will also be a consideration in developing the pace. If anxiety is high, the therapist may need to slow things down to assist in containing the client's fears. If the client's anxiety is extremely low, there may be a lack of motivation to change, and the pace may need to be increased.

Specific techniques that hasten the pace of therapy include asking open-ended questions, leading in a particular direction, identifying the process in the session, and focusing on the here-and-now. Techniques that slow down the pace include tracking and obtaining clarification, mirroring behavior, active listening, and reflecting.

Dealing with Crises

Sometimes therapy begins with a crisis, a situation with unique circumstances that tend to be short term, overwhelming, and understandably stressful. Sudden and unexpected external events such as the death of a family member, an automobile accident, or a natural disaster are examples of events that could cause a client to be under severe stress or in crisis. Crisis can occur around developmental or maturational issues such as the birth of a child, a child reaching adolescence, or the last child leaving home. Each individual or family will react to the situation differently and cope with it idiosyncratically. The crisis state is characterized by severe disruption in the client's or family's normal level of functioning. Common symptoms include physical and psychological agitation, poor appetite, loss of sleep, emotional distress, anxiety, and an inability to solve problems. Although the objective reality of a crisis such as a natural disaster may be the same to most people, responses to the event are highly subjective. A client's level of vulnerability will depend on his or her subjective interpretation of the event, available resources, and previous history in coping with stress. When a crisis involves suicidal or homicidal ideation, child abuse, or elder or dependent adult abuse, we must not only attend to the needs of the client, but also act swiftly to carry out our ethical and legal responsibilities.

Even within a family each person will respond to a crisis differently, which can exacerbate family difficulties. For example, a family was about to go to court to settle a case involving an automobile accident in which their 17-year-old son was at fault. The event was causing a severe amount of stress for the parents, who had an exhaustive argument prior to the court appearance in which they both became very caustic and verbally abusive. The potential threat to their already unstable financial picture caused considerable fear and insecurity. The parents' response to the upcoming court hearing was to become agitated and conflictual, while the young man's response was to withdraw and deny the importance of the problem. Their reactions caused further difficulties between the family members, and thus a situational crisis ensued.

Families respond in their characteristic ways to a potential crisis. A crisis may escalate very quickly in a family in which anticipation of a worst-case scenario adds to the problem. In another family a crisis can be avoided through use of effective problem-solving skills. The family's ability to respond to a crisis will depend on their ability to handle stress and conflict.

Crisis intervention tends to be short term and present-focused. The therapist typically needs to assume an active and directive role in assisting clients when they are under severe stress. Rappaport (1970) has identified four goals for crisis intervention:

1. Relieving the client's immediate symptoms.
2. Restoring the client to his or her previous level of functioning.
3. Identifying the factors that led to the crisis state.
4. Identifying and applying remedial measures.

Crisis intervention techniques will vary, depending on the client's state and the nature of the crisis. Affective interventions will focus on assisting the family in expressing their feelings about the situation, as often there is little opportunity to do so during the actual event. A debriefing period should allow clients to express their feelings and the therapist to provide support for what the family has been through. Normalizing their response to the situation may also be helpful. Cognitive interventions may focus on altering negative beliefs, guilt, or self-incriminating thoughts. For example, if a family is involved in an accident in which one member dies and another lives, assisting the surviving member in alleviating guilt may be an important initial intervention. By providing an opportunity to take action, behavioral tasks can help the client begin to regain a sense of control over his or her life. Beginning to rebuild shortly after a disaster can prove helpful in coping with psychological and material losses. Assisting the family in using community resources from agencies, churches, synagogues, or social programs may also be valuable.

Offering Psychoeducational Information

Another basic resource that can be provided by therapists is verbal and written information about common presenting problems. Handouts on common topics, such as effective communication or stages of grief; lists of respected self-help books; and directions to reputable websites on useful topics can be invaluable for clients. The division between academic information and self-help references has become blurred in recent years, and many wonderful books and articles are available to help families with particular life issues.

SKILLS UNIQUE TO THE SYSTEMIC/RELATIONAL THERAPIST

Up to this point, we have described skills that most general psychotherapists employ in the therapy room. Therapists who work from a systemic or relational perspective have unique ways of intervening and achieving change. A complete exploration of these skills and interventions is beyond the scope of this chapter, but we would be remiss not to highlight some of the key features of systems-oriented therapy that accompany the basic counseling skills described earlier.

Common Factors in Couple and Family Therapy

The therapeutic process with couples and families can be elusive. There are certainly trends and factors that can be identified as helpful in creating change and reducing stress in clients. Different theories suggest that we focus on varying aspects of the client's or family's functioning. For example, narrative therapists elicit and develop their client's story and try to thicken alternative narratives to weaken the problem-saturated story. Structural family therapists expand the symptom to include the system and restructure the family system to create change. Different therapies target different variables and build their view of change around them. But what do the different theories have in common? Are there variables that can be identified as factors transcend different specific theories?

Lambert (1992) identified key factors that impact the process of change and found that 40% of the change process is associated with client factors. These factors include the environment, the client's socio-economic status, their motivation, and their belief system. The alliance between the client and the therapist accounted for 30% of the variance impacting the process of change. The other factors were hope and expectancy (15%) and therapists' fidelity to their treatment model (15%). The choice of treatment model receives a great deal of emphasis in our clinical training, but, as we discussed at the beginning of this chapter, it's the relational and client factors that have the most significant impact in creating change.

Sprenkle, Davis, and Lebow (2009) identified four common factors unique to couple and family therapy: (1) conceptualizing difficulties in relational terms; (2) disrupting relational patterns; (3) expanding the direct treatment system; and (4) expanding the therapeutic alliance. Consistent with our message throughout this chapter, they also note that individual and relational therapy rely "heavily on the quality of the relationship between therapist and client" (p. 34). Below we discuss a couple of these common factors, as well as other skills unique to the systemic family therapist.

Identifying and Interrupting Negative Interactional Patterns

Family therapists identify relationship patterns by carefully listening for interactional themes and observing family interactions in session. To interrupt negative interactional patterns, therapists address the behavioral, cognitive, and emotional domains of family relationships. For example, emotionally focused therapists identify and label primary emotions (e.g., hurt) underneath secondary reactive emotions (e.g., anger) to soften the interactions between family members and interrupt negative patterns. Therapists working from a structural perspective may identify communication patterns that have become rigidified and unhealthy. For example, a 15-year-old girl calls her non-custodial mother when she was unhappy at home with her father and stepmother. The therapist worked with the family to interrupt the pattern by facilitating more direct communication between the daughter and her father. The identification and interruption of unhealthy relationships patterns helps the therapy move from content to process and provides a thread from session to session, a skill we discuss in more detail later in this chapter.

Inviting Absent Family Members to Sessions

It's rare for an entire family to arrive for the first therapy appointment. More commonly, therapists initially make contact with part of a system, such as an individual, couple, or parent and child. Most systemic family therapists attempt to engage family members who do not participate in the first or second session, either by asking the client to invite other family members to a session or by the therapist contacting family members directly to seek their involvement. For example, if a mother and child present to therapy due to the child's unwillingness to attend school, a therapist might ask for the father's involvement at subsequent sessions.

If the therapist is seeing an individual who is married or living with someone as a couple, it may make sense to invite their partner in for a collateral session. The invitation can be based on the suggestion that their perspective may prove helpful to the therapeutic process and help to obtain a clearer picture of the relationship issues. When inviting the partner, it's important not to frame the invitation as couple therapy, for a couple of reasons. A partner may interpret the invitation as a suggestion that he or she is to blame for the problem, which increases the likelihood that he or she will reject the invitation. In addition, you want to protect your therapeutic relationship with your client, who may worry about loss of her individual therapist. Couple therapy may be indicated. If so, a decision will need to be made about who will provide the couple therapy.

Developing a Genogram

In Chapter 4, we discussed the use of a genogram for family assessment. Family therapists use genograms for a variety of purposes in therapy. In some cases, it takes on a very minor role, such as helping to organize a therapist's private notes about a client's family-of-origin. For example, during a first session a therapist might draw a genogram in her notes to keep track of who is in the family. In other cases, the genogram takes on a starring role and becomes a focus of treatment, which is a common method in the transgenerational approaches to family therapy (Kerr & Bowen, 1988). We see the genogram as much more than a note-taking tool, but not solely as a treatment technique. The construction of a genogram is an essential part of our work with clients, helping us better understand a family's current challenges and strengths. We have seen many students skip this part of the therapy and regret it later when they're stuck or when important family-of-origin information arises later in treatment and they feel foolish for not knowing the information.

In its simplest form, a genogram is a visual map to identify members of a family, including gender, generation, and age. Figure 6.1 provides a summary of the most commonly used symbols for the graphic depiction of a family (McGoldrick et al., 2008; Pendagast & Sherman, 1977; Williams, Edwards, Patterson, & Chamow, 2011). We won't describe each symbol, but rather highlight a few of the most relevant symbols. Each family member is represented by a square (male) or a circle (female); ages are written in each symbol. The identified client or patient (IP) is indicated with double lines. Siblings are listed based on their birth order, oldest to youngest from left to right. The youngest generation is drawn at the bottom, with the oldest generations above the younger generations. Marriages are indicated with a solid line; the husband goes on the left. Committed relationships are indicated with a dotted line. Previous or subsequent marital or committed relationships are drawn on the left or right side. At times, you will want to record information that either doesn't have a symbol or you won't be able to remember the symbol. In situations like this, give yourself permission to improvise by writing statements on the genogram or creating your own symbols. The genogram does not need to look perfect; it just needs to communicate the important information.

Early in your work with a client, preferably in the second session, you will be setting aside time to collect information for a three- or four-generation genogram. By this time, most therapists have already been constructing a genogram in their private notes in order to organize all the information they've received. Including the family in a discussion about their extended family changes the genogram from a note-taking tool to an intervention tool. Because your client will be focused on the presenting problem, questions may be raised about why precious time is being used to gather information "in the past." You need to be prepared to present a rationale for why the information is important (e.g., "What we learned in our families growing up often influences our attitudes and behaviors in our current relationships"; "I want to know about the strengths and resources in your family that will help you overcome this problem"). If you don't view the information as important, it will be very difficult to convince your client that it's important.

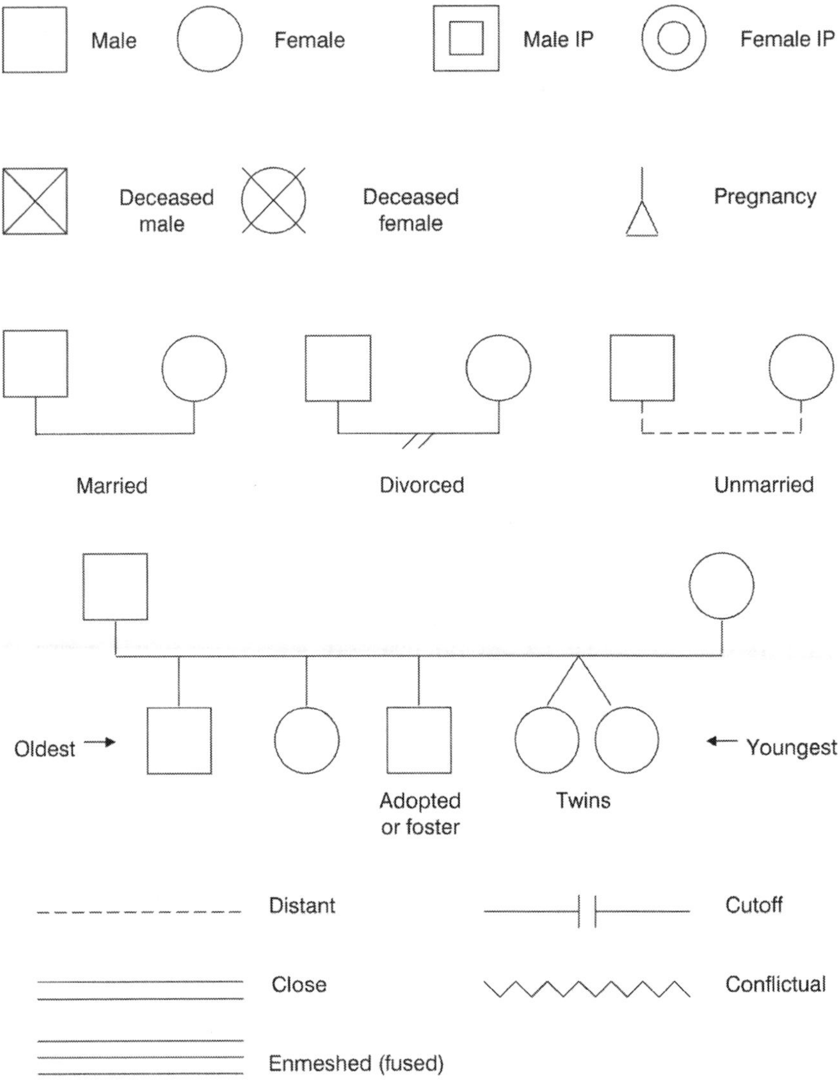

FIGURE 6.1. Common genogram symbols. From Williams, Edwards, Patterson, and Chamow (2011). Adapted with permission from The Guilford Press.

Most clients will understand the importance of doing "a good history" because it's consistent with their experiences seeing other healthcare professionals.

Once you and your client agree to do a genogram, your next challenge is how to stay on task. Some therapists prepare for these interviews and then get sidetracked when clients present a flurry of new issues since the previous session. In order to help your clients stay focused, we recommend constructing the genogram on a large piece of paper that everyone can clearly see. You can keep the genogram in your file and post it on the wall during each session. Another advantage of a large posting is that you can involve children in the drawing of symbols and lines, which engages them in therapy and may provide diagnostic information about how they diagram particular relationships.

The first phase in the construction of a genogram is breadth:

* Gather the gender, ages, and names of each family member, starting with the youngest family members and moving up.[1]
* For family members who have died, list the person's age at the time of death, along with an *X* to indicate the loss. Also, indicate how the person died.[2]
* Connect the family members with lines indicating biological or legal relationships.
* On the relationship lines, make a note of the beginning and, if needed, ending dates of relationships.

The second phase in the construction of a genogram is depth. Here is a list of the information we gather:

* Descriptions of each relevant family member. "Let's start with your father. Tell me a little bit about him." For clients who need more structure, you may want to ask, "What are five words that describe your father?" Regardless of how you gather the information, you will want to make sure that positive descriptions are included with negative descriptions.
* A description of how family members would describe your client or clients. "If your parents and siblings were here, how would they

---

[1] A common question is whether you need to include every distant relative. Although in some cases it might be necessary to get this specific, we recommend focusing on the closest family members.

[2] Unless it's relevant to the presenting problem, avoid spending too much time at this stage on the circumstances of a death. You can acknowledge the significance of a loss and ask the family if you can revisit the experience at a later date.

describe you?" or "What are five words your parents and siblings would use to describe you?" These descriptions can frequently capture roles in a family (e.g., scapegoat, star, black sheep, comedian).

 • Descriptions of dyadic relationships. "Tell me about the relationship between you and your father? What about the relationship between you and your sister? What about the relationship between your parents? How have these relationships changed over time?"

 • Description of family time together. "What was a typical day in the life of your family? What did your family do for fun together?"

 • Description of the family emotional climate. "How were anger, sadness, and joy expressed in your family? If you had a problem, who did you go talk to? If your parents were unhappy with your behavior, how did they discipline you? These descriptions can capture rules in a family—rules that are explicit (e.g., "No dating until you're 16") and implicit (e.g., "We don't talk about a family member after they've died").

 • Family belief systems and mantras. "What were some of the core beliefs in your family?" For example, families may carry beliefs related to gender (e.g., men should not be vulnerable or show emotions other than anger) and what is normal or abnormal ("We have a great relationship; we never argue") (Rolland, 1994).

By this point, you will have heard many descriptions of family members and relationships and general themes will begin to emerge that may or may not connect to the presenting problem. Themes are often identified as patterns in the family's functioning that occur across generations.

Although a genogram is a valuable tool to identify the vertical stressors (e.g., relationship patterns, addictions, violence) in the life a family (McGoldrick & Shibusawa, 2012), it obscures the temporal dimension of family history (Friedman, Rohrbaugh, & Krakauer, 1988). In other words, the genogram lists dates and events, but doesn't place them in their proper order for appreciation. For example, a divorce, a move, and the diagnosis of a parent's illness may have occurred in close time proximity, which may have also been the time when a presenting problem started. We now turn our attention to another skill unique to the systemic family therapist: the timeline.

Developing a Timeline

Like a genogram, a timeline helps clients place their concerns in context. A timeline records the significant normative events (e.g., transition to adolescence) and nonnormative events (e.g., unexpected job loss) in a family's life. For example, a family might learn that a child's problem behavior began at a time of increased family stress during several concurrent transitions, including the arrival of a new sibling and a move to a new home and school.

Similar to the construction of the genogram, you will want to post a sheet of paper on the wall and allow the family to identify the most important events, along with dates, in the life of their family. Stanton (1992) succinctly and clearly describes the process:

> It consists of drawing a long horizontal line and dividing it into equal time segments representing years, months, weeks, even days, depending on the therapist's preference. At points along the line various nodal or life cycle events are designated by short vertical markers extending downward from identifying inscriptions (e.g., Louise loses job," "Bert and Marie get married," "William dies"). There is no limit to the kinds of nodal events that can be highlighted. They usually include key births, deaths, engagements, marriages, separations, divorces, school changes, launchings, layoffs, promotions, financial setbacks, relocations, immigrations, and the onset of severe medical events such as illnesses, hospitalizations, and surgery. Any kind of loss, gain, or change is grist for the mill. (p. 332)

Once events are plotted on the timeline, you can begin to hypothesize the significance of particular transitions.

Mobilizing Hope, Agency, and Communion

When clients meet us for the first time, demoralization can be common themes in their presentation. They can express regret and shame about their past and despair for their future. Sometimes this can be an indication of depression, but more frequently it's an expression of the burden, discouragement, and isolation they feel in daily living. A primary goal in the first few sessions is to help the client feel more hopeful, empowered, and socially connected.

Based on Michael White's narrative therapy, Griffith (2013) suggests the questions below to mobilize hope:

* When did you last feel hopeful? What was that like?
* Who in your life helps you stay hopeful?
* When times are hard, what keeps hope alive?
* Who have you known in your life who would not be surprised to see you staying hopeful amid adversity? What did this person know about you that others may not know?

To mobilize agency:

- When was a time when you knew that you were managing your life well, despite problems?
- What should I know about you as a person that is not a part of the problem you've described to me?
- Who helps you to stay strong despite the challenges you face?
- How have you managed to keep these problems from taking total control of your life?

To mobilize communion:

- When did you last feel the close presence of someone who cares for you?
- Who knows what you are going through? To whom do you turn when you need help?
- With whom do you feel most comforted when you are hurting?
- In whose presence do you most feel a bodily sense of peace?
- As you cope with this problem, how do you stay connected to people who matter in your life?

This sample of questions helps facilitate a conversation with clients to elicit strengths and resources that may have gone unnoticed and can unlock options in situations that feel overwhelming and unresolvable.

BECOMING MORE SOPHISTICATED IN USING INTERVENTIONS

In addition to using basic counseling skills and intervening systemically, family therapists must consider issues of process and content, timing, and clients' anxiety levels when selecting specific interventions. O'Hanlon (1982) has identified 13 classes of intervention that delineate different options for intervening in personal and interpersonal patterns of behavior, perception, and experience. These interventions are focused on altering patterns of behavior as they affect symptoms. For example, if the family presents constant arguing as the problem, the intervention is used to disrupt the pattern by altering how often arguments take place.

Interventions can focus on the process or content of a dialogue or interaction. The content of an interaction is what is actually said, while the process is how it is said (Satir, 1967). For example, a father and his 15-year-old son might be discussing the young man's desire to get his driver's license. This issue is the content, or *what* is being discussed.

The process, or *how* it is being discussed, includes underlying feelings of concern, the tone of the discussion, and the communication pattern. Interventions that focus on content help to clarify issues, provide more information, and define problems. Interventions that focus on process aid in exploring or uncovering feelings and revealing themes or patterns of interaction. For example, if the therapist notices that family members are discussing a very emotionally charged issue with an absence of feeling, the therapist might intervene to identify this process. Solid therapeutic interventions involve both content and process.

A therapist considers several critical factors when choosing interventions. The timing of the intervention must be considered in evaluating its effectiveness. Timing affects how a particular strategy, a homework assignment, or a directive will be received by the family. Using a particular intervention too early in therapy, when there is insufficient trust in either the therapist or the process, can cause it to fail.

In addition to trust, it is helpful to consider motivation for change in determining appropriate timing. If a client is highly motivated, he or she likely will be more receptive to interventions that accentuate change. If the client is resistant to change, then interventions that pace the client, such as tracking and active listening, might be in order. In the initial therapy session, where the primary goal is assessment, a "no change" stance can be beneficial. The "no change" stance assumes that until the therapist has completed an adequate assessment, introducing change is premature. It really does not make good therapeutic sense to suggest change before fully comprehending the problem.

Assessing and managing anxiety in a session can prove helpful in evaluating the choice of an intervention. Some interventions, such as open-ended questions, can increase a client's anxiety simply because the client doesn't immediately know the answer. Questions that are more orienting in nature, such as basic information regarding family or work history, are likely to decrease anxiety. A moderate level of anxiety is to be expected in therapy and assist in moving toward change. It is helpful for the therapist to note the level of anxiety in the session and anticipate which interventions are likely to heighten or diminish it.

CONCLUSION

The basic treatment skills discussed in this chapter must be coordinated with the art of matching these skills to particular clients with particular problems, keeping in mind the kind of therapist you are. This is a lifelong and challenging component of being a family therapist. Good therapy is like good art—basics need to be mastered first:

understanding yourself, your clients, and your context at multiple levels provides the setting in which a masterpiece is created. We close this chapter on treatment skills by offering, in Table 6.1, a list of self-assessment questions. Beginning therapists may find these helpful in gauging and guiding their early work.

TABLE 6.1. Self-Assessment Questions Regarding Treatment Skills

<u>To create a therapeutic relationship</u>

1. Do I show a concerned interest for my clients?
2. Have I structured a safe therapeutic environment in the room and set guidelines for working outside of the session?
3. Can I understand my clients' experience to some extent at both emotional and cognitive levels?
4. Do I continue to be curious about this case?
5. Do I need to be clear about my status as a trainee or intern, or my lack of expertise in a particular area?

<u>To assess and intervene</u>

1. Do I ask the appropriate questions to assess (e.g., lineal and circular questions) and intervene (e.g., strategic and reflexive questions)?
2. Can I normalize the clients' concerns in some way?
3. Will reframing the presenting problem help to change the way it is understood?
4. Do the clients perceive me as increasing their social support system?
5. Can I confront the family when necessary?
6. Am I aware of the pacing needs for these clients?
7. Have I considered referrals that would be useful?
8. Would psychoeducational material (e.g., reading, handouts, Internet website) be useful for these clients?
9. Do I have a treatment plan in place?

<u>To develop my family therapy skills</u>

1. Am I thinking and acting in a systemic manner?
2. Do my interventions match my systemic understanding of the problem and family?
3. Would it be useful to read an article or chapter on this treatment approach or problem? Do I need to attend a workshop to deepen my understanding?
4. Do I consult with a colleague or supervisor if I get confused?
5. Am I managing the legal and ethical concerns of this case well?

CHAPTER 7

Working with Families and Children

Lisa S sat wide-eyed and trembling on the edge of her chair, occasionally hiding with one hand a persistent tic in her left eye. It was her first visit to a therapist's office, and since 9-year-old Lisa was by nature a shy and nervous child, she left the talking to her mother and father. Mr. and Mrs. S leaned toward the therapist, and painfully revealed their daughter's daily panic attacks and their own frustration in trying to solve Lisa's "problem." By the end of the interview, the therapist had compiled a rich history and a number of hypotheses about Lisa's disorder. Although Lisa was clearly the IP, there was no question that family work would be part of treatment. Having carefully listened to and empathized with his new clients, the therapist began to talk teamwork.

Perhaps our deepest conviction in working with children is that, with remarkably few exceptions, primary caretakers are absolutely key to the assessment and effective treatment of childhood problems. This "umbrella" assumption is a common value of family therapists, but is at times not put into practice by new therapists who feel anxious involving multiple family members. Without family involvement, our interventions with children may become 50-minute exercises whose impact quickly dissipates in the 10,000 minutes that lie between sessions. Whether we lean toward a view of childhood problems as somehow functional within the family or are inclined to see childhood disorders from a more individual perspective, our work with children almost always involves addressing the hopes, fears, attitudes, and abilities of the grownups with whom our child clients live. Indeed, a collaborative set in which parents or primary caretakers share their own assessments and carry insights, information, and actions learned in therapy into the home is basic.

ASSESSMENT OF CHILDREN AND ADOLESCENTS

Art historians are likely familiar with that period of time in which European painters depicted children as miniature adults. Similarly, sociologists and anthropologists report on those eras in which children were surmised to think, feel, and behave as adults in undersized bodies. Today, of course, the differentiation between "child" and "adult" is as complex as it is well documented. In psychopathology, however, we continue the struggle to define, identify, and treat mental disorders that, previously described and treated among adults, behave quite differently in children.

In our work with children, we are reminded daily of how childhood itself complicates differential diagnoses (Costello, Mustillo, Erkanli, Keeler, & Angold, 2003; Hofstra, Van der Ende, & Verhulst, 2000). The common behavioral symptoms seen in troubled children cut across neat diagnostic categories and, in so doing, engage all our skills of assessment and appropriate treatment planning: "Are this child's mood swings a sign of ADHD? Bipolar disorder? Should a DSM diagnosis even be made? Or are these symptoms an offshoot of marital conflict and 'poor parenting'?" In any case, diagnoses are made with caution, and assessment is ongoing and comprehensive, involving biological evaluations (e.g., electroencephalograms [EEGs] and magnetic resonance imaging [MRI] to detect brain abnormalities), as well as social (detailed information gathering regarding family, school, and peer relationships) and psychological ones (use of paper-and-pencil instruments and projective tests).

While a biopsychosocial-systems approach enriches our assessment of childhood *and* adult disorders, we cannot overestimate the importance of assessing family issues, particularly when the IP is a child. A systems view in child assessment carries several common premises: (1) the view of child and family disorders as constellations of interrelated systems and subsystems; (2) the need to consider the entire family situation when assessing the impact of any single variable; (3) the idea that similar behavior may be the result of different sets of initiating factors; (4) a recognition that intervention is likely to lead to multiple outcomes, including readjustment of relationships within the family system; and (5) the notion that family systems and subsystems possess dynamic properties and are constantly changing over time (Estrada & Pinsof, 1995).

In addition, a large body of literature suggests that the development of child and adolescent problems does not occur in a vacuum but is strongly influenced by certain marital and family characteristics (Achenbach, 2008; Essex et al., 2006; Shapiro & Gottman, 2005). For example, factors such as marital discord, parental psychopathology, social-cognitive deficits in family members, socioeconomic disadvantage, disrupted parent–child relations, lack of social support, and social isolation are all variables that strongly influence the course of a child's individual disorder. This literature gives a strong argument for a systemic assessment.

Having considered these important family variables, the therapist working with Lisa S and her parents would have discovered some enlightening facts and expanded his hypotheses for later treatment. We learn, for example, that Lisa's father has a history of panic attacks and agoraphobia; that both parents are inadvertently maintaining Lisa's symptoms by avoiding using the words "death" and "dying," which often precipitate attacks; that Mr. S has unresolved grief issues from a death in his family; and that Mr. and Mrs. S strongly disagree about how to parent their daughter but avoid discussions or arguments about these differences. We also find that about the time Lisa's attacks began, her father had lost his job due to his agoraphobia and a role change had occurred in which Dad now stayed home to care for Lisa and Mom left the house to work.

Certainly, individual assessment and diagnosis of children is important. In Lisa's case, we can use DSM and find that our client meets the criteria for panic attacks. Based purely on individual symptoms reported by Lisa and her parents, we can then design a treatment program based on known effective interventions for anxiety disorders. However, by taking a systemic as well as an individual approach in our evaluation, we can supplement Lisa's treatment by addressing the family issues that clearly impact her symptoms. Thus, our assessment has expanded and enriched the treatment.

While family therapists are primarily concerned with systemic assessment and intervention, it will be increasingly important for all clinicians to have an up-to-date and working knowledge of individual diagnoses for children and adolescents. Common disorders in childhood include depressive disorders (disruptive mood dysregulation disorder; major depressive disorder), neurodevelopmental disorders (ADHD; autism spectrum disorder; learning disorder), anxiety disorders (separation anxiety disorder; generalized anxiety disorder), and disruptive disorders (oppositional defiant disorder; intermittent explosive disorder). Other problems that are frequently diagnosed in children and adolescents include posttraumatic stress disorder (PTSD), adjustment disorder, eating disorders, and substance abuse. Many children have problems that are comorbid. For example, a young child may be diagnosed with ADHD and later be diagnosed with a conduct disorder and substance abuse problem. We recommend you review the latest edition of DSM for diagnostic criteria.

Family therapists are well advised to become familiar with such instruments as the Child Behavior Checklist (see Conners, 1997), in which multiple sources provide information about a child's behavior, and the Conners' Rating Scales, a neuropsychosocial instrument for assessing hyperactive children (Conners, 1997). In addition, since child and adolescent assessment often focuses on development, many pencil-and-paper instruments and projective tests are used to assess intelligence and development, including the Wechsler Intelligence Scale for Children, third edition (WISC-III; Wechsler, 1991), the draw-a-person test, and the house–tree–person tests (Buck & Jolles, 1966). Many of these tests are used in the educational batteries of school districts. While most family therapists will not be administering these instruments as part of their therapy, it is important that they know what psychological evaluation instruments are available and make appropriate referrals for further evaluation, especially when they suspect a child has a developmental disorder or other learning problem.

Rather than trying to summarize the evidence-based literature for every diagnosis, we encourage you to read three articles from the *Journal of Marital and Family Therapy*: "Family-Based Interventions for Child and Adolescent Disorders" (Kaslow, Broth, Smith, & Collins, 2012), "Empirically Supported Family-Based Treatments for Conduct Disorder and Delinquency in Adolescents" (Hengeller & Sheidow, 2012), and "Family Therapy for Drug Abuse: Review and Updates 2003–2010" (Rowe, 2012). Each article respectfully acknowledges the important role of families and family therapy in treatment.

EMERGING RESOURCES FOR TREATING CHILDREN AND ADOLESCENTS

While parents' support and family-based treatments can serve as the foundation for child and adolescent interventions, other new resources also offer hope. New knowledge from neuroscience points to the critical importance of attachment for brain development (Jensen & Nutt, 2015; Siegel, 1999). In addition, brain research has led to a new understanding of many disorders. For example, some research suggests that at least some types of ADHD may be simply a case of delayed brain development (Duncan et al., 2007; Shaw et al., 2007). Other research on ADHD examined family-based interventions since ADHD frequently occurs in multiple family members. For example, researchers have noted that conflict and hostility in families make ADHD symptoms worse. To alleviate stress and conflict in families with ADHD, some families are being taught meditation and mindfulness skills (Baruchin, 2008).

As research in neuroscience continues, family therapists can be aware of resources and referrals for their clients. For example, children and teens with learning challenges might benefit from neuropsychological evaluations. Usually these evaluations assess intelligence, academic achievement, visual–motor skills, and emotional health. Skills such as the ability to pay attention, the ability to remember information, and the ability to decide and execute one's plan are all important domains of a neuropsychological evaluation. If parents or schools have concerns about a child's functioning in any of these areas, a neuropsychological evaluation can offer critical information to guide the treatment.

Psychotropic medications are growing in popularity as a treatment for children and adolescents. While medications sometimes offer relief to families that have tried other options, concerns still exist about using medications to treat child and adolescent problems. Questions about the influence of the medications on child development, especially brain development, remain. In fact, several mental health organizations have issued position papers suggesting that nondrug treatments be considered first. These treatments should include techniques that focus on the adults in a child's life, including parents and teachers (Carey, 2006).

Genetics and heritability are other areas of study that are influencing our understanding of children's and teens' problems. For example, mental health professionals know that disorders like autism and ADHD have high heritability, 76% for ADHD and 90% for autism. In addition, genetic researchers are interested in gene–environment interaction. What type of environment influences gene expression? Stated more simply, what type of environment "turns on" the gene, and when does the environmental influence start?

In recent years, geneticists have demonstrated that few gene mutations are causal in terms of mental illness (Mukherjee, 2016). While our bodies are always creating new mutations, few "candidate genes" turn out to be causal. Thus, therapists can focus on environmental risks for mental illnesses such as schizophrenia, bipolar disorder, and others. Implied in the focus on risk is the possibility of prevention. Pregnancy to young adulthood are key times to protect children from risk factors such as maternal depression by providing secure attachments and modulating the amount of stress that children face. For example, researchers have suggested that maternal smoking correlates with more serious mental health symptoms. Thus, the impact of the environment starts in the womb.

What can family therapists take from this exciting new research? While a child's genetics won't change, therapists can influence the child's environment. Armed with new knowledge about the importance of a healthy family environment, family therapists can feel confident when they help families reduce stress, reduce conflict, and increase close bonds.

THE FAMILY LIFE CYCLE REVISITED

One significant context that needs to be understood when assessing and treating problems in childhood and adolescence is the family's stage of development and how it interfaces with the problems that exist in a family. Building on early studies of the family (Duvall, 1955) and applying this information to the needs of the family therapist, Carter and McGoldrick (1989) categorized the family life cycle into six stages with a key emotional process and several developmental tasks at each stage (see Table 7.1).

The family life-cycle concept has been criticized for its exclusiveness: In today's world, a minority of families transition through these stages in a prescribed sequence. For example, many children in their 20s remain at home with their parents, for a variety of reasons. Rather than emphasizing a sequential order of stages, we are interested in how families cope with transitions from one stage to another, particularly their efforts to achieve second-order change. Second-order change necessitates a redefining of the family system in behavioral, cognitive, emotional, and relational domains. Carter and McGoldrick's (1989) version of the family life cycle gives special attention to these transitions between stages.

Combrinck-Grahams's (1985) alternative to stage models of development describes a process of family movement through time. She states that families naturally oscillate through times of greater closeness (centripetal periods), such as the birth of a new baby, and times of greater distance (centrifugal periods), such as a child's transition into adolescence. Centripetal periods are characterized by greater family cohesion and greater focus on internal family life. Centrifugal periods display an opening of external family boundaries, allowing individual family members to pursue goals and interactions with the extrafamilial environment.

These models provide a reminder to therapists that families often present to therapy when they are in the midst of a developmental

TABLE 7.1. The Stages of the Family Life Cycle

Family life-cycle stage	Emotional process of transition: Key principles	Second-order changes in family status required to proceed developmentally
1. Leaving home: single, young adults	Accepting emotional and financial responsibility for self	a. Differentiation of self in relation to family of origin b. Development of intimate peer relationships c. Establishment of self; work and financial independence
2. The joining of families through marriage: the new couple	Commitment to new system	a. Formulation of marital system b. Realignment of relationships with extended families and friends to include spouse
3. Families with young children	Accepting new members into the system	a. Adjusting marital system to make space for child(ren) b. Joining in childrearing, financial, and household tasks c. Realignment of relationships with extended family to include parenting and grandparenting roles
4. Families with adolescents	Increasing flexibility of family boundaries to include children's independence and grandparents' frailties	a. Shifting of parent–child relationships to permit adolescent to move in and out of system b. Refocus on midlife marital and career issues c. Beginning shift toward joint caring for older generation
5. Launching children and moving on	Accepting a multitude of exits from and entries into the family system	a. Renegotiation of marital system as a dyad b. Development of adult-to-adult relationships between grown children and their parents c. Realignment of relationships to include in-laws and grandchildren d. Dealing with disabilities and death of parents (grandparents)

(continued)

TABLE 7.1. *(continued)*

Family life-cycle stage	Emotional process of transition: Key principles	Second-order changes in family status required to proceed developmentally
6. Families in later life	Accepting the shifting of generational roles	a. Maintaining own and/or couple functioning and interests in face of psychological decline; exploration of new familial and social role options b. Support for a more central role of middle generation c. Making room in the system for the wisdom and experience of older adults, supporting the older generation without overfunctioning for them d. Dealing with loss of spouse, siblings, and other peers and preparation for own death; life review and integration

Note. From Carter and McGoldrick (1989). Copyright 1989. Reprinted by permission of Pearson Education, Inc., New York, New York.

transition. The therapist hypothesizes that the presenting problem may have a lot to do with the family being stuck in its progress toward achieving a particular developmental stage or coping with movement in a particular direction (centripetal or centrifugal). For example, a 14-year-old daughter of very controlling parents may start acting out by breaking curfew and hanging out at school with kids the parents deem unacceptable. This behavior signals a difficulty in the family system's transition to the "family with adolescents" stage (centrifugal motion), where there is a need to increase the permeability of the family boundaries to include the teenager's growing independence.

The first task at each transitional stage is for the therapist to normalize what is going on in the family, framing many of the presenting problems as common and understandable. A therapist can use the life-cycle information to connect more fully with the family, as it helps him or her to understand their dilemmas more completely. In normalizing, a therapist must be careful not to trivialize the pain, fears, and emotional power of these developmental shifts. When done well, normalizing can be offered as a first "gift" to the family from the therapist, toning down the emotional turmoil within the family. The therapist's expertise in understanding what the family is about helps establish a solid working alliance. Thus, life-cycle information boosts the therapist's authority, which is especially helpful if he or she is significantly younger than the other adults in the therapy room.

Knowing the key emotional issues at each developmental stage provides guidance to the therapist. What must the family members manage effectively in each stage? Therapists can connect to family members' deeper emotional issues by using information about the family life cycle. For example, the key emotional transition for two individuals to make in forming a committed relationship or marriage is "commitment to a new system." Without a new system that cultivates a place for each partner to be included and respected, a kind of competition takes place wherein each person attempts to win the battle for dominion over a particular area of life, be it housecleaning, finances, or friendships. A therapist, aware of the necessary emotional transition, can direct the couple to find ways in which each person can be comfortable with a decision. The therapist facilitates the couple's transition from a "me" to a "we." Of course, there is no right way to transition from one stage to the next. Each family will be guided by its own family histories and the belief systems of its race, culture, and ethnicity.

Next, we explore some of the key themes in four stages of family development: (1) families with young children; (2) families with school-age children; (3) families with adolescents; and (4) launching children. Applying this material in your therapy sessions means that you ask yourself a few key questions each time you assess a new family. Those questions include:

- What are common or expected developmental tasks for this family given their family life-cycle stage?
- How might the family's presenting problems influence their abilities to successfully navigate the developmental tasks?
- How might the developmental tasks be influencing the family's presenting problems?

You might also want to consider the overlap between individual development, family development, and the presenting problems. Thus, you might ask yourself the following questions:

- What are common or expected developmental tasks for the *individuals* in this family?
- How might the individual needs and the family's developmental needs be influencing the family's presenting problems?

For example, a therapist saw a family consisting of a 19-year-old woman and her parents. During high school, the 19-year-old had been diagnosed with an aggressive form of cancer. For several years, she endured painful, exhausting treatments and at times the family wondered whether she would survive. She had to quit school and the basketball team. Her mother became her primary support and they traveled to a city several hours away for treatments. Her father worked harder to help cover her skyrocketing healthcare costs.

When the mother and daughter came in for therapy because they were having conflict over the daughter's wish to start college in a city 2 hours away, the daughter had been in remission for over a year. While the treatment had been successful, the illness had wreaked havoc on the family. The couple had ignored their marriage for several years while they focused on helping their daughter. Now, 3 years later, they found they had little in common. In contrast, the mother's life had evolved around her daughter's health needs and she had gradually given up her individual life and her relationship with her husband. As the daughter's health improved, she began to seek more autonomy, while her mother remained resistant to letting go—partially because she feared that if she wasn't watching carefully, the cancer might reappear and partially because she wasn't sure what to do with her own life now that her daughter no longer needed her constantly.

At the launching stage of the family life cycle, this family's normative transition had gone awry because of the demands of the cancer and its painful treatments. Thus, considering the family life cycle and the tasks of both individual development and family development helped the therapist create a nonpathologizing plan to help the family get back on track.

Families with Young Children

Frank and Laura were on the verge of divorce when they agreed, as a last resort, to give therapy a try. When they appeared in therapy with their 19-month-old daughter in tow, it soon became apparent to the therapist that the couple's smooth sailing days had ended when they struck the rocky shores of new parenthood. Since the birth of their baby and Laura's 6-week maternity leave, the couple had continued their prebaby work schedule. The baby was put into quality home childcare, but mom and dad felt guilty about this and spent all of their evening hours and weekend time devoted to their little girl. Before long, chronic irritations deteriorated into outright fighting. Frank and Laura had a hard time remembering why they married in the first place. Clearly, without finding a way to protect their marital relationship, divorce looked imminent.

This couple's story is a reminder that couple issues are paramount in this stage of the family life cycle. New parents must take time and energy to develop an emotional attachment to the baby, as well as meet his or her physical needs. A family's response to the new baby can range from a "hardly noticing" to a "drop everything" stance. In the former, or closed boundary, stance, the parent or couple won't be able to meet the needs of a dependent child since a baby requires significant family resources. Neglect of one form or another can result. On the "drop everything" end of the spectrum, a family opens its arms wide to the child at the expense of all other relationships, including the couple's own. Though well suited for the very early aspects of this stage, a child-centered family often struggles with the growing independence needs of its members at later stages of the family life cycle. Problems of marital distress or individual functioning (depression) could result.

Fights over childrearing, household tasks, and financial responsibilities are common at this stage. Particularly when couples haven't formed a new system in the previous stage of the family life cycle (the joining of families), the practical urgency and plentitude of stressors and decisions here can seem overwhelming. Many studies have shown that after the birth of a child, marital conflict increases and marital quality decreases (Belsky & Kelly, 1994; Shapiro, Gottman, & Carrere, 2000).

Gender issues often come to the forefront at this stage. Sue and Joe, who lived together for 5 years, had been separated for 2 weeks when they sought therapy. Their 4-year-old son and 2-year-old daughter were the motivation behind this move, yet as we explored what brought them in, the couple's children seemed to make up the major battleground. Both Sue and Joe needed to work in order to make their rent payments, but Sue resented this, saying that Joe didn't make as much money as he could in his sales work. Sue, whose mother stayed home until Sue was in sixth grade, longed to be able to do the same. Joe, raised by his mom in a single-parent household, believed Sue needed to work in order to provide their children with the house and yard he never had. Clashes about role expectations, especially gender role expectations, come to a powerful crescendo at this stage. An understanding of these practical, emotional, and interpersonal issues that appear in families with very young children can guide therapeutic interventions and help new parents make a successful transition from one life-cycle stage to the next.

While this early phase of family life brings more parents than children to therapy, therapists will occasionally meet with families whose IP is an infant or toddler. Three-year-old Jason came to therapy for repeated aggressive behavior against his 1-year-old sibling, for destroying toys and household belongings, and for trying to climb out of a moving car. His single mother presented Jason to the therapist with a simple plea: "I don't know why he does it! But you've got to make it stop!" Clearly, how the therapist explores Jason's problems and ultimately how he or she treats them are limited by Jason's age.

Family therapists who work with very young children can base their initial assessment and treatment on the child's developmental stage. The literature on children's emotional, cognitive, and social development from infancy to adulthood is voluminous, and we would do a disservice to its scholars to encapsulate developmental theory here. While we encourage beginning therapists to learn about or refresh themselves on the needs and expectations of each stage of childhood and adolescence, our focus is on brief reminders about developmental issues and practical steps to take when a young child toddles into your office.

Armed with the knowledge that infants and toddlers require secure attachments in order to build a trustful orientation toward life, we can assess very young children in terms of their early attachments and the sense of autonomy they show, among other variables. Our knowledge about cognitive development also shapes our expectations: for example, realizing that "time out" can be understood by a toddler, while "telling the truth" is much less clear to someone who is 3-years-old. In Jason's case, for example, we learned that frequent separations from his mother and maltreatment by intermittent caretakers marked this youngster's first years of life. Furthermore, his mother's lack of information about the cognitive capabilities of her toddler likely made the situation at home more difficult. Lengthy explanations of why siblings should not be hit or thrown had little impact on Jason's aggressive behavior. Immediately, we have clues to the route family therapy can take—reestablishing a secure attachment between Jason and his mother, and helping this single parent learn appropriate methods of dealing with her child's behavior.

Beginning therapists can also benefit from a number of practical guidelines for working with very young children. These involve space, safety, shared responsibility, and expectations.

Space

Most therapy offices don't fit the needs of both adults and children. Traditional play therapy rooms may be too cramped or full of potential hazards (paint, clay) for an adult to relax. In contrast, adult-oriented rooms with immobile furnishings may be boring and/or increase anxiety in children. Ideally, therapy rooms should accommodate full family interactions as well as provide separate spaces for play and for separating out family subsystems, if needed. A larger room, sparsely furnished with movable chairs and pillows, could accommodate all. It's also helpful to have play areas with toys that encourage interaction between children and adults (hand puppets, crayons and paper, simple games). All of these assist therapy.

Safety

Safety needs to be established during the therapy session, and everybody can help make this possible. Therapists need to check the therapy room and remove potentially dangerous items before the session starts. Parents often believe the therapist will take responsibility for setting limits and discipline during the session. It's helpful to assign the major responsibilities to the parents instead, using rules they have at home. This offers a way to strengthen the parental position in the family hierarchy and gives the therapist an opportunity to see how the family functions.

Shared Responsibility

Although setting a collaborative tone with most families is helpful, allowing for a flexible sharing of the work with young children is essential. Therapists need to be able to sit on the floor and play with the children when this activity is useful. Parents can take their child for a walk as a break when necessary. Often cotherapy teams can assist greatly in managing the subsystems of a particular family. One therapist can take a child into another room, while the other therapist works with the parent. Also, selecting session times that don't interfere with naps and mealtimes is helpful. Asking parents to bring a favorite toy might be useful too. Finally, creatively dividing up the family system for different sessions over time—one oriented for a parent–child focus, one for parents only—can assist in better management of therapeutic goals.

Expectations

For children in particular, nothing is sacred about weekly, 50-minute therapy sessions. Shorter or longer sessions or meetings divided into smaller segments can help the therapist's work with a family. Toddlers, in particular, will rarely be able to sit for more than a few minutes of talk, necessitating the need for play therapy involving games, artwork, or storytelling. Action in the therapy session and participation between family members are also helpful for older children and adults.

In addition, family therapy often makes sense as "brief therapy." After a longer intake/assessment session, for example, a therapist might offer several interventions to be tried out over several weeks and request that the family report the results at a later session. Home visits too can often result in very helpful information on ways of adapting the environment to alleviate problems with a young child. In short, flexibility and teamwork are crucial to working with families with very young children.

Families with School-Age Children

Family life-cycle concerns at this stage are similar to the previous ones in that they reflect a need to adapt to change. What often differs at this stage is the expansion of the family's contact with larger social systems. If children have been in half-day preschool, the transition now is to full-day school. If children have been in full-day childcare, they now have full-day school and participation in sports activities after school and on weekends. Furthermore, evaluation of the child now involves comparisons with peers, and the ability or inability of a child to fit in becomes more prominent. The school system connects intimately with the life of the family. Problems or successes at school can impact the family system.

During this and the previous stage, relationship issues with extended family are also renegotiated. What will be the role of the grandparents, aunts, uncles, and cousins? Previous issues within the family that haven't been resolved are revived during this time. For example, when molestation or other kinds of abuse have occurred in the family, fears and boundary concerns come to the fore. For parents, the issue in therapy may relate to contacts their children will have with relatives. Glenda presented to her therapist the dilemma of what to do when her mother invited her 8-year-old daughter to spend the night for a weekend. Her stepfather had molested Glenda yet her mother was still married to him. She had an ongoing relationship with her family, but always watched her daughter when Grandfather was around. Glenda had worked on her past in group therapy but hadn't brought up her concerns to her family directly. Family therapists will frequently be called upon to help clients navigate transgenerational difficulties at this stage.

Connection with the School System

For the children in this stage, the focus is around starting school, moving out into the world, and building self-esteem by managing their environment more intentionally. Feelings of being a failure or success permeate activities such as tying shoelaces and learning to read. Development of initiative versus guilt and industry versus inferiority provide the basis of many daily concerns for the child. Peer relationships become more and more central, and comparisons to others— "Tommy's the best kickball player at school" or "June can read two books a day"—seem to pervade many social interactions. The task for parents, teachers, and therapist is to find places where a child can experience competency and some level of proficiency. If this is not the case at school, parents can look to sports, art, music, and relationships outside school for experiences that will help a child develop a healthy self-concept.

It's not surprising to find therapy clinics brimming with 6-, 7-, and 8-year-old children whose first months at school have been met with frustration or failure. This is the time when problems with attention, hyperactivity, anxiety, oppositional behavior, and learning become evident to those outside the family. Frequently, young children make their way into therapy on the recommendations of teachers, school administrators, and counselors. In some cases, the mere suggestion by school authorities is all the impetus distraught parents need to finally seek help.

This is an important point for beginning therapists to remember. By the time parents bring their youngsters to therapy, they are well acquainted with their child's behavioral problems and have likely tried "every trick in the book" to solve them. It's not unusual for us to see parents who report being fed up, exhausted, angry, lost, guilty, and in myriad other states when they arrive in our offices. Frequently, these beleaguered parents want you—the therapist—to fix the problem. Returning to our guiding principle, however, we're reminded that without the parent as an active participant, our chances of success are minimal. Our first task, then, is to support and join with the parents, to empathize with their struggle, and to enlist their expertise as we present the real need for a team approach. Whether the treatment plan focuses on parent-management training (as is typical with problems involving very young children) or is combined with recreating parent–child bonds and nurturing the warm relationships that often get lost in stressful circumstances, our ability to engage and work with parents is at the heart of therapy with these children.

Often, parents do not understand their child's problem or how they might help. Thus, psychoeducation can be an important part of your work. In the era of the Internet and self-help, parents have often begun the process of self-education before they ever start therapy. If not, you can provide parents with educational resources. In addition, parents sometimes do not know how to advocate for their child or obtain the resources their child needs. Again, your role might be to help the parent help the child, for instance, by helping the parent work more effectively with the child's school. Finally, parents may be dropping a child or teen off for therapy because their own lives are overwhelming—emotionally, financially, or structurally. Try not to fall into the trap of feeling critical of the parents and internally aligning yourself with the child, thus subtly believing that you are the child's secret protector. Instead, search for an empathic understanding of the parent's life. What brought the mother to this place? In what ways does it make perfect sense that this dad does not want to be involved in his child's struggles at school? If you can genuinely develop empathy and understanding of the parents' struggles, you can begin to help them help their child.

At the same time, our sense is that therapy will progress further, and parents will commit more to the process, if we can creatively engage children at these ages—they are therapeutic allies, information resources, and affective conduits for the family. Probably the easiest way to involve children at this age is through drawing and role playing. Therapists who aren't able to create a child-centered therapy room can often hide a large art pad and markers for artistic purposes under the couch. A basket full of puppets, dolls, and dress-up items can facilitate interaction at multiple levels within the family.

As with younger children, action needs to replace talk during some of the therapeutic encounters. Sessions can be broken up into sections where the child is "excused" from the therapy (although still in the room) while the therapist talks with parents directly. Therapists must be sure to edit any information that would be inappropriate for the child to overhear. The child can then be reengaged toward the end of the session for a summary of what the family might do during the week to continue improvement. After a session, stickers or other small items to reward the child's participation might encourage involvement in the future.

Besides working with the family itself, therapists must be mindful of other professionals that need to be involved for therapy to proceed effectively. For example, since at this stage therapy is often initiated due to school concerns, contact with a teacher or other school personnel can significantly enhance work in the family therapy session. Minuchin, Montalvo, Guerney, Rosman, and Schumer (1967) recognize that demands from multiple systems (family, child, and school) often create problems, rather than the child being the problem.

Active information gathering from the school, childcare, or sports or religious organizations with which the family is involved can be useful in shaping appropriate interventions. Whether the presenting problem occurs only in one setting or across multiple settings helps the therapist to orient his or her approach with the family. The following case demonstrates how interventions involving outside settings are both important and beneficial.

Brittany was a 12-year-old girl enrolled in the seventh grade. She was brought to therapy by her parents because she was having problems in school. She had done well in elementary school, achieving mostly A's and B's. After entering junior high school she hadn't performed well academically, getting C's and D's at the end of the first semester. She complained that she didn't like most of her teachers. She would do most of her homework but often "forgot" to turn it in. The parents reported no problems at home. She did most of her chores when she was asked and enjoyed playing softball and playing piano.

Brittany was a soft-spoken, bright, and articulate girl who felt "badly" about her school performance. She blamed most of the problem on a couple of her teachers who, she said, "don't like me and are boring." She often felt intimidated by the teachers and the school environment. She found going to different classes and having lots of teachers to be disruptive and chaotic. She was also struggling with making new friends and was feeling that she didn't fit in. Her response to feeling overwhelmed by the new school environment was to withdraw. She became afraid of failing, so decided not to turn in her homework. The more she got behind in her classes, the more her feelings of failure and futility increased.

The parents responded that they were "concerned, frustrated, and helpless" about Brittany's school problems. The father was often out of town because of his work and he didn't have enough contact with Brittany to "truly understand the problems." The mother was frustrated in her attempts to help Brittany. She had tried to help the girl with her homework, but they would end up quarreling. She felt that Brittany wasn't interested in talking about school and would either withdraw or become defensive. Brittany's mother had contacted the school counselor but felt that the counselor was of little help. The counselor suggested that Brittany might need a tutor and that her test scores indicated that Brittany was "full of potential and easily capable of doing the work."

The therapist began working with the family, although the father's attendance was sporadic due to his work commitments. Brittany and her mother had a fairly close relationship. They spent a significant amount of time together and genuinely enjoyed each other's company. They shared interests in music and sports, and played tennis together. Their primary difficulty revolved around Brittany's school problems and an inability to communicate without arguing about school.

Brittany was having considerable difficulty in making the adjustment from the stable elementary school environment to the fluctuating schedule at the junior high school. She felt insecure and overwhelmed by the constant changes in her classes, the lack of individual attention, and the sheer number of students. The therapist contacted the school counselor in an effort to increase the school's interest in Brittany, and to obtain more structure and stability for her. The counselor said the school would cooperate in providing weekly progress reports on Brittany's work. The counselor also agreed to provide a student mentor for Brittany. The mentor would be an eighth-grader who could help tutor Brittany and help familiarize her with the school. The mother was encouraged to contact several of Brittany's teachers and coordinate their efforts in determining whether Brittany turned in her homework.

Brittany responded very positively to the structure and interest she was given. Her adjustment to the new school was slower than that of most students and she needed some special attention. The therapist was able to intervene to work as a liaison between the school and the family and to support positive solutions to Brittany's adjustment.

Families with Adolescents

The primary emotional task for families at this stage is increasing the family's boundary permeability, or transition to centrifugal motion, to allow for children's growing independence. A family's ability to successfully make this transition is partly influenced by their level of flexibility over time—how have they been changing and preparing for this transition? Although the focus commonly revolves around adolescent independence, the ability of parents and children to maintain a close connection is equally important as children navigate new relationships, responsibilities, and choices.

Second only to the life-cycle period with young children, this stage is associated with a high number of divorces. One reason is the convergence of many powerful and sometimes competing needs of family members. First, the adolescent must be permitted to move in and out of the family system more fluidly. Friendships and relationships outside the family take on growing significance and the family sometimes becomes secondary in the young person's life. When family values conflict with the teenager's behavioral choices, the family might over- or underrespond. In either case, family therapy can enhance positive adaptation to this stage.

Issues besides adolescence are present at this stage—midlife concerns for parents often come to the fore. Regrets, missed opportunities, possibilities for beginning new dreams, reassessing the quality of the marital relationship, all these and more add to the challenging mix. Furthermore, stresses from taking care of older parents emerge. Such caretaking consumes time and financial resources. Adults in these families often term themselves "caught in the middle" between the financial and emotional needs of their older and younger members. The following case illustrates the interplay between difficulties around adolescence and midlife issues:

The C family was having difficulty with their youngest child, 15-year-old Derrick, who hadn't been coming home at night, was doing poorly at school, and had been caught with marijuana on several occasions. Derrick was a star football player on his high school team. He was a bright, likable, and outgoing young man who appeared self-assured. He came from a family of four children, in which the other three were out of the home—two in college and one in the navy. This was a middle-class, African American family that had come to a point in its development in which everyone seemed to be going off in separate directions.

Derrick's mother was a 54-year-old woman who had worked hard most of her life at her civil service job while raising her four children. She was very involved in her church, and after her parents died she had become the matriarch of her family. She had a younger sister who was a single mother and was trying to raise three children. Mrs. C spent a great deal of her time helping her sister. She also helped out with her husband's printing business. Mr. C was a 57-year-old man who had retired from the navy about 12 years ago. He had worked hard to develop his own business, which had lots of financial problems. Mr. C was rarely at home and spent his time at work or with his friends.

Mr. and Mrs. C were concerned about Derrick's behavior, but both acknowledged that they were tired of raising children. They had worked hard and fulfilled their responsibilities. They were helping all of their children financially and felt burdened by this. They expressed a desire to slow things down and spend some time together, and they had been talking about wanting a less hectic lifestyle. Mr. C wanted to sell his business and move to Arizona. Derrick wasn't sure where he fit into the picture; he felt his parents really didn't care what he did, as long as he stayed out of trouble. He said that he got very little attention from them and "that's okay, they don't really know what I'm doing." Mrs. C expressed a lot of concern and frustration with the situation but didn't know what to do. She said she just didn't have the energy to deal with Derrick.

Derrick's difficulties seemed symptomatic of his confusion over recent changes and his perceived lack of security in the family. There was a considerable difference in needs and priorities between Derrick and his parents. They readily admitted that they couldn't keep up with him. Derrick's difficulties in school, marijuana use, and staying out at night could be seen as a cry for attention from his parents and a request for help. Therapy initially needed to validate each family member's position and use their concern for each other as an effective motivation to effect some change. Normalizing their situation given their different needs and developmental stages was also important.

Transformations

Precisely when adolescence begins and ends is open to debate. But one of the most clearly pronounced signs of its beginning is the development of the physical capacity to procreate. Secondary sex characteristics overtly signal this transition, and social definitions become more sexually oriented. Children can grasp ideas and concepts beyond their own concrete experience, that is, they are able to think more abstractly, although this capacity is measured in different ways across cultures. On the social–emotional front, teenagers struggle with self-definition. They "try on" roles, like trying on jeans at a department store, in order to find the right fit. Without this process, individuals become confused about who they are in life. Parental overreaction to this natural developmental stage can stigmatize a child as "a problem" and lead the adolescent to retreat from family connections. Underreaction too can hinder this stage, leaving nonfamily agencies such as the school or police to provide the only limit setting for the adolescent.

Therapists attempt to balance the family need for maintaining structure with the transformational needs of launching an adolescent member. This balance is aided, in part, when the therapist manages the IP label appropriately, creates a metaphor or ritual to capture the family's evolution, and is flexible in responding to the idiosyncrasies of the family.

For example, a 17-year-old adolescent and his family came to therapy with the presenting problem of his drug use. The boy had been experimenting with various drugs and his schoolwork had declined. The family focused on the son's problems so intently that everything seemed to revolve around him—who or who did not do the chores, fights between siblings, and conflict between the parents. The therapist created a family "sculpt" exercise in order to show the family its developmental dilemma. She first asked the client to sit in a chair in the middle of the therapy room and asked each family member to stand in emotional proximity to him. A closely connected "huddle" resulted. She then removed the son from the middle and stated that she was going to work with him on his issues, and asked the rest of the family to stand where they would like to be in the family. Confusion resulted. The family members looked lost, unable to glimpse a vision of life without the IP's presence. Debriefing following the session evoked important and unacknowledged emotions from various family members about the "positive" function the client served for the family. The family had become developmentally stuck and unable to move forward because of their fears of separateness and individuality.

Most commonly, teenagers are brought to therapy to be "fixed" by the therapist. Although the rest of the family members acknowledge, at some level, that they impact the adolescent, often the focus is "teen versus the family system." Family therapists do well to bring up the complexities of this developmental stage with the family. Psychoeducation helps the family broaden its frame of reference and normalizes the anxiety for everyone. For example, information about teen brain development may be instructive. In their informative book *The Teenage Brain: A Neuroscientist's Survival Guide to Raising Adolescents and Young Adults,* Jensen and Nutt (2015) help readers understand adolescent brain development and its impact on learning and memory, stress, addiction, as well as other areas. Information on brain development may lessen criticism, increase empathy in families, and lead to productive discussions about ways to help teens.

"How are we going to help this child become an adult?" is a useful question to be presented to the entire family. Probing how the parents went through this stage can elicit normalizing information not discussed by the family previously. Having parents describe what their own parents did well or poorly during this stage provokes some systemic reflection.

The therapist should keep in mind, however, that the family isn't the only important concern during this stage. If an adolescent has been displaying addictive patterns, relationships outside of the family might be affecting the teen, and may involve drug use or unsafe sexual activity. When the therapist thinks about multiple systems rather than family systems alone, other factors are seen as important to therapeutic work. Referral to a chemical dependency program or inviting friends into therapy might be helpful in managing these important influences. Creatively engaging people from within and without the family to understand the presenting problem assists in solid clinical treatment.

Technology

Over the past decade, technology has taken center stage in the lives of families, particularly families with adolescents. A staple for the contemporary teenager is her cell phone, which provides potentially limitless contact with friends, instant access to information, and infinite games for entertainment. For parents of adolescents, cell phones are a source of both helpful connection and worrisome interference. We commonly hear parents complain about their inability to have meaningful conversation with their adolescent because she's solely focused on her phone. They also worry about the ability of others to have unfettered access to their children, despite their best efforts to monitor cell phone use.

Video games, too, can play a central role in the lives of preteens and teens, especially boys. Nathan, age 13, plays several hours of video games every day. When his parents encourage other social activities, he says that he is playing with his friends online. He and his parents have considerable conflict over the amount he plays and how this behavior impacts his school work and sleep. Many families identify with this problem, struggle with how and when to set limits, and worry about how technology impacts their family. We encourage you to open discussions with your adolescent clients and their family members about the role of technology in their lives and define reasonable expectations that can respect parents' need for safety and teens' needs for social connection and entertainment.

Treatment of Adolescents

Most civilizations have heralded the passage from childhood to adulthood. Western culture, however, is generally bereft of meaningful ways to mark this transition. Perhaps the most significant ritual for teens in the United States is acquiring a driver's license. Therapists have found that bringing a ritual into the therapeutic process can assist in creating second-order change (Imber-Black, 1988). Rituals can awaken family members to respond in new ways. One therapist assigned a family the task of creating a "birthday ritual" for each quarter-, half-, and full-year birthday beginning at age 15 and ending at age 18. Using these "birthdays" as points for change, the family negotiated one new privilege for their daughter and one new responsibility. The parents and teenager talked about ways in which they needed to both offer more adulthood status and she needed to show more adulthood behavior. Issues such as curfew, driving, chores, screen time, and allowance were "ritually" discussed on these dates until a mutual agreement was found. A celebration of adulthood was prescribed for her 18th birthday.

As so often happens, therapists and clients are challenged by the same things during therapy. Families with adolescents need to be flexible, and so does the therapist. Therapists encounter teenagers who may angrily sulk during most sessions and then suddenly rage at everyone. Parents of teenagers may present as flexible, yet undermine any new suggestions developed during therapy.

Therapists need to keep in mind their "window of opportunity" to influence a family positively. Settling into a long-term therapy posture probably won't fit the needs of the family. Even a weekly therapy schedule might need to be reevaluated. Working with various subsystems of the family, as with very young children, can be quite valuable.

Encouraging adolescents to do reverse role plays (in which the teen plays the parent) or to write poems and letters to express their feelings to the family might enhance therapy too. Maintaining a balance between structural expectations (regarding physical safety or time together) and flexibility around the presenting concerns helps develop a strong therapeutic alliance and will model to the family what they need to be doing in their home as well.

Launching Children and Parents in Transition

Families are challenged to accept multiple comings and goings in the family system's membership. In-laws, grandchildren, returning divorced children, aging parents, and death must be accommodated during this life stage. Couples often shift into a dyadic relationship for the first time in life, and are challenged to create a non-child-oriented relationship. Adolescents grow into adults who have their own children, and relationships with them shift from parent–child to adult–adult connections. Illness, retirement, or disability challenge the family's resources at many turns. Additions and losses pervade the emotional terrain. In Chapter 8, we discuss in more detail the issues relevant to therapy with clients in later life.

Family therapists can act as consultants during these transitions. Clients often request a few brief sessions to "sort out what to do next": "Shall I kick my 27-year-old cocaine-addicted son out of my home?" "Shall we bring Grandma in to live with us after her stroke?" "I thought I was going to have time to travel with my husband, but now we're helping to raise my grandchildren while my daughter works—I'm not sure I want this, but I feel guilty saying that."

We are in changing societal times with few clear directives on how to handle these complex and emotionally charged issues. Each family needs to redefine itself in response to its unique set of beliefs, structural framework, and emotional capacity.

Social–emotional needs of those being launched from a family include the development of intimate relationships and some sort of generativity in the world. Friends and lovers must be found and relationships established. Often individuals seek therapy when limited in this important developmental domain. Being able to use one's gifts, abilities, and interests for the benefit of self and others takes on a prominent focus. Having at least some degree of financial independence from one's family seems to be a part of the process. If these needs aren't met, people experience isolation and stagnation. Often it is in midlife that these concerns are recycled and reviewed once again, although losing one's job or suffering a business failure elicits reassessment too.

Later in life, social–emotional needs involve reviewing one's life choices and evaluating whether one feels integrated regarding what has been accomplished. Peer relationships continue to be a vital connection to good health, although family contacts are important in emergencies. Solid friendships in later years promote well-being at many levels. Gender concerns reemerge as one reviews personal and professional connections. Some men in our culture feel too separated from family connections, while women ponder if they could have been something more than what they were. In either case, a life review in connection with continuing family and friendship ties enhances relationships between all members.

Helping clients access resources is an important skill a therapist can apply when working with families in the launching stage. Although useful throughout the lifespan, knowledge of community and extended family resources can be critical during this period. The therapist can encourage clients to use some of their own resources and use community resources in achieving positive adjustment for the entire family. Financial, emotional, and practical information can be provided that helps ease some of the strains of this stage. This case illustrates these points.

John, age 20, began to have difficulties while away at college. A history major, he had dreams of becoming a lawyer after he finished college. He began drinking heavily during his junior year, and his friends reported to his family that he was acting a bit odd at times. On one occasion, he jumped down a long flight of stairs screaming that the "monkeys are trying to bite me." Hospitalization for a broken ankle and for his first schizophrenic episode followed. John took a leave of absence from college, never to return. When he went home, however, his family found it difficult to cope with him.

In a case like this, a family therapist may be included in the decision-making process. The therapist will need to assess the resources of the family as well as the values they hold regarding care for their ill relatives, and may encourage them to broaden their support to include extended family and friends. Also, he or she may be able to access important community resources for the family and assist them in learning to network. Medical specialists, funding sources, self-help and support groups, board-and-care homes, transitional housing options, respite care, and practical nursing can be invaluable resources for the family.

VARIATIONS IN FAMILY DEVELOPMENT

Of course, the stages of the family life cycle described above address just part of a family's development over time. In addition to the transitions associated with family members joining or leaving a system, families encounter many other unpredictable transitions over time, such as job loss, geographical relocation and migration, serious illness, divorce, and many other challenges that have a major impact on family life. The following sections describe family adjustment to divorce and explore two variations in family structure: single-parent families and stepfamilies.

Divorce

Family adjustment to divorce comprises additional stages in the family life cycle—stages that are almost normative in a society where divorce is so common. Stress occurs at predictable times for divorcing families, and the response to the stress influences how members adjust to shifting family compositions. Family therapists need to keep in mind that emotional cutoffs often hinder adjustment and that, even though there are exceptions, having an ongoing relationship between parents and children is usually the best way to proceed.

The family therapy literature provides numerous examples of how divorcing families go through predictable stages (Ahrons & Rodgers, 1987; Everett & Volgy, 1991; Kaslow, 2000). Most of the stage models share a general framework, which includes (1) predivorce issues, such as feelings of ambivalence; (2) the decision to divorce; and (3) postdivorce adjustment, restructuring, and, in many cases, remarriage (Livingston & Bowen, 2006). For example, Ahrons and Rodgers (1987) found that divorcing families go through the following stages, although not necessarily in sequential order:

1. Decision to divorce, usually by one member before the other
2. Family system is told about the impending divorce
3. Actual physical separation
4. System reorganization
5. System stabilization into a new form

Most researchers indicate that it takes 2–3 years to go through these phases. Successful postdivorce families may often look like the following:

Custodial parent

- Maintains parental contact with ex-spouse.
- Supports contact of children with ex-spouse and his or her family.
- Rebuilds own social network.

Noncustodial parent

- Maintains parental contact and supports custodial parent's relationship with children.
- Establishes effective parenting relationship with children.
- Rebuilds own social network.

However, research also indicates that only about half of divorcing families are able to develop cooperative coparenting arrangements. The other half of divorced parents continue to fight with their former spouse over the children or neglect this continuing aspect of their relationship. Family therapists often see the emotional fallout on the children from these negative experiences.

Divorce almost always involves some level of conflict. The research affirms again and again that children exposed to continuing parental conflict are negatively affected. Individuals and families will not be able to move beyond their presenting problems unless they can manage conflict constructively. Therapists must advise and set limits on the amount of conflict permitted within the family (Margulies, 2007).

In addition, therapists must determine how able a family is to operate in a coparenting relationship. When parents are unable to cooperate for the sake of their children, therapists must consider how to define relationships between parents and children separately. Complete cutoff with a parent might occur, but should not be an acceptable solution for the family. Effective coparenting by coparents who can cooperate and continued contact with noncustodial parents, typically fathers, will play a significant role in helping children adjust to divorce (Ahrons, 2007).

Therapists should guard against colluding with particular family members because doing so can close off relationships that might be therapeutic. For example, a mother might say that her ex-husband has "no interest" in their difficult teenage daughter. If you contact the father, however, you may find he does have an interest and can assist the family and support his ex-wife in parenting the teen. Each case regarding connections with noncustodial parents needs to be considered carefully.

Often extended family—aunts, uncles, grandparents, and cousins—had significant relationships severed as a result of divorce. These relatives can often function as family resources during difficult transitional stages. Therapists should ask about these people and encourage contact when appropriate.

When working with families experiencing divorce, it's important to remind family members that it takes time and patience to negotiate these stages successfully. Some don't manage well because of the continuing battles between family members. Noticing and encouraging successful developmental steps and normalizing struggles will help families use their resources to the fullest.

Mediation and Child Custody Evaluation

Family therapists have become an important resource for the legal system in determining the separating and postdivorce world of the family. Many states require families to work with family court mediators, a large number of whom have family therapy training, to assist a family in negotiating divorce and custody settlements. Mediators have helped to relieve our overburdened court system in many states. Specialized training allows mediators to become an important link between the legal and family systems.

Most states' legal systems have moved from the "tender years doctrine" of generally awarding mothers custody to a "best interests of the child" standard. The Uniform Marriage and Divorce Act (National Conference of Commissioners on Uniform State Laws, 1970) offers these guidelines in Section 402:

> The court shall determine custody in accordance with the best interest of the child. The court shall consider all relevant factors, including:
>
> 1. the wishes of the child's parent or parents as to his custody;
> 2. the wishes of the child as to his custodian;
> 3. the interaction and interrelationship of the child with his parent or parents, his siblings, and any other person who may significantly affect the child's best interest;
> 4. the child's adjustment to his home, school, and community; and
> 5. the mental and physical health of all individuals involved.
>
> The court shall not consider conduct of a proposed custodian that does not affect his relationship to the child.

Judges often rely on the advice of experts to determine the "best interests" standard; this relational information can be obtained from a family therapist's observations and opinions. Parents as well as the court can seek the services of family therapists for this purpose. Sometimes interns and therapists are surprised to discover the "true" motive for a person seeking therapy after it has been going on for a while— the client requests a letter or report from the therapist to be used in a divorce court or custody proceeding!

Therapists need to be informed about the divorce and custody laws of their state in order to work competently in this arena. If one wants to learn how to do custody evaluations, it is best to be mentored by someone who has done them over several years and is recognized by the court. Therapists need to be aware of the research outcomes regarding high-conflict divorce. Finally, therapists need a clear contract regarding their role in any divorce or custody case. Often, it's best to be hired as an expert to the court rather than be triangulated into serving as an expert for one parent against the other parent. Family therapists have much to contribute to the legal–family interface (Gould & Martindale, 2007).

Single-Parent Families

Whether the result of divorce, death, or a choice to parent alone, single-parent families, usually headed by the mother, share many common challenges that have the potential to go unrecognized in the therapy room. When a child from a single-parent family is presented to you for therapy, you will benefit by identifying and addressing these challenges, most notably the possibility of financial stress and the fact that many single-parent families are coping with loss, whether it be the loss of a partner/coparent or the loss of a dream about a family's future (Anderson, 2003).

Due to work and family demands, single parents frequently feel overwhelmed and depleted by their varied roles and responsibilities. In addition, children of single parents may carry a greater share of the domestic responsibilities because their sole parent is working outside the home. Because strands of American culture have often been critical of single-family structure, it is common for single parents to live with the guilt of "not being good enough."

Minuchin, Colapinto, and Minuchin (2006) offer a clinical approach to working with single-parent, low-income families that includes structurally defining parental roles when parents, live-in partners, and grandparents have a say about the household's children; encouraging the development of the biological mother's personal resources; and increasing access to social and economic resources. The following case provides a glimpse of what life can be like for clients who are single mothers living in poverty, as well as possible interventions.

Ms. G was a single mother who was raising three children: 13-year-old Gilbert, 10-year-old Alex, and 7-year-old Elise. Ms. G's husband had left the family when Elise was 2 years old, and he had provided no support and had no contact with the children. This family lived in a small two-bedroom apartment. The mother worked long hours cleaning office buildings, and she had little money to pay for anything but the bare essentials. Her long hours made supervision of the children difficult, so she often left Gilbert in charge. This became an increasingly difficult situation because he resented the responsibility and would leave his brother and sister alone for long periods.

Ms. G sought counseling at the recommendation of the school counselor. Gilbert had become a "behavior problem" at school. After entering junior high school a year and a half before, he began cutting classes and showing little interest in his schoolwork. His mother said that he was hanging out with "gang bangers," but she didn't think that Gilbert was involved in a gang. She had tried to get his uncle to spend time with Gilbert but his work schedule made this difficult. Gilbert seemed angry with and disappointed by any authority figures. His grades kept dropping and his teachers had added Saturday school as a steady part of his weekly routine.

Ms. G felt frustrated and helpless in trying to handle Gilbert. She said she was almost ready to give up and concentrate on the younger ones. She couldn't afford to pay for childcare after school and so had begun to send the younger children to the local Boys and Girls Club, but she was afraid of the effects that the older neighborhood children would have on Alex and Elise.

Ms. G had been receiving some help from her mother until they began having difficulties about 2 years earlier. Ms. G had begun dating a man that her mother disliked, and this caused considerable conflict between the two women. The children's grandmother wanted to maintain contact with them but Ms. G's anger and resentment caused her to severely limit their visits.

Ms. G's lack of financial resources and emotional support was quite apparent. The therapist's job was to assist her in making effective use of community resources and in considering family therapy that would include the children, Ms. G, and her mother. Single parents like Ms. G often lack the time and energy to make use of community resources and feel overwhelmed in attempting to fulfill all of their responsibilities. Providing support and identifying outside resources is an essential element in working with this type of case.

While single-parent families often face daunting problems, most of them are competent and successful. Lindblad-Goldberg (1989) has identified successful single-parent families as those in which parents, usually mothers, showed less depression, experienced more control over their lives, displayed more effective executive authority with their children, launched their older children from the household, communicated more effectively, developed close family ties, cognitively highlighted positive life experiences rather than negative ones, and used social networks creatively. When working with single parents or children of single parents, it is imperative that you address their hardships and highlight their strengths and resilience.

When working with single-parent families, it's important to assess what Becker and Liddle (2001) call the "self of the parent." Assessing the self of the parent means asking about her hardships, such as exhaustion and work stress, as well as her efforts to care for her individual needs. Beginning therapists are frequently hesitant to do this assessment because they want to focus on the presenting problem and feel blocked by the single parent's reluctance to self-disclose. If you want to understand the interaction between a single parent and her child and build a therapeutic alliance, you will need to learn more about her personal concerns outside of her role as parent (Becker & Liddle, 2001).

Stepfamilies

Mr. and Mrs. A presented with arguing and disagreements over raising their two boys. They were a recently married couple, and each spouse had an 11-year-old boy. Most of the couple's other disagreements seemed to be resolvable, but discussions involving the boys would quickly escalate, with Mr. A becoming very angry and Mrs. A crying and feeling attacked and hopeless. Each partner accused the other of being overly protective of his or her own child. The husband's response to the conflict was to become openly angry, raise his voice, and become opinionated and a bit self-righteous. The wife would cry, withdraw, and say that she had never been talked to like this before. Both agreed that if this problem was not resolved they could not stay married.

Unlike first marriages with no children, stepfamilies face the daunting task of merging two families with different beliefs, traditions, and practices; they also must sort out a variety of roles and responsibilities (Bray & Kelly, 1998). Loyalty issues are paramount. Although it's rare for a client to label a problem as a "stepfamily problem," stepfamily dynamics are a common, important undercurrent in many presenting problems.

You might assume that family membership is easy to define. In fact, family members in stepfamilies frequently have different definitions of who is "in" and "out" of the family. In other words, the boundaries are ambiguous. The differing definitions are due to acceptance (or a lack of acceptance) of new members and their roles in the family. For example, Stephanie, a single mother of three boys (Terrance, age 13; Vincent, age 10; and Jacob, age 5) remarries 3 years after their death of her husband, the father of her children. Terrance is angry with his mother for inviting a new person, especially a male, into their family home and is resentful at this man for trying to replace his father, even though that's not the new husband's intention. Jacob is fond of Tom, his new stepfather, and likes having a new playmate in the home. In this example, Terrance treats his stepfather as an uninvited outsider, while Jacob warmly welcomes him as a new family member. Terrance's anger and resentment likely stem from his powerful status while his mother was a single parent, as well as his continued loyalty to his deceased father. Power issues and loyalty conflicts are common in stepfamilies and can be a roadblock in a stepfamily's efforts to form a family identity.

All newly married couples need to find ways to protect their developing relationship; this is particularly vital for new couples in stepfamilies (Visher & Visher, 1988). Newly married couples in stepfamilies are not only coping with the adjustments associated with early marriage, such as developing problem-solving skills, but also the stress of new stepparent–stepchild relationships as described above. Couples without children have the luxury of time to prepare their relationship for children; stepfamilies are thrust into these parent–child roles immediately, which may leave little time to nurture the new couple relationship. According to Hetherington and Stanley-Hagan (2002), marriages and children in stepfamilies fare better when spouses focus on establishing a supportive, positive marriage. Loyalty can be tested when conflict arises between stepparents and stepchildren and biological parents are pulled in to the conflict.

Family loyalties and role ambiguity are complicating factors in decisions about parenting responsibilities. If divorced, biological parents must work out parenting issues while living in separate households and new stepparents must work on developing a relationship with stepchildren and determining their parental role. The research suggests that children tend to reject stepparents who discipline and try to control them early on (Ganong, Coleman, Fine, & Martin, 1999). Like many new parents, couples in stepfamilies may have had very little discussion about parenting roles and methods and rely on assumed or stereotyped roles without considering the effects on the children. For example, a biological mother may hand over disciplinary responsibilities of her two boys to their new stepfather because "men are the disciplinarians," even though the children may rebel against this arrangement. Spousal disagreements about parenting practices may also be the first crisis in a new stepfamily. Understanding these common themes and effectively communicating an understanding are key ingredients to successful therapy with stepfamilies (Pasley, Rhoden, Visher, & Visher, 1996).

CONCLUSION

In this chapter, we have reviewed information on the predictable and unpredictable changes in the lives of families with children. Knowledge of a family's development and the presenting problems associated with each developmental stage and transition assists us in providing solid clinical work. Family therapists need to recognize their strengths and limitations when assisting families through their growing pains. At a time when social transitions are complex and abundant, it is impossible to provide a single model of family that fits every family. Rather, we walk alongside families to help them invent a new form of family structure that will work for them.

CHAPTER 8

Working with Older Adults and Their Caregivers

Maria, a 68-year-old Latina, arrives for therapy with her younger sister, Anna. Maria's family doctor referred her to therapy for depression and anxiety. As Maria sits down with her sister and the therapist, she expresses confusion about the purpose of the appointment. Anna reminds Maria that Dr. R suggested she talk to a counselor about her sadness and worries. Anna vaguely recalls the discussion and expresses exasperation about being "left in the dark." As the interview progresses and Anna displays more comfort, the therapist learns that Maria had a stroke 3 years earlier, which required her sister to assume full-time caregiving responsibilities. Their relationship is clearly strong, but the therapist also sees tremendous stress. Maria communicates frustration that her daughter doesn't visit her and wishes Anna would allow her to be more independent. Anna listens attentively and sympathizes with Maria's struggle, but holds firm to the limitations placed on Maria as a result of the stroke. They live in a studio apartment and have little time apart from one another. Maria is convinced nothing will change, but she says she likes the therapist and is willing to schedule another session.

When we informally ask our students if they entered the field of family therapy to work with older adults like Maria and Anna, few raise their hands. Once they begin their clinical work and have contact with older adults, their attitudes change and, for some students, a specialization emerges. Initially intimidated by the wisdom of clients who are old enough to be their grandparents, our students quickly join with older clients and listen to them express appreciation for the benefits of therapy.

Between 2010 and 2020, the proportion of the world's population over 65 years old will increase from 13 to 16% (Karel, Gatz, & Smyer, 2012; Vincent & Velkoff, 2010). The increase will undoubtedly impact the demographics of our caseloads. To date, the mental health problems of older adults have been underidentified by healthcare professionals, family members, and clients themselves. The stigma surrounding mental illness contributes to older adults' reluctance to seek help. When older adults do seek help and a mental health diagnosis is made, evidence indicates that a variety of interventions can be effective in alleviating distress for the clients and their family members (Forsman, Nordmyr, & Wahlbeck, 2011).

As we did on our earlier chapter on children and adolescents, we must confess that one chapter can never capture all of the salient issues for older patients and their family members. Much of what we've written in other chapters applies to older adults as well. In this chapter, we present additional skills that may be necessary for the variety of older adults you might encounter. We start with an individual perspective to document what the research literature says about anxiety and depression in later life. We then turn to a family perspective and focus on illness, disability, caregiving, and loss. Although written as separate sections, we view them as parts of a whole, which is consistent with our biopsychosocial-systems approach.

ASSESSMENT AND TREATMENT OF OLDER ADULTS

"Can I really make a significant difference with my older client?" is a common question we hear from our students. The question isn't intended to be pessimistic or critical, but rather communicates their struggle with knowing how to proceed with elderly clients. Ageism and generational values on the part of the therapist, clinic, and client can be major barriers to a good outcome in therapy. Ageism may be expressed as beliefs such as "too old to change" or "depression is normal in later life," which often prevents older adults from seeking help or getting referred for help and also reduces expectations about therapy outcomes. Some older clients may feel that they don't deserve therapy; it should be reserved for those who are younger. Despite these constraining beliefs, many older people are interested in counseling services.

In addition to stigma, lack of access and/or knowledge of mental health services can be barriers to treatment. Older adults coping with mental health issues are less likely than younger and middle-age adults to receive mental health services or receive care from a mental health professional (Karel et al., 2012). In our work in medical settings, we frequently encounter older adults who would never seek out a therapist in the community. They come to see us because their doctor recommends us and our services and we share space with those doctors, which allows the older patient to feel more comfortable in a familiar clinic.

The effort to increase access to mental health services by placing therapists in medical settings is called "collaborative care." Collaborative care is a growing movement around the world that links doctors and mental health professionals, either through a traditional referral system or by immediately assisting with care in coordination with other healthcare professionals as they are in the process of seeing their patients. When a doctor detects emotional stress or determines a health behavior change is needed, he or she can perform a "warm handoff" during the patient's visit to the onsite mental health professional, which can result in patients receiving timely mental health services compared with usual referral to similar, but distant services. While more studies are needed to deepen the support for collaborative services across the full range of mental health needs, there is strong evidence from the United States and the United Kingdom that such care improves outcomes for older adults with depression (Gilbody, Bower, Fletcher, Richards, & Sutton, 2006).

Physicians refer their older adult patients to therapy for a variety of reasons:

1. As a supplement to psychotropic medication in the treatment of depression and anxiety
2. To foster adherence to medication use
3. To help distressed caregivers (e.g., treating a dementia caregiver experiencing depressive and anxiety symptoms)
4. To alleviate psychosocial problems related to aging (e.g., to help achieve contentment and acceptance of aging or to resolve disputes within a family brought on by the illness of an older family member)
5. As part of a collaborative care intervention in the treatment of depression and/or anxiety and comorbid physical illness (e.g., neurocognitive disorders)

Once a referral is made, the therapist establishes a relationship with the patient and a dialogue continues with the referring physician as they jointly form a treatment plan to help the patient and family. Of course, older adults and their family members also seek therapy through traditional channels for issues other than depression, anxiety, and/or illness, such as coping with retirement and other late-life transitions.

Anxiety and Depression in Older Clients

The combination of extended years of shifting roles in families as older adults gradually grow increasingly dependent on their adult children and the multiplying demands on caregivers suggests that both elderly family members and caregivers will be at increased risk for depression and anxiety. Symptoms of anxiety and depression are common in all countries throughout the lifespan, with up to 13.5% of older people having depression and between 1 and 15% diagnosed with anxiety disorders (Beekman, Copeland, & Prince, 1999; Bryant, Jackson, & Ames, 2008; Prina, Ferri, Guerra, Brayne, & Prince, 2011).

As we mentioned earlier, depression in older adults frequently goes undiagnosed and untreated. Depression may go undetected for a number of reasons, including (1) the presentation of multiple somatic complaints that focuses attention on physical concerns and hides emotional distress; (2) viewing sadness and despair as a normal part of aging, which it isn't; (3) and the reluctance of older adults to acknowledge psychological distress (e.g., stigma). Missing a depression diagnosis can be fatal. Although older adults are less likely to attempt suicide in comparison to younger adults, elderly white men are more likely to complete a suicide (Centers for Disease Control and Prevention, 2006).

A robust literature is emerging that shows therapy, often integrated into primary care, is effective for older adults. Similar to the evidence-based treatment literature among younger age groups, cognitive-behavioral therapy (CBT), problem-solving therapy, interpersonal therapy, and supportive psychotherapy show positive results for decreasing depression. CBT, psychoeducation, and relaxation training show positive results for decreasing symptoms of anxiety (Ayers, Sorrell, Thorp, & Wetherell, 2007). For moderate-to-severe depression and anxiety, medication may also be helpful if side effects can be tolerated (Givens et al., 2006).

Although family therapy isn't represented in this treatment literature, we never work with older clients in isolation from their family members, caregivers, and other treatment providers. Our systems orientation is critical in understanding the relationship between our clients and their family members and the relationships between our clients, their family members, and their physician. If you have the opportunity to refer an older client to a family physician and/or psychiatrist, we recommend choosing someone who is knowledgeable about older adults and able to form a caring, trusting relationship.

With a BPS-systems model as a guide, we describe a range of effective interventions for older adults coping with depression and anxiety. Some of our suggestions may not sound like family therapy (e.g., exercise), but we've found that our older clients and their family members respond positively to practical behavioral suggestions, rather than relying solely on therapeutic conversations, insight, and identification of negative interaction patterns. Consistent with our message to you in earlier chapters, your effectiveness with older adults is increased by a good therapeutic relationship with your client, his or her family members, and his or her primary care physician.

Enhancing Social Contact

Social support affects the onset, course, and outcome of depression, and individuals with distress can benefit from emotional and social support (Cohen, 2004). In addition, research suggests that sustained loneliness can be devastating to a person's health and well-being (Cacioppo & Patrick, 2008). Cacioppo and Patrick (2008) have shown that loneliness can increase cortisol levels, a stress hormone; increase blood flow; and weaken the immune system. Also, there is mounting evidence that links loneliness to illness and cognitive decline. In spite of these numerous negative effects, many older adults in the United States live alone.

While social support and social ties of any type can be beneficial and decrease loneliness, family ties and strong marriages can produce even more health benefits (Cohen, 2004; Iveniuk & Suhumm, 2016). In fact, recent research found that older adults who had more family members and were closer to their family members were less likely to die than older adults who had numerous close friends. Being married, having a larger network of family and friends, participation in social activities, and feeling close to one's friends and family all correlate with a longer life (Iveniuk & Schumm, 2016).

Thus, one key focus of therapy with an older client can be to increase his or her social ties. The therapist can help the client identify potential networks in his or her life (e.g., antique car club, knitting club, religious group). Also, the therapist can look for direct ways to strengthen marital and family ties. Problem solving (how to get to a group meeting when the client no longer drives), identifying interpersonal priorities, and identifying resources can be important parts of a family therapist's work with an older client. A systematic review of the literature showed that compared with usual care or no treatment, increasing social ties (befriending) had a modest but significant effect on depressive symptoms in both the short and long term (Mead, Lester, Chew-Graham, Gask, & Bower, 2010).

Cognitive-Behavioral Therapy

CBT, and the related problem-solving therapy (PST), emphasize behavioral techniques, repetition, a slower pace, identifying a highly specified focus, and giving homework assignments to disrupt negative beliefs that an older adult possesses that may lead to low mood and low self-esteem. For example, PST trains older clients to select and solve daily problems that seemed insurmountable to them initially, with the goal of increasing their self-efficacy and overcoming feelings of helplessness, which form the core of depression. With continued rounds of problem solving with highly specific action plans arrived at through client–therapist collaboration, self-esteem and confidence hopefully rises, thereby countering demoralization and lowering overall depressive symptoms (Arean et al., 2010). The hoped-for result is that the newfound confidence in problem solving will continue to additional problems, which if also successfully handled will maintain the patient's confidence and continue to relieve depressive symptoms over the long term (Gould, Coulson, & Howard, 2012a, 2012b).

Additional Therapies

Low-intensity aerobic exercise (e.g., walking, swimming) is an effective treatment for mild-to-moderate depression (Bridle, Spanjers, Patel, Atherton, & Lamb, 2012). Exercise may also be effective in decreasing symptoms of anxiety (National Collaborating Centre for Mental Health, 2009). Although this may sound outside of our scope of practice, in collaboration with a physician and family members, we think it's acceptable and therapeutic.

Reminiscence or life review therapy helps patients to either accept past negative events and resolve past conflicts or recollect past coping strategies. A number of studies involving elderly patients with depression demonstrate that those receiving reminiscence therapy showed fewer depressive symptoms, less hopelessness, and improved life satisfaction (Arean et al., 1993; Serrano, Latorre, Gatz, & Montanes, 2004). We return to the theme of life review later in this chapter.

Illness and Losses in Later Life

Whether they're coping with a specific mental health disorder or not, all older adults are coping with a variety of transitions (e.g., retirement, moves) and losses (e.g., friends, family). Most are coping with a variety of physical ailments and illnesses. Four areas that deserve special attention by family therapists include health, finances, social ties, and purpose/meaning. If an older adult has adequate resources in these four broad areas, aging need not be a period of depression and hopelessness. However, for most people, aging gradually involves multiple losses in each of these areas.

Physical Decline and Disability

Martha, age 78, lived alone after the death of her husband 10 years previously. She lived independently, enjoyed her friends, and gardened and walked each day. One day, her daughter called her several times and could not reach her—an unusual experience. A friend was asked to check on her, and she found Martha unconscious on the floor. Taken to the hospital immediately, Martha was diagnosed with a small cerebral hemorrhage that disabled her permanently. She was unable to walk independently, and thus could no longer live alone or take care of herself. The family faced the decision of what to do next.

In a culture that encourages independence and celebrates youth, attention to physical decline becomes pronounced in later years. Along with physical concerns, cognitive abilities may be affected by aging. Severe cognitive impairment affects 4.9% of adults over age 65 and 16–30% of those over age 85 (Regier, Boyd, Burke, & Rae, 1988; Skoog, Nilsson, Palmertz, Andreasson, & Svanborg, 1993). Although aging people maintain a high ability for new learning, new information may be processed more slowly and memory and reaction time can be impaired. A small, but significant, number of people are seriously impacted by dementia, including Alzheimer's disease.

The fourth edition of the *Diagnostic and Statistical Manual of Mental Disorders* (American Psychiatric Association, 2000) renamed a section that was previously called "Organic Disorders," "Cognitive Disorders." The purpose of this change was to clarify that these disorders have both environmental (e.g., years of education) and biological (e.g., genetic mutations) etiologies. In the most recent edition of the DSM (American Psychiatric Association, 2013), the term "neurocognitive disorders" is used to indicate the growing influence of neuroscience research on our understanding of aging and mental illness.

Clinicians conducting assessment are always interested in the following questions: "Can this client function independently?"; "Can he dress himself, plan his day, and cook his meals?"; "Can she do the tasks of daily living?" Usually, the answers to these questions depend on the patient's "executive functioning" and memory. Executive functioning refers to skills such as planning, organizing, and executing a plan. If your client shows deficits in these areas, you should refer him or her to a physician immediately.

If you have concerns about your client's cognitive functioning, you could consider doing two simple tests: (1) You could ask your client to draw a clock and set the hands to a specific time; (2) You could ask your client to remember three unrelated words such as *ball*, *toy*, and *choir*. Continue talking for a few minutes and then return to the three words. If the client cannot recall the words or cannot draw the clock, this is important screening information to document and to provide in your referral to a physician.

DSM-5 (American Psychiatric Association, 2013) talks about three mental disorders that often occur with aging: mild neurocognitive disorder, delirium, and dementia. Mild neurocognitive disorder is a new category in DSM-5 and its utility has not yet been proven. In fact, some clinicians are reluctant to use this diagnosis because cognitive decline is a natural part of aging and a clinical label may both frighten your client and not reflect the client's mental health accurately. Major neurocognitive disorders refer to dementias that can be caused by strokes, Alzheimer's disease, or other physical illnesses. The most important risk factor for dementias is age; approximately half of clients in their 80s will have some type of dementia. Dementias usually rob clients of cognitive skills such as the ability to understand language and also maintain memories. Both retaining old memories and forming new memories can be lost because of dementia.

Delirium refers to a sense of confusion and trouble keeping track of conversations. The client appears disoriented. He or she may be confused about where he or she is and who you are. A client's delirium is a medical emergency, and the client should be seen by a physician immediately. Because these disorders are brain disorders, a therapist's initial role is to make sure the client gets quick medical attention. Once a diagnosis is made, a family therapist can help the client and his or her family members sort out his or her limitations and plan for the future. While deliriums sometimes reverse and the client reverts to his or her previous level of functioning, dementias usually do not reverse and the client starts a slow, steady decline.

Therapy in cases of dementia and cognitive impairment can be complicated because these problems are progressively deteriorating conditions that are unlikely to remit as a result of therapy. Treatment often focuses on accepting and understanding illness, coping skills, and management of changes, including optimizing quality of life, minimizing disruptive behavioral symptoms, adjusting to functional impairment, and preventing self-harm. As family therapists, we are interested in relational functioning, how families cope with changes, and the well-being of family caregivers.

FAMILY CAREGIVING

If an older adult experiences the loss of problem-solving skills, executive functions, and memory loss, it becomes increasingly difficult to participate in normal daily activities (Qualls, 2000, 2016). The older adult may begin to feel that he or she has little to contribute and may even feel like he or she is only a burden. He or she may also feel increasingly isolated. As the aging person faces losses, family members become caregivers and compensate for these losses in a variety of ways, such as driving the loved one to his or her doctor's appointments or providing financial management. Newly appointed caregivers, most frequently wives and daughters (Wolff & Kasper, 2006), often need assistance deciding how to respond to age-related changes. For example, a common question from caregivers is how to balance the aging person's desire for independence and the family's need for safety.

Losses in ageing have consequences for family relationships. Some of the common areas that need family restructuring include roles (Can they be renegotiated?), authority (Who's in charge?), and shifting responsibilities (Qualls & Williams, 2013). As aging parents become more disabled and dependent on others, adult children frequently take on a parent-like role while also managing their usual responsibilities, such as paid employment and caring for their children. In addition to increased decision making on behalf of their aging parent, family caregivers may begin providing assistance with daily life tasks (e.g., bathing and grooming), psychological support for coping with pain, and administering complex medical tasks (Fingerman, Miller, & Seidel, 2009; Qualls, 2016). With their new position on the front lines of healthcare, family caregivers also become a spokesperson during encounters with healthcare professionals, partly to ensure treatment adherence.

As family caregivers respond to changes by taking on more and more responsibilities, stress builds and the potential for caregiver burnout is high. You may see several sources of stress, including conflict about who should or shouldn't be providing care and how care is administered, sibling competition and resentments (e.g., over financial decisions), and difficulties defining the limits of care that can be provided by family members (Zarit & Heid, 2015). For many families, decisions about placement in assisted living is especially difficult.

Janet, a 35-year-old African American woman, came to therapy to get help coping with the stress of caring for her mother with early-stage Alzheimer's disease. Janet is married and has a young daughter. She has one sister, who lives in another state. Her mother currently lives in an apartment with a roommate, who's coping with her own physical disabilities. Janet's sister wants to move their mother to assisted living, but Janet says keeping her mother in the home she's known for 30 years is paramount. She's now facing the dilemma of knowing her mother needs a higher level of care, but can't fathom the idea of moving her. She's thinking about moving to a larger home that can accommodate her mother. When she shared the idea with her sister, they argued and her sister abruptly ended the call. The stress is taking its toll on Janet's family and her physical well-being; her doctor recently told her she has high blood pressure.

When working with clients like Janet, we need to help them consider options (e.g., placement) and identify their needs. A helpful metaphor to guide responses to illness and disability in later life comes from narrative therapy—externalizing the problem. In the case of chronic illness and disability, externalization means "finding a place for the illness and keeping it in its place" (Reiss, Steinglass, & Howe, 1993). Opening up this discussion with families recognizes the reality that illness and disability can change a person's, and a family's, life forever. However, the older adult and his or her caregivers can have some influence over the effects of the illness. "Keeping it in its place" suggests that illness doesn't have to spill over into every area of well-being. Sources of pleasure and meaning can be protected with thoughtful planning and the establishment of boundaries that free up time (Zarit & Heid, 2015). Caregivers benefit from defining space that is free of illness talk and caregiving activity, which means structuring breaks or brief vacations from caregiving by reaching out to others for assistance, if possible. We recommend the book *Meditations for Caregivers* (Jacobs, 2016), which is a helpful resource for caregivers about finding hope and meaning in their care for others.

Although a focus on caregiver stress and burnout is critical, we would be remiss not to mention love, commitment, and resilience in the face of illness and disability. As we listen to frustration, exhaustion, and sorrow, we also listen for joy and gratitude. For example, we've heard adult children caregivers talk with great pride about caring for their aging parents. On a recent visit to Japan, we listened to an adult daughter talk about her many responsibilities caring for her bedridden father living in her home. She identified a variety of hardships, but labeled her caregiving experience as a "gift." She said she was spending precious moments with her father at the end of his life.

Anticipatory Loss

The concept of anticipatory loss is useful to therapists as they seek to better understand illness and the caregiving experience. Rolland (1990) describes anticipatory loss as a broad term that encapsulates the multiple losses over the course of an illness, many of which were described earlier. As families move from the initial diagnosis to the chronic phase, they cope with losses that have already befallen or are currently being experienced, such as the loss of normal family life. Family members also anticipate future losses. The experience of anticipatory loss appears like other grief reactions and includes fluctuating emotions such as denial, sorrow, yearning, and guilt, as well as other emotions like hope and acceptance.

Losses experienced with progressive illnesses, such as Alzheimer's disease, are often ambiguous, or lack clarity (Boss, 1999). While their family member still lives, the person that family members remember and love slowly slips away. At the beginning of the slow progression toward death, the older adult and his or her family caregivers may understand his or her fate. But slowly, the older adult becomes unaware of his or her surroundings, including the ability to recognize the family members who love him or her. This period, which can extend for many years, can drain the family of emotional, physical, and financial resources. In addition, the family members may have difficulty acknowledging and communicating about these losses. While a family therapist cannot change the course of these illnesses and inevitability of the losses, he or she can help the family navigate the many decisions and transitions that occur naturally as the client declines.

End of Life

With few, if any, models as a guide, family members are eventually thrust into the challenging position of discussing end-of-life care and making difficult decisions (Qualls, 2000). In *Being Mortal* (2014), Atul Gawande illustrates how often the wishes of the patient are missed or overlooked as caregivers, family members, and medical providers respond to inevitable changes. One reason the older adult's preferences might be overlooked is that losses lead to increasing dependence on others. Gawande suggests that the best way to know a person's priorities near the end of life is to ask them the questions below:

- "What is your understanding of your illness?"
- "What are your fears?"
- "What are your priorities if time becomes short?"

Activities like the card game "Go Wish" can also help clarify what is most important to the older adult. The game helps clients find words to talk about what is most important to them if their life was shortened by serious illness.

How else can family therapists help clients and family members nearing the end of life? Dignity therapy has emerged as an effective intervention (Chochinov et al., 2005). Dignity therapy asks older adults to tell the story of their life, enabling them to create something that will exist after they're gone. Over the course of approximately four sessions, the therapist elicits information through questions such as "Tell me about your life history" and "When did you feel most alive?" The most commonly discussed topics include autobiographical information, love, and lessons learned in life (Montross, Winters, & Irwin, 2011). A written document is then created and edited with the assistance of a therapist and usually given to family members. Dignity therapy is not simply "telling one's life story." Rather, the process allows a person to reevaluate past events and potentially forgive themselves and/or others. Family members report that the document is a helpful source of comfort (McClement et al., 2007).

Resources to Cope with Illness and Loss

A significant part of our work with older adults and their family caregivers is pointing them in the direction of resources. Table 8.1 identifies specific resources on the Internet to help older adults and their family members clarify adaptations that must be made to keep illness and losses in their place and protect other sources of meaning and hope. Table 8.1 also lists resources for therapists. Encouraging families to use these resources can create a sense of agency as the older adult comes to terms with necessary transitions and simultaneously identifies what he or she values most about his or her life.

The use of these resources is not intended as a substitute for therapist knowledge about key issues, such as the unique characteristics and demands of specific illnesses, but rather as a supplement to comprehensive, integrative treatment.

Grieving Families

Although the death of an elderly family member may be expected, either due to our beliefs about the inevitability of death or as the eventual outcome of a long-term illness, it still doesn't come without stress, shock, and significant grief (Brown, 1989). In addition to losing a beloved elder, family members lose their caregiving role, which may

TABLE 8.1. Resources for Clients, Caregivers, and Therapists

Resources for Therapists

Supporting Someone Who Is Grieving

This brochure is helpful to understand how to approach and communicate with someone who is grieving. It can also be used as a tool when supporting family members who are caring for others who are grieving.

www.caringinfo.org/files/public/brochures/Supporting_Someone_Who_is_Grieving.pdf

Caregiver Family Therapy (CFT)

CFT is a form of therapy aimed to improve family functioning for those involved in family caregiving, and institute problem-solving methods in reducing burden on the family. This website gives a brief summary of the therapy, as well as resources including online training links.

www.apa.org/pi/about/publications/caregivers/practice-settings/intervention/family-therapy.aspx

Caregiver Family Therapy: Empowering Families to Meet the Challenges of Aging by Sara Honn Qualls and Ashley Williams

This book explains the concepts behind CFT and gives clinical examples to help providers care for the needs of caregiving families. This link directs you to a brief summary of the book and instructions on how to purchase it. *www. apa.org/pubs/books/4317295.aspx*

Go Wish

The Go Wish card game is an intervention that gets people thinking about what is most important in life if it were to be shortened by severe illness. One, two, or more people can play it.

www.gowish.org/article.php/how_to_play

Evidence-Based Effective Practices with Older Adults

This article discusses the effectiveness of certain therapies for aging adults with various illnesses and later life transitioning. Some of the therapies included are group therapy, life review therapy, and reality orientation.

www.healthcare.uiowa.edu/icmh/evidence/documents/EBPOlderAdults.pdf

Center for Music Therapy in End of Life Care

This organization provides resources on the effectiveness of music therapy in bereavement and offers workshops to learn more.

www.hospicemusictherapy.org/resources/published-research/

(continued)

TABLE 8.1. *(continued)*

Dignity Therapy

This article from the *Chicago Tribune* describes dignity therapy in aging adults and how it can provide meaning and purpose in end-of-life stages. It tells the story of a few patients who benefited from this meaningful story-writing therapy.

www.chicagotribune.com/lifestyles/health/sc-health-0111-dignity-therapy-20120111-story.html

Respecting Choices

Respecting Choices is an internationally recognized, evidence-based advance care planning model of care.

www.gundersenhealth.org/respecting-choices

Alzheimer's Association

This national program can be a resource for clients, clinicians, and caregivers. The Alzheimer's Association (AA) provides 24-hour advice and information sharing through their hotline (1-800-272-3900). AA also offers care to clients through support groups, online message boards, and an online tool, Alzheimer's Navigator, which assists individuals with managing their disease. Interested clinicians can find resources, information, and studies through AA's online library and network. Finally, caregivers are offered support and information through the Alzheimer's and Dementia Care Center.

www.alz.org

Resources for Clients

National Institute on Aging

This website provides aging adults with up-to-date information on a variety of health topics, including depression and doctor–patient communication.

www.nia.nih.gov/health

Transitions in Later Life

This website is sponsored by a British foundation that offers collections of journal articles specific to learning about emotional well-being when transitioning to later life, including topics on retirement and increasing physical frailty.

https://transitionsinlaterlife.wordpress.com/resources-journal-articles/journal-articles-on-emotional-well-being-in-transitions-in-later-life/

Benefits Check Up

A great resource for patients to research what benefits they are eligible for such as Medicare, food programs, and more.

www.benefitscheckup.org

(continued)

TABLE 8.1. *(continued)*

The Positive Aging Newsletter

This site, sponsored by the Taos Institute, offers readable newsletters, which provide summarized research, news stories, and books related to positive aging. Both caregivers and patients can benefit.

www.taosinstitute.net/positive-aging-newsletter

Cycling without Age

This is a program in which young people give rickshaw rides to older adults so they can feel "the wind in their hair" even if they have little mobility. It is an environmentally friendly means of connecting generations that began in Denmark, and now is available in other countries, including some cities in the United States.

http://cyclingwithoutage.org

Positive Aging Resource Center

This is a helpful website that offers practical tips for emotional, physical, and mental health pertinent to the aging community. It is mainly for patients, but also has a section for caregivers.

www.positiveaging.org/index.html

Fierce with Age

This is Dr. Carol Osborn's blog, which offers recommended reading, inspirational videos, and even online retreats for the aging population with particular emphasis on spirituality and resilience.

http://fiercewithage.com

Exergaming with Xbox Kinect

Video games have been developed as an affordable, simple means of exercise for older adults. Participation in the games have been associated with improved balance, strength, walking, and motor control (see the article by Kamel Boulos, 2012, in the journal *Games for Health*, a potential resource for the aging population.)

The Friendship Line

This is a nationwide program that offers counseling to older adults through their 24-hour hotline (1-800-971-0016) as well as in-home and outpatient psychotherapy. The Friendship Line is particularly helpful for individuals who find it difficult to connect with their community, are grieving, or are suicidal. Volunteers are trained specifically to work with depressed older adults and engage in friendly conversation.

www.ioaging.org/services/all-inclusive-health-care/friendship-line

(continued)

TABLE 8.1. *(continued)*

Resources for Caregivers and Families

Aging Parents and Common Sense: A Practical Guide for You and Your Parents

This online booklet gives great advice for caregivers who may be struggling with financial planning, living situations, and understanding their parent's aging process. It also gives tips on healthy communication for caregivers and how to deal with some tough conflicts that are associated with aging.

www.caregiving.org/pdf/resources/Aging%20Parent-Guide_5thEd.pdf

There Is No Right or Wrong Way to Grieve after a Loss

This pamphlet explains what grief is, how to experience grief, and how to know when grief is ending. *www.caringinfo.org/files/public/brochures/ There_is_no_Wrong_or_Right_Way_to_Grieve_After_a_Loss.pdf*

National Hospice and Palliative Care Organization

This website gives a lot of resources on advance care planning, end-of-life care, grief and loss, and other resources on caring for a loved one.

www.caringinfo.org/i4a/pages/index.cfm?pageid=3406

Family Caregiver Alliance

Based in California, this organization gives great advice on educating caregivers about their loved one's needs as well as where to find support groups to take care of themselves as well.

www.caregiver.org/resources-health-issue-or-condition

Caregiver Action Network

This organization offers support to caregivers through education, peer support, and outlets to share their stories.

http://caregiveraction.org

Well Spouse Association

This foundation offers emotional support to spousal caregivers via local chapters and educational resources. It is specifically designed for caring for those who are the caretakers of their spouses at the end of life and helping them through the many transitions.

www.wellspouse.org

The Emotional Survival Guide for Caregivers by Barry J. Jacobs

Written by a clinical psychologist and family therapist specializing in counseling medical patients and families, this is an excellent book for caregivers

(continued)

TABLE 8.1. *(continued)*

struggling with role reversals and coping through struggles associated with caring for a loved one. This link takes you to his website, which features a book summary and information on purchasing the book.

www.emotionalsurvivalguide.com/book.htm

Coping with the Death of a Loved One

This online workbook provides an outlet for caregivers to learn about the different stages of grief, rituals that one can do to help the grieving process, differences among ages and genders, and even exercises to complete throughout their bereavement.

www.counsellingconnection.com/wp-content/uploads/2011/04/COPING-WITH-THE-DEATH-OF-A-LOVED-ONE.pdf

The Caregiver's Handbook by the National Care Planning Council

This handbook gives caregivers information on common problems in caregiving, caring for the caregiver themselves, and legal/financial affairs.

www.longtermcarelink.net/eldercare/the_caregivers_handbook.htm

The Caregiver's Handbook: Caring for Your Parents

This handbook gives information on how to get started with the initial conversations caregivers have to have with their elderly parents. It provides resources on finances, legal affairs, health care, insurance, housing, staying active, and caring for the caregiver.

www.seniorshelpingseniors.com/Library/Files/PR/Caring%20For%20Your%20Parents%20Handbook%20-%20PBS%20Documentary.pdf

National Alliance for Caregiving

This site focuses on research and advocacy to improve the quality of life for caregivers in the United States. It offers caregiver support through national programs and advice regarding topics like finances or military families. Finally, clinicians can seek professional support in working with family caregivers through this website.

www.caregiving.org

Caring.com

This website assists caregivers in discerning types of support and living situations for their loved ones. It distinguishes between assisted living, independent living, senior living, and in-home care, while identifying local placements by state. Ideas for financing a particular living situation are also described. Finally, the site offers caregiver wellness tips and support groups.

www.caring.com

be met with a tremendous void as well as an aching guilt: "What could I have done differently to extend her life?" "Why couldn't I reduce his suffering?" "Why do I feel relief that she died?." Family members may also encounter different styles of grieving (e.g, stoic vs. emotionally expressive) that leave them feeling confused and potentially isolated.

Historically, our understanding of grief has come from an emphasis on stages, phases, and tasks that individuals experience during grief. For example, Bowlby (1980) and Parkes (1972) describe a general grief process that starts with disorganization (e.g., emotional numbness, denial), followed by a period of extremes (e.g., searching for the deceased, accommodating the loss), and then eventually resolving or accepting the loss (e.g., saying goodbye). The family therapy literature has articulated stages that families must proceed through to effectively cope with the death of family members: (1) shared acknowledgment of the death or loss—someone is "gone"; (2) shared expressions of the range of emotions—allowing for variations; (3) reorganization of the family system to accommodate loss—the practical ability for the family to continue to function; and (4) reinvestment into a future life direction without the loved one—finding new ways to continue a meaningful life.

Therapy for grief has evolved over the years (Neimeyer & Holland, 2015). Whereas early approaches focused on psychoeducation about stages, accepting the loss, and moving on, current approaches to bereavement treatment emphasize understanding the unique and complex ways that people grieve and recognizing that some losses will never reach full closure. Contemporary models are also eschewing the goal of "saying goodbye" by helping clients maintain a relationship with the memories of the deceased loved one. The dual process model (Stroebe & Shut, 2010) and the two tracks of bereavement model (Rubin, 1999) help clients move forward in two parallel ways: (1) by honoring the continued relationship with the deceased via emotional processing of the loss (e.g., retelling the story of the death, reviewing photos, imagined conversations with the deceased, letter writing) and (2) by reengaging in a satisfying life (e.g., reconnecting with special people and activities).

Based on his narrative approach and belief that death ends a life but not a relationship, White (1988) offers the metaphor of "saying hello" and a menu of questions to help clients reclaim their relationship with the person who has died:

- "If you were seeing yourself through John's eyes right now, what would you be noticing about yourself that you could appreciate?"
- "How did John know these things about you?"

* "What difference would it make to you if you kept this realization about yourself alive on a day to day basis?"
* "What difference would it make to your relationships with others if you carried this knowledge with you in your daily life?" (p. 30)

Once clients have transitioned through the initial trauma of loss, employing the questions above may help them reengage with their memories of the loved one and celebrate the relationship.

CONCLUSION

Therapy with older adults and their family members necessitates patience and flexibility. As you begin therapy with an older adult, we encourage you to adapt your work to fit his or her needs. For example, the pace of therapy may need to be slower. Providing memory aids, such as handouts and session summaries, also can be helpful. Accounting for age-specific stressors (e.g., chronic illness and disability, loss of loved ones), and consequently sources of support during assessment is also important. In-home therapy may be a valuable option for those who lack reliable transportation and/or have a medical or physical disability. Most importantly, and consistent with our message throughout this book, view your older client in the context of his or her family. Family caregivers will be a valuable source of information, as well as an area for further assessment to ensure that their own needs are being understood and addressed.

CHAPTER 9

Working with Couples

Mary is a 29-year-old Caucasian female who has been recovering from alcoholism for the past year. Bob is a 32-year-old Caucasian male who is also recovering from alcoholism. Bob is being treated for depression by a psychiatrist who is prescribing Lexapro for him. Mary has been to two individual therapists through her health maintenance organization but feels dissatisfied with them because they don't really understand "the disease" of alcoholism.

This couple has been living together for the past 6 years. They have separated several times during that period. They were married 1 year ago. Bob says that he is increasingly unhappy in the marriage and has decided that he wants a separation. Mary has said that she "can't stand the thought of being without him" and wants to keep the relationship together. She reports "always feeling insecure" and doubting herself. She feels very confused by Bob's "double messages" because he says he wants a divorce but continues to act friendly and interested in Mary. He invites her to do things with him and desires to be with her sexually. He also tells Mary that he doesn't love her anymore. They argue and bicker about lots of little things but seem able to discuss important concerns. Still, many conflicts go unresolved.

Mary is requesting couple therapy to "try to either resolve these issues or get some closure." Bob is reluctant to go to therapy but has indicated that he will try it for one or two visits. They saw a couple therapist previously but didn't continue beyond the first session because Mary felt that the therapist sided with Bob and didn't really understand the whole situation.

This case presents a complex web of symptoms and concerns. The individual issues include alcoholism, Bob's depression, and Mary's insecure attachment reactions. The couple's issues include their confusion about whether to stay together, their inability to resolve conflict, and their ineffective communication patterns. The case is complicated by their previous unsatisfactory attempts at therapy. How does a therapist understand and work with such a couple?

This chapter focuses on couples who seek help for their continuing relationship. We explain the key principles that beginning (and probably all) therapists need to follow to do effective couple therapy. We then move on to special topics in couple therapy and suggest ways to understand and deal with them.

KEYS TO PROVIDING SOLID COUPLE THERAPY

What makes a good couple therapist? There are some unique aspects of doing couple therapy that can make the therapist's job difficult. Knowing about some of these and, more importantly, anticipating them can ease some of the difficulty. Implementing the key principles described below will increase the likelihood that couple work will be successful.

Key Number 1: Joining with the Couple System

Effective couple therapists must have the ability to manage a three-person relationship. Managing this three-person relationship, however, can present a challenge for beginning therapists. A new intern, in commenting about her first couple session, said, "I felt beat up, totally stuck in the middle. Anytime I tried to listen to the husband, the wife interrupted and told me her version. I didn't know what to do." The therapist literally becomes the emotional and relational hub for the couple's interactions and can provide the foundation for solid couple work depending on how well he or she works with a triangle, or three-person relationship. Therapists can connect to the couple in several ways, as shown in Figure 9.1.

Creating an Empathic Connection with Each Partner

In Figure 9.1A, the therapist attempts to connect empathically with each person. For example, he or she might ask at the beginning of the first session, "What brings you in today and how might I help you?" This question might prompt one partner to say, "I'm not happy in my

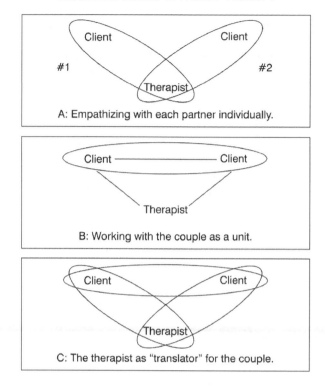

A: Empathizing with each partner individually.

B: Working with the couple as a unit.

C: The therapist as "translator" for the couple.

FIGURE 9.1. Therapeutic triangles.

marriage and I haven't been for a long time. I don't know what to do. I've tried, but nothing seems to work." The therapist might empathically respond, "So you're sad and frustrated with the way your marriage is right now and you're confused about what to do next." The client responds, "Yes, that's it." When the therapist builds the relationship with each person during the first session, then each one usually experiences a beginning bond with the therapist and will want to continue in therapy. Without this empathic connection with each partner very early in the therapy, clients often will not return. Also, it will be vital to create a "shared couple agenda" in order to proceed successfully in the couple work together.

It's important to remember that when the therapist takes an individually empathic position, it impacts the triadic relationship. The partner who is not being attended to feels "left out" for a moment. Often the unattended person will interrupt the process to receive attention or to "correct" the point stated by the partner. If the therapist allows interruption to occur repeatedly without taking charge of the interactions, he or she will begin to feel bumped back and forth between the two individuals, much like a tennis ball between two players. It's wise for the therapist to direct this interaction, to tell the couple that each of them will get their turn, and to emphasize that it's important for the therapist to understand each person's concerns.

Unfortunately, beginning therapists often get stuck at this stage. They know how to connect with each partner—in a sense, to begin individual therapy with each—but don't know where to go next. Instead of managing the entire triangle, the therapist listens only to each partner individually during the session. Often the tension between the couple heightens and the interaction becomes more conflicted. Without knowing how to manage the case triadically, the therapist might even recommend that each person be seen separately. Although this is useful at times, most often couple work needs to be done with both partners present. Separating the couple mostly helps the therapist's anxiety, not the couple's need to work on things together. In order to be effective, the therapist must be able to move fluidly to other positions.

Working with the Couple as a Unit

As Figure 9.1B shows, another dimension in doing conjoint therapy is to make the couple's relationship rather than each person the focus of your work. Rather than attend to the personal therapist–client relationship, the therapist takes a position of orchestrating new behaviors between the couple. Much of traditional couple therapy, especially any with psychoeducational or "skill training" components, takes this triadic stance. Skills and positive interactional experiences are needed to create and maintain a new couple system.

For example, a couple comes to therapy presenting with fights over parenting and money. The therapist determines several strengths in their relationship and decides to begin therapy with a solution-focused therapy approach. The therapist begins to identify when they "don't fight" and to describe these interactions in detail. She also explores and "rates" when their fights are "less destructive" to their relationship. She encourages the couple to notice when they are doing "not fighting" behaviors and employing "less destructive" fighting styles. After several weeks, the couple reports "less intense" fighting around money and parenting. They also reveal that spending weekly "fun time" together sets a better tone in their relationship to discuss problematic issues surrounding money. In this case, the therapist focuses on developing new relationship patterns that address the couple's presenting problems. Individual experiences are less of a focus; the therapist is more goal-directed and works with the couple as a unit.

When a beginning therapist is unsure of how to proceed when doing work with a couple or when a couple negatively escalates their interaction, the therapist can interrupt the process by restating the powerful assumption of this triadic position—for example, he might say, "What we're trying to do here is create a new kind of relationship where both of your concerns and needs can be honored. Rather than living together as opponents, let's work on being on the same team." Another comment from this perspective might be "We all know that partnering is hard work. In many ways, you've never been 'married' on this issue and this is the first time you're trying to find a really useful way to work it out."

These kinds of comments often lessen the tension between the couple since both are joined in wanting to make the relationship work. If this doesn't calm them, it may mean that at least one person has already emotionally left the relationship and has given up attempting to be a partner (Gottman & Notarius, 2000). Alternatively, it might indicate the therapist's need to return to the previously discussed "empathic" position with respect to one of the partners. In such a case, the therapist should attend to and possibly reengage the more disengaged partner.

The Therapist as "Translator" for the Couple

Figure 9.1C illustrates a final triadic position the therapist can take to manage couple therapy effectively, that of an interpreter or translator. In this focus, the therapist functions as the one who understands that each partner's behaviors, perceptions, and experiences influence the couple's functioning. The therapist creates new ways for the couple to understand each other, often taking a mediating or reframing position. For example, couples commonly battle with each other because each person is trying to re-create his or her family of origin in the new relationship. Often both partners want to get back to their own way of understanding their cultural and familial ways of doing things.

What the therapist needs to keep in mind is that the couple is in the process of creating a "new system" of relating with each other. Interactions that respect some combination of each person's history and values can help to create this new system. Without this new-system perspective, the couple continues to fight. The therapist can facilitate the creation of the new system by helping each partner better understand where their mate is coming from.

Basic to being a "translator" for the couple is an understanding that requires each person to be validated as "different" in some way. These differences will either promote a healthy, differentiated system or will disintegrate into a power play wherein each partner wants to win control of the relationship. The therapist, rather than taking sides, promotes a relationship based on the unit of the couple rather than on each person individually. The therapist simultaneously translates and verbalizes how each partner brings into the relationship different ways of being and doing.

For example, a young couple comes in with complaints about how they are spending their money. One partner came from a structured family where money was carefully accounted for, while the other partner's family allowed all members to spend as they wished. Each partner argues for his or her own "right way" to oversee the family budget and criticizes the other for being either tight or irresponsible. The therapist can first acknowledge the strengths and possible liabilities of each person's family-of-origin lessons about money. Then he or she might reframe the couple's battle as "very healthy—each person has a different expertise that can benefit the relationship and both need to be heard." Then the therapist can wonder out loud if the couple might find a way to embrace each other's expertise, and, in so doing, strengthen the marriage. In this way the therapist first translates, then mediates, for the couple.

Key Number 2: Building a Commitment to Therapy

Therapy is more likely to be successful if both partners are committed to the relationship. Unfortunately, one of the frequent challenges facing couple therapists is that one or both individuals may be ambivalent about continuing their relationship. Often one partner will present as wanting to save the marriage, while the other is doubtful it can be saved and is seriously thinking of leaving. Angelica came to therapy very distraught that her husband had left her and said that he wanted a divorce. He agreed to come for a few sessions to see if there was a chance to save their marriage. Her hope was reconciliation and she said, "I will do anything to get him back." Obviously, the greater the difference in a couple's motivation and desire to repair the relationship, the more challenging it will be for reconciliation to occur.

Even if individuals are highly ambivalent about continuing their relationship, it may be possible to build a commitment to coming to therapy. One way to do this is to initially do a marital or relationship evaluation. Typically the therapist contracts to do the evaluation with the couple for a limited number of sessions. The evaluation is framed as a way of better understanding why the relationship is not working. To the ambivalent partner, you can suggest that gaining this understanding is important even if the couple separates or divorces. Otherwise, individuals are at risk for making similar mistakes in future relationships. To the committed partner, you can say that understanding why the relationship is struggling may give insight into how it might be fixed.

Using the metaphor of a home inspector for the evaluation resonates with many couples. Much like what a house inspector does for potential homebuyers, you will carefully examine the relationship to determine what elements of the relationship need to be fixed, as well as elements that seem to be working well. After the evaluation has been completed and presented to the couple, each partner can decide if he or she wants to invest in making the necessary changes to save the relationship. The goal of the evaluation is to give couples new insights into their own dynamics, rather than simply to list all the problems that exist in the relationship. The evaluation should also include the strengths that you observe in the relationship. Sometimes offering new insights gives the ambivalent partner some hope that the relationship may be salvageable.

After doing a marital evaluation, you can often build a commitment to therapy if you can identify goals for each individual that provide a win–win scenario. In a win–win scenario, individuals benefit from working on the goals regardless of whether the relationship succeeds or fails. In one case, the husband was pursuing his wife for greater connection or closeness. His wife, however, felt smothered by his pursuit. The more he pursued, the more she distanced herself from him emotionally. The therapist pointed out this central dynamic, and suggested to the husband that if he continued to pursue his wife, then he would push her out of the marriage. Thus, the husband was encouraged to examine his dependency needs, which seemed to drive his pursuing behavior. Doing so put the husband in a win–win situation. Working on their attachment issues could help them reduce his pursuing, and perhaps save their marriage by interrupting the couple's vicious cycle. However, if his wife did decide to leave, reducing his dependency needs would make the divorce less painful for him. In a similar manner, the wife was encouraged to explore her ambivalence about intimacy, a pattern that was also evident in her previous relationships. Resolving this issue could potentially help her feel better about the marriage. If she decided to divorce, however, then resolving this issue would still benefit her by helping her avoid replicating this dynamic in future relationships.

An alternative to doing a marital evaluation would be to follow an approach called "discernment counseling" (Doherty, Harris, & Wilde, 2015). Like a marital evaluation, it is particularly helpful for "mixed agenda" couples, where one wants to stay in the marriage ("leaning in") and the other is considering ending the marriage ("leaning out"). A highly intentional and structured counseling experience, discernment counseling provides a way for a couple to access the assistance of a therapist's expertise and a safe "holding environment," while clarifying what to do with their marriage. Specifically, discernment counseling helps couples determine if they want to keep the relationship as it is (maintain the status quo), move toward separation or divorce, or pursue a 3- to 6-month course of couple therapy with divorce off the table during therapy. Discernment counseling itself is brief, lasting only one to five sessions.

In contrast to a marital evaluation, in discernment counseling most of the work is done meeting with each partner separately. After the initial conjoint session, 1.5- to 2-hour sessions are split between individual counseling with each partner, alongside conjoint summarizing opportunities led by the counselor. For "leaning out" partners, conversations focus on making a good decision and helping them identify their contribution to the problems. For "leaning in" partners, conversations focus on helping them understand their partner's complaints and developing strategies for saving the marriage. Similar to the early family therapy metaphor of a crucible (Napier & Whitaker, 1978), the discernment counselor provides a holding place for the "hot issues" that each partner brings. A therapist can become a discernment counselor with specialized training or refer a couple for discernment counseling when appropriate (see *discernmentcounseling.com*).

When working with issues of commitment, it is important that you leave the decision up to the client as to whether to continue the relationship. You need to be careful not to push the ambivalent partner to commit to the relationship, or you may create resistance. Conversely, you should not tell an individual to leave a relationship because the problems seem so severe. If you feel that a relationship is unhealthy, then you should clearly state your concerns and what steps the individuals need to take in order to make the relationship healthy.

Key Number 3: Identifying and Altering Vicious Cycles

In our experience, one of the most powerful predictors about whether couple therapy is successful is the therapist's ability to identify and alter a couple's negative interactional pattern. These interactional patterns typically take the form of a vicious cycle that the couple repeats over and over, which creates conflict and erodes goodwill within the relationship.

For example, Sandra and Tom, both in their late 40s, presented for couple therapy to work on saving their marriage. Tom, it was recently discovered, had had an affair with another woman. The couple reported intense conflict every time they attempted to talk about the affair. The couple appeared stuck in their efforts to move forward. When exploring the conflict over the affair, the therapist discovered that the couple was caught in a vicious cycle. Sandra would approach Tom with questions about the affair. Her questions were an attempt to understand why he had the affair. Tom would begin to retreat from her questioning. When asked why, Tom stated that he wanted to put the affair behind him. He also reported that he was fearful the answers would make his wife even more upset or distressed. Sandra, in contrast, viewed his avoidance of her questions as a possible sign that he didn't care about her or that he was protecting the other woman. As a result, his avoidance heightened her distress. The more distressed she became, however, the more convinced Tom became that it was unsafe to talk about the affair. Interrupting this cycle helped the couple begin to feel better about the relationship and got them back on the road to recovery.

Although vicious cycles can take many different forms, the demand–withdraw cycle and the overfunctioner and underfunctioner cycle are two of the most commonly encountered patterns. In the demand–withdraw cycle, one partner appears to take the lead more often in working on the couple's relationship. Frequently this is the woman, since women have been socialized to take care of relationship issues more than men. A variation of the demand–withdraw cycle is the pursuer–distancer cycle. In both cases, the pattern develops when one partner initiates and the other responds by backing away.

Jamie and James illustrate the classic pursuer–distancer cycle. Jamie seeks out connection with James by asking him to sit down and watch a TV program with her (and in a frustrated tone of voice), but she becomes hurt when he does not give her the attention that she feels she needs or deserves. Jamie expresses her hurt by becoming angry and critical of James for not being a more caring husband. James, who already harbors insecurities about his role as a husband, responds to Jamie's criticisms by withdrawing even more from the relationship. This, of course, further fuels Jamie's hurt, perpetuating the cycle.

Another common pattern is the overfunctioner and underfunctioner cycle (Williams & Jimenez, 2012). The overfunctioner takes on more responsibility in the relationship and is often critical of the other partner for not doing enough. The underfunctioner, in many cases, is happy to let the other partner assume responsibility, reinforcing the overfunctioner's belief that he or she must compensate for the underfunctioner's lack of initiative and responsibility. Interrupting this cycle often requires that the overfunctioner step back, which can create intense anxiety on his or her part (particularly since the underfunctioner may not step in immediately). In addition, you will need to explore possible reasons why the other partner underfunctions. Is it simply because he or she is happy not to have the responsibility, and knows the overfunctioner will do it? Or are there other factors that must be addressed? For example, a lack of skills or confidence may be contributing to the individual underfunctioning, as well as possible mental health disorders (e.g., ADHD, depression). The underfunctioner may also resist doing what the overfunctioner wants unless given the freedom to do it his or her own way.

The ability to identify negative interactional patterns or vicious cycles is an important skill that family therapists need (see Chapter 6). In many cases, you will be able to directly observe the couple's dynamic in session, particularly if the couple becomes upset when discussing a recent conflict or issue. When anxiety is high in the couple system, couples are likely to fall into their vicious cycle. Circular questioning (see Chapter 6) can often uncover these patterns. For example, in the pursuer–distancer example above, you might ask James what his wife does first before he begins to withdraw.

Certain family therapy theories such as emotionally focused couple therapy address these interactional patterns at both the relational and the intrapersonal levels (Johnson, 2004). Therefore, it is important to map out the underlying thoughts or feelings that drive each person's behavior because they are often targeted when the therapist attempts to alter the cycle. A cognitively oriented therapist, for example, might challenge the underlying meaning that each individual attaches to the other's behavior. The therapist might help Jamie see that James withdraws because of his insecurities about being a good husband, rather than due to a lack of caring. Emotionally focused therapists would encourage each party to express his or her primary emotions and underlying attachment needs, which can alter the dynamics (Johnson, 2004, 2015). Jamie, for example, would be encouraged to express how hurt and insecure she feels when James is not available. If Jamie can express these primary or vulnerable emotions, James may be able to be empathetic to her feelings and needs. The infinity cycle is one useful tool to visually tie the behaviors each partner displays to their underlying emotions and attachment issues (Brubacher & Lee, 2012).

Past relationships or family-of-origin experiences can impact how individuals respond to their partner, creating potential sensitivities (Christensen, Dimidjian, & Martell, 2015). For example, a husband's loud voice may trigger his wife's memories of emotional and physical abuse as a child, leading her to become fearful and withdrawn. The therapist must determine how much historical information is necessary for the partners to work together. Bringing these historical factors into the discussion can sometimes reduce defensiveness on the couple's part, an initial step toward reducing reactivity in the interaction.

Therapists often discover that labeling the interactional sequence for the couple can begin the change process. The vicious cycle now becomes the enemy rather than each other. The therapist encourages each partner to focus on what he or she can do differently to interrupt the vicious cycle. When couples begin to behave differently, they often notice that a virtuous cycle emerges. For example, as James begins to engage more with Jamie, she validates his efforts. This validation is reassuring to him, reducing his desire to withdraw.

Key Number 4: Moving from Blame to Focus on Self

Couples who present for therapy frequently blame each other for all the problems in the marriage or relationship. As long as they remain in this blaming mode, therapy is likely to remain stuck (and frustrating for the therapist). Thus, you will need to get each individual to shift his or her focus away from the partner and focus on what changes he or she needs to make.

This can often be done in one of several ways. First, it may be possible to identify how the problems in this relationship are similar to those encountered in earlier relationships. This is usually compelling evidence that the individual must have some role in the problem since it repeats itself across a number of his or her relationships.

Second, pointing out the couple's cycle illustrates how each partner contributes to the dynamic. Seeing one's part in the cycle can help individuals shift from blaming their partners to focusing on their own thoughts, feelings, and behaviors. Some therapists even go so far as to frame the cycle (and not each other) as the enemy.

Third, individuals can be reminded that they don't have control over what their partners do. They have control only over themselves. If necessary, you can push this point further by pointing out that they are giving their partner a lot of control over their personal happiness. This observation often encourages individuals to focus more on what they can do themselves to regain a sense of control over their own happiness.

Key Number 5: Strengthening Cohesion and Caring

Couples who come to therapy have often allowed conflict to erode their relationship. Over time, the couple may distance themselves from each other in response to the conflict or to avoid further conflict. Conversely, couples that stop doing pleasurable activities together (e.g., focusing on children) may find that the relationship is more vulnerable to conflict. Regardless of the cause, often an important part of therapy with couples is to strengthen the couple's caring or cohesion.

Building cohesion and caring is often done through prescribing behavioral homework for couples. Getting couples to do pleasurable activities together or go on dates is often a highly effective intervention. Helping couples identify and do more caring behaviors for their partners is also beneficial. Couples who successfully carry through on these homework assignments report greater relationship satisfaction and a greater sense of hope.

Key Number 6: Identifying and Managing Individual Psychopathology

As you will read in the next chapter, therapists must give consideration to how mental illness can impact individuals and families. This is also true for couples, and can complicate treatment. Therefore, when doing couple work, it is important to assess if one or both individuals have any mental illness or substance abuse problems, and the extent to which they are impacting the relationship.

In some cases, you may find that the problems in the marriage or relationship are heavily influenced by an undiagnosed mental illness. Mark and Eve, for example, came to therapy after experiencing problems in their 4-year marriage. In the first session, Eve stated that her husband was generally a very kind and considerate man, but around football season he became "Mr. Nasty." She also reported that he would begin to become inactive except for watching a lot of television. Interestingly, the couple also reported that their relationship was great in the summer but would then begin to deteriorate in the fall. With further assessment, it was discovered that Mark had a severe case of seasonal affective disorder, which would begin to reappear each fall and go into remission by late spring.

For couples where mental illness is a serious issue, it is important that you encourage individuals (or in some cases, both partners) to get appropriate care or treatment for their disorder. If a mental illness has not been properly managed in the past, then getting appropriate treatment may significantly improve the relationship. One couple reported that conflict in the relationship declined 50–70% after the husband was put on medication for bipolar disorder. A client should be encouraged to learn as much as possible about his or her partner's mental illness. In addition, practicing good self-care should be emphasized, since living with someone with mental illness can be stressful, particularly if the partner is in a caretaking role.

Negative interactional patterns or vicious cycles can arise around mental illness or substance use. Current research has suggested that anxiety disorders may negatively impact the stability and functioning of couples through escalating quarrels, restricting relational behaviors, or decreasing attention to the needs of the nonanxious partner (Snyder, Castellani, & Whisman, 2006). Empirically supported ways to counteract marital dysfunction due to anxiety disorders involve exposure techniques, relaxation techniques, and cognitive restructuring, as suggested by Baucom, Hahlweg, and Kuschel (2003). As an alternative example, a couple may have conflict over one partner's use of alcohol or drugs. The conflict creates tension for the individual using alcohol or drugs, which he or she may try to alleviate by drinking or using more often. This, in turn, leads the other partner to attack the individual, creating additional conflict in the relationship. Thus, you may need to concurrently address psychopathology and relational dynamics.

The bidirectional influences of psychopathology and relational dynamics have led to an increased focus on how couple therapy can help treat mental illness or substance abuse. Couple therapy, for example, has proven to be effective in treating depressive symptoms of individuals in distressed relationships (Whisman & Beach, 2015). Behavioral couple therapy has also been demonstrated to be an effective treatment for substance abuse (Fals-Stewart, Kashdan, O'Farrell, & Birchler, 2002). There is an added benefit to increasing overall marital satisfaction found when practicing behavioral couple therapy, as opposed to practicing therapies that are focused on the individual (Gupta, Coyne, & Beach, 2003).

Key Number 7: Managing Emotions

Emotions are an important element in doing couple work. Emotions are like water and fire—they can be constructive or destructive elements depending on the circumstances. Intense emotions like anger and rage can disrupt the couple's connection. Conversely, sharing more vulnerable emotions may enhance a couple's intimacy and connection. Therefore, couple work often involves helping couples effectively manage their emotions. Research indicates that managing emotions in couple therapy appears to be a central thread across multiple effective modalities (Whelton, 2004).

One of the more difficult aspects of doing couple work is that fighting between partners might escalate, particularly when emotions run high. Couples can bring this high level of conflict into the session itself, which can be very stressful for beginning therapists. Therapists often must teach couples how to contain or manage negative emotions both within and outside the therapy sessions.

When couples become highly conflictual in the therapy session, you must be comfortable interrupting the interaction. At times, particularly if the couple is "flooded," or in a highly emotional state, this may require you to be quite forceful in getting them to stop. The couple should be encouraged to calm down and collect themselves before resuming the discussion. In some cases, it may even be necessary to separate the couple and meet briefly with each of them individually until emotions settle down.

Couples who report that their conflicts escalate should be taught to recognize when one or both is getting flooded. When couples become flooded, they tend to engage in destructive behaviors that damage the relationship. Gottman (1999) has observed that the Four Horsemen—strong predictors of divorce—can invade a relationship when the couple becomes flooded with negative emotions. Criticism is the first horseman, which occurs when individuals attack their partner's character or motives rather than make a specific complaint about their partner's behavior. Contempt, the second horseman, happens when individuals resort to name-calling, mock their partner with sarcasm, or do other behaviors that convey disrespect and disgust for their partner. Gottman believes contempt is particularly corrosive to relationships. Defensiveness and stonewalling are the other two horsemen. Defensiveness is evident when individuals make excuses or counterblame their partner rather than take any responsibility for the problem. Stonewalling refers to when one partner shuts out the other. Attempts to engage this partner are like speaking to a brick wall. There is also the potential for domestic violence when couples escalate using the Four Horsemen, which should be carefully screened for among all couples.

Once a couple is able to recognize that one or both are getting flooded, then someone should ask for a time-out. During the time-out, the couple separates until they have emotionally and physiologically calmed down. Whoever asks for the time-out initially has the responsibility for reinitiating a conversation about the topic. Otherwise, the time-out can be used inappropriately to avoid talking about significant issues.

More behaviorally oriented approaches teach couples communication skills to help conflict from escalating. The Prevention and Relationship Enhancement Program (PREP; Markman, Stanley, & Blumberg,

2010), for example, teaches couples the "speaker–listener" technique. Using this technique, one partner is the speaker while the other takes the role of listener. After the speaker has had the opportunity to speak as desired, the couple switches roles. The speaker uses skills such as "I" statements to facilitate communication, while the listener uses active or reflective listening to confirm that the message has been correctly received and understood.

Couples may also need help expressing the more vulnerable emotions they feel underneath their anger. Helping couples access these more vulnerable emotions is an important element of work in emotionally focused therapy (Johnson, 2004, 2015) and integrative behavioral couple therapy (Christensen et al., 2015), two popular approaches to couple therapy with good empirical support. For example, in emotionally focused therapy, a distinction is made between primary and secondary emotions. Primary emotions include sadness, fear, and hurt. Although anger can be a primary emotion if in response to a boundary violation, anger is most often a secondary emotion that individuals express rather than the more vulnerable primary emotions that are underneath the anger. Many individuals, for example, become angry if they become anxious or their partner does something to hurt their feelings. Unfortunately, individuals often have a difficult time dealing with another person's anger, either withdrawing or getting angry in return. In contrast, individuals generally want to comfort those who are sad, fearful, or hurt. Thus, getting clients to express their primary emotions rather than anger often leads to a positive response from the partner. Expressing vulnerability to one's partner and getting a validating response strengthens the couple bond. Helping clients to access and express their primary emotions can create powerful moments of change in therapy.

Individuals can also vary on how they relate to emotions, which can impact intimate relationships. Gottman and Gottman (2015) have described two general approaches to how individuals manage emotions, which they call "meta-emotions." Emotion-coaching individuals value emotions and view them as a useful guide to understanding life. As a result, they reflect on the meaning of emotions and develop a rich vocabulary for describing them. In contrast, emotion-dismissing individuals do not value emotions, and prefer action rather than dwelling on their feelings (e.g., "Suck it up and get on with life"). As a result, they often avoid looking at their emotions and have a limited vocabulary for describing them. While many individuals with an emotion-dismissing approach are good at suppressing emotions, a subcategory of emotion-dismissing individuals view themselves as overly emotional. These "emotion-out-of-control" individuals view strong emotions as dangerous and are disapproving of strong emotions both within themselves and in others.

A meta-emotion mismatch between two partners can create conflict for the couple. For example, an emotion-coaching partner may want to share and talk about emotional experiences as a way to connect. However, the emotion-dismissing mate may disregard the partner's emotions, perhaps even becoming impatient or critical of them. The emotion-dismissing mate is essentially rejecting the partner's bid for connection, creating distance or conflict. To help a couple like this bridge their meta-emotion mismatch, the Gottmans recommend that you teach the couple how to make their emotional bids and needs explicit, ask open-ended questions, and make statements that show empathy and interest for what the other is saying.

Given the importance of dealing with emotions in couple therapy, therapists should examine their own meta-emotion style. Are they emotion-dismissing or emotion-coaching? What messages about emotions did they receive from their own families of origin? The answers may influence how one works with couples. For example, an emotion-dismissing therapist may not like certain therapies like emotionally focused therapy that target the emotional experiences of individuals.

SPECIAL TOPICS

The principles described above will be a useful guide as you navigate the challenges of helping couples overcome relationship distress. However, you will also need to be prepared to address issues like affairs, sexual issues, or pornography, which frequently arise when working with couples. Furthermore, you will need to be sensitive to the unique needs that certain types of couples bring into therapy. This section explores how to work with specific issues or populations that the couple therapist will frequently encounter.

Domestic Violence

Both in theory and in practice, marital and family therapy has only recently begun to fully address domestic violence. It is important that therapists assess all couples for domestic violence. Despite the frequency, potential lethality, and cost of domestic violence, many therapists fail to detect it. In addition, there is continuing debate on the best way to treat domestic violence.

As discussed in Chapter 4, the therapist must determine what type of violence is occurring in the relationship since it has important implications for treatment (Greene & Bogo, 2002). It may be possible to conduct couple therapy if the violence falls under the category of common couple violence (sometimes also referred to as "situation couple violence"). If couple therapy is pursued, it is important that there be a commitment to stopping the violence. If both partners engage in any physical aggression, then both must commit to stopping these actions. The therapist must also encourage individuals to take full responsibility for their behavior and recognize that violence cannot be part of a healthy relationship. Of course, taking this posture makes it more difficult to therapeutically align with a partner who uses physical aggression. One approach is to discuss with the violent partner how stopping the violence is in his (or her) best interest. The therapist might identify, for example, how continuing the violence damages the individual's relationship with his or her partner, or puts the individual at risk for police involvement.

If you determine that it is safe to do conjoint treatment, then the initial focus should be on reducing the risk for violence and ensuring safety. Encouraging couples to take time-outs when emotions rise is an important intervention. Teaching individuals how to self-soothe may be necessary. A referral for anger management is sometimes helpful to supplement the work being done in couple therapy. It is also prudent to have a safety plan in place in the event that violence reoccurs. Throughout treatment, you should continually reassess if the couple has experienced any episodes of violence. A subsequent incident of violence during treatment should lead you to reevaluate whether conjoint treatment is contraindicated for the couple.

If the violence falls under the category of patriarchal terrorism (sometimes referred to as "intimate terrorism" or "battering"), couple or conjoint work is definitely contraindicated. The goal at this point is to encourage individuals to seek appropriate treatment prior to doing couple work. For the violent partner, this may include doing either individual therapy or group therapy for batterers. Victims of domestic violence should be encouraged to develop a safety plan and seek out additional support or resources. Referrals for shelters or legal aid may be necessary.

Therapists need to examine their own beliefs and reactions to domestic violence, especially given its emotional intensity, the potential danger involved, and the effect of any prior victimization of the therapist. Moral, legal, and ethical concerns related to this issue must be well thought out by therapists in order for them to respond professionally. For example, the therapist may have a legal and ethical obligation to file a child abuse report if children witness domestic violence and it leads to emotional or physical harm. Solid supervision must be available when a beginning therapist first encounters this difficult and, sadly, all-too-common aspect of couple work.

Dealing with Infidelity

Disclosure of an affair is a frequent catalyst for couple therapy (Blow & Hartnett, 2005). However, studies attempting to determine the prevalence of affairs have found varied or unclear results ranging from 15 to 65% in heterosexual couples (Blow & Hartnett, 2005; Lawson, 1989). Research indicates that women and men participate in and understand extramarital affairs differently; women tend to engage in emotional relationships, while men engage in sexual ones, although this distinction is changing (Brown, 1991; Treas & Giesen, 2000). Gordon, Khaddouma, Baucom, and Snyder (2015) describe a treatment approach for addressing affairs that has some initial empirical support. Also, having a cross-cultural understanding of infidelity may help a therapist treat the couple more effectively (Penn, Hernandez, & Bermudez, 1997).

Another form of infidelity can occur through the Internet (Vossler, 2016). This type of infidelity is based on online activity that threatens the couple's relationship. The behaviors can include cybersex, emotional involvement with potential partners online, flirting with people in chatrooms, and secretly seeking out potential sexual partners. A key element in treating this problem is addressing the betrayal (Hertlein & Piercy, 2012). Once it is discovered, most clients feel that their trust has been breached, and this trust must be reestablished. The experience of violation is highly subjective. The person who has been involved in the behavior may minimize the problem, while the other partner usually feels threatened by the behavior.

Two components seem evident in all forms of infidelity: (1) breaking the couple's agreement regarding sexual and/or emotional exclusivity and (2) secrecy. A partner might react to an "emotional" affair as strongly as to a "physical" affair. The therapist must understand the couple's relational contract and the meaning of the breach of the contract. Therapy could be hindered by not knowing about an affair. Thus, some therapists will ask privately if an individual is engaged in an affair. The risk, however, is that the therapist will be triangulated by one of the partners into keeping the secret from the other. Many couple therapists don't believe that keeping secrets for very long is clinically or ethically responsible behavior. Some choose always to see the couple together and to disclose all information, including telephone conversations, to both partners. Clinicians should be guided by their theoretical orientation and professional or ethical judgment.

If infidelity is identified or disclosed, a crisis intervention often needs to follow. Safety issues, such as suicide risk, should be assessed and dealt with if necessary. Many couples consider separating after the disclosure of the affair. Thus, therapy may need to review some of the pragmatics of life, such as addressing where each partner will be living or sleeping over the next several days, practical care of children, and short-term finances. A structured separation (discussed later in this chapter) may be a reasonable response. After this, a clearer definition of the problem can be made to determine if individual or couple therapy should be started. It may be inappropriate to work on the couple's relationship if the affair is continuing. Individual work with a partner who is ambivalent about both marital and extramarital relationships may be necessary before a commitment to couple work is made.

Ending the affair is only the first step in this delicate restoration process. The couple is faced with a number of other tasks: They must find ways to reestablish trust in the relationship; examine the reasons for the affair, which may include both individual and relational factors; deal with the negative emotions generated by the affair; and find a way to learn from and let go of (forgive) the infidelity in order to commit to a newly defined relationship (Gordon et al., 2015). When addictive components to the infidelity process are identified, sometimes referral to group or 12-step programs can assist in the recovery process. In addition, children may have knowledge of the affair or be asked to keep it a secret for a parent, especially if the infidelity has gone on for some time. This issue might need to be explored.

Dealing with Pornography

Couple therapists will inevitably work with couples where pornography is a source of conflict. The Internet has contributed to a growth of problems in this area because it has increased access, affordability, and anonymity for those wanting to use pornography (Cooper, 1998; Griffiths, 2012).

When problems with pornography arise, it is important to assess the meaning each partner assigns to the use of pornography. Some individuals who use pornography view the behavior as normative, and do not consider it a problem. These individuals may be reluctant to address the issue, and may even view their partner as the one who has a problem. Other individuals view using pornography as contrary to their values, or believe that its use is excessive or compulsive. These individuals are more likely to be motivated to examine and change their behavior.

Pinpointing the concerns that the other partner has about their mate's pornography use is crucial. Do they view all pornography as objectionable, or is the concern specifically related to the content or frequency of the mate's pornography use? Some individuals do not object to pornography per se, and are open to it if used in the context of the couple's relationship. However, these individuals are upset that their mate uses pornography for personal sexual gratification outside the couple's relationship. Some individuals believe that a mate's use of pornography is a form of betrayal similar to an affair.

A partner's use of pornography may raise a number of other fears or concerns (Maltz & Maltz, 2010). Some individuals fear they will not be able to compete with the men and women depicted in pornography, leading them to feel sexually insecure or self-conscious. In some instances, partners may be upset with the amount of time and money that the mate spends on pornography. Partners may also lose sexual desire or respect for their mate, especially if they are disturbed by the content of the pornography (e.g., fetishes, violence toward women). This can help perpetuate a vicious cycle where the mate spends more time with pornography in response to the couple's declining sexual intimacy. Partners may fear that their children will be negatively impacted if they discover the pornography, or perhaps even that the mate will sexually abuse the children.

A potential challenge in addressing pornography is defining whether the individual has a problem with pornography that deserves treatment. Is the individual's use of pornography normative, or is there evidence that it is excessive or problematic in other ways? Answering this question will require that you look at the frequency, content, and function of the pornography use. Also, does the individual continue to use pornography despite potential negative consequences both inside and outside the relationship? Determining the extent to which a problem exists is further complicated by the fact that the therapist's own views on pornography may inform the assessment. For example, therapists who object to pornography may be more likely to view the individual's use of pornography as problematic (Ayers & Haddock, 2009). Therefore, it is important that therapists examine their own values regarding pornography and be aware of how these views may impact the therapeutic process.

Even if you conclude that the partner's use of pornography is not problematic individually, it still presents a problem relationally for the couple. In these situations, you will need to help the couple negotiate a contract or agreement around this behavior that is agreeable to both. Couples need to negotiate expectations on a number of different issues in their relationship (e.g., number of children, gender roles, division of household chores), with pornography use being another example. During this process, you can help the individuals to share what the pornography use means to them, including the values, beliefs, fears, or experiences that inform each person's perspective. For example, a woman who has experienced previous sexual trauma may disclose that she finds pornography highly objectionable because she believes it is another form of sexual exploitation like sexual abuse. Hopefully, the couple will be able to negotiate an agreement or understanding that is acceptable to both, although the possibility always exists that the issue is a deal-breaker for the relationship.

If the individual's use of pornography is problematic and there is agreement that it needs to be stopped, then a number of different strategies can be used. Maltz and Maltz (2010) outline six basic action steps that need to be taken for treating a porn addiction. First, individuals need to tell someone about their problem with pornography to break the cycle of "isolation, secrecy, and denial." Second, individuals need to seek out some form of treatment for the problem. A variety of options exist, including individual counseling, couple therapy, or doing group therapy (e.g., 12-step programs or Smart Recovery). Third, individuals need to create a porn-free environment. This requires removing all pornographic materials from the home, as well as taking steps to keep it out in the future, such as installing computer programs that restrict access to pornographic sites. Fourth, individuals should seek out a network of people to call upon for 24-hour support and accountability. Fifth, learning how to care for one's emotional and physical needs is an important step in recovery, especially for those who use pornography to cope with negative emotions. Finally, individuals need to examine and change their attitudes regarding sex. Maltz and Maltz recommend that individuals develop an intimacy-based approach to sex, which focuses more on developing a loving connection with one's partner rather than focusing exclusively on sexual gratification from viewing pornography.

Couples often need help in rebuilding their relationship if one of the partners struggles with pornography (Zitzman & Butler, 2005). Rebuilding trust is an important element of the work, which is facilitated by encouraging open communication. However, shame over the use of pornography may be a barrier to open communication. Trust is also built by seeing the individual make an effort and progress in addressing the pornography problem. Partners may benefit from education about the potentially addictive dynamics that can emerge around pornography use. This may help partners show more compassion and support for their mate, especially if they are able to separate the problem from themselves and avoid personalizing it (e.g., "He uses pornography because he does not find me sexually attractive"). Couples also need reassurance that they can successfully work through the problem, and may even grow stronger as a couple by learning new insights and skills for the relationship.

Sexual Difficulties

In our role as supervisors, we've found that it's common for beginning therapists to ignore the sexual aspect of their clients' relationships. The new therapist often assumes that because the couple doesn't mention problems with sex their sexual relationship is fine. Making such an assumption is a mistake. Many couples that seek therapy are coping with sexual problems and may be waiting for you to ask about the issue because they're too embarrassed or uncomfortable to introduce the concern themselves. A good question to ask when you start your assessment of a couple's sexual relationship is "How does (presenting problem) affect your sexual relationship?" The more comfortable you appear during this assessment, the more likely it is they will reveal the details of their problems (Weeks, Odell, & Methven, 2005).

When sexual problems become a focus of your assessment, you should take a sexual history. Ideally, it's best to explore this history with the couple together and separately. The onset and context of a sexual complaint should be explored so that contributing factors can be clarified. For example, if a man states that he has little desire for sex with his partner, it's important to know if it's a primary problem (no history of sexual desire) or a secondary problem (positive history of sexual desire). In addition, does your client experience feelings of desire in some situations (e.g., during masturbation), or is desire completely absent? Of course, the therapist needs to know if the partners have undergone medical examinations to rule out or clarify any biological causes. It's also important to check if clients are using alcohol, drugs, or prescribed medications that might interfere with sexual functioning. The construction of a sexual genogram (Belous, Timm, Chee, & Whitehead, 2012; Hof & Berman, 1986) can also be helpful during assessment and treatment to understand sexual beliefs, behaviors, and patterns from each partner's family of origin.

Once you've completed your assessment of a couple's relationship, you'll have some indication of the severity of their sexual issues. For most couples, their sexual problems will comingle with other relationship problems, such as commitment, communication, and conflict management. For these couples, improving the couple's relationship can lead to an improvement in the couple's sex life. For other couples, however, their sexual difficulties will require more significant attention and treatment. Because sex therapy is an advanced skill, you will need to decide if it fits in your scope of competence. If it doesn't, you

can refer the couple to a therapist certified by the American Association of Sexuality Educators, Counselors and Therapists (AASECT). At
the very least, it's important for you to have a basic understanding of
sexual anatomy and physiology, which can usually be acquired in an
introductory human sexuality course or in most family therapy training programs.

Structured Separations

Therapists should also be familiar with how to facilitate a structured
separation with couples. Of course, structured separations can be
used with couples obviously moving toward ending their relationship.
Orderly separations are likely to be less destructive than separations
that are disorderly and not anticipated (Ahrons, 1994). However, structured separations can also be used as a possible couple therapy intervention. A structured separation can be helpful for highly conflictual
couples that need a cooling-off period to interrupt a repeated negative
interaction cycle. Some partners will view any separation as "the end
of the marriage" and will have great difficulty with the notion that
some structured time apart may be useful. Establishing clear boundaries and negotiating times for contact will be helpful in lowering their
anxiety.

When doing a structured separation, expectations regarding visits,
telephone contacts, dating, parenting, financial and household responsibilities, and therapy need to be discussed. Specificity in establishing
frequency of contacts and who shall initiate the contacts might be necessary. When used as a therapy intervention, Granvold (1983) recommends that a structured separation be done initially for 6 weeks, evaluated, and extended as needed.

Evaluating the style and severity of conflict is necessary when
working with couples who are separating. If the conflict is severe and
chaotic, then the couple should have limited contact with one another
and possibly be instructed not to try to solve problems outside therapy, at least initially. If they're less conflicted and able to spend time
together in a congenial atmosphere without quickly escalating into difficulties, then they might gradually increase the amount of time they
spend together. Spouses need to be able to adhere to the rules of the
separation agreement and reestablish trust in each other. If boundaries
are violated, then that trust becomes difficult to create. Consequently,
rules and boundaries should be fair and realistic for both parties.

Nichols (1988) identifies three tasks for the couple involved in the
decision to divorce and these same tasks seem appropriate when working with a structured separation:

1. Accepting the reality that a separation/divorce is occurring (regardless of how or by whom the decision is made).
2. Coping with the initial emotional/psychological reactions.
3. Performing the initial planning for the contemplated actions.

The therapist can assist the couple in orchestrating the separation and accomplishing the tasks identified by Nichols.

It is typical for one partner to be asking for a separation while the other desires to stay together and "work things out." A prelude to a prolonged physical separation can be one of the spouses taking a vacation or even structuring time apart. However, if one of the spouses is adamant about insisting upon a separation, then the therapist can be a helpful mediator. The therapist must be sensitive to each person's concerns and avoid developing a coalition with one of the partners.

Divorce Therapy

For some couples, a structured separation is a prelude to divorce. The decision to divorce will lead most couples to terminate couple therapy given that they view marital counseling as a means to preserving rather than ending a marriage. However, some couples will seek out help during or after a divorce. The large majority of these couples do so because they want to maintain or develop an effective coparenting relationship after the divorce.

Divorce does not necessarily mean the end of conflict between two partners. One reason that divorce therapy can be helpful is to reduce the level of conflict between the couple. Many of the strategies that therapists use in couple therapy can be applied to divorce therapy (Lebow, 2015). For example, many couples benefit from learning structured communication skills like the speaker–listener technique (Markman et al., 2010). It may also be helpful to change the negative attributions that individuals may hold toward their partners. High-conflict couples may need to learn strategies for managing anger and how to exit escalating interactions. More psychologically minded couples may be capable of exploring why their marriage failed, resolve past hurts, and gain new insights that will help them in future relationships.

Divorce therapy may also need to address how the couple's conflict and divorce are impacting their children. Parents need to be aware that children may blame themselves for the divorce, or fear that the non-custodial parent will stop loving them. It will be important to reduce the children's exposure to the couple's conflict. Couples also need to avoid triangulating the children by making negative comments about the other parent, creating distressing loyalty conflicts for the children.

Divorce is both an emotional and a legal process. Ideally, couples will be able to reach agreement regarding how to divide their possessions, allocate their assets, and share custody of their children. Divorce mediation is a proven approach to help couples reach agreements without involving the courts. Therefore, couples seeking divorce should be encouraged to use this pathway for developing a mutual agreement. Unfortunately, some couples cannot reach an agreement and must rely on the courts to make decisions on important matters like child custody. Involving the courts and potentially aggressive lawyers can make the divorce highly contentious, complicating the therapeutic process.

Premarital Counseling

In contrast to couples seeking help with divorce, therapists will occasionally encounter engaged couples wanting premarital counseling. You should assess why couples are seeking out premarital counseling because it may impact how you work with the couple. Some couples want therapy because their relationship is in distress, possibly even threatening the couple's plans to marry. For these couples, therapy closely resembles the work that a therapist might do with other distressed couples that are married or are in a committed relationship. Other couples seek out premarital counseling on their own initiative to learn new insights or skills to give their future marriage the best chance of success, but are not experiencing serious problems. A third group of couples come because they are required to do some form of premarital counseling. These are typically couples that want a religious wedding, and are required by their place of worship to obtain marriage preparation. For the latter two sets of couples, the focus of the work is primarily on prevention rather than treating relationship distress. This section examines how to work with couples where the focus is more on prevention.

One popular approach to marriage preparation is to administer a premarital inventory to the couple. The inventories ask questions about several topics that may impact future marital success, such as communication, conflict resolution, managing finances, sexuality, extended family, personality, and other areas. The inventories can be invaluable in helping couples uncover unstated expectations for the relationship. Premarital inventories are used to help couples explore and discuss their relationship; they are not used as a test to evaluate whether they should marry or not.

Three of the most popular premarital inventories are FOCCUS (Williams, 2016; *www.foccusinc.com*), PREPARE (Olson & Olson,

2016; *www.prepare-enrich.com*), and RELATE (Loyer-Carlson, 2016; *www.relateinstitute.com*). All three instruments have been evaluated through research and have empirical support (Larson, Newell, Topham, & Nichols, 2002). Both FOCCUS and PREPARE require that a trained facilitator administer and go over the results with the couple. RELATE, however, does not require a facilitator. Couples can take RELATE online, and are then sent the results directly. If you anticipate doing a lot of work with premarital couples, you may want to become trained in using FOCCUS or PREPARE so you can get referrals through their listing of trained facilitators. However, if you do premarital counseling infrequently, then the most expedient option would be to have couples take RELATE on their own and share the results with you.

The inventory will provide you and the couple with a wealth of information about the relationship. When reviewing the results, you may need to be selective about what questions are discussed, especially if there are a limited number of sessions devoted to reviewing the inventory results. It is important that you highlight the couple's strengths in addition to possible growth areas. Couples also need to be reassured that all couples have areas where they can grow and improve. You may be able to provide the couple with some initial guidance on how to address these growth areas. Sometimes the issues or concerns that are uncovered may need to be delved into more deeply through therapy. You should also pay special attention to inventory items that are possible red flags for serious issues, such as relationship aggression, mental illness, or substance abuse. Further assessment may be required to determine if these are significant concerns that must be addressed.

Another popular approach for working with premarital couples is to teach them effective communication and conflict resolution skills. Several programs have been developed that teach couples these skills. Relationship Enhancement (Scuka, 2016), Couple Communication (Miller & Sherrard, 1999), and PREP (Tonelli, Pregulman, & Markman, 2016) are three examples of programs with strong empirical support. PREP is the most comprehensive in that it explores other elements of the couple's relationship (sexuality, friendship, values) besides communication and conflict resolution skills. PREP also has the strongest empirical support in terms of long-term follow-up of outcomes. Therapists working with premarital couples can draw upon these programs or other training to provide skills in these areas.

Beyond teaching couples communication and conflict resolution skills, you may also want to provide couples psychoeducation about marriage in other areas. For example, couples may benefit from learning about the five love languages (Chapman, 2015), which describes the different ways that individuals like to be shown love. You can help the couple identify each partner's preferred language, and encourage each to speak the other's love language. PREP (Markman et al., 2010) also emphasizes the importance of couples maintaining a strong commitment to their relationship, and discusses factors that may weaken or strengthen a couple's commitment. For example, the PREP program recommends that couples make the relationship a priority and continue to do the things that initially led them to dedicate their lives to one another.

Some premarital counselors will assess each partner's personality or temperament using various approaches (e.g., Myers–Briggs, Big Five, or Taylor–Johnson Temperament Analysis). This can be a fruitful area to explore, especially if differences in personality are likely to cause misunderstanding or conflict for the couple. Learning acceptance around these differences will be important for the couple's future marital success (Christensen et al., 2015; Gottman & Gottman, 2015).

Exploring how the couple's families of origin could influence the relationship can also be helpful. For example, doing a genogram with each partner may uncover possible transgenerational themes, patterns, or expectations that will impact the couple's dynamics. The premarital inventories discussed earlier also have questions that may provide a springboard for exploring family-of-origin factors.

Some couples will come to premarital counseling with important cultural and religious differences. The potential impact of these differences, both positive and negative, needs to be explored. For example, a couple may have different expectations around gender roles based on their cultural or religious socialization. Furthermore, cultural or religious differences may also impact the couple's relationship with their extended families. For instance, some individuals experience a lack of acceptance from their extended family for marrying someone outside their religion or race/ethnicity.

Gay and Lesbian Couples

Most of the information in this chapter applies to any couple. However, there are some important differences when working with gay and lesbian couples. Although same-sex couples may come to therapy for issues common to all couples, therapists should also pay attention to issues such as minority stress, relational ambiguity, and the lack of social support that same-sex couples frequently face (Green & Mitchell, 2015).

First, you need to consider the stress encountered by gay and lesbian couples due to prejudice, discrimination, and marginalization in our culture. Although there has been increasing acceptance of lesbian, gay, bisexual, and transgender (LGBT) individuals, there is still a large segment of society that holds negative views of gays and lesbians and believes same-sex relationships are wrong. Some LGBT individuals will experience hate crimes and commonly encounter verbal harassment for their sexual orientation (Herek, 2008). Others may tolerate LGBT individuals, but are not fully accepting of them. This can lead to LGBT individuals feeling invisible or marginalized. LGBT individuals have also historically faced discrimination in several forms. For example, until recently, many same-sex couples did not have the ability to get legally married. Despite gains in this area, LGBT individuals are still vulnerable to job and housing discrimination (Herek, 2008).

LGBT individuals may internalize society's negative views about their sexual orientation. External prejudice and discrimination, in combination with internalized negative views, creates *minority stress*. Minority stress can create problems for same-sex couples in various ways, such as creating ambivalence about committing to a same-sex relationship or displacing one's frustration about external prejudice and discrimination onto the partner. For couples struggling with minority stress, building greater self-acceptance will be key.

A second consideration is *relational ambiguity,* which sometimes exists in gay and lesbian relationships. Issues over how "out" to be with others can impact a couple's ability to publicly express their commitment to one another. Another challenge in defining couple identity is the dearth of relationship role models. Since almost all gays and lesbians grew up in homes dominated by heterosexual relationships, they have few models to draw from in defining roles and responsibilities in their relationships. You can play a helpful role in assisting gay and lesbian couples to clarify their identity as a couple.

A third consideration is examining the same-sex couple's level of *social support*. For example, families of origin may shun, distance, ignore, or attack couples attempting to identify and honestly express their commitment, which can leave same-sex couples isolated from broader family ties. As a result, some same-sex couples build a "family of choice" through friendships rather than family members. Helping build a cohesive social support system will be important for some same-sex couples coming to therapy.

Green and Mitchell (2015) consider the therapist's personal comfort with love, intimacy, and sexuality in gay and lesbian relationships to be the most important prerequisite for helping same-sex couples.

Personal comfort means appreciation for gay and lesbian culture, the ability to listen empathically to the experiences of gay and lesbian couples, and the willingness to talk about the range of issues that these couples bring to therapy, including sexual difficulties. Therapy with same-sex couples is similar to working cross-culturally with any client: it requires respect for differences and openness to new learning.

The following case example demonstrates that therapy with a lesbian couple, like other family therapy, requires attention to individual, interactional, intergenerational, and community systems.

Susan and Brenda, both in their late 20s, have been living together for the past 2 years. Presenting problems include constant arguing, frequent conflict, and a lack of intimacy. They say they fight about virtually everything from household responsibilities to money, sex, and how to spend their leisure time. Both report being very dissatisfied with the relationship. The arguments have led to several threats of separation. Although neither reports any physical abuse, there have been threats of physical harm, and Brenda reports being afraid of Susan.

The arguments can generate a great deal of emotion, including anger, fear, and rage. Susan says that Brenda is not committed enough to the relationship, that she won't engage enough in discussions about the relationship, and that she withdraws from contact and closeness. Brenda feels intimidated, bullied, criticized, and threatened by Susan. She sees Susan as being unhappy with whatever she does, and feels that she's not ever good enough to meet Susan's high expectations. They do report periods in which they get along well and enjoy each other's company, as long as they keep things superficial.

Susan works full time as an elementary school teacher. The job is demanding and she likes it very much. She says that she "gives to others all day long" and wants to be given to at home sometimes. She comes from a family of three children, and is not particularly close to her younger brother and sister. She describes her mother as "good, caring, and warm." Her father physically and verbally abused her. She says that she "still hates him" and is frightened that when she gets angry she becomes just like him.

Brenda works part time as a reference librarian. She is an only child and spends much of her time with her ailing grandmother. She has a history of depression and is being treated with antidepressants. During the couple therapy, her depressive symptoms worsened and she felt so overwhelmed that she wasn't able to function in the relationship. She was referred to individual therapy, which proved quite helpful. Brenda feels insecure in the relationship with Susan. She reports having felt pressure from Susan to marry.

Susan and Brenda feel frustrated with each other. There has been a lot of blaming and protection of their own feelings. They say they are both committed to the relationship but can't handle the conflict. Susan is active in the gay and lesbian community and has been out since she was a teenager. Brenda is out with some close friends but keeps her sexual orientation a secret from her family and at work, which frustrates Susan.

The couple will benefit from discussing their perspectives on being out. It also will be helpful to look at how out they are to their respective families, friends, and work colleagues. Defining roles and expectations within the relationship will be another area of focus. The therapist should remain sensitive to their differences and help to mitigate them. Treatment of this couple will need to focus on managing conflict more effectively, including interrupting their negative interactional cycle. Personal and family histories will prove valuable in evaluating their style of conflict and developing some ways to contain and manage it.

WHEN COUPLE THERAPY MIGHT NOT WORK

Couple therapy is not always the therapy of choice. Although therapists might differ in how they decide for or against couple work, several indicators point to the limits of conjoint sessions. One might be the individual pathology presented by one of the partners. For example, severe depression, psychotic thought processes, or active alcoholism or drug abuse in one partner, or explosive violence between the couple, are potential warning signs that couple therapy might be inappropriate. One way to assess whether presenting problems are conducive to conjoint sessions is to determine if a connection or therapeutic relationship can be made between the therapist and the individual or system. If the therapist fails to develop some structure around the couple's interactions, if one of the pair comes drunk or high to the session, or if an individual's affect so influences the session that it severely hinders any interventions, then the therapist would be wise to separate the couple. A referral of one or both of the partners to other resources before embarking on conjoint therapy may also be considered.

Sometimes there is wisdom in using individual therapy, or individual group sessions, along with couple therapy. Simultaneously working at an individual and systemic level is merited in complicated cases. The major limits, of course, are the financial and therapeutic resources available for the work to be done. Prioritizing and delineating an overall treatment plan that shows therapy can be provided from different and complementary system levels (biological, individual, relational, cultural) often helps the couple engage in the tough work of therapy. It is important that you review assessment information and treatment planning ideas (Chapter 5) when feeling stuck with a couple.

CONCLUSION

Couple therapy can present several challenges for the beginning therapist. Maintaining a balanced relationship with both partners, building
a commitment to therapy if the couple has divergent goals about the
relationship, identifying the couple's cycle, and managing the couple's
affect are some of the tasks required to do effective therapy with couples. Domestic violence and infidelity can also present challenges in
doing couple therapy, and in some cases may be a contraindication
for couple work. However, couple therapy also offers rewards. Given
the importance that most people place on having a loving and satisfying intimate relationship with another human being, helping couples
achieve this goal is especially rewarding.

CHAPTER 10

When a Family Member Has a Mental Illness

"I'm convinced there is nothing we cannot cure." One of the authors heard this comment from a senior therapist who had just returned from an upbeat training seminar in the 1980s. At that time, the author was an inexperienced student therapist. Nevertheless, she questioned the possibility of "cure" for many of the serious and long-standing struggles her clients faced.

Many years later, we have learned that some mental illnesses are intractable despite our best treatment efforts; they are chronic illnesses whose symptoms wax and wane over the life cycle. Families with a mentally ill member may appear at your office door after years of struggle. The illness may have consumed the family's resources and the individual's identity. Nevertheless, family therapists have much to offer these overextended families. Regardless of the diagnosis, a number of common factors influence families with mentally ill members. Loneliness, poverty, lack of social support, and increased stressful life events can make the patient or family's situation worse. Family discord, including frequent hostility, conflict, and overinvolvement, can also hurt clients. In contrast, a strong sense of family identity, closeness, and shared values and beliefs can strengthen and protect families. While keeping these relational qualities in mind, family therapists must also know about individual assessment and diagnosis when working with families of the mentally ill. Increasingly, research has shown that an individual with a mental illness can worsen or improve depending on environmental factors such as family cohesion or family stress.

INDIVIDUAL AND FAMILY CONCEPTS

In the last 50 years, significant gains have been made in describing mental disorders and discovering effective treatments. The National Institute of Mental Health (NIMH) has sponsored important research examining mental disorders that affect millions of people and suggested major changes to how psychopathology is conceptualized. Instead of using the *Diagnostic and Statistical Manual of Mental Disorders* (DSM), the NIMH leadership has proposed a dimensional approach that examines the full range of psychological variation from normal to abnormal. The Research Domain Criteria (RDoC) include biological sources, developmental trajectories, and environmental effects (National Institute of Mental Health, 2016). Fundamental assumptions guide the changes being made. Historically, DSM and our understanding of mental illness was guided by what patients said (symptoms) and what we observed (signs) during the clinical interview. Recently, the growing influence of knowledge about biological etiologies has helped therapists recognize that waiting for signs and symptoms to appear is often too late. New advances are being made in neuroscience and genetics that help explain the biological roots of some mental illnesses.

If someone has colon cancer, physicians try to identify the illness and treat it before it has spread. Similarly, new models of mental illness focus on preventing the illness or detecting mental illness before it has reified. Recognizing that mental disorders are developmental disorders has led to a new interest in prevention as opposed to simply treating mental disorders that often become chronic illnesses (Insel, 2014). In addition, many mental disorders are brain disorders that change over the life cycle (Insel & Quirion, 2005). Also, they are genetic disorders that are influenced by the environment (epigenetics). Both the onset and course of a mental illness can be strongly influenced by environmental influences. These environmental influences can ultimately change the genome so that mental health researchers today speak of "epigenetic inheritance"—changes created by the environment of the parent's genome that the parent passes down to his or her child.

Since most mental disorders start between childhood and early adulthood, recognizing the influence of the family has never been more important. Family therapists have known for years that high expressed emotion in families can worsen schizophrenic symptoms (McFarlane, Dixon, Lukens, & Lucksted, 2003). Children who experience multiple traumatic events in their upbringing are particularly vulnerable to both mental and physical health problems. The longitudinal ACE (Adverse

Childhood Experience) Study indicates the strong association between household dysfunction and later life problems. For example, an ACE score above 6 is associated with a 30-fold increase in attempted suicide (Felitti et al., 1998). Today, mental health professionals from many disciplines are interested in how the family can ameliorate or worsen the risk of mental illness (van der Kolk, 1997).

Other evidence suggests that health services should focus on prevention and early intervention. Research at the Harvard Center on the Developing Child suggests that toxic stress can permanently damage children's developing brains and that families can buffer their children from the destructive effects of toxic stress (Patterson & Vakili, 2014; Shonkoff & Garner, 2012). The multidisciplinary, developmental research on toxic stress shows how early experiences and environmental influences such as good parenting can have lasting effects on a person's capacity to respond to stress throughout his or her life. Long after childhood is over, the effects of toxic stress during childhood can influence an adult's life trajectory including his or her risk of developing mental illness.

In addition, health researchers have begun to use a metric called a DALY (disability adjusted life year) to measure the impact of mental illness on overall health. DALYs reflect the years of life lost due to an illness including mental illnesses and the years lived with a disability. Research has shown that depression is the fifth leading cause of poor health and that anxiety ranks higher than breast cancer as a cause of suffering (Lozano et al., 2012; Patel, Chisholm, Dua, Laxminarayan, & Medina-Mora, 2015). Thus, there is a growing worldwide recognition of the destructive impact of chronic mental illness. In fact, the World Health Organization (WHO; 2010) has created a low-cost program, MH Gap, to treat common mental illnesses in countries that have no government funding or private insurance to treat mental illness.

A burgeoning body of literature examines research on effective treatments for individual disorders. Cognitive-behavioral treatments, interpersonal treatments, and family-based treatments have been used in field trials for specific disorders. There is a growing awareness that one treatment might not work for every problem and initiatives to match specific therapies with certain disorders. In addition, there is an increasing focus on prevention, especially for children and adolescents. As we learn more about gene–environment interactions, clinicians hope that early interventions, at the onset of mental health problems, can protect the child and keep the illness from beginning or worsening.

In addition to the research on talk therapies, there is a significant literature on the effectiveness of pharmacological treatments

(Patterson, Albala, McCahill, & Edwards, 2010). New medications are coming out almost daily to treat disorders that were once considered untreatable. At the same time, there is a growing awareness that most psychotropic medications are not a miracle cure. At best, they work for some patients some of the time. Because of their negative side effects such as dry mouth or constipation, taking the medications as prescribed only happens about 50% of the time (Bulloch & Patten, 2009). Other research examines how an individual's genetics may influence his or her response to psychotropic medication (Brown & Bussell, 2011; Miller, Rose, & Van Amburgh, 2016). Precision medicine suggests that physicians use specific treatment protocols that are matched to the patient's genome. Matching the treatment to the patient's genome has occurred most frequently in cancer treatments thus far but will increasingly be used to create treatment regimens for mental illnesses in the future.

We know that mental illness can run in families and that transmission may not only result from dysfunctional family patterns, but also involve biological determinants. More often than not, when one mentions family history in a psychological assessment, it refers to genetic transmission. Individual diagnosticians are very interested in relatives both in the present and past who have a history of mental illness because this suggests genetic transmission in the patient.

Research on genetic transmission was enlightening news to families of the mentally ill. After years of subtly being blamed for their family members' problems through concepts such as the "schizophrenogenic mother," families were both saddened and relieved to learn the illness has a genetic component. While these discoveries relieve the family of guilt and responsibility for "causing" mental illnesses, they also can transmit some discouraging news about prognosis and transmission to future generations.

Families will be interested to know that while they did not cause mental illness in one member, they can influence its course. Research on "expressed emotion" and "communication deviance" in schizophrenic families demonstrates that family qualities like overinvolvement, hostility, and critical attitudes can influence the schizophrenic family member to relapse. More recently, emotional dysregulation, hostility, and conflict in the family have been examined in relation to depression, dementia, schizophrenia, and a variety of other disorders (Beach & Jones, 2002; Gross, 2007; Miklowitz, 2008; Peris & Miklowitz, 2015). This research has demonstrated the powerful impact family behaviors and mood can have on individual members and their illnesses.

Family therapists can consider psychiatric consultation for the family member with mental illness. The consultation can provide information that the therapist can integrate into the overall treatment plan. In addition, the psychiatrist might recommend psychotropic medication to treat the symptoms of the individual's mental disorder.

Beginning family therapists can glean useful therapeutic tools from the world of individual diagnosis and simultaneously incorporate the strengths of family therapy. Therapists do not need to choose one ideological position to the exclusion of all other perspectives. Beginning family therapists can use multiple sources of information and perspectives to create an optimal treatment plan for their clients.

Even if you recognize the key concepts of individual diagnosis or family process, it can still be overwhelming to sort out the distinctions when you are doing assessment. A suicidal teenager who is not sleeping or eating because she is upset about her grades and her parents' fighting may be hard to identify when her parents bring her to see you "because she is just not motivated in school." In fact, a common struggle that new therapists face is sorting through the family's view of the problems, the referral source's views, and individual members' views. Discernment about assessment and treatment can be especially challenging if you are unfamiliar with individual diagnostic criteria or if you hold personal allegiance to one school of therapy.

One of the most common struggles we observe in new students is their ready acceptance of the problem definition, especially if an authority such as a parent, school principal, or physician refers the family for a specific, detailed problem. In addition, if a couple or family comes for therapy and defines the problem relationally, the therapist may be reluctant to consider individual diagnoses. In like manner, if the family describes the problem as a problem with an individual, the therapist may be averse to exploring family dynamics. We observed a diagnostic challenge when a couple came for marital therapy because they were fighting. The wife's complaints included the husband's disorganization, inability to be on time, inability to keep a job, and explosive anger. While the therapist started working on conflict resolution and communication skills with the couple, he also noted the husband's chaotic life. The husband was never on time to the sessions and on several occasions forgot the session entirely, even when the wife reminded him the day before. After a while, the therapist began to wonder if the husband had ADHD. While maintaining a focus on the couple, the therapist gently explored the husband's learning history more carefully. Ultimately, a diagnosis of adult ADHD resulted in dramatic changes in the husband's life, the wife's life, and the marriage.

INDIVIDUAL DIAGNOSIS IN A FAMILY CONTEXT

Epidemiological research suggests that more than 50% of the population will have a mental disorder at some time in their lives (Kessler, Berglund, et al., 2005). Although this statistic includes a problem as simple as an adjustment disorder, the frequency of mental health problems suggests the need for effective treatments. While most people who have a mental health problem improve spontaneously and without treatment, there is a small minority, approximately 14%, who have recurring episodes of mental illness, often at least three major episodes during their lifetime. Researchers and clinicians also note that one patient frequently has several problems (comorbidity). Epidemiological data and clinical experience suggest that mental problems of various durations and intensities are frequent, debilitating, and painful for both the person and his or her family (Kessler, Eaton, Wittchen, & Zhao, 1994; Wang et al., 2005).

People often have mental health problems that do not meet DSM diagnostic criteria. The individual diagnostician who closely follows DSM diagnostic outlines risks overlooking serious problems that do not fit neatly into a category. This poses a more serious risk for children and adolescents because their problems fit DSM criteria less frequently than adult disorders and can be strongly influenced by developmental issues that might be overlooked by the diagnostician completing a DSM symptom checklist. A contextual, holistic approach to mental health problems can correct for many of these weaknesses.

The most common DSM disorders are mood disorders (such as depression), anxiety disorders, and substance abuse problems. Frequently, a patient suffers from two or more of these disorders simultaneously. While everyone suffers from depression or anxiety at some time in his or her life, illness does not refer to these everyday problems but to known, recognizable syndromes. Specificity of symptoms, duration, and intensity distinguish a syndrome from the common problems of living.

However, clinicians and patients often find the distinction between a syndrome and everyday problems unilluminating. A patient who is going through a divorce, working as a single parent, and worried about losing her job doesn't care whether she meets four or five criteria for major depression to justify this diagnosis. She just wants to feel better. In addition, patients with non-DSM problems such as chronic pain, marital problems, or physical illness simply want relief, not a diagnosis.

As a result, clinicians primarily use DSM criteria when it comes to filling out forms or for reimbursement purposes. However, when doing treatment, they focus on the most comprehensive view of the problem(s), which often expands beyond a DSM diagnosis. While the vast majority of family therapists are trained in individual diagnosis (Denton et al., 1997), they may initially disregard individual symptom assessment in order to obtain a more holistic understanding of the patient and his or her family's problems, and to briefly enter the patient's world with as few distractions as possible (Beach & Gupta, 2005). As one psychiatrist explained, "It is not a person as an isolated and self-contained entity that one is studying, or can study, but a situation, an interpersonal situation, composed of two or more people" (Sullivan, 1953, p. 245). Similarly, family therapists tend to conceptualize an individual case through the lens of relationships.

The practical, ethical, and logistical dilemmas of using both individual and family diagnosis have never been clearly delineated. Family therapists have discussed some of the inherent strengths and weaknesses of combining individual and family approaches in assessment and treatment (Beach & Jones, 2002; Beach et al., 2006). For the most part, the family therapist has been left the task of working out the nuances of integrating these approaches. Using diagnostic taxonomy to describe mental health issues while acknowledging the context wherein these issues take place can prove challenging for professionals (Strong, 2015). How can a family therapist effectively integrate information on individual diagnosis and still maintain a systemic, holistic perspective? Perhaps this can be done by maintaining an attitude of openness—a willingness to consider the possibility of individual diagnosis while still maintaining the strengths of a family therapy approach.

Research on health and illness suggests that loneliness, together with lack of social support, is one of the strongest predictors of decline and further suffering, regardless of the problem. Loss of an important relationship through death, divorce, or other means is rated as one of the most significant stressors a person can experience. Family therapy's strength is its recognition of the importance of these relationships, regardless of the other mental health problems an individual experiences. Being isolated and having no social support can signal problems.

Research on bipolar illness and other affective disorders suggests that while individual symptoms can be recognized and perhaps treated with medication or by other means, the symptomatic person still desires the support and love of family (Beach & Gupta, 2006; Clarkin & Glick, 1992; Fredman, Baucom, Boeding, & Miklowitz, 2015; Miklowitz, 2008). In addition, the individual can be either hurt or helped by familial responses. A family therapist can successfully combine, in his or her work, the basic tenets of systemic thinking with careful attention to individual problems and the clinical literature on both systemic and individual perspectives.

Clearly, the therapist must pay attention to the symptoms of the identified patient as well as to the characteristics and symptoms of other family members. Questions to think about include the following: "Does this person have a known, recognizable cluster of symptoms that meet specific diagnostic criteria?" "Should this individual receive treatment for these symptoms, in addition to any other therapeutic goals?" "Do I, as the therapist, have the skills and knowledge to recognize and treat this problem, or should I consider referral to someone else?"

Increasingly, therapists are using psychiatric screening instrument to assess common disorders such as depression or anxiety. These brief, valid instruments work well in the busy office of a primary care physician or a community clinic overwhelmed with patients. But they are only a first step. Besides using some common screening instruments (see Appendix), the therapist should do a more comprehensive evaluation of both the individual and his or her family. Screening instruments can help ensure that the therapist does not miss important symptoms and can sometimes help the client feel hope when he or she realizes that there is a name and description for what he or she has been feeling.

While most family therapists can recognize symptoms of common problems such as depression or anxiety, they may not spot less frequently occurring syndromes. For example, family therapy students may be unfamiliar with signs indicating Tourette's syndrome or trichotillomania. There are several remedies for this situation.

First, family therapists should make every effort to keep up with the literature on individual diagnoses. In addition, they can maintain an attitude of curiosity and alertness to clinical situations they haven't encountered in the past. Frequent reflection on one's clinical caseload and increased supervision for beginning therapists invite further exploration of clinically unfamiliar situations. When the unusual happens, the therapist can begin by consulting colleagues and reading.

Referral to a psychotherapist with expertise in a specific diagnosis is always an option. For example, many family therapists will not treat a family whose adolescent has an eating disorder unless they have significant previous experience in that area. They recognize the severity of the condition, and while they may continue family therapy for other issues or related problems, they make sure the adolescent gets an appropriate referral to a psychotherapist or physician who knows how to treat eating disorders.

Finally, family therapists need to be aware of individual diagnoses because the healthcare system demands it. As more therapists are paid by the government or other large payer organizations, they will be expected to diagnose and plan treatment according to commonly accepted protocols. Even when family therapy is a common and highly regarded treatment, familiarity with individual diagnoses will be essential to obtain treatment authorization and fulfill insurance form requirements.

While it would be impossible to describe every individual problem and its treatment here, the rest of this chapter focuses on four of the most common individual disorders: depression, anxiety, substance abuse, and impulse control. These disorders are the most commonly occurring ones in the general population, and often disorders start at a young age (see Table 10.1). At times, these problems are described as discrete entities, but family therapists recognize that even these disorders are best viewed in a holistic context. A contextual approach makes room for consideration of primary symptoms, other social and emotional problems, and the family's extant strengths and deficits.

TABLE 10.1. Most Common Mental Health Disorders.

Disorder	Prevalence	Mean age at onset
Anxiety	28%	11 years
Impulse (ODD, CD, ADHD)	25%	11 years
Mood	21%	30 years
Substance	15%	20 years
All disorders	46%	½ by 14 years; ¾ by 24 years

Do patients seek help and when?

Disorder	Proportion that ever seek help	How long after onset of symptoms
Anxiety	60%	9–23 years
Mood	88%	6–8 years
Impulse	40%	
Substance	40%	

Predictors of *not* seeking treatment: early age of onset, elderly, male, married, low education, minority.

Who receives the most treatment? Patients with comorbid illnesses—7% of population with three or more diagnoses.

Predictors of never getting treatment: elderly, minorities, poor, no insurance, rural patients.

Note. Data from Kessler, Berglund, et al. (2005) and Kessler, Chiu, Demler, and Walters (2005).

Two other disorders that we do not describe in much detail but deserve mentioning are psychotic disorders and somatization disorders. While being able to treat patients with psychotic disorders is a critical skill, these treatments are not covered in detail in this book because psychoses are less common than other disorders. Nevertheless, we recommend that all family therapists recognize the hallmark signs and symptoms of psychoses: hallucinations, delusions, loss of interest in life, changing speech patterns, and a flat mood. Hallucinations refer to sensory experiences, and the most common hallucination is hearing voices. Delusions refer to false beliefs, for instance, believing that your neighbor has implanted a radio in your head. If you are treating any family members that complain of these symptoms or have other types of odd thinking, it is time to refer the patient to a psychiatrist for a more careful evaluation. (Suggestions for working with physicians and more information about psychoses and other major mental illnesses are described in *The Therapist's Guide to Psychopharmacology* [Peterson, Albala, McCahill, & Edwards, 2010].)

Referral to a psychiatrist does not mean that you will no longer treat the patient and his or her family. Often, once a psychotic patient's most disruptive symptoms are treated, usually by medication, the family is at a loss for how to proceed. Diagnosis of a major mental illness such as psychosis can be a devastating experience for a family. They may wonder what to expect in the future, feel impatient, and even angry with the patient. Family therapists can play a significant role in helping families deal with the day-to-day challenges of coping with mental illness. Families need information about what to expect and they need another asset that you can provide—hope. If you become knowledgeable about psychoses, you can guide the family through many challenges. Often, the challenges deal with boundaries, both real and interpersonal. For example, clients wonder where their ill family member should live, or they may experience interpersonal problems such as feeling irritated or embarrassed by the ill member's strange behaviors. It is not uncommon for families to feel abandoned by the mental health system once the patient has received a diagnosis and medication. Before clients begin feeling abandoned, you can offer education, guidance, hope, structure, and the support of a therapeutic relationship that might last for many years.

The second diagnosis that we do not describe in detail is somatic symptom disorder. Instead of referring to the specific disorder, we want to focus on somatizing symptoms, regardless of the diagnosis. "Somatic" means "relating to or affecting the body." As part of a holistic, biopsychosocial approach, therapists are interested in patients' physical symptoms, not just their relationships or thoughts. While you want to remain aware of scope-of-practice issues and not treat a problem outside your expertise, many physical symptoms are one part of a carousel of issues you can address. Depending on the circumstances, physical symptoms may demand immediate attention. For example, a depressed patient may not be able to sleep. An anxious patient may be losing weight because he has lost his appetite. A wife may no longer be interested in sexual relations despite her husband's efforts.

Regardless of the individual or family diagnosis, prominent physical symptoms deserve the therapist's attention, even if only for a referral to a physician. Physical symptoms may indicate a much larger problem, such as clinical depression or substance abuse. In addition, physical symptoms including sexual problems, chronic pain, eating problems, and sleep problems may become, at least temporarily, the focus of treatment. It is not necessary for you to be an expert in all areas. Instead, you simply need the skills to recognize these issues when they arise in the session, make them a clinical focus, and know how to enlist help from colleagues like physicians when the problems are outside your expertise. In addition, you can encourage your patients to take a holistic approach to their health. While you continue to focus on family dynamics and individual psychopathology, you can encourage your patients to exercise, lose weight, or smoke less—general health habits that are known to affect both physical and mental health.

DEPRESSION

When individual diagnosticians talk about mood disorders, they refer to specific criteria or symptoms—something beyond the "blues" that everyone experiences at one time or another. Controversy exists about when grief or a reaction to stress crosses an invisible line and becomes depression. One way to assess the seriousness of your client's mood is to think about three questions:

1. How long has your client been sad?
2. How severe are his or her symptoms, for example, thoughts of suicide?
3. Is your client's mood keeping him or her from doing the daily tasks of living?

The most common syndromes include bipolar disorder, cyclothymia, persistent depressive disorder, and major depression (Belmaker & Agam, 2008). Depressive symptoms appear in other disorders, such as atypical depression, adjustment disorder with depressed mood, and schizoaffective disorder, but describing these varied conditions is beyond the scope of this book. For family therapists, it is important to note that child and adolescent depression have different pathways and presentations. For example, depression in children frequently presents with irritability.

The prevalence of depression in the general population is high and on the rise (Belmaker & Agam, 2008; Kessler, Berglund, et al., 2005). As previously mentioned, depression is the fifth leading cause of poor health (Lozano et al., 2012; Patel et al., 2015) Up to one in eight individuals may require treatment for depression in their lifetime. However, the majority of depressed people never receive any treatment; if they do, it is usually from their primary care physician, not a family therapist.

Besides being painful, depression can be debilitating and recurring. After a first episode, a client has a 50% chance of another. A second episode increases the risk of more episodes to 70%. For any single episode, one in three clients will get well, a second client gets somewhat better, and a third client doesn't respond to the treatment at all so new treatments must be tried (Frances, 2013).

Bipolar depression is characterized by swings between elated moods (manic or hypomanic episodes) and depressed moods, while cyclothymia is characterized by a more mild manifestation of the same swings. Dysthymia, now called persistent depressive disorder in DSM-5, refers to a type of depression that has lasted for at least 2 years and whose symptoms are less debilitating than major depression. Major depression, meanwhile, is a condition in which intense feelings of sadness, loss, and helplessness prevail, to the point of impairing daily functioning.

Depression occurs twice as often in women as in men (Denton & Burwell, 2006; McGrath, Keita, Strickland, & Russon, 1990). Possible explanations include women's characteristic style of internalizing problems (thinking instead of doing) compared to men's more aggressive and externalizing style. The social circumstances of women (living in poverty, or suffering abuse) also play a role. Many mental health experts consider depression in women almost epidemic.

Major risk factors for depression include a family history of depression (regardless of whether this is due to interactional or biological factors), lack of social support, stressful life events, and suicides by family members. In addition, depression frequently is found in individuals who suffer from anxiety or have substance abuse problems. While most patients recover from depression without treatment, they are at high risk for relapse. In addition, the most rigorous study ever completed on treatment for depression found that only 19–32% of recovered patients stayed well for more than a year (Patterson et al., 2010; Shea, Gibbons, Elkin, & Sotsky, 1995).

The symptoms of bipolar illness (manic–depressive disorder) are often dramatic and intense, and the majority of bipolar patients will experience about 11 episodes of either mania (elated mood) or depression (sad, tearful, hopeless mood) during their lifetime (Fredman et al., 2015; Miklowitz, 2008). In addition, manic—depressive illness is seldom "cured," but managed throughout a person's life. A family who witnesses an initial episode in one of its members can expect more of the same in years to come. These bouts can leave a family reeling and wondering when the next "crazy" episode will happen. One family powerfully described their confusion when police told them that their college-age son threw a microwave oven through a store window. Their story chronicles years of treatment, confusion, feeling blamed, and eventual healing after their son was diagnosed with bipolar illness (Berger & Berger, 1991).

Family therapy has been examined as a treatment for major depression and persistent depressive disorder, and researchers have explored using couple group therapy in cases where one member of the dyad has bipolar disorder (Beach & Jones, 2002; Clarkin & Glick, 1992; Cordova & Gee, 2001; Moltz, 1993). A close relationship with a depressed person is difficult at best. The relationship can be challenged by the sad, hopeless quality the depressed person emanates or the dramatic swings in mood and behavior of the bipolar patient. In addition, the depressed person may look to significant others to help them cope or, even worse, they may withdraw from relationships completely. The stress generation model captures this vicious cycle between relational distress and depression (Beach & Whisman, 2012). Relational conflict increases stress levels and can lead to decreased social support. This, in turn, exacerbates depressive symptoms, which contribute to relational distress, and the cycle continues. Disrupting this unhelpful pattern will require attention to the relationships in which the individual is embedded.

The family's response to the depressed person can be a key influence on the course of the depression (Kung, 2000; MacFarlane, 2003). Some research on depression has examined marital therapy, especially behavioral marital therapy, as a form of treatment (Beach & Jones, 2002; Uebelacker, Weishaar, & Miller, 2008). Results of these outcome studies demonstrate that for adults who received marital therapy to treat depression, the marriage improved and the depression abated. Treating depression with marital therapy makes sense, especially when one considers that the most prevalent client is a wife or mother, in her late 20s to early 40s, who is socially isolated and depressed about her relationship with her husband.

In discussing social and family relationships of depressed persons, Gotlib and Beach (1995) state:

> Whereas depressed persons exhibit social skills deficits in their interactions with strangers, their interactions with their spouse and children are more likely to be characterized by hostility and anger . . . it is clear that depression in one family member has a significant influence on the emotions and behavior of other members and . . . on the family as a unit. Conversely, negative interactions with spouse or other family members are powerfully related to level of depressive symptomatology. (p. 418)

While no research suggests that families cause depression in individuals, studies indicate that family members affect the course of the illness (Beach & Gupta, 2006; Keitner, Ryan, Miller, & Kohn, 1993). Many researchers suggest a reciprocal relationship between depression and family interaction, stating that it is impossible to identify a single etiology. However, researchers agree that empathic family support can play a critical role in healing. On the negative side, criticism and continued hostility seem to have a harmful effect on both the depressed person and the family. For women, equality in decision making and companionship in marriage protect against depression and a variety of other health problems (Cohen, 2004). In addition, some research suggests that depressed patients tend to relapse at lower levels of criticism than do schizophrenic patients (Keitner et al., 1993). Clearly, family support (especially spousal support) is critical in the course and treatment of depression (Cordova & Gee, 2001; Miklowitz, 2008; Peris & Miklowitz, 2015).

For some couples, spouses of depressed persons may be empathic to their partner's suffering at first but over time become impatient and even hostile. The therapist and family confront a challenging situation when the hostile spouse identifies the reason for that hostility as the partner's helpless behavior and the depressed spouse claims a need for the partner's love and support to improve. The influence of criticism, contempt, defensiveness, and withdrawal in couples with a depressed partner are important because these same themes predict marital deterioration and divorce (Gottman, 1994). In addition, distress and psychopathology in parents predict the same in children. Depression is not an isolated illness residing within an individual, but a serious condition that affects every family relationship, and even the continuing existence of the family.

Family therapists can empathize with the burden spouses feel in helping the depressed client. Common issues family members may present with include the degree of responsibility one must assume for the depressed member, suppressing or denying one's own feelings or needs, generalizing the illness and blaming all negative behaviors and family interactions on it, and arguing with the spouse about treatment recommendations such as medication compliance and therapy.

A family therapist's ability to provide support, education, and information about depression can affect not only the individual patient but the marital and parenting relationships as well. Family therapists can assess not only for the individual symptoms of depression but for the impact the depressed person's mood and behaviors have on other family members and the group's overall well-being. Spouses and children of depressed parents can be considered an integral part of the treatment.

In particular, the intertwined relationships among an individual's depression (especially a woman's), the marriage, and parenting need careful examination. Treatment should be multifaceted, addressing each of these issues and their overlap. There may be no other mental disorder whose course has been demonstrated to have as clear a relationship to marital quality as depression. In addition, children's therapists lament that adult therapists often overlook the impact of parental problems on children's development. Family therapists treating depressed parents have the opportunity to assess and treat the children who are affected by their parents' emotional states.

Studies looking at a marital format to treat depression suggest that women with unipolar depression, who are distressed about their marriage, can be effectively treated with marital therapy (Beach & Gupta, 2006; Prince & Jacobson, 1995). The client's perception of the problem is important in deciding what type of treatment to pursue. The therapist can assess how central the marital relationship is in the patient's beliefs about why she is depressed.

Evidence suggests that parent–child disputes are prominent in families with a depressed member (Gotlib & Beach, 1995; Uebelacker et al., 2008), and that depressed children grow up in homes with one or more depressed parents. Thus, family therapy can potentially ameliorate a damaging situation for multiple family members, not only treating the individual symptoms of the depressed person but also potentially improving the marriage and the parent–child relationships.

Current research and information about depression give beginning family therapists several guidelines to follow when working with depressed people and their families:

* Check for a family history of depression.
* Consider medication for the depressed family member as an effi-
  cient, cost-effective treatment option.
* Consider how the marital relationship influences the member's
  depression (by asking him or her).
* Note other family members' responses to the depressed member (e.g., distancing, empathizing, hostility, overinvolvement,
  criticism).
* When a parent is depressed, assess the impact on the children.
* Look for depression masked as other symptoms (e.g., irritability,
  anger, withdrawal).
* Consider treatment options including individual therapy (especially cognitive-behavioral treatments), couple therapy, family
  therapy, and group therapy, and match treatment to the specific
  needs and wishes of the clients.
* Use psychoeducation to inform family members about depression.

Marital and family therapies to treat depression generally work
best for clients with mild depression and have been shown to be less
effective for those who were part of an inpatient sample of severely
depressed persons (Prince & Jacobson, 1995). Marital and family therapies may be used in conjunction with other treatments, such as phar-
macotherapy and/or individual therapy.

ANXIETY

Everyone gets anxious and nervous at times—it's part of the human
condition. But true anxiety disorders are more intense and specific
than the general worry we all experience. Fortunately, treatments for
these disorders have some of the most successful outcome evidence.
New work is going on daily in discovering better pharmacological and
cognitive-behavioral treatments for anxiety disorders and much has
been learned about emotion regulation and anxiety in recent years
(Amstadter, 2008; Gross, 2007). While most mental health problems
have a 50–70% treatment success rate, some of the anxiety disorders
have a 70–90% cure rate, particularly panic attack with agoraphobia.
With these statistics in mind, a family therapist might consider referral
to an individual therapist with expertise in pharmacology or cognitive-
behavioral treatments for the individual, while simultaneously continuing to treat the family.

Not all anxiety disorders can be treated effectively, however, and recent research suggests that changes in the brain are associated with some anxiety disorders (Etkin & Wager, 2007). For example, post-traumatic stress disorder (PTSD) is often difficult to cure but can be managed. Nevertheless, compared to many disorders where the goal is symptom management, one can, at times, talk about cure for some anxiety disorders. When the new edition of DSM was published in 2013, the editors separated anxiety disorders that had previously been listed under the overall heading of anxiety disorders into three sections: anxiety disorders, obsessive–compulsive disorders, and trauma and stressor disorders. Obsessive–compulsive disorder often starts in child-hood, has biological foundations, and consists of repetitive thoughts and behaviors such as washing, checking, and counting. Trauma and stress-related disorders range on a continuum of severity and symptoms. Ideally, a response to a stressor (e.g., a serious car wreck) will be short-lived and the client, with the support of family and friends, will return to his or her old self. But therapists increasingly recognize that symptoms and impairment can be lifelong depending on the circumstances of the original event. Controversy surrounds the issue of whether someone who simply witnesses trauma, instead of experiencing the event personally, can be diagnosed with a trauma diagnosis. Trauma is an area where researchers are generating new knowledge about both its causes and effective treatments. An interested therapist can easily find helpful information in books and workshops. A book that our students have found particularly helpful is *The Body Keeps the Score* (Van Der Kolk, 2014).

Frequently, people suffer from both an anxiety disorder and another major problem, such as depression or substance abuse. At times, a client may suffer from all three, using the substance to deal with the other two problems. Physicians who prescribe medication often try to delineate the specific symptoms of each disorder, and prescribe medication to treat them. They also try to understand which cluster of symptoms is dominant. Thus the patient's primary diagnosis might be generalized anxiety disorder with symptoms of depression.

These distinctions, while important, may be less critical to a family therapist. While the therapist can profit from identifying specific symptoms of each disorder, the client is treated as a whole person, and symptoms are seen as part of a whole life, not discrete entities. The patient's perspective and family context are equally important.

Anxiety disorders are common, and occur almost twice as often in women than in men (Castle, Kulkarni, & Abel, 2006). Prevalence of anxiety disorders does not vary, however, on the basis of race, income, education, or rural versus urban living. Once again, we note that women tend to internalize (and become anxious) while men are more likely to externalize or act (perhaps get drunk or become violent) when they are distressed.

Anxiety disorders are the most frequently diagnosed problem of children and adolescents, and some research suggests that anxious children become anxious adults (Beidel & Turner, 2007; Dadds, 1995; Kessler, Berglund, et al., 2005). Children's worries are different from adults' worries, and they have different kinds of fears. They may not want to go to school (school phobia), they may be afraid of strangers, or they may not want to leave their mothers (separation anxiety). Regardless of the age-appropriate symptoms, anxiety in childhood can be a frightening and debilitating problem.

Since anxiety disorders generally involve how or what an individual is thinking and his or her physiological responses to these thoughts, it's easy to understand why they might be thought of as problems of the individual. Indeed, sometimes anxiety disorders can be effectively and efficiently treated with individual therapies. Pharmacological treatments and cognitive-behavioral treatments are effective for people suffering from anxiety, and have little or no focus on the patient's family.

Cognitive-behavioral treatments focus on changing how people think and behave. An underlying assumption is that if a person changes his or her thinking or behavior, physiology and emotions will change too. Gradually exposing someone to the situation he or she most fears and giving him or her new ways of thinking about it have proven especially useful treatments.

These methods are similar to the structural family therapy techniques of reframing and enactment. In addition, solution-focused therapists suggest "making one small change" in the way one normally behaves regarding a problem. Narrative therapists talk about someone's "inner dialogue" and "re-storying" one's life. These family therapy approaches share many similarities with cognitive-behavioral techniques.

The major focus for marital therapy in anxiety disorders is often agoraphobia and panic. New research is just beginning to incorporate spouses in the treatment of obsessive–compulsive disorder, social phobia, generalized anxiety disorder, and PTSD. Existing evidence on outcomes for these disorders suggests that social support— especially family support—leads to superior outcomes. Negative family interactions—such as criticism, anger, hostile confrontation, and a spouse's belief that the client could control his or her own symptoms if he or she wished—were all predictors of poor outcome (Craske & Zoellner, 1995; Gross, 2007; Kase & Ledley, 2007).

The role of family therapy may be even stronger when treating children with anxiety disorders. Mental health researchers hope that early intervention can keep children's brains from "locking in" patterns of anxious behaviors and thoughts. Based on the saying "Neurons that fire together, wire together," clinicians hope that early treatment protects against permanent, damaging brain changes (Hebb, 1949). Research suggests that fearful, apprehensive responses instead of feelings of mastery and competence are learned by children—often by watching their parents (Beidel & Turner, 2007; Morris & March, 2004). Some research suggests that anxious children grow up in homes with at least one anxious parent. While the family therapist needs to be careful not to fall into the historical trap of blaming the parents for the origins of the child's problems, he or she needs to understand how each parent responds to anxiety-producing stimuli and what the family's response to fearful situations has been in the past. Family treatments, especially those employing cognitive-behavioral principles, can be effective since family members share many beliefs, including a worldview. In addition, the powerful influence of emotional support of spouses and parents can be directed toward recognizing and praising mastery and competence instead of reinforcing worry.

Family therapists are aware of covert and overt rules and beliefs in the family as well as hidden agendas. Beliefs and hidden agendas strongly influence a person's response to anxiety. For example, a lonely parent may be as ambivalent about a child's going to school as is the youngster. The parent then subtly reinforces "school refusal" behavior. A client who is easily threatened and needs to control the lives of his or her family may be content to do all the work for an agoraphobic spouse. Recognizing that change in one part of the family brings change for each member, the family therapist can assess for individual responses as well as the interaction between family members regarding the client's anxiety.

Many of the guidelines used for treating depression also hold true for treating anxious clients and their families. In addition, current research and information about anxiety disorders provide several clinical guidelines for working with anxious clients and their families:

* For panic disorders and phobias, consider cognitive-behavioral treatments.
* Consider the role family or marital conflict has in influencing the member's anxious symptoms.
* Consider covert or hidden relational interactions that influence the member's anxious symptoms (e.g., the partner's need to control or "protect" the anxious member).

- Consider the place or function of the anxious symptoms in the family system and the marital system.
- When treating anxious children, evaluate how the parents cope with stress and what coping skills they have taught their children.

ALCOHOLISM AND DRUG ABUSE

Substance abuse, whether it involves alcohol, illegal drugs, or prescribed medication, can occur when the therapist least expects it. Unless the therapist works at a drug and alcohol treatment center, few couples or families identify substance abuse as the presenting problem—exactly the opposite usually occurs. The family presents because a child is acting out in school and the school has required therapy for behavior problems. A couple requests marital therapy after years of tension and the wife's recent ultimatum, and the therapist begins treatment only to discover a substance abuse problem.

Individual therapists can simply ask the patient about substance use, but a family therapist may have to search for the abuse before it becomes apparent. The family may be so used to the abuser's behavior that it no longer considers it a problem, at least overtly. Family members may be frightened, ashamed, or intimidated into denying (at least verbally to an outsider) that there is a substance abuse problem. They can only get to therapy by requesting help for something else. The most important advice for a beginning family therapist is this: Consider the possibility of a substance abuse problem during your assessment, regardless of the presenting problems, and reconsider the possibility every time a constellation of symptoms, explanations, or descriptions does not make sense.

The professional debates surrounding substance abuse can be confusing to a new therapist who is trying to learn the basics. Current controversies surround the issues of whether an alcoholic can ever drink again, whether alcoholism is a biological disease, whether recreational drug use leads to abuse and addiction, whether an "addictive personality" exists, and whether this personality develops from childhood trauma. Diagnosis is further confused by the ongoing arguments about whether substance abuse and substance dependence should be viewed on a continuum or seen as distinct categories. Another ongoing controversy surrounds "behavioral addictions" such as gambling, sex, shopping, and video game addictions. Neuroscience has shown that similar neural networks light up on scans for all of these disorders. Underlying this common pathway is the idea that a behavior that began as a pleasurable activity has now become so ingrained that the person feels out of control (Frances, 2013).

The beginning family therapist might consider these ongoing controversies intellectually interesting. However, for the therapist developing basic clinical skills, these arguments can distract from the primary goal—to get the person to stop using or abusing the substance. One therapist explained the goal of substance abuse work by comparing it to surgery: "I simply want to cut the harmful substance out of the person's life and then I'll do a pathology summary later, when the person is no longer being harmed." Substance abusers, family members, and other professionals can get caught up in myriad debates surrounding substance abuse and never focus on the simple behavioral issue of stopping the problem. Addressing marijuana use in therapy can be a controversial topic as well. It is important for a beginning therapist to consult his or her supervisor on how to handle the function of the substance use as well as how to decipher what place it holds in the couple or family system.

Substance abuse is much more common in men than women. As a result, behaviors that reflect lapses in judgment and reasoning and lack of control, such as violence and sexual abuse, are much more common in men. If a family therapist scratches the surface of many deviant social behaviors committed by men, he or she will usually find comorbid substance abuse.

Substance abuse is a serious and common problem in the United States, and is related to drunk driving, suicide, homicide, violent crime, child and spouse abuse, and "household accidents." In addition, the biological effects of substance abuse, including cirrhosis, hepatitis, and seizures, can permanently damage a person's health. Alcoholism can be a true systemic illness—fetal alcohol syndrome is one of the only illnesses in which the mother is responsible for the damaging behavior and the child feels the effects, forever.

Assessments of alcoholism and substance abuse were addressed in an earlier chapter. The purpose here is to review clinical and research literature that examines the role of alcoholism in the family and effective family treatments. Alcoholism and substance abuse are among the DSM categories that have received the most investigation by family therapists, perhaps because of evidence that alcoholism and substance abuse are "family diseases" in the sense that the abuser's behavior affects everyone in the family and, in turn, the abuser is affected by family members. Thus, many treatment programs involve family members and view interventions into family interaction as part of the treatment. For example, a goal of behavioral couple therapy is to increase relationship factors that are conducive to abstinence (O'Farrell & Fals-Stewart, 2006).

Research on alcoholic families suggests that a family's rituals, routines, and beliefs are strongly influenced by alcohol. In essence, the family can take on an "alcoholic identity" and collude to allow the alcoholic behavior to continue. At times, positive effects of the alcohol, not just damaging effects, are experienced by the family. For example, a family may be reluctant to encourage a husband and father who is more relaxed and engaging when he drinks to stop the drinking.

Some researchers take a developmental view of substance abuse. They suggest that seeds of an alcoholic family identity are planted early in the marriage, as a couple decides on patterns to follow and beliefs to hold—largely an implicit process (Steinglass, Bennett, Wolin, & Reiss, 1987). The role of alcohol and drinking in the family, while influenced by family-of-origin patterns, is one of the "decisions" a new couple makes. In essence, several small "agreements" to accept alcohol and alcoholic behavior can lead to a big "yes," and thus an alcoholic family is formed.

We believe that every alcoholic family must contend with the following characteristics of alcoholism: It is chronic; it involves use of a psychobiologically active drug; it is cyclical in nature; it produces predictable behavioral responses; and it has a definite course of development. However, families are more diverse than they are alike in their responses to these issues, and the role of alcohol must be assessed for each individual family.

Research reviews and meta-analyses of alcohol and drug studies have examined the efficacy of different psychosocial interventions (Dutra et al., 2008). Psychosocial treatments evaluated included contingency management, relapse prevention, cognitive-behavioral therapy, and other combined treatments. In general, contingency management, a system of rewards and punishments for specific behaviors, proved the most effective. Motivational interviewing, a treatment that focuses on understanding the client's level of motivation, has proven effective also (Arkowitz, Weston, Miller, & Rellnick, 2008). Principles from these models can be applied in a family format.

Specific situations might influence the efficacy of family treatments for alcoholism (Edwards & Steinglass, 1995; O'Farrell & Fals-Stewart, 2006; Rowe & Liddle, 2007). Families have a strong influence in motivating alcoholics to get treatment and to alter their drinking behavior. Family involvement, especially inclusion of nonalcoholic family members in the assessment phase, can be a routine component of alcoholism treatment. The impact of family treatment seems to vary according to gender (it is more helpful for men than for women to have spouses involved), investment in the relationship (an investment here produces greater motivation to change drinking behaviors), and support for abstinence from the family.

Most of these studies had control groups and several types of treatment groups. They generally found family therapy to be as effective as or more effective than other treatments. Family therapy was almost always superior to no-treatment control groups. Research suggests that involving the nonalcoholic spouse in treatment significantly improves outcome and can lead to more abstinence, happier relationships, less domestic violence, and fewer marital separations (Jacobson & Gurman, 1995; O'Farrell & Fals-Stewart, 2006). In addition, children can benefit from family-based treatments for substance problems.

Interestingly, many successful drug treatment programs derive from a structural/strategic tradition, while effective alcohol treatment programs derive from a behavioral therapy tradition (Fals-Stewart, O'Farrell, Birchler, Cordova, & Kelley, 2005; Rowe & Liddle, 2007). Both of these theoretical approaches share an active, problem-solving method with a focus on the present situation. Facilitating communication and problem-solving skills among family members is a key element of these treatments. While there is still much to be learned about treating substance abuse problems and alcoholism with family therapy, one can conclude that an active, focused style is essential for effectiveness.

Beginning clinicians often ask, "Is family therapy or marital therapy enough, or should it be used in conjunction with other forms of treatment?" The answer depends on the specific circumstances of the family. Many family therapy treatments are combined with individual treatments, education programs, and pharmacological treatment. In general, research shows that behavioral couple therapy produces greater abstinence and better relationship functioning than typical individual-based treatments alone. For many patients with the necessary resources, a combined treatment approach may be ideal.

Some family therapy programs combine aspects of other therapies into the family approach. For example, Liddle uses an individual therapist to form an alliance with substance-abusing adolescents and a separate family therapist to do the family treatment (Liddle & Dakof, 1995; Rowe & Liddle, 2007). One way to decide whether family therapy should be the sole treatment is to assess the intensity of the family's impact on the problem. For example, family therapy is more effective than other treatments for younger teens but not to the same degree for older teens (Sprenkle & Bischoff, 1991). In addition, behavioral marital therapy or spouse involvement in treatment for alcoholism is more effective for couples who report some marital distress before treatment. The old adage "If it ain't broke, don't fix it" comes to mind. Some research, however, suggests that even couples without marital distress see improved marital satisfaction and communication skills, and prevent deterioration of the relationship, when marital therapy is used to treat substance abuse (Alexander, Holtzworth-Munroe, & Jameson, 1994; O'Farrell & Fals-Stewart, 2006).

In determining whether marital or family therapies should be the sole treatment for a substance problem, the therapist can ask the abuser how much he or she would like the family to participate. On the other hand, limited resources or a structured treatment program may make this decision moot. In general, marital and family therapy should make up part of the treatment, given the growing evidence of its effectiveness.

Another benefit of including family therapy, besides ameliorating the substance abuse, is improvement in family members' satisfaction with marital and family relationships. When treatment ends, the family has a shared experience and new beliefs to refer back to in times of stress. The spouse can provide reminders of the benefits of the treatment several years after it is over. The potential effects of spouse and family involvement, even when the IP has a substance problem, are noted in the superior follow-up results of family therapy groups compared to other treatment groups.

If the goal is lasting change, not just a quick fix, it makes sense to include the most important people in the abuser's life in treatment because family members will still be with the patient long after therapy has ended. Literature on alcoholism and substance abuse suggests the following clinical guidelines:

* Regardless of the presenting problem, consider the possibility and role of substance abuse.
* Assess the role of alcohol or the substance in the family. For example, one family reported that their father was "the most fun and relaxed" when he was drinking, and thus the family saw the drinking as serving some positive functions for them.
* Consider the possibility of "enabling behaviors" by other family members.
* Assess how pervasive the substance is in influencing family beliefs, rituals, and routines.
* Accept that various family members will have different views on the seriousness of the substance problem. Some members may minimize the problem and others may focus on the substance use as the key problem in the family.
* Consider the possibility of violence or abuse occurring in the family because they are frequently comorbid with substance use.

- Consider stopping family therapy and refocusing treatment on stopping the member's substance abuse.
- Consider the source of the substance. For opioids, patients often get prescriptions, at least initially, from physicians trying to treat patients' chronic pain.

IMPULSE DISORDERS AND NEURODEVELOPMENTAL DISORDERS

Research suggests that mental health specialists have overlooked the frequency of impulse control disorders, which generally refer to the following DSM diagnoses: oppositional defiant disorder, conduct disorder, intermittent explosive disorder, and the most well-known disorder in this category, ADHD (Dell'Osso, Marazziti, Hollander, & Altamura, 2007; Grant, 2008). These disorders can be found in two categories of DSM—neurodevelopmental disorders and disruptive impulse disorders. All of these disorders could be viewed as brain disorders that change over time and usually start in childhood. In addition, all of these disorders can be characterized by impulsive behaviors, emotional dysregulation, and an inability to self-soothe.

These disorders are much more common than had been realized in earlier years, and are not confined to active schoolboys who can't sit in their chairs. Instead, these problems can be lifelong and share a common feature—struggles with emotional dysregulation (Gross, 2007). Unfortunately, within the group of most commonly occurring problems, impulse problems are most likely to be overlooked and undertreated. In addition, impulse problems most frequently occur in males, not females, and men are much less likely to seek treatment than women. If schools do not help identify children with impulse problems, the next public institution to address their struggles is often the legal system.

Oppositional defiant disorder and conduct disorder are usually diagnosed in childhood or late adolescence. Both refer to behavior problems, usually in boys. Oppositional defiant disorder is less serious than conduct disorder. Most of these problems initially manifest in the home and then appear in other settings such as schools. In fact, research correlates certain qualities of the home environment with the occurrence of these problems. For example, oppositional defiant disorder is commonly found in children growing up in homes with serious marital discord. Children with ADHD often grow up in homes where drug or alcohol dependence by one or both parents is an issue. Other research suggests that large family size, poor mental health of the mother, a father who has a criminal record, and high family conflict all correlate with the presence of impulse control disorders in children. Studies have also found that impulse disorders run in families, often because of genetic links. Thus, ample opportunities exist for a family therapist to intervene and help families and patients whose lives go awry because of these disorders.

While a boy's impulse problems may be more visible than a girl's internalizing depression, they are still frequently ignored or not treated. In addition, when children with unrecognized ADHD grow up, it is highly unlikely that they will ever be diagnosed and treated. This is in spite of good evidence suggesting the deleterious effects of ADHD and impulse control disorders in general. While we know that adult ADHD is associated with loss of jobs, families, and income and a host of other negative effects, usually the patient is blamed for his "personal failings" (Kessler et al., 2006). In fact, research suggests the correlates of adult ADHD include being divorced and unemployed.

Most impulse problems start at a young age (Pallanti, 2006). In fact, parents often report that they cannot remember a time when their child's behavior was not impulsive. However, recent neuroscience findings suggest that children who have behavior problems at young ages are not doomed to lives of failure. In fact, the origins of at least some types of ADHD indicate delays in brain development, not a learning deficit. And these young brains often catch up, especially with a supportive, healthy home and school environment.

Impulse control problems are an area where family therapists can make a big difference if they are identified before a child reaches adulthood. But even this process can be challenging. For girls, impulse control problems might manifest in aggression toward other girls and be ignored by adults as "teenage angst." Girls with attention problems are often daydreamers, rather than hyperactive, and poor academic performance can be attributed to lack of motivation. Thus, many girls with impulse problems are never diagnosed. In addition, once a young person reaches adulthood, his or her learning style is often set and employment struggles or other deficits are attributed to "laziness" or "lack of motivation." Even if the child's problems are correctly identified, parents are often reluctant to consider medication, the mainstay of treatment for ADHD.

Impulse problems are often connected to underlying emotions such as anger or aggressive feelings. ADHD has a core group of symptoms including impulsivity, inattention, emotional dysregulation problems, and motor restlessness. Oppositional defiant disorder has core symptoms such as defiance and hostility, while conduct disorder can be characterized by willful disregard for the rights of others and includes behaviors such as cruelty, destruction of property, lying, and theft. Even if impulse problems don't lead to criminal behavior, the symptoms can still lead to an adult life of frustration, anger, and failure.

Family therapists can make a significant difference in helping families that struggle with impulse problems. Besides considering medication for at least some diagnoses, such as ADHD, family therapists can focus on emotion regulation in the family. How are frustration, anger, and disappointment handled in the family? Often, parents with their own emotional struggles, such as a depressed mother or a violent father, will overrespond or underrespond to their children's needs for soothing, emotional validation, and structure. These patterns often start early, when the child is an infant, and continue to adulthood.

If parents have the emotional resources and ability to help their children, research suggests that parental soothing and structuring can make a difference by helping children learn how to identify their feelings, master their behaviors, and calm themselves down. In turn, these abilities can lead to lifelong skills in "executive functioning"—being able to organize one's life and cope with stress. In general, the earlier parents get started on addressing both their own emotional struggles and their children's challenges, the easier the task. Family therapists can serve as coaches and consultants to parents—giving them the information and tools they need to create a home environment where children can prosper. In addition, family therapists can help parents advocate for their children's needs in school systems and try to ensure that the learning environment is optimal. Family therapists should be familiar with the laws and policies that guarantee children access to resources for neuropsychological testing and other assessment measures. They can help the family obtain an individualized educational plan (IEP) for the child.

However, if impulse control disorders remain undiagnosed, problems persist into adulthood. Family therapists can look for patterns of loss and failure in their adult patients that initially seem unexplained. Frequent job changes, incomplete educations, disrupted relationships, poor driving records, and histories of substance abuse are all warning signs that the patient may suffer from an impulse disorder. Often, instead of feeling stigmatized by a diagnostic label, patients feel relief when they are finally given an explanation for their painful history. As one patient said, "I'm so glad there is a name for what I have because before now the only name I had for it was 'loser.'"

Research shows that some small changes early in a child's life can have a significant effect as the child ages. Thinking in simple cost–benefit terms, it makes sense to help parents with their own issues and then to help them parent effectively. In fact, a major study documenting the presence of mental disorders beginning at early ages suggests that public health interventions should be more focused on children and adolescence (Kessler, Berglund, et al., 2005). With these ideas in mind, family therapists can consider the following goals when working with families with impulse struggles:

- When you are treating a child or teen for impulse problems, expand your assessment to the parents. Both genetic and environmental influences often lead to multiple family members struggling with control of their impulses.
- Make sure you are up to date on the literature, especially for ADHD, and make psychoeducation a significant part of your treatment.
- Work with the family on both behavioral interventions for creating structure and emotional interventions for creating soothing and self-regulation.
- Involve other systems such as the schools, and teach the parents how to advocate for their children.
- Use outside resources. Consider neuropsychological testing, psychotropic medication, tutoring and coaching, and other measures to help the family.

CONCLUSION

Alcoholism or drug abuse, anxiety, impulse struggles, and depression are four of the most common individual disorders a therapist will encounter in clinical practice. A therapist must not view these disorders in a vacuum but rather within the context of existing and past social and emotional problems and the family's extant strengths and weaknesses. In addition, a therapist must keep in mind that the family of an individual with a mental disorder is often inextricably involved in the perpetuation or containment of this disorder and that psychoeducation and support are crucial to the well-being of the whole family as well as that of their afflicted member.

CHAPTER 11

Getting Unstuck in Therapy

"I've been working with this family for several weeks, but not much seems to be changing. Now what do I do?" Supervisors and seasoned colleagues often hear this question from beginning therapists. Clearly, therapy is not always a smooth ride for any of its participants, and therapists frequently encounter a multitude of complications and obstacles along the way. Consider the case of the Smith family:

The Smiths initially presented their 16-year-old daughter's sexual acting-out as their primary problem. Her mother discovered a letter detailing her sexual fantasies and possible encounters with a young man who lived a few hundred miles away. The family sessions included two teenage daughters, ages 16 and 13, and the parents. The family—bright, verbal, and well educated—could express its ideas well, but had considerable difficulty with direct communication and expression of feelings. After several family sessions, the family stabilized and everyone agreed that many of the difficulties were the result of long-standing marital problems.

Couple therapy began as a slow and painful process for the spouses in this family. Considerable sexual tension, a lack of feeling disclosure, and a history of fighting culminated in hurt feelings and emotional withdrawal. The husband had a history of going into rages in which he couldn't control his emotions and would break things in the house. These incidents, described by his wife as "childlike temper tantrums," resulted in the wife withdrawing, becoming depressed, and locking herself in their bedroom. Both individuals harbored a great deal of resentment for unresolved conflicts dating back to their courtship. The husband insisted that the problem was essentially the wife's. His contention was that her withdrawal and lack of affection caused most of the difficulties. There was no evidence of alcohol abuse. The wife had taken antidepressants on several occasions that were prescribed by her family doctor—she refused to see a psychiatrist.

The couple therapy continued for several weeks with little change. The wife refused to talk about her family-of-origin issues, other than to say she was abused. She indicated that she felt her husband wouldn't understand her early history and would only use the information against her. The husband was willing to discuss his family of origin, but saw little relevance in it for his marriage. The husband's frustration with the lack of contact and change increased. The wife's depressive symptoms intensified, and included crying spells, sleep problems, withdrawal, excessive worrying, and lethargy. She felt that the marital sessions were "too much" and were just creating more stress and difficulty. The husband threatened divorce if his wife didn't change.

Family therapists expect people to be ambivalent about change. The struggle for change is inevitable within any relationship context, including the therapy room. The challenge of facilitating new ways and ending old ways is central to all therapeutic processes. In the following sections, we identify common sources of "stuckness" in therapy and provide options for thinking about and dealing with them.

UNDERSTANDING CLIENTS' AMBIVALENCE ABOUT CHANGE

Beginning therapists need to recognize that all clients have some ambivalence about change. Fortunately, the fact that clients even come into therapy usually shows some willingness to try something new or to apply energy in a different way. Furthermore, the therapist's very participation with a client or family can produce and promote change. True change, however, might not be welcomed by the people requesting it. All people have a tendency to go back to the ways things have always been done—homeostasis. Familiar is comfortable.

There may also be outside factors, which can be identified as constraints to change. For example, a family may be very interested in therapy but may have severe transportation difficulties. The family could also have limited time available due to heavy work commitments, or they may have limited financial resources to pay for the therapy. All of these constraints may make therapy more difficult, but can be seen as outside factors inhibiting the process rather than resistance.

Resistance is a normal part of therapy, not an exception. Younger therapists sometimes think they have failed when they encounter resistance. In order to talk intelligently about client resistance, we need a definition. For resistance, we use the working definition offered in the excellent text *Mastering Resistance* (Anderson & Stewart, 1983), which states:

> Resistance can be defined as all those behaviors in the therapeutic system which interact to prevent the therapeutic system from achieving the family's goals for therapy. The therapeutic system includes all family members, the therapist, and the context in which the therapy takes place, that is, the agency or institution in which it occurs. Resistance is most likely to be successful, that is, to result in the termination or failure of family therapy, when resistances are present and interacting synergistically in all three components of the therapeutic system. (p. 24)

Various theoretical orientations label clients' ambivalence about change and their resistance differently. For example, structural family therapy would find resistance in the family's failure to accommodate its structure to the changing developmental needs of its members, while transgenerational family therapies might assess resistance as an integral part of dealing with unfinished business in one's family of origin. Resistance in either case is a predictable partner of change. By definition, then, a family therapist must clearly keep in mind both a theoretical approach and the family's goals for therapy in order to interpret resistance accurately. Resistance comes with the territory of therapy and must not be viewed as failure, but instead as an expected aspect of the work.

The client system fears change since it is something new and unpredictable. For example, a client might be an alcoholic, single mother who is coming into therapy because of her child's school problems. If the mother fails to look at the possible influence of her drinking (an examination usually carried out later in the therapeutic relationship) on the child's school problems, we have resistance. A client system might also be a couple that continues to practice abusive interactions between sessions, even though alternative interactions have been offered and practiced in therapy. Changing old and comfortable coping and communication patterns is threatening. The future is unknown to the client.

The therapist can provide significant emotional support to the client by recognizing ambivalence. Verbally acknowledging that change is hard, scary, and uncomfortable helps. Also, giving the resistance "back to the client" is an important method of diffusing rather than escalating resistance. Telling the client, "You're changing too much," "You're proceeding too fast," "There must be other, more important concerns that keep you from trying new things," or "Maybe the old way wasn't so bad after all" drops the pressure from the therapist and allows the client to reevaluate the desired area for growth.

Although this section has focused on how a client's ambivalence about change can create resistance, the definition of resistance offered above also notes that resistance can come from other sources such as the therapist him- or herself or the agency context. Therapists can demonstrate resistance by pursuing goals that are different from what the clients want to work on. Therapists must also consider how the agency context may contribute to resistance in the therapeutic system. To truly understand resistance, the therapist must consider how all three components interact together.

THERAPIST–CLIENT AGENDA AND TIMING MISMATCH

Resistance can arise from a mismatch between the therapist's goals and the family's goals. Especially enthusiastic at the start of their work, family therapy practicum students often want to "change the world" and "fix" the family. The therapist–client mismatch becomes particularly clear when a therapist begins to direct the family toward something they don't want. For example, a 10-year-old child of a single mother is brought to therapy because of chronic lying at school and at home. The therapist focuses on the task of involving the father, who has visited with the child only five times in her life, in solving the problem, and the mother doesn't return to therapy. When a therapist focuses more on a theoretical perspective or his or her own agenda than the working relationship with the client, a mismatch is more likely to occur.

In addition to being clear about the type of change desired by client and therapist, timing of interventions must be considered. Family therapy highlights the need to be intentional about when certain tasks need to be done and who needs to be a part of the change. This concern is revisited throughout therapy. A remarried couple might need to solve differences and work on better communication skills before inviting an ex-wife to join in sessions concerning a college-age daughter. If the ex-wife was brought in before the remarried couple dealt with their own conflicts, a therapist might see resistance. The therapist must handle the important issues of matching agendas and timing to proceed effectively.

One way to help avoid a mismatch between the therapist and clients' expectations is to regularly assess how clients feel therapy is going. For example, clients can be asked what they have found most helpful in therapy, as well as what they have found least helpful. Regularly checking in with your clients will help uncover if a significant mismatch is occurring, giving the therapist an opportunity to make any necessary adjustments.

MATCHING LEVEL OF DIRECTNESS TO THE CLIENT

Another potential sources of resistance can occur if the therapist's level of directness does not match the client (Beutler, Harwood, Michelson, Song, & Holman, 2011). Some clients will respond well to a therapist who gives direct advice or instruction on how to change. These clients will be compliant in doing what the therapist asks, such as completing assigned homework.

However, other clients will passively or actively resist the therapist's suggestions. One possibility the therapist should consider is that the client does not like to be told what to do, which can be an underlying source of resistance. For example, Jay told his therapist that he hated being assigned "homework" in therapy because it reminded him of battles with his parents when he did not do his school homework as a child. These clients will typically respond better to a more indirect approach to therapy that bypasses their resistance to being told what to do.

Alternatively, paradoxical interventions (e.g., prescribing the problem) may be effective because the client will resist the therapist by changing, or accept the therapist's formulation to continue to do what he or she is doing. The Rodriguez family has come to therapy for three sessions without the father. He has refused to attend, saying that therapy is a waste of his time and he is much too busy with work. However, he always asks the family about their sessions and wants to know what changes are occurring. After continuously being invited to the sessions, it is suggested that he is told, for a time, that he is no longer invited. The family is asked not to talk with him about the sessions but allow him to remain curious. He is also told that he may be talked about in the sessions.

The paradox is used after Mr. Rodriguez has demonstrated his resistance and it has been determined that he will not be compliant. He is told the invitation is no longer available. Because he is already choosing to not be involved, nothing has changed if Mr. Rodriguez accepts that he is no longer invited. However, Mr. Rodriguez has shown some interest in the sessions. Should he become curious and feel left out, he may wish to come to the sessions. Mr. Rodriquez may resist the therapist's idea that he cannot participate in therapy, and insist that he should be able to attend.

THE THERAPIST'S RELUCTANCE TO INTERVENE

Another key area of "stuckness" comes when the therapist is reluctant to intervene. The rules of talking in therapy are different from those in polite conversation. What might seem like interrupting someone in casual discourse may be an intervention in therapy. Some clients will talk continuously with a lack of clarity. The therapist may need to intervene in order to help them refocus or to keep them on track. In intervening, the therapist is looking for an opening to redirect the client and maintain continuity.

Sometimes trainees do not risk an intervention until everything is totally clear. Lack of experience and anxiety over dealing with presenting issues can result in gathering too much information or spending many sessions unfocused. Clients need to experience some progress early in the therapy—without this, they might not come back. One idea is to offer some therapeutic "gift" to the client early, even before the direction of therapy has been decided. These gifts include interventions such as normalizing, reframing, amplifying positive interactions in the family, or congratulating the family on their courage in seeking help.

Also, after two to three sessions, the therapist may want to use the clinical reasoning process discussed in Chapter 5 to understand the presenting problems and to focus on possible interventions. Once this is done, you just need to jump in and risk trying something.

THERAPISTS' LACK OF CONCEPTUAL CLARITY

Another common therapist contribution to problems in the therapeutic process stems from a lack of clarity about how to conceptualize a case. One way that this problem can manifest itself is if the therapist remains stuck in the content that the client shares. As family therapists, our goal is to focus more on the process rather than on the content, which we accomplish through helping our clients change how they relate to one another and the problem. Therefore, try to observe the family's interactions and comment on them as a way of staying focused on the process. As you gain more experience as a therapist, this will become easier to do.

A lack of conceptual clarity can also arise if the therapist is not intentional or consistent in how he or she applies theory to a case. Beginning therapists jump at the opportunity to translate what they've learned in class into a therapy session. After joining and assessment, the therapist might take a grab-bag approach to interventions. For example, John and Jean enter therapy after an argument in which they decide to call off their engagement. Sweethearts since high school, they and their fairly enmeshed families have found increasing tension around wedding plans—styles and expectations differ. A therapist begins to work on the couple's communication and problem-solving skills during the first two working sessions, but then shifts to a structural perspective in order to more appropriately separate a mother–daughter alignment. In a subsequent session, we find the therapist encouraging the expression of grief. While none of these clinical interventions or understandings is incorrect, the therapist might begin to lose focus on the theoretical perspective, appropriate interventions for that theory, and therapeutic goals. When this happens, supervisors often hear practicum students say, "I'm lost."

Your theoretical orientation helps to define what domain of therapy is central to your work with a particular client. Affective, behavioral, cognitive, and/or relational domains may be affected. It's important for the therapist to keep in mind which of these domains therapy will impact. For example, in experiential therapies the domain of affect needs to be emphasized. Thus, a therapist might have difficulty debriefing a family sculpture that depicts a child who feels left out when the family is one that doesn't readily allow for expression of sad feelings. Experiential therapy also requires family members to be in the therapy room in order for authentic and honest self-disclosure to be accomplished. It would be insufficient to address being left out if the child was not present. In contrast, from a strategic perspective where behavioral sequences are central, the parents of an oppositional adolescent son might resist "catching their child following the rules" when he does follow them. The son wouldn't necessarily need to be in the room in order to facilitate change in this family.

Therapists who are focused and intentional about what they offer to a family will help clients manage their resistance positively. Therapists who lose focus on therapeutic goals and domains of therapy (as addressed by their theoretical orientation) will frustrate both themselves and their clients. This process can be complicated when new therapists receive conflicting feedback from different supervisors, each with different therapeutic agendas.

The most helpful way to stay on track in facilitating change is to set clear goals with the family during the first few sessions and then select theoretical perspectives that will best serve reaching those goals. A conscious blending of several theories is often appropriate; however, goals need to be prioritized—which are of first, second, or third importance? The therapist and family should handle these issues in the initial sessions at regular intervals. Without prioritizing the goals, session agendas are unclear for everyone.

CHANGE AND ACCEPTANCE

Therapy can also become stuck if the clients or therapist have an unrealistic expectation about what can be changed. Therapists (and clients) often work from the mind-set that change must happen for clients' lives to improve. However, not everything is open to change. For example, an individual's temperament or personality is not likely to change, at least to a significant degree. Likewise, chronic struggles with mental or physical illness will be a reality for some clients. Pursuing change where change is not possible will create frustration and feelings of being stuck in therapy. Therefore, it is important for both the therapist and the client to have realistic expectations about the prospects for change.

The "Serenity Prayer" teaches us to accept the things that cannot change, have the courage to change the things that can, and possess the wisdom to know the difference between the two. Part of our role as therapists can be to help clients know the difference between what can be changed and what must be accepted.

For situations where change is not possible, developing acceptance requires a shift from solving the problem to learning how to better manage the problem. Helping clients find ways of coping with the problem, including incorporating self-care, can help reduce distress. Developing acceptance may also mean increasing awareness and understanding of the problem. For example, psychoeducation around mental illness can sometimes alleviate negative attributions that either family members or clients have toward themselves. Mason was a 12-year-old boy who struggled academically due to his ADHD. Mason viewed himself as stupid because of his difficulties in school. Mason's therapist, Shonelle, helped him see that he struggled with school because of his ADHD, not because he was stupid. Because Mason loved cars, Shonelle used the metaphor that even a high-performance car would not run well if one part of the engine was not working properly. She helped Mason recognize that it was his difficulty maintaining attention due to his ADHD that was the problem, rather than his overall intelligence.

COUNTERTRANSFERENCE: HOW THERAPIST ISSUES INTERFERE

Sharon was a 25-year-old intern who had been working comfortably with latency and teenage youngsters at a family service agency. One afternoon, Sharon met with the mother of a 7-year-old female client. The woman was very critical of the child and had unrealistic expectations concerning her daughter. Sharon thought the mother was expecting the girl to be "perfect," and she felt protective of the child. She identified with the little girl and noticed that the mother's criticism and demands reminded her of her relationship with her own mother. Recognizing this connection, Sharon was able to disengage from a power struggle with the mother and maintain her composure through the rest of the session. Later, she sought supervision and was able to get help in separating her reactions to the client's mother from those toward her own mother.

These processes, which regularly come into play in therapy, stem from what analytically oriented therapists term "transference" and "countertransference." Often ignored or relabeled in family therapy texts, they relate to a phenomenon that is commonly discussed in supervision. Family therapy, in its attempt to establish its own specialization separate from its psychoanalytic roots, tends to be more technique-focused and less concerned about the therapeutic relationship. More recent writings in family therapy, such as those about narrative therapy, have asked important questions concerning the interpersonal context of therapy. Certainly, it is in the interpersonal arena that self and family are shaped.

In very simple terms, transference denotes the interpersonal material brought into the therapeutic relationship by the client, and countertransference denotes the interpersonal material brought into the therapeutic relationship by the therapist. Object relations theories understand these components as the essential working domain for therapy, since in transference the client offers a re-creation of the affective, behavioral, and cognitive issues that need to be reworked for positive growth to take place. Countertransference too must be internally monitored and interpersonally used for therapeutic progress to occur.

Whatever terms are used, part of the process of therapy (especially when it lasts for some time) involves the way feelings, behaviors, and cognitions from the past are played out in the current therapeutic setting. For example, a single mother comes into therapy for treatment of her depression. After several weeks of work in which the therapist empathizes with her situation and encourages access to underused resources in her life, she becomes more quiet and occasionally says, "I know you're going to get mad at me, but. . . ." The client expects that the therapist will react to her just as her own mother had—with criticism and disappointment at her lack of progress.

Feelings, thoughts, and behaviors also emerge from the therapist's past. Almost weekly, in supervising practicum students, we hear the words "I thought I had my father (or mother, or boyfriend, or ex) in the room with me during part of the session."

In managing transference and countertransference, it is important first to normalize personal reactions during therapy. Note that these phenomena will probably occur more often when doing individual therapy than when doing couple or family work because in the latter several persons can serve the purpose of projective identification, that is, expecting someone other than the therapist to act as someone significant from their own background.

Second, several common, though varied, themes can be understood in this process, including helplessness, control, and sexuality. Most often these themes develop when there's some form of anxiety in the system—a normal reaction to any change process. Some clients present with a "help me" cry that seems stronger than "I need help"; these clients readily stay in a victim stance even when they're no longer being victimized. A common therapist reaction is to feel overwhelmed by the client. For example, one intern remarked, "I found myself making phone calls to this family and worrying about them before I went to sleep at night. They were all-consuming."

We do have many clients in this work who are in great pain and need, so compassionate reactions must be a part of what we do. However, good therapy requires that a working relationship be established in which each member of the system shares in therapy's progress. Without this working alliance, a client might remain stuck as a victim and the therapist will be "burned out" by the client system. Each client's responsibility for the therapy will need to be reviewed and clarified if the helplessness theme continues.

A control issue is present when one member of the system demands or dictates to everyone where the therapy should or should not go. If the client initiates control, then commonly the therapist feels criticized or incompetent. Young therapists, in particular, often look for approval from their clients as a way to feel adequate. Working with a demanding and critical client can distract the therapist from the job of facilitating change within the entire system. Furthermore, the therapist might be pulled to react as other family members have acted, perhaps passively. It's important for the therapist to know his or her limits and actively acknowledge them. Beginning therapists need to feel comfortable about stating they are just that—beginning. As long as the therapist is backed up by solid, supportive supervision, this is fairly easy to do.

Therapists can inadvertently contribute to this controlling theme. Feeling internal pressure to be "in charge" may undermine a therapist's ability to share with clients the responsibility for doing the work necessary for change. Also, paradoxically, controlling persons need to be "reframed" as the most vulnerable or out of control. Controlling persons often are highly needy or anxious individuals and must be treated with care. If a therapist discovers that this is his or her style, it would be critical to examine the roots of this attitude in order to facilitate a more therapeutic alignment with the family.

The third theme is sexuality. Particularly in opposite-gender therapeutic relationships, romantic or erotic messages may be verbally or nonverbally introduced into the session. Therapists might be attracted or scared by this. Many interns have disclosed that they have sexual dreams about their clients. Several important aspects of the sexuality theme can be noted. First, gender issues are a part of all human relationships; this can't be avoided. Furthermore, some people sexualize these gender factors, especially when they have been abused or are needy in this area. Finally, the emotional legacy from one's family-of-origin influences how comfortably or uncomfortably this domain will be addressed within the therapeutic relationship.

As a general rule, seeking therapy or peer consultation must be a part of professional development no matter how much experience one has. Therapy will be "loaded" if one's family-of-origin issues touch the clients with whom one works. All therapists have an Achilles' heel in their work, but using vulnerable parts of ourselves in our work can enhance and enrich the therapy greatly.

Finally, recognizing what type of work one does well, given certain family-of-origin experiences, provides a solid focus for one's energies. Learning about oneself is a lifelong journey, and this profession provides a wonderful context for continuing down this path.

DEALING WITH CANCELLATIONS AND NO-SHOWS

A 19-year-old client who has been coming to therapy for depression missed an appointment because he had a job interview; he forgot to call the therapist and cancel the appointment. A younger adolescent client failed to make her morning appointment because she overslept, and she blamed her mother for not waking her up. A family being treated for anxiety in two children begins canceling and rescheduling appointments, and 4 weeks have gone by without a session.

Cancellations and missed appointments offer important information to the therapist and must be acknowledged and evaluated. Since systemic thinking assumes a relational nature to therapeutic work, cancellations and missed appointments need to be interpreted relationally. Therapists need to respond to both, usually by telephone, to determine the meaning of the no-show or cancellation. Sometimes the meaning is quite concrete and practical: it's simply a missed appointment—"I had a flat tire and couldn't get it fixed in time for our appointment." It's useful to review one's policy on cancellations and missed appointments at this time and to clarify any misunderstandings. Most agencies and practices have a 24-hour cancellation policy in which clients are billed for the appointment unless they cancel at least 24 hours before the appointment. This policy may be waived for emergencies; however, what constitutes an "emergency" must be defined.

No-shows or cancellations can indicate a reevaluation of the therapeutic process itself. Goals need to be evaluated throughout the therapeutic process, preferably with the clients' involvement. But when clients have concerns about the therapy process, they might communicate their discomfort by canceling or missing appointments. For example, a couple comes to therapy to decrease the number of fights they have. This goal is partially addressed by encouraging solid communication skills such as "I" statements and active listening. After a bit of relief, the couple starts canceling or consistently rescheduling their appointments. The therapist requests a reevaluation session to discuss if therapy has satisfied the couple's goals and could be terminated, if appointments might be set at more infrequent intervals, or if other goals need to be addressed. It's important to set a collaborative tone for the reevaluation process since client and therapist goals might not match.

Cancellations and no-shows might also indicate that parts of the client system are questioning the therapeutic process. For example, as a depressed adolescent begins to speak more assertively about his needs, perhaps even yell sometimes, the rest of the family might wonder if therapy is doing any good, since this "isn't the behavior we wanted." Cancellations and missed appointments can simply indicate the system's ambivalence about change.

No-shows and cancellations might also result from a disruption in the therapeutic alliance. This is particularly true for clients with certain family-of-origin issues, such as abandonment, or with Axis II DSM-5 diagnoses, such as borderline or avoidant personality disorders. Some clients might be extremely sensitive to a therapist's taking sides during a family session, experiencing the therapist's validation of another family member as invalidating them. Clients express this indirectly by not showing up for an appointment or by "forgetting." Again, depending on the therapist's theoretical orientation, this aspect of the client's reaction will be explored in more or less depth. All therapists need to determine, on an ongoing basis, the solidity of the therapeutic alliance in order to proceed successfully in therapy.

Clients who lack significant motivation or stability in their lives are more likely to cancel or no-show. Clients who are mandated to go to therapy can be expected to be sporadic in their attendance. Those who have been transferred from another therapist are also susceptible to missing appointments until they develop a relationship with the new therapist. Having realistic expectations regarding the client's level of motivation and desire for the therapy will help you manage your caseload more effectively.

Cancellations and missed appointments also result from practical constraints, especially for clients who are socially and economically disadvantaged. For example, a client may have to choose between paying for therapy and paying for groceries or rent. Also, lack of access to transportation can constrain one's ability to attend therapy. It's important to be sensitive to these realistic limitations and to negotiate ways of increasing resources to keep therapy accessible. There's nothing magic about scheduling therapy once a week. This format stems from early analytic patterns of scheduling three to five sessions each week. Systemic interventions can be creatively managed, as highlighted by the approach of some Italian family therapists (the Milan group), who might do several hours of intensive family work and then not see the family for several months.

The key is that the therapist participates actively in understanding the meaning of the no-show or cancellation and manages this meaning therapeutically.

DIFFICULTY GETTING OTHER FAMILY MEMBERS TO THERAPY

The family members who do not make it into treatment may be absent for several different reasons. The first area to investigate is communication between family members. Were they asked to be a part of therapy? How was this discussed? Sometimes therapy can be viewed as another issue to fight about, and it becomes the problem rather than a vehicle for solving problems. Each family member makes a choice in coming or not coming to therapy, exercising some power in the family's decision-making process. If a family member is involved in a power struggle, it may be helpful for the therapist to intervene as a mediator to invite the member to come to the session. Offering to make telephone contact with a reluctant client can serve as a bridge to therapy.

Family members may not come in because they don't think they have a problem. It's not unusual for one member of a couple to want to go to therapy while the other is reluctant or ambivalent. The reluctant partner often feels that he or she does not really have a problem, so "Why should I go?" It can be useful for the therapist to indicate to this partner that he or she has a valuable perspective and pertinent information to offer, regardless of who appears to have the problem. It is reassuring to some clients to hear that they don't have to be part of the problem to be a part of the solution. Furthermore, the therapist might point out to reluctant clients that they are in the best position to relay their own story. Absence could mean their voice may go unheard or their position be misrepresented.

Some family members may be reluctant to attend sessions due to their discomfort with others in the family. In some situations, it may be useful to first work with subsystems and join effectively with them before bringing in all of the family members at once. In some families, being together and having direct communication is a rarity and may need to be "worked up to" on a gradual basis over several sessions.

Reluctant clients may be skeptical of the value of therapy or they may have had a previous negative experience in therapy. Their previous experiences and views about therapy should be explored and understood. It can be helpful to suggest that the client commit initially to only one visit. This session should provide an opportunity for the person to be heard as well as a chance for him or her to hear what other family members have to say. The focus of this session will likely be on providing a safe place for communication and not on making changes. A positive experience may open the door to the reluctant client agreeing to participate in future therapy sessions.

Therapists must also examine if they are reluctant to encourage other family members to participate in therapy. Therapists may find it easier to do individual therapy because there is only one person with whom to develop a relationship. Doing therapy with a whole system can be more challenging because you must join with multiple individuals who may have very different perspectives and needs. Managing sessions can also be more of a challenge with multiple people in the room. However, including family members allows you to more readily access and change relational patterns that may need to be addressed to resolve the issues.

HANDLING SECRETS

Some therapists prefer the "clarity" of individual therapy, which simplifies the clinical contract. However, systemically oriented therapists understand that involving more than one person is a powerful resource in the change process. But with this power comes the issue of confidentiality and the potential problem of secrecy. Most important for the systemically oriented therapist to understand and avoid is the easy trap of collusion, or re-creating the same relational dynamics that brought the clients into therapy in the first place.

The following example illustrates how collusion can develop. An anxious client calls you to make an appointment for therapy in order to talk about her husband. You schedule the appointment with her alone and listen to her story, which includes news that she's been having an affair with a family friend for the past 5 months. She thinks her lover is going to end the relationship and she's very uncertain as to what to do next. "Part of me wants to make my marriage work, of course, but my husband can't know about the affair, so I want you to promise not to tell him when I bring him in for some marital counseling." If the therapist quickly reassures the client that information is confidential and then begins therapy without addressing the impact of the secret, collusion has occurred. More important, the therapist has given over an important domain of powerful information to the client, without participating in defining how the secret might affect clinical work. Like resistance, collusion will occur. The therapist, however, must determine and actively participate in the control of pertinent information. Without this control, the therapist is working with one arm tied behind his or her back.

Some therapists manage this dilemma by not allowing any confidential information to be disclosed—all sessions are with all family members and any phone contact will be disclosed in the next therapy session. Some therapists respect the confidential nature of information and determine that sometimes they will hold the confidence providing it doesn't interfere with therapeutic work. Some family therapy theories would say that secrets are mostly powerful in a negative way. Bowenian theory might see secrets as helping to create pathology in a subsequent generation; therefore, disclosing any secret would be therapeutic. Other theories, such as emotionally focused therapy, might be less interested in how truth was managed in the past and wholly interested in the honest sharing of emotional and behavioral information within the therapy session.

Again, one's clarity of theoretical focus, as well as what is needed to maintain the therapeutic alliance, must be evaluated in order to manage family secrets constructively.

DEALING WITH CLIENTS WE DISLIKE

Sooner or later you will have a client whom you dislike. This is a problem that all therapists encounter. Unfortunately, disliking a client can potentially undermine therapy by disrupting the formation of the therapeutic alliance. If a therapist dislikes a member of the couple or family, then this may lead to the therapist not being balanced in terms of advocating for all parties equally. Therapists may dislike a client for a number of different reasons, which may require them to respond with different strategies (Linn-Walton & Pardasani, 2014; Williams & Day, 2007). For example, therapists may dislike clients who challenge their competence or credibility, who threaten their emotional or physical safety, or who have little motivation for change.

Another possible reason that a therapist may dislike a client is due to countertransference issues. Does the client remind you of someone in your life with whom you had a difficult relationship (e.g., parent, sibling, significant other)? Or has the client harmed someone (e.g., child abuse, domestic violence, infidelity), reminding you of a similar experience? Does the client belong to a group of people (e.g., race/ethnicity, sexual orientation, religious affiliation) toward whom you have negative feelings? Answering yes to any of these questions might point to countertransference issues, which should be addressed through supervision and perhaps personal therapy. In more extreme cases, a referral to another therapist might be in the client's best interest.

In many cases, a negative response to a client may be diagnostic, providing important assessment information. For example, if you feel irritated by a client who is constantly blaming others, then it may help to recognize that the client has a poor external locus of control. A client who is irritable and critical may be suffering from depression. In other situations, you may find that your relational dynamic with the client you dislike parallels the process or dynamics that others within the family or couple have with the client. Recognizing the underlying clinical issue or parallel process often gives you greater objectivity about the client, reducing your dislike for him or her.

Our perception of a client can also be shaped by how others see the individual. Other people's negative feelings about a client could negatively affect our view of the client, particularly if we hear these negative views prior to meeting the individual. Conversely, it may be helpful to identify what others who like the client value about the individual. This may open us up to seeing some of the individual's positives that we have overlooked.

The therapist's initial response to a client may be one of dislike or anxiety, but looking further at the underlying reasons for a client's behavior or attitude may help change the therapist's perspective. An angry or blaming person may be experiencing hurt, rejection, or fear underneath. Individuals with fragile self-esteem may have developed maladaptive ways of coping with this (e.g., being narcissistic) that make them difficult to like. Clients may initially present with a protective shield in order to help manage their fears and anxieties about the therapeutic process. One such client was a 40-year-old man who came to his initial session proclaiming that the therapist had three visits to make things better or he would stop coming to therapy. The client's statement was his way of maintaining control and managing his anxiety. Initially, it was important to join with the client, to help him feel safe and reassure him that he was in control of making changes. Once this occurred, he was able to be more vulnerable in disclosing his concerns. His timetable became less of an issue once he felt understood by the therapist and felt that he could impact what happened in the therapy.

A variety of other approaches can also help you deal with clients whom you dislike. Actively seeking out client strengths can help counter negative feelings for a client. In some cases, a negative attribute (stubbornness) can be framed in a more positive light (perseverance). Therapists sometimes struggle with liking individuals who have harmed others (e.g., child abuse, domestic violence). In these situations, it may be helpful to separate the person from the problem. One phrase that illustrates this philosophy is "God hates the sin, but loves the sinner." Separating the person from the problem allows one to be compassionate for the individual, yet avoid minimizing the destructiveness of the behavior. You may also need to develop greater empathy for the client by trying to learn more about his or her life. Often you will learn about challenges, life experiences, or other contextual factors that influence the client's behavior. Understanding the multigenerational context of an individual may be especially helpful in developing a greater (and more empathic) understanding of the client.

Supervision is also recommended if you struggle with liking a client. Your supervisor may be able to offer a different perspective on the client. In many cases, clients whom therapists dislike are also difficult to treat. Your supervisor may be able to offer some guidance on how to approach a difficult case, which might reduce your frustration with the client.

HOW AGENCIES CONTRIBUTE TO BEING STUCK

Traditionally, agencies and institutions have developed to serve the needs of individuals. Agencies and institutions that focus on individuals will need to adapt to accommodate the different epistemology of systems thinking when working with couples and families. For example, does the agency allow a therapist to keep a "family file" or does each family member need to be assessed individually—that is, given a diagnosis or mental status exam? Does the agency have senior supervisors familiar with the theory and practice of family therapy? Practically, do the rooms of the agency provide enough space or evening and weekend office hours to serve the needs of the family? Without considering these concerns, an agency's organization might interfere with effective treatment of the whole family.

Beginning family therapists need to be aware of the agency's level of commitment to systems-oriented therapy before beginning their work. In this way, expectations and change can be facilitated positively. As in doing good therapy, know who is supportive of family therapy, explore their position within the agency as a whole, and enter the system respectful of its power base. When significant change is needed, be willing to serve as a helpful partner in that change, perhaps by offering to review and edit intake forms. Offer your own perspective about the cases you observe or nondefensively ask for feedback regarding alternative theoretical positions, after explaining how you're dealing with a case. Find family therapy supports outside the agency if you're working as a Lone Ranger (even he had Tonto).

Interestingly, the most resistant cases appear when all systems involved—client, therapist, and agency—get stuck together. This is called "isomorphism," a reference to the creation of similar relational structures across several systems. Client, therapist, and supervisory systems exist from the beginning of therapy. Since systems tend to re-create themselves at several levels, and beginning therapists are accountable across several systems, at times problems at one system level can be observed at another level. For example, a wife presented the problem of feeling powerless to change her husband; the therapist tried several interventions to help her respond differently to her husband, but she continued to do things in the same style; the supervisor directed the therapist to use another modality of therapy with this woman, but the therapist wanted to stay with the current agenda for a few more sessions. What we see at these three system levels is isomorphism, or similar interactional styles developing across systems. Isomorphism sometimes can be positive, but it also can signal areas of stuckness in the therapeutic relationship. Consider the case of Carl, a family therapist, and his client Bob. Carl has some difficulties in his work setting, which in turn have a direct effect on Bob's process of recovery.

Bob, a 32-year-old Caucasian male, reluctantly admits himself to an inpatient substance abuse program. His wife has been threatening to divorce him, and his employer indicates that Bob's work performance has suffered due to his alcohol-related absences. Bob feels that he drinks recreationally and can handle his problems. He does agree that he shouldn't drink so much during the week and thinks he can control it. He has even "quit completely several times, for 2 or 3 months." He thinks his wife should be more understanding of the stress that he's under because of his work and concentrate on her own problems. His fear of losing his job and his wife motivates him enough to enter a treatment program. His presentation is sarcastic, and he's resentful that he has to be there. He says that he'll stay for a while because he promised his wife. When asked about his goals he says, "I'm still trying to figure out why I'm here and who is in charge."

Bob's therapist is Carl, a 40-year-old Caucasian marriage and family therapist and a recovering alcoholic who has been working in the substance abuse field for the past 7 years. He has been sober for 12 years. Carl is a very committed professional who believes in combining the 12-step program with psychotherapy in order to help clients achieve sobriety. He works long hours and gets a great deal of satisfaction from his job. He feels that he has a realistic picture of what can be accomplished in treatment given "the time limits and nature of the disease of alcoholism."

Carl has worked with many clients like Bob who present an initial high degree of resistance to treatment and "denial as to the extent of their problem." Carl expects that Bob's hostility will begin to dissipate once he gets involved in some group meetings and begins to accept his problems.

In their first meeting, some of Bob's anger is directed at Carl. Bob insists that Carl can't really understand him and that he is only interested in keeping him in the hospital so that he can keep his job. Carl's response is to maintain his distance from Bob's anger and ask Bob further questions about his feelings about being in treatment. This helps to stop the attacks, but Bob continues to be fairly hostile throughout the session. In their second session Bob talks about his initial group meeting. He begins with sarcastic comments about some of the members and talks about why he doesn't think he belongs there. Further questions by the therapist help to identify some of Bob's feelings of identification with two of the group members who feel ambivalent about the treatment process. Carl's questions throughout the remainder of the session help Bob to disclose some of his fears about treatment. Carl leaves the second session feeling as though he has begun to develop a therapeutic alliance with Bob and the treatment process has begun.

Bob's treatment progresses well during the first week. He has quickly begun to like and respect Carl and is making good use of the treatment process. Carl also feels good about Bob's progress and begins to cautiously self-disclose about his own battle with alcohol. Carl sees some of himself in Bob, so he finds it a bit easier to talk with him than with most of the patients.

Toward the end of Bob's first week in treatment Carl begins to have some difficulties with his supervisor and some of the facility's policies. There has been a growing amount of required paperwork. The hospital has become more restrictive about overtime and has developed policies to discourage it. Carl's supervisor feels that his work with the patients is good but that his documentation is not up to par and he must improve in this area. Carl feels that his supervisor is more concerned about protecting his job than providing quality care, and he and the supervisor have a heated argument over this issue.

In his next meeting with Bob, Carl is still upset about his meeting with his supervisor. Although he knows better, he begins to talk about some of his frustrations with the hospital and his job. This becomes the topic of discussion for most of the session. Bob is very interested in Carl's difficulties with his job and asks lots of questions. Toward the end of the session he indicates that he has had some of the same kinds of problems with his boss.

At his next group meeting, Bob announces that he's going to leave the treatment program. He says he has learned that the program "doesn't have its priorities straight" and he doesn't "belong there."

The key for a beginning therapist, or any therapist, is to recognize when an isomorphic process is occurring. Unchecked, isomorphisms can be detrimental to therapy. With recognition comes the ability to be a more effective agent of change for the client.

Another potential way that agencies can contribute to being stuck is maintaining a strict adherence to a particular model of doing therapy. An agency or organization may be committed to using a particular framework because it has been demonstrated to work well with a particular problem or population. In some cases, the supervisor rather than the agency may be insistent that you work from a particular model. While a particular model may have demonstrated effectiveness for a particular population or issue in general, there may be specific clients in which the model may not provide the optimal fit with their needs. If confronted with this issue, you may need to advocate for why your client may need a different or modified approach. Your supervisor or agency will probably be more amenable to you modifying the treatment plan if you can maintain many of the essential ingredients to the treatment model. If you feel that the required treatment model cannot be modified to provide a good fit with your client's needs, you may need to consider making a referral.

SUPERVISION

Many normal obstacles interfere with successful therapy, especially in the beginning. Central to removing these barriers is a willingness to learn from one's mistakes and be open to information. Supportive, safe, and "live data" supervision (using videotape or direct observation of a session) offers vital information in helping beginning therapists avoid problems and find a solid footing.

Ideally, you will have access to a supervisor who has both strong clinical and supervisory skills. Individuals who are Approved Supervisors through the American Association for Marriage and Family Therapy, for example, have received special instruction in supervision (including supervision of their supervision).

Although the supervisor's qualifications are important, you must also be willing to do your part to make the supervision experience worthwhile. This requires that you be willing to share issues and cases that are a source of struggle for you. You need to be willing to seek live supervision or show videotapes of cases in which you feel stuck or frustrated. Therapists who only present cases in which they feel competent are missing an opportunity to grow and stretch themselves through supervision. Although it can be difficult to bring in cases where you are struggling, by doing so you are demonstrating your commitment to growing as a therapist. Also, be aware that you are likely to see your work in a much more negative light than your supervisor or peers in group supervision.

Preparing for the supervision ahead of time can prove very beneficial for both the supervisee and the supervisor. It can be helpful to come with thoughtful, pertinent questions. Supervision is likely to be most productive if you come prepared with a focus and specific questions. For example, you might ask for help on conceptualizing the case, or seek assistance on how to best handle an issue that arises in therapy. Or you may want to discuss with your supervisor how a case is impacting you (e.g., confidence, countertransference). Typically, the better the questions, the more likely one is able to gain a useful and clear direction.

Although supervision is generally invaluable to beginning therapists, it can also present challenges. In some instances, your supervisor may offer suggestions that do not seem to resonate with what you think your clients need. Rather than simply ignore the advice, it is best to explore with your supervisor why you think the suggestions may not be a good fit for your particular client. Most supervisors will appreciate any feedback you can provide that gives a clearer sense of your clients. Hopefully, the subsequent dialogue between you and your supervisor will lead to new, more helpful insights on how to intervene.

If you are getting supervision from more than one person, you may receive different or conflicting advice on a case. In some instances you will be able to resolve the problem by listening to your clinical intuition. By virtue of spending a lot of time with your clients, you may have an intuitive feel as to which approach will offer the best fit. If you do not have an intuitive feeling as to which approach is best, then this may be a sign that further assessment is needed. Collecting additional information may help clarify which conceptualization is a better fit with the case. You may even consider presenting both perspectives to the clients, and ask for their feedback on which conceptualization is most valid or helpful. Finally, you might consider bringing the issue of conflicting advice back into supervision with one or both supervisors. Supervision can then explore the possible advantages and disadvantages of each approach, as well as possible ways to resolve the contradictory perspectives.

Therapists may encounter problems in supervision if there is not a good fit between the supervisor and therapist. "Goodness of fit" between therapist and supervisor can be determined by a number of factors. An issue of fit can arise if the supervisor and therapist conceptualize cases from different theoretical perspectives. Issues of fit can also arise out of a mismatch between the supervisor's approach and the therapist's needs. A therapist who is interested in exploring self-of-therapist issues in supervision, for example, may feel frustrated by a supervisor who focuses primarily on theory or conceptualizing cases. Supervisors can also differ in the extent to which they are directive or nondirective, hierarchical or collaborative, or in the balance between offering positive feedback and constructive feedback. These and other factors can influence the extent to which the therapist perceives the supervisor as a good fit with his or her needs. As stated above, you should be explicit in stating what you need from supervision, which will hopefully help the supervisor make the necessary adjustments to better meet your needs. If possible, you can also consider seeking additional supervision from others who may offer a better fit with your needs.

SELF-SUPERVISION QUESTIONS

In addition to getting supervision from a qualified supervisor, you should begin to develop your own self-supervision skills. In other words, you should develop self-reflective methods and questions that can be used in place of getting supervision from another individual. Watching videotapes of your own sessions is helpful in providing a more objective viewpoint on what happens in therapy. Often therapists who have watched their videotapes prior to receiving supervision will report gaining important insights into their work.

You can also develop a list of self-supervision questions that are helpful when you get stuck in a case—a checklist of items that can frequently cause difficulties. A list of sample self-supervision questions is provided in Table 11.1. For example, a therapist who feels frustrated by the lack of movement in a case may discover upon going through the checklist of questions that he or she is working much harder than the clients are. This might lead the therapist to explore the clients' motivation for therapy or possible negative consequences of change. Used in this manner, a checklist of questions can help you troubleshoot a case on your own.

GETTING UNSTUCK USING RESEARCH AND LITERATURE

The family therapy literature is a rich source of information for dealing with difficult cases. Reading the research or literature is particularly helpful in cases where you have limited experience with a particular

TABLE 11.1. Self-Supervision Questions

When feeling stuck or encountering client resistance, ask yourself:

1. Am I, as the therapist, working harder than the clients? If so, why?

2. What are negative consequences of change with which my clients may be struggling?

3. Does the problem serve some positive function or purpose?

4. Have I clearly assessed the client's goals, and does the client see me as working on those goals?

5. Have I developed a strong therapeutic relationship with the client?

6. Does the client see therapy or the therapist as credible?

7. Is my frustration a possible sign of my own personal issues interfering with therapy?

8. Are my reactions or responses isomorphic to the system?

9. Have I appropriately balanced the responsibility for change between clients? (Or do I find myself siding with one client over another?)

10. Have I identified two or three key therapeutic issues or themes, or am I trying to focus on too many things at once?

11. Am I being sensitive to cultural or contextual factors that might be impacting therapy or the therapeutic relationship?

---

problem or population. For example, a therapist who has not worked with a couple experiencing infertility could read books, research, or other literature on the issues that infertile couples often face.

The 5 As (Ask, Acquire, Appraise, Apply, and Analyze and Adjust) is a useful step-by-step model for using research or other literature to inform your clinical work. In Step 1 (Ask), you create questions that can be answered by the research or literature. Are you primarily interested in issues of assessment, or are you looking for treatment approaches with regard to a case? Being specific in constructing your questions can help you narrow your search more efficiently.

After creating your questions, you need to conduct a search to locate research or literature to answer your questions (Step 2; Acquire). PsycINFO (*www.apa.org/psycinfo*) offers the most comprehensive database of psychological research and literature, and is usually an excellent starting point. PsycINFO can be accessed through many university or college libraries. However, you may want to consider other databases as well. GoogleScholar (*https://scholar.google.com*) can be used to search for scholarly articles on the Internet. Useful research may also be found by searching medical databases, particularly for issues related to health or psychopathology. Evidence Based Mental Health (*ebmh.bmjjournals.com*), for example, is an online journal that summarizes mental health research from medical and psychiatry journals. Medline offers the most extensive listing of the biomedical literature, and can be accessed for free through PubMed (*www.ncbi.nlm.nih.gov/pubmed*). You may also want to familiarize yourself with databases that provide summaries of the research, such as the Cochrane Database of Systematic Reviews (*www.cochrane.org*), Campbell Collaboration (*www.campbellcollaboration.org*), and UpToDate (*www.uptodate.com*).

If your initial search uncovers a limited number of articles, you may be able to locate other relevant literature by examining the reference list. The titles in the reference list may also include other potential keywords you can use to expand your search. Some databases allow you to see what other articles subsequently cite the current article, which may help you identify additional relevant works.

In other cases, you may find an abundance of articles that might apply to your question. If the amount of literature is large, you may want to consider limiting your search by date of publication, type of publication (e.g., peer reviewed), age of the population (e.g., adolescent, adult), or some other criteria. Furthermore, if there is a lot of research on a topic, then it is likely that you will be able to find reviews of the literature or meta-analyses. Finding these can be a significant time saver because they conveniently locate and summarize the key literature or research for you.

In the third step (Appraise), you will need to evaluate the quality of the research if the article summarizes an empirical study. Obviously, greater confidence can be placed in studies with stronger methodologies. Table 11.2 lists questions that a reader with a basic understanding of research can ask to discriminate studies that are generally strong from those with major weaknesses. However, more indirect measures of quality can also be used to evaluate the quality of research. Greater confidence can be put in studies that are published in peer-reviewed journals. In addition, more prestigious journals typically have higher-quality studies because they can be more selective in the research they publish.

In the fourth step (Apply), you will need to use what you have learned from the research or literature to inform your clinical work. There are a number of factors that you will need to consider when applying information from the research or literature. First, you will need to assess how directly the research or literature relates to the issue your client is addressing. Literature that is indirectly related to your client's issues might still inform your work, but you will need to be tentative in applying the findings. Second, you need to ask how similar your clients

TABLE 11.2. Questions for Evaluating Research

<u>Introduction and literature review</u>

1. Are the purpose and importance of the study clearly articulated?
2. Does the literature review cover the relevant research?
3. Is the literature cited current?
4. Does the literature review critique the existing literature, or simply summarize it?

<u>Methodology</u>

Measurement issues

1. Are the instruments in the study adequately described?
2. Is there evidence of internal and/or test–retest reliability for measures used in the study?
3. Is there evidence for interrater reliability if coding systems are used?
4. Is there evidence that the instruments are valid (e.g., content, criterion, concurrent, and/or construct validity)?
5. Are there other measurement concerns (e.g., reactivity, sensitivity)?

Sampling issues and external validity

1. What steps were taken to make sure the sample was representative of the population of interest? Was probability (random, systematic, strata, multistage cluster) or nonprobability (e.g., convenience) sampling used?
2. Does a low response rate threaten the representativeness of the sample?
3. Are the demographics of the sample adequately described?
4. Does the sample adequately represent diversity (e.g., race/ethnicity, gender)?
5. Are the possible threats to generalizability (external validity) addressed in the research?

Issues of internal validity

1. For experimental studies, does the study include both a treatment and a comparison group (control or alternative treatment)? Are subjects randomly assigned to the groups?
2. Does the outcome study take into account possible confounding variables such as placebo effects, attention effects, or mortality rates?
3. Is there evidence that the treatments were delivered as intended, or that participants were compliant in following the treatment?
4. For correlational research, does the researcher inappropriately imply cause and effect relationships? Is there consideration of spurious relationships?
5. Are threats to internal validity from cohort effects addressed in cross-sectional research?

(continued)

TABLE 11.2. *(continued)*

Methodological issues for qualitative research
1. Does the researcher identify the theoretical framework and other potential biases that may influence interpretation of the data?
2. Is the researcher role in relation to the participants clearly defined (e.g., participant vs. nonparticipant, concealed vs. nonconcealed)?
3. For qualitative research, were the criteria for selecting participants clearly described?
4. Does the researcher specify the types of data collected, and how they were collected?
5. Does the researcher specify how the data were analyzed?
6. Does the researcher report how he or she established reliability and validity (e.g., triangulation of data, saturation, having participants examine the findings)?
7. Do the illustrative quotes or descriptions support the conclusions?

Other considerations
1. Are there any ethical concerns about the study (e.g., benefits outweigh risks, informed consent, voluntary, privacy)?
2. For outcome studies, are the treatments adequately described?
3. Were appropriate statistical tests used to analyze the findings?

<u>Results and discussion</u>
1. Does the researcher draw appropriate conclusions from the results, or do they go beyond what they should given the limits to the internal or external validity of the study?
2. Does the article clearly identify the limitations of the research?
3. Does the researcher address clinical significance or rely exclusively on statistical significance?
4. Are implications (or contraindications) for treatment discussed?
5. Are recommendations for future research included?

Note. From Williams, Patterson, and Miller (2006, pp. 31–32). Copyright 2006 by the American Association for Marriage and Family Therapy. Reprinted by permission from John Wiley & Sons.

are to the ones who have been studied or described in the research or literature. The more different they are, then the more cautious you will need to be in applying the findings. In addition, you may need to make modifications to account for differences due to culture, age, gender, sexual orientation, or other attributes. Fourth, client preferences must be taken into account. Therapists can describe to the clients what the treatment options are, and seek their input on what might be the best approach. Finally, additional steps may be necessary before you can successfully apply the research to the case, such as obtaining treatment manuals, training, or assessment instruments from the authors.

Taking the above factors into consideration requires that you use your clinical judgment. Therefore, while research and other literature can offer helpful guidance, it stills requires that you use your clinical expertise to discern how to best apply what you have learned to your specific clients' needs and situation.

As you apply the findings from the research or literature, you will ideally evaluate the effectiveness of your approach and make the necessary adjustments (Step 5; Analyze and Adjust). This step is vital if you have needed to adapt or modify the treatment approach to your client's specific situation. Beyond asking clients about their progress in therapy, various instruments (e.g., Outcome Rating Scale, Outcome Questionnaire–45, Systemic Therapy Inventory of Change) are also available that the therapist can use to evaluate if therapy is progressing.

In addition to using journal articles and books, therapists can locate a lot of useful information on the Internet. However, if you use information from the Internet, you need to be certain the information is from a reliable source. Information from sites sponsored by organizations (e.g., universities, medical organizations) or the government are likely to be more reliable than sites created by individuals.

CONCLUSION

Finding oneself stuck, for whatever reason, in the midst of the therapeutic process is ubiquitous in the early stages of one's work. Keep in mind that every point of "stuckness" provides a chance to increase competence and confidence. This chapter has identified some of the most common places therapists encounter challenges, and we've talked about ways to become "unstuck." Heightening awareness of the therapeutic process and developing specific skills, and knowing what steps to take when we meet obstacles, are the essential parts of our work.

CHAPTER 12

Termination

Cassandra is reviewing her session notes from her last meeting with Sophia and Greg. As Cassandra waits for Sophia and Greg to arrive for today's session, she reflects on how far the couple has come in therapy over the past 6 months. When the couple began therapy, Sophia was close to divorce after she had learned of Greg's affair. A remorseful Greg said he would do whatever it would take to save the marriage. Sophia admitted that she loved Greg, but wondered whether she could ever trust him again after such a significant betrayal. In the early sessions, Cassandra worried whether the couple would survive the crisis. However, the couple was eventually able to make progress, particularly after Greg was able to articulate the reasons behind the affair with Cassandra's help. The couple also examined how they could use the crisis precipitated by the affair to strengthen their marriage, addressing some unmet needs that Sophia and Greg had swept under the rug in order to avoid conflict. Although Sophia admitted that she still occasionally struggled with trust issues, she told Cassandra in the last session that she was fully committed to the marriage now. Cassandra was now wondering where to go in therapy with the couple. Should she be ending therapy, or should she continue to do more work around the trust issues? When Cassandra had hinted that therapy might be winding down 3 weeks ago, the couple expressed fears about being able to handle things on their own. Was this a sign that the couple needed more support through therapy, or was this anxiety about ending therapy normal? Should she directly raise the prospect of ending therapy in today's session? How should she bring closure to therapy that will be most helpful to Sophia and Greg?

An important part of therapy is termination, despite the fact that it does not receive much attention in the literature—this is comparable to learning how to drive but never learning how to properly park the car and turn off the engine. A successful termination to therapy can be important for several reasons.

Terminations can be an effective way of empowering both the clients and the therapist. A successful termination should consolidate or reinforce the therapeutic gains of the client. For those who need to be referred or transferred, a successful termination can increase the likelihood that they will have a productive experience with the new therapist. For you as the therapist, a successful termination can help you understand how you were most helpful to the client, thereby building your confidence.

Terminations can also be important because they bring closure to the therapist–client relationship, an especially vital consideration in cases in which the therapist and the client have developed a strong connection over time. If properly handled, terminations can help clients and therapists deal with losses associated with ending the therapeutic relationship. Terminations can also be an opportunity for the client to learn that relationships can end with a positive outcome. This realization can be especially useful for clients who have had trauma or difficulty around loss or abandonment issues.

This chapter discusses three types of termination: mutual termination, therapist termination, and client termination. Mutual terminations occur when both the client and the therapist agree on the termination, which typically occurs when both feel that client goals have been achieved. Therapist and client terminations happen when one party makes the decision unilaterally.

Although these terminations will be discussed as three distinct phenomena, it is perhaps more accurate to view them on a continuum. Client and therapist terminations could be considered the two ends of the continuum, with mutual terminations representing the midpoint. Therefore, the therapeutic considerations outlined under each type may also apply to the others, depending on the situation.

MUTUAL TERMINATIONS

Most therapists strive for mutual terminations, where both you and your client are in agreement that the presenting issues have been properly resolved and that continuing therapy is no longer necessary. In rare cases, both you and your client may agree that therapy should no longer be continued, but not necessarily because the issues are resolved. In one such example, both the therapist and the client agreed that the client should discontinue therapy until she had finished a particularly difficult semester, given that most of her energy was devoted to finishing her studies. The client resumed therapy after completing her semester and had more energy to devote to her personal growth at that time.

When to Terminate

Although clients will sometimes bring up the topic of termination, more often the therapist must initiate the discussion about ending therapy. Therefore, it is important that you recognize when it is time to begin termination.

Mutual terminations generally result from having successfully achieved the goals for therapy. It will be easier to recognize when to conclude therapy if these goals have been clearly defined. If not, you may need to rely on other indicators. If your clients have difficulty finding issues to discuss in therapy, this is often a sign that therapy is close to ending. Likewise, if you and your clients spend a lot of time in session on nontherapeutic talk or social chatter, termination should be considered. Missed appointments may be another indicator that therapy is coming to a close. The client may not feel the same urgency to come to therapy if he or she is aware of significant improvement.

One of the difficulties that can arise when working with couples or families is that not all family members may feel equally ready to terminate therapy. Sometimes this is simply due to family members having different levels of confidence in their ability to handle problems without the therapist's guidance. One might consider spacing out the sessions until all family members have developed the confidence to end therapy.

In other cases, family members may not be in agreement about terminating therapy because they have different expectations about what they want to achieve through therapy. In these situations, you are faced with the same dilemma as when clients enter therapy with different expectations. It is often possible for you to help the couple or family achieve some compromise. For example, one couple had made significant progress in reducing their high level of conflict in their relationship. The husband reported being satisfied with the changes that had been made and expressed interest in discontinuing therapy. While the wife agreed that their relationship was much improved, particularly in terms of the original goal of reducing conflict, she also expressed a desire to continue in therapy to improve the couple's sexual intimacy.

A compromise was reached wherein the couple contracted to work on improving their sexual intimacy, but agreed to come to therapy every other week rather than weekly.

Termination Goals

In terminating therapy, it's helpful to keep three goals in mind. First, help clients consolidate the gains they have made through therapy. Termination should reinforce the new skills, behaviors, or ways of thinking that the clients have learned.

Second, empower clients, giving them greater confidence in their ability to manage issues on their own in the future. Another result of empowerment is that there will be a leveling of power between the therapist and the clients, reducing the clients' dependence on you and increasing their self-reliance.

Third, be sensitive to potential losses associated with terminations. Many clients develop a close relationship with their therapist and feel a strong sense of loss when ending the relationship. This is most likely to occur when working with individuals, but couples and families can experience loss too. The sense of loss may be particularly keen for clients who have limited social support to compensate for the loss of the therapeutic relationship.

Like clients, you may also experience a sense of loss during termination. Therapists can develop a very strong connection with clients, triggering feelings of sadness that the relationship is ending. These feelings can be compounded by other losses you may be experiencing. For example, when therapists leave their training program upon graduation, many report sadness about ending relationships not only with their clients, but also with their colleagues and friends from school. You need to be prepared to acknowledge and deal with these feelings as they arise.

Termination as a Process

Terminations are more successful if they are conceptualized as a process rather than as an event. Therapists should be thinking about how and when to prepare clients for termination prior to the final session. In fact, one could argue that termination should be in the therapist's mind from the initial sessions. A therapist who is aware that a client has a very limited support network could anticipate that the client is likely to develop a strong dependence upon the therapist. This will make termination a more acute loss for the client if this high level of dependence is left unaddressed. In fact, a client who is overly dependent upon his or her therapist may actually manufacture problems so as to prolong the therapeutic relationship. Therefore, the therapist would be wise in this situation to help the client develop a social support network during therapy. This will not only empower the client by giving him or her more resources, but will reduce the feelings of loss associated with termination because the client will have others to turn to for emotional support.

Therapeutic Interventions in Termination

You can use several interventions to help achieve the goals for termination. One common intervention is to begin spacing out sessions. This strategy can give your clients time to consolidate the gains they have made, while simultaneously building their confidence in their ability to manage problems on their own between sessions.

In helping clients consolidate what they have gained from therapy, a number of questions can be asked. You can request clients to articulate what has changed for them and what they believe accounts for the change. You can also put them in the expert role by highlighting how successful they have been in addressing their problem, and then asking them for advice about how you might work with other clients who have a similar difficulty. The latter approach has the advantage of both empowering your clients and helping them consolidate therapeutic gains. When asking clients to indicate what has brought about change, it's important that you give them permission to acknowledge things that may have happened outside of therapy. For example, one couple acknowledged that in addition to what they learned in therapy, having extended family move out of the couple's home greatly improved their marriage. Some clients have difficulty answering the question of what they are doing differently. One possible approach to this problem is to ask them what they could do to make things worse, which often gives them insights into what positive changes have occurred (Hoffman, 1981). In other cases, you may need to help highlight for your clients the changes they have made.

It's often helpful to warn clients that temporary relapses may occur after therapy ends. Clients can be told that change is frequently "two steps forward and one step back." This helps them feel less threatened by temporary setbacks. Furthermore, clients can be instructed to use the temporary setback to review what they have learned and perhaps gain new insights to create the next two steps forward.

Clients respond very positively when you can share something special that they have taught you. This not only empowers your clients, but also helps make them feel the relationship has been reciprocal. For example, one therapist told a couple how a particular metaphor that had emerged out of their work together had been helpful in his work with other clients.

Some therapists also like to give small gifts to clients to mark termination. The gifts should be of small monetary value so clients do not feel obligated to give a gift in return. Instead, the gift should be rich in symbolic meaning. One therapist gave a couple an onion to symbolize the different layers of the couple's relationship they had explored and the emotions that were brought forth. Gifts not only communicate that the therapist values the client, but they can also symbolize an important therapeutic theme in the work. Jasmine worked with Devon, a shy, 9-year-old boy with significant self-esteem issues. Over the course of 20 sessions, Jasmine was able to draw Devon out and help him see his strengths. At the conclusion of therapy, Jasmine gave Devon a geode stone. The rough, plain exterior of the stone represented how Devon initially viewed himself, whereas the beautiful crystals on the inside symbolized the hidden gifts he had uncovered through his work in therapy.

Special Issues in Termination

One special issue that can arise at termination is whether to accept gifts from clients. Therapists (and the agencies where they work) can have different views on this topic. Some therapists believe they should not accept gifts from clients under any circumstances. The advantage of this approach is that you are never placed in the position of having to decide if a gift is inappropriate (e.g., too expensive). The potential disadvantage is that it may hurt the client's feelings if you refuse to accept a gift, particularly if it was meant to be a symbolic gesture. Therefore, some therapists believe that it's permissible to accept gifts from clients provided they aren't expensive. Therapists must weigh the monetary and symbolic meaning of the gift before accepting it. This makes the judgment surrounding whether to accept a gift or not more complicated, but gives the therapist more latitude on how to respond. Each therapist must make a personal choice on which philosophy he or she will adopt regarding gifts from clients.

Another issue that can arise at termination is that clients may want to continue to have a relationship with you outside of therapy. We recommend that you avoid this situation. Once a therapeutic relationship is established, it is extremely difficult to transition to any other type of relationship. The therapeutic relationship is built around the client talking and the therapist listening. It is not typically a mutual sharing, but the client disclosing while the therapist provides a safe place to be heard. Maintaining contact with a client beyond termination can be valuable as a follow-up, but transitioning to anything other than a client–therapist relationship can be complicated, confusing, and constitute a dual relationship. It is also not uncommon for clients to return to therapy because of new problems that arise. If you keep up a relationship with your clients after termination and they need to resume therapy, it puts you in the uncomfortable position of having a dual relationship with them. Therefore, another reason to avoid a friendship relationship after termination is to preserve your clients' right to return to therapy if needed.

Avoiding relationships outside of therapy not only protects the clients, but can also protect you. If problems arise in the relationship outside of therapy for any reason, you are vulnerable to having your professional behavior questioned. A therapist who gets romantically involved with a client after terminating therapy could be accused of taking advantage of the client if the relationship sours.

Finally, another issue that therapists sometimes face is clients who do not wish to terminate, but who would like to continue therapy on a less frequent basis. Some therapists see this request as a sign that the client is too dependent upon the therapist. Other therapists believe that this arrangement is completely appropriate and desirable for some clients. Some therapists advocate booster sessions to help maintain treatment gains.

When clients ask to continue therapy, you should carefully evaluate the motivation behind the request. The request may signal excessive dependence upon you, particularly if your clients ask to see you on a frequent basis (more than once or twice a month). These clients typically have few people other than their therapist with whom they feel closely connected. You may then want to help your clients develop their support network to reduce their dependence on you.

However, the request to continue therapy doesn't always signal dependency issues. Some clients want to see their therapist periodically to help keep their family relationships healthy. For these clients, therapy is like going to the dentist for a 6-month preventative checkup. Other clients genuinely want to continue to grow, and they see therapy as a way to facilitate that growth. Therapy assumes more of a coaching or mentoring role, rather than resolving a crisis or pressing problems. Therefore, a therapist could feel comfortable seeing these clients periodically as a preventative measure or to facilitate the clients' desire for continued growth. For example, after a successful course of couple therapy, Eli continued to see one couple once every 3 months to facilitate their continued growth and enrichment of their relationship.

THERAPIST TERMINATIONS

There will be times when a therapist may unilaterally decide therapy should be discontinued. As with client terminations, there can be a variety of reasons leading to a therapist termination. A common reason is that you are moving or terminating employment with an agency. In some instances, a therapist may wish to end therapy with particular clients due to specific issues in the case. The therapist may feel unqualified to deal with these issues, or feel that personal issues interfere with the case.

You might also suggest terminating therapy if an agreement cannot be reached on the therapeutic contract or you strongly suspect the clients are not ready for change. However, you should work closely with these clients to make termination of therapy as much of a mutual decision as possible. In one case, for example, a therapist felt it was necessary to address the husband's severe mistrust of his wife as part of the couple's dynamics. However, the husband never agreed with the therapist's assessment that this was an important issue to address, thereby creating an impasse in therapy. The therapist discussed with the couple how the lack of agreement on this key issue probably precluded a successful outcome to therapy. The couple agreed, resulting in a mutual decision to terminate therapy and a referral to another therapist for a second opinion.

When terminating therapy, you should give your clients as much notice as possible. An abrupt termination of therapy is often stressful for clients, particularly for those who have abandonment issues. Giving advance notice will provide your clients time to prepare themselves emotionally for the termination. Clients whom you anticipate will struggle with terminations might be informed as early as 2–3 months in advance, if possible. This permits you to solicit and process your clients' fears regarding changing therapists. Advance notice of termination may also motivate your clients to work harder in therapy to avoid having to transfer to another therapist.

If clients need to continue in therapy, it is important you make a proper transfer or referral. When making an outside referral, you should try to provide your clients with at least three referrals so they have some choices. This increases the likelihood of the clients finding a suitable therapist. In other cases, clients can be transferred to another therapist within the same agency or practice.

Effectively transferring a case requires attending to the needs of the clients, the departing therapist, and the incoming therapist (Williams & Winter, 2009). Clients have multiple needs or concerns with regard to being transferred. For example, they need assurance that there will be continuity of care after you leave them. If feasible, it is ideal if the new therapist can join you for at least one session prior to termination so that he or she can be introduced to the clients. You may even elect to do some type of intervention to mark the transition. For example, the incoming therapist may initially take an observing role during the transfer session, but deliver a summarizing message at the end of the session to mark his or her assumption of responsibility from that point forward. If a break in therapy is required because the new therapist is not immediately available, then your clients should be told when he or she will be available and whom to contact in the event an emergency should arise before then.

Clients may have several reservations about starting over with a new therapist. Many, for example, may not want to tell their story over again. Even if you talk to the new therapist about the case, he or she will inevitably need to cover some history that was discussed in the previous therapy. Your clients' concerns about retelling their story can be validated, yet at the same time you can suggest that a fresh perspective may be gained by sharing some of the story again with a new person. Clients may also worry about whether they will like their new therapist. If you have had input on whom the new therapist will be, you can assure your clients that the incoming therapist has been selected with their needs in mind. It is also possible that your clients are concerned about whether the new therapist will like them. Offering reassurances that the new therapist will enjoy working with them can alleviate these fears, particularly if you can note the ways in which you have enjoyed working with the clients.

As with other terminations, it is important for you to review the progress your clients have made to date in meeting their goals. The transfer can be framed as closing one chapter and beginning a new one with the new therapist. As mentioned earlier, clients may experience a sense of loss over ending therapy. This will be particularly true for individuals who have a strong attachment to or dependence upon you. Some clients may also have anger about being transferred, which may or may not be expressed overtly. In some cases, this anger may be directed primarily at the new therapist. It is important that you or the new therapist not respond defensively to this anger or disappointment should it occur. Indeed, validating the feelings of loss and anger over a transfer may help the new therapist solidify the therapeutic relationship.

As the departing therapist, you also have important needs that should be considered in the process. As in other terminations, you may experience a sense of loss over therapy ending. A formal transfer or termination session can help bring proper closure for both you and the clients alike. You may also worry about the future welfare of your clients. In some cases, therapists may experience guilt because they worry that their clients' needs won't be met as a result of therapy ending. These feelings may be particularly strong if the therapist is unable to hand his or her clients over to another therapist that he or she knows or has confidence in.

The needs of the therapist receiving the transfer should also not be overlooked. The new therapist hopes that you can pass on a good understanding of the case. Ideally, both of you will be able to discuss the case prior to your departure. The new therapist can also review your case notes or consult with your supervisor to learn more about the case. Therapists receiving transfer clients can also struggle with issues of credibility, especially if they are less experienced. Ideally, you will be able empower the incoming therapist by highlighting his or her strengths or capabilities. With time, the new therapist can earn the clients' trust and credibility. The new therapist also needs to be able to renegotiate the contract for therapy. The goals for therapy, which may have changed over time, should be reviewed. Other expectations for therapy may also need to be renegotiated (e.g., approach to therapy, who will be in therapy, time or frequency of appointments). Asking clients what they liked and disliked about therapy can give the new therapist insight into what expectations they may be bringing into therapy.

CLIENT TERMINATIONS

Unilateral terminations, whether initiated by the client or the therapist, are usually frustrating for the party who was not consulted. What can make client terminations even more difficult is that they can occur without warning, and the client may never offer an explanation for leaving therapy. The client may simply not show up for therapy, or cancel the appointment and never reschedule. Therapists' reactions to client terminations may include blaming the client ("They were unmotivated"), being relieved ("They were a difficult case"), acceptance ("This happens to all therapists, it is just part of doing therapy"), or blaming him- or herself ("I must have done something wrong").

When a client does not return to therapy, beginning therapists frequently worry that they have done something wrong. Although this is a possibility that should be considered, you should not automatically assume that a termination is a sign of failure on your part (Ogrodniczuk, Joyce, & Piper, 2005; Skovholt, 2010). This point was poignantly made for one of us during two internship cases. One couple who had suddenly dropped out of therapy came back unexpectedly after 5 months. When he expressed surprise at seeing them return, they explained how a job change and subsequent temporary move made it impossible to continue therapy. However, they were now eager to resume therapy because they had found it to be helpful earlier.

A short time later, a new couple came to see the therapist. The couple reported that another couple had recommended they see him. He was surprised that this particular couple had recommended him because they had left therapy unexpectedly. In both cases, the therapist had worried that the couple dropping out of therapy was a sign of a treatment failure on his part.

Clients can terminate therapy for a variety of reasons (Barrett et al., 2008; Knox et al., 2011; Renk & Dinger, 2002; Roos & Werbart, 2013). For some clients, from their point of view, their problem has been resolved and they no longer see the need to continue therapy. Or the clients may feel that things have improved enough and do not wish to invest additional time or money in therapy.

Other clients simply lose momentum coming to therapy. They may cancel an appointment (e.g., due to illness) or promise to call later to reschedule (e.g., after returning from vacation or a business trip). Some of these clients may have obtained enough relief that they no longer feel compelled to reinitiate or continue with therapy, or they allow other things to take priority.

Some clients discontinue therapy because of factors not directly related to therapy itself. Financial hardships may keep some from returning, like the man who informed his therapist he could no longer afford the gas it took to come to therapy. Transportation difficulties, moving, changing jobs, or illness may be other reasons that clients stop therapy unexpectedly. A single mother who brought three young children to the first session did not return for a second session. When a follow-up phone call was made, she said getting to the agency by bus with three young children was stressful, and that she had found an agency that provided home-based services as an alternative.

Clients may drop out of therapy if their motivation is undermined by a lack of hope or ambivalence. Individuals may question whether to invest the time and money in therapy if their expectations that change will occur are low. Ambivalence can also be a factor in early termination of therapy. For example, couples are more at risk for early termination if one or both partners are ambivalent about working on the relationship (Mondor et al., 2013).

Of course, some clients will not return because they are dissatisfied with therapy. Clients are at risk for dropping out if the therapist has been unable to establish a strong alliance or therapeutic relationship with them (Sharf et al., 2010). This can be more complicated in couple or family therapy where the therapist must form a therapeutic bond with multiple individuals. In some cases, the therapist may have damaged the therapeutic relationship in some manner. Clients may also leave therapy if they feel change is not happening quickly enough. Their dissatisfaction may be rooted in unrealistic expectations of what therapy is, or because the therapist has been ineffective in creating change.

Although client terminations are an inherent part of doing therapy, there are steps you can take to help minimize the likelihood that clients will end therapy prematurely (Barrett et al., 2008; Ogrodniczuk et al., 2005; Rainer & Campbell, 2001; Swift, Greenberg, Whipple, & Kominiak, 2012). First, you must be attentive to the therapeutic relationship, both in building it and in maintaining it. Second, you should monitor whether your clients feel that therapy is being beneficial. Various instruments are available to measure the client's perception of the therapeutic relationship and progress in therapy (see Williams et al., 2014, for a review of these instruments). Some instruments are brief and easily incorporated into therapy, such as the Session Rating Scale (SRS) and the Outcome Rating Scale (ORS), which are four-item instruments that measure the therapeutic relationship and progress in therapy, respectively. Ongoing assessment will help you quickly identify a problem if it arises, giving you the opportunity to address client concerns. Third, you should assess your clients' expectations for therapy in the beginning session. If your clients' expectations on what therapy will address are not met, then your clients will become dissatisfied and prematurely drop out. Problems can also arise if the client's expectations are unrealistic. For example, some clients may believe that their problems can be solved in just one or two sessions. Some clients may need education about therapy (e.g., length of therapy, the role of the therapist and client in therapy) so that their expectations are appropriate. Fourth, be attentive to factors that impact motivation, such as ambivalence and a lack of hope. Instilling a sense of hope, for example, may prevent clients from prematurely leaving therapy before sufficient progress can be made. Finally, be aware of external factors that may impact your clients' ability to participate in therapy (e.g., financial hardships). You may be able to help your client problem-solve around these issues, reducing the likelihood that they will need to prematurely leave therapy.

If a client ends therapy without an explanation, you should ideally follow up with the client to determine the reason for the termination. Your next step will depend on the reason given for termination. You might be able to negotiate a lower fee for clients who stop for financial reasons. If you have harmed the therapeutic relationship, you can attempt to fix the relationship, or at a minimum provide referrals for your clients. In some cases, you might want to invite your clients in for a termination session to bring a proper closure to therapy.

CONCLUSION

Terminations can be a difficult time for clients and therapists alike, particularly if both parties did not mutually agree to end therapy. When the therapist must initiate termination, there is the potential for clients to feel abandoned or insecure about starting therapy with another therapist. Conversely, therapists may question whether they were effective in helping clients who appear to have prematurely left therapy. Even when terminating therapy is mutually agreed upon because the goals for therapy have been successfully achieved, there can still be a sense of loss from ending the therapeutic relationship. An effective termination will deal with the losses, help clients consolidate the gains they have made, and give them greater confidence about the future.

CHAPTER 13

Family Therapy in the Future

Ralph briefly reviews the intake sheet. The client writes "Ongoing, unresolved issues" in the blank space for the presenting problem. Ralph wonders what the client means by this brief comment. During the initial interview, he gets a history of Andrea Beckham's many attempts to address the struggles she has faced since she was diagnosed with bipolar disorder at age 22. At that time, she had a job with good insurance and she received therapy and medication. She also attended psychoeducational support groups with some family members. It was going well until her company downsized and she was laid off. She could no longer afford her expensive medications and the private clinic was too expensive. She tried to get government-sponsored health insurance but did not qualify.

Eventually, she gave up and decided to hope for the best as she looked for a new job. At the time of the intake with Ralph, a year had passed since Andrea lost her insurance and Andrea's life had gotten worse. However, a friend recently told her about the community clinic that used a sliding scale for payments and she decided to try again. At the end of the session, Ralph hesitated to tell her that there was an eight-session limit and that the clinic had recently lost its funding to pay a psychiatrist for medication evaluations. He was not sure what to say when Andrea said, "I finally feel hope after not knowing what to do during the past year."

PERTINENT ISSUES FOR BEGINNING CLINICIANS

Beginning family therapists exit graduate school and enter the mental health marketplace with a noble goal: to help clients alleviate their distress and suffering. But in the therapist's office of the 21st century, the challenge of doing therapy goes beyond the basics encountered during training. Clinical work in many settings means cooperating and sharing care with other healthcare providers, giving increased attention to to clients with individual and DSM diagnoses, adhering to treatment guidelines provided by someone else, and complying with utilization reviews. More than ever, family therapists may find themselves playing double advocate roles: searching out creative options for clients whose healthcare plans limit modality and length of treatment, and helping the profession prove its legitimacy, thereby ensuring that family therapy is one treatment option.

Affording healthcare services, including mental health, is a worldwide issue. As countries struggle with economic reforms, leaders note the stresses that families face. In the global economy, government leaders look for ways to support families and children, including creating mental health services that support families. Whatever form the new systems take, family therapists can be certain the effects will be felt by themselves and their clients.

In the United States, there is tremendous variability by region in the availability of mental health services. We are hopeful that legislation supporting parity for mental and physical health and government-sponsored health insurance initiatives mean that more clients can receive treatment. Parity suggests that a client should have the same coverage (payment) for mental conditions that he or she has for physical conditions (Glied & Frank, 2008). Historically, many payers will not cover clients' mental health services even when they pay for physical care. Even if some mental health payment is offered, most insurance plans impose special limits on the amount of mental health care they will pay for.

Parity arguments usually revolve around cost sharing and "medical necessity." Even with private insurance, mental health clients are likely to pay a higher percentage of their income for their mental health care than for physical care. "Medical necessity" generally refers to care that is accepted medical practice or meets community standards of care. Thus, payers do not want to pay for communication problems but are willing to pay for treatment of DSM diagnoses like anxiety, ADHD, depression, bipolar disorder, and schizophrenia.

In this chapter, we leave you with a glimpse of the present and future "business" of family therapy, the implications (pro and con) for your work with clients, and some pointers that will help you navigate the unpredictable waters of ongoing healthcare reform. In addition, we talk about trends in mental health services that will influence your work. Finally, we end the book with a discussion of the impact of your work as a therapist on you personally.

HEALTHCARE REFORM:
IMPLICATIONS FOR YOU AND YOUR CLIENTS

The World Health Organization (WHO) has created a pyramid (Figure 13.1) that represents the optimal mix of services for mental health care. WHO is concerned with mental health services both in countries that have virtually no funding for mental health services and in countries like the United States that have multiple funding streams: government funding, private funding, and self-pay mental health services. The WHO Pyramid reflects the belief that self-care and informal community care are adequate for many people needing mild mental health services. At

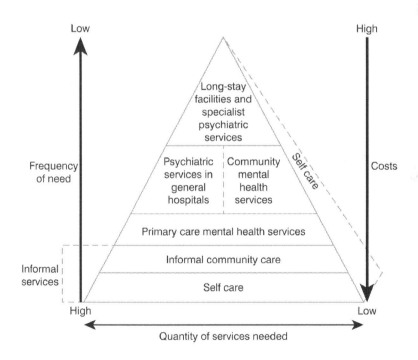

FIGURE 13.1. The WHO Pyramid.

the next level, primary care is viewed as an ideal context for delivering basic mental health services. As one moves up the pyramid, the expenses increase and fewer people both need and receive services. The WHO Pyramid is an excellent reminder that mental health does not exist in isolation. As WHO suggests, there is "no health without mental health" (Prince et al., 2007). In addition, mental health services will always reflect the resources and beliefs of stakeholders in specific communities.

In recent years, the United States has made significant efforts to improve both mental health services and overall health services. But as worldwide health policy experts have grappled with how to deliver good care, several controversies remain unresolved:

- *Individual versus universal treatments*—Should mental health providers offer individualized care (a single therapist delivering care to his or her client) or population- based care (delivering a packaged treatment to a group of individuals with shared characteristics)? How does this decision affect the cost of treatments?
- *Social interventions versus biological interventions*—Which type of intervention produces the most good for the least cost? For example, should we use limited financial resources to provide parent education or provide free psychotropic medications?
- *Diagnosis versus distress*—What is the threshold for reimbursed treatment? How many symptoms does one need to qualify for care? How will this care be paid for? (Patel et al., 2013; Patel & Saxena, 2014).
- *How should mental health care be paid for?* Who should pay—individuals, employers, the government, or others? How will payment plans affect access to care? Should preventative mental health care be a "covered benefit"?

These questions remain unresolved and the discussions by therapists, policymakers, legislators, insurance boards, and other authorities will have important implications for the work that future therapists do.

Healthcare changes may be both good and bad news for consumers and providers of mental health services, and family therapists should be aware of both sides of the story (Edwards, Patterson, Scherger, & Vaikili, 2013). The good news is that in 2018 a significant number of Americans who were previously uninsured now have access to care. Increasing access to care is a goal that resonates with the values of family therapists. The bad news is that there could be more pressure to identify a single client instead of treat family relationships and provide treatments that are based on individual symptoms.

At the same time, clients and therapists may be caught in the ongoing battle to balance cost-effectiveness with quality care. The potential here is for postponed treatment, bureaucratic obstacles that lead clients to give up, and severely limited choices regarding whom the clients can see. In addition, numerous chronic problems and certain acute ones may not qualify for treatment. Similarly, time-limited therapy may be the rule, despite the fact that resolution of some problems requires long-term treatment. Finally, in an environment where cost-effectiveness is so crucial, there may be an overreliance on drugs. The ease with which certain popular drugs are prescribed, and the use of these as diagnostic tools, may prevent clients from pursuing other types of treatment.

While these issues are significant for adult clients and their therapists, they are even more challenging for therapists who treat children and adolescents. Evidence for the critical importance of excellent care for children and adolescents comes from a national study examining the frequency of mental health problems (Kessler, Berglund, et al., 2005; Kessler et al., 2007). In general, the research suggests that half of all mental health disorders start by age 14 and three-fourths start by age 24. The mean age for anxiety disorders and impulse disorders to start is 11 years old.

In spite of numerous efforts, children and adolescents are still frequently treated individually and the impact of their families on their problems is often overlooked. Nowhere is this more apparent than in the rush to provide psychotropic medications for children and adolescents as the first-line treatments. While we recognize the tremendous difference that medications have made, such as stimulants to treat ADHD, we hope that you will continue to advocate for the critical importance of family-based treatments for developing children and adolescents.

Master's-level family therapists may have an advantage in the emerging healthcare market, as do master's-level nurse practitioners and certified physician assistants. Providing quality care for common problems in the least expensive way will be fundamental to the new healthcare organization. Family therapists are likely to practice on a team with clinical psychologists, psychiatrists, and primary care physicians in order to address the healthcare needs of a population. The closer the family therapist is to the primary care physician, the better a biopsychosocial approach to healthcare can be maintained.

When the primary care physician and the family therapist work together, a greater efficiency of care will augment service delivery. New models for integrating mental health providers with primary care physicians could flourish. At present, the strongest research supporting collaborative care has come from treating depressed primary care patients (*http://aims.uw.edu*; *www.cfha.net*; *integratedprimarycare. com*). In addition, government organizations and foundations have created models of care for clients with little or no private insurance. Most models of collaborative care share a problem-solving focus, are brief (five to seven sessions), and may or may not include psychotropic medications as part of the treatment. While the traditional private practice model that focuses on self-pay clients will continue, we anticipate that healthcare reform will financially support the new models of care based on principles of good collaboration between healthcare professionals.

The positive side of new payment models is that the therapist need not withhold treatment because the family cannot afford therapy. The negative side is that some treatments deemed necessary by the therapist may still not be covered, while others may be time-limited. Family therapists need to use authorized sessions creatively, perhaps using alternatives to the standard of the weekly 50-minute hour. Since new payment models may put the burden of cost containment partially on the provider, family therapists must have some knowledge of case management and practice economics. Family therapists must be trained to think about issues regarding treatment efficiency, effectiveness, cost, client satisfaction, utilization, and access.

Thus, they must be able to work as part of an interdisciplinary team, which might include a primary care physician, a dietitian, a nurse practitioner, a psychiatrist, and any other healthcare specialist deemed necessary for effective treatment. Embedded in working as part of an interdisciplinary team are issues of loss of autonomy, establishing parity or hierarchical relationships with other healthcare providers, and credibility regarding the services provided by family therapy (compared to the more clearly measured outcomes of biological sciences and medical model treatments). Family therapists must understand how other specialists think about problems—for example, the psychiatrist's focus on individual physical symptoms or the family physician's focus on pragmatic, efficient treatment (Patterson et al., 2010; Patterson & Magulac, 1994). The ability to actively consult with and understand other professionals while communicating the role of family therapy is essential.

As part of healthcare reform, a specific diagnosis and treatment plan will be important. Because of utilization management, evidence-based outcomes research, and other macro-accountability methods, a clear articulation of the problem, possible treatments, chosen treatment, and expected outcomes is critical. In other words, family therapists need to convey appropriate information to payers and must be aware of specific criteria. For example, obtaining treatment authorization often includes the following: documenting a DSM diagnosis, level of impaired functioning, level of care needed, and prognosis. Proving medical necessity means addressing both diagnostic and functional criteria. In addition to providing a DSM diagnosis, therapists may need to give evidence of clinical instability, which includes potential lethality to self or other, current medical status, and ability to perform basic self-care. In documenting authorizations, therapists will also address interpersonal relationships and a client's ability to maintain vocational and other activities—problems here might be classified as "functional impairments."

While some diagnoses (e.g., phobias) have strict diagnostic criteria and convincing treatment outcome research, other issues frequently discussed in therapy are broader and may not be covered. For example, most plans would not pay for marital therapy to treat communication problems. However, a distressed spouse might tell his primary care physician that he is depressed and is not eating or sleeping because of a painful marriage. Part of the treatment for depression might be marital therapy. Whatever the identified problem and treatment goals, therapists need to use behavioral terms that reflect symptom reduction. Treatment modality also needs to be identified and rationalized using evidence-based guidelines.

In practical terms, family therapists need to identify and document the focus of treatment early and use behavioral terms. Progress notes must be legible and up to date, and should demonstrate some measure of change noted from session to session. Furthermore, therapists need to show reviewers that applicable treatment guidelines or current standards for treatment are being followed.

The relationship between continued therapy and client improvement is an important consideration. Group therapies that prove as effective as individual therapies may take precedence because they are cost-effective. Using the Internet to provide client education and care could become more common. Since family therapists have been working with family groups and systems, they should already have the necessary skills to make this transition.

Finally, client satisfaction is important and can be measured using brief questionnaires. This should be an area where family therapists excel, since relationship skills have always been a basic ingredient of family therapy. Research suggests that patients' most frequent complaints and reasons for changing doctors include (1) the physician does not care, (2) the physician does not listen, and (3) the physician does not explain in a way that is understandable (Desmond, 1993). In like manner, therapists must communicate their caring and concern to their clients.

In the past, the family therapist's focus was on helping families function more effectively, usually by altering their interactions. Today, new family therapists must also think about cost-effectiveness, research effectiveness versus the practical efficacy of using a treatment in the "real world," criteria for treatment authorization, treatment guidelines, time-limited therapies, utilization reviews, and accountability. The approach may be interdisciplinary and biopsychosocial, and family therapists will become team members who share with other professionals a concern for the client's total health. By expanding beyond the boundaries of traditional family therapy training and gaining understanding of the forces shaping healthcare services, beginning family therapists can help themselves and their clients.

EMERGING TRENDS IN TREATMENT

While family therapy will always maintain its focus on family-based treatments and the BPS model, the field is also being shaped by broader influences and global changes. In this section, we identify some of the most important forces affecting family therapy. While these areas are not always addressed in traditional curriculums, we believe that they will affect your future clinical work.

Evidence-Based Treatments

The previous section discusses payers' and the governments' interests in supporting proven, effective treatments. Physicians and therapists share these goals. Indeed, these goals have emerged as a movement in the United States. In every health discipline, professionals have supported the move toward evidence-based treatments (EBTs) (Hunsley & Mash, 2005; Mash & Hunsley, 2005). EBTs refer to the integration of best research evidence with clinical expertise and client values when making treatment decisions (Sackett, Strauss, Richardson, Rosenberg, & Haynes, 2000). In Chapters 5 and 10, we discuss more about the process of finding the best treatment and give specific suggestions for the process. Evidence-based family therapy treatments include functional family therapy, multisystemic family therapy, structural family therapy, cognitive-behavioral couple therapy, emotionally focused therapy, and others. The movement toward EBTs suggests that reimbursement in the future will be tied to EBTs that have been proven effective for a specific problem. At present, problems are generally organized around DSM diagnoses.

If you have had little exposure to EBTs, opportunities exist for you to train yourself. In addition to learning the steps we mention in Chapter 10 under "Doing a Literature Search," training modules on the Internet can give you the basic skills to conduct a search on a client's problem or conduct a systematic review (*ebbp.org/training.html*). In addition, there are many EBT resources on the Web, including conference presentations, discussion groups, and expert discussions. Several of the authors of this text have also written a text on EBTs in family therapy—*Clinician's Guide to Research Methods in Family Therapy: Foundations of Evidence-Based Practice* (Williams et al., 2014).

Family therapists may have concerns about the limits of EBTs (Patterson, Miller, Carnes, & Wilson, 2004; Williams, Patterson, & Miller, 2006). For example, therapists may feel that it takes too much time to conduct literature reviews. Another concern could be that the freedom to match the treatment to the individual client's circumstances is lost. Some therapists feel that EBTs are too reductionistic and don't capture the complexity of their clients' lives. Therapists are not alone in expressing concerns. One prominent physician states: "Numbers can only complement a physician's personal experience . . . as well as his knowledge of whether a 'best' therapy from a clinical trial fits a patient's particular needs and values" (Groopman, 2007, p. 6).

In spite of these concerns, we believe that the public and payers will increasingly demand EBTs. Thus, academic journals, professional organizations, and government agencies have created websites that provide information about EBTs. They have done the time-consuming research review for the therapists and succinctly summarized the findings into suggestions. Chapter 10 provides Web addresses for some of these summary sites. We recommend that you become familiar with this information and simultaneously maintain your focus on your clients' individual needs and circumstances.

Technology

In the previous section, we mentioned opportunities to teach yourself new skills by using resources on the Web. Technology, especially the Internet, has changed the way people obtain and use information. In addition, tele-medicine—medical care delivered over the phone or Internet—is becoming a paid-for benefit in some insurance plans. For family therapists and their clients, the Web provides exciting new opportunities and some risks.

Many clients will have conducted their own search and will bring downloaded information about their problem to their initial therapy session. However, when searching for treatment options, they might have a difficult time distinguishing between safe, effective treatments and fraudulent ones. At times, our clients have mentioned the search they did using our name or our clinic's name so they would know about who we were before they had their first session. In addition, some treatment programs now exist exclusively online, and the only contact a client has with a therapist may be an occasional phone call. For instance, MoodGym is one of many online depression treatment programs, and there is evidence to suggest that these programs work even without a therapist present (Haldane, 2006). An article in the *New York Times* highlighted the strengths of online treatments. According to the author,

> Online therapy . . . can help people who stay sick because there are no therapists nearby, who fear being judged or embarrassed in therapy, who can't take time off from work, or for whom the cost of treatment is too high. It allows people to carry therapy around in their pockets, use it at 2 A.M., and pay nothing or nearly nothing. (Rosenberg, 2015)

There is a growing list of digital resources, including mobile device applications, available to clients and therapists. Some online treatment programs take clients through a step-by-step treatment program, for example, a treatment package for anxiety using CBT techniques. Other resources include applications that can be downloaded to a phone so clients can meditate as they sit on a bus on the way to work.

The Internet is also a risk for our clients. Clients may ignore their family members because they spend each evening on blogs or in chatrooms on the Web. They explore pornography and other high-risk websites. Clients may obtain wrong information about their problems or possible treatments on the Web.

In terms of opportunities, the Web offers a quick way to conduct a literature search on a specific topic. Besides the sites mentioned in Chapter 10, many Web resources are available for family therapists. For example, Google Scholar (*www.scholar.google.com*) is a free Web search engine that can search a wide variety of academic literature from many disciplines. Government-supported search engines like PubMed (*www.pubmed.gov*) and MedLine are free and offer access to a broad array of health literature. MedLine, the largest component of PubMed, indexes approximately 5,200 American journals and journals from over 80 other countries. A free tutorial is available on how to search PubMed (*www.nlm.nih.gov/bsd/disted/pubmedtutorial*). Simply searching the government websites of agencies such as the National Institute of Mental Health (*www.nimb.nih.gov*) or the Substance Abuse and Mental Health Services Administration (*www.samhsa.gov*) can also be helpful. Other article databases include Thomson ISI's Web of Science (*www.isiwebofknowledge.com*) and Wiley InterScience (*www3.interscience.wiley.com*). Many journals now publish their entire content online. Some of these resources require paid subscriptions and others are free.

Besides using search engines, family therapists can attend lectures and receive online training. Besides the EBT training mentioned earlier, therapists can participate in live lectures on mental health problems via the Massachusetts General Hospital Psychiatry Academy (*www.mghcme.org*). Webcasts, audio and video podcasts, and expert online forums are available for free just by logging in. Training centers are also putting lectures online. For instance, a family therapist can watch a lecture summarizing the unique role of marriage as a source of social support by going to the Pittsburgh Mind–Body Center (*pmbcii.psy.cmu.edu*).

Video conferencing and other new communication tools are also available for therapists. Our colleagues are using Skype to provide supervision to family therapists in another country. One of the most exciting opportunities that new technologies provide is the chance to work with family therapists from around the world without having to travel to another country. Long-distance meetings and teaching can take place using video conferencing.

Initiatives in medicine and mental health are exploring service delivery via the Internet and using cell phones, text messaging, and e-mail reminders for health promotion and prevention. Recent research has demonstrated that phone therapy had a much lower attrition rate than traditional therapy, and some clients prefer technology as a medium for therapy because of its convenience and anonymity (Mohr, Vella, Hart, Heckman, & Simon, 2008). Family therapists who want to provide services to clients in rural areas are exploring the use of technology to conduct therapy sessions (Bischoff, Hollist, Smith, & Flack, 2004). Today, clients can find therapists who are willing to provide therapy via the Internet and some therapists see advanced technology as a way to expand their practices.

However, family therapists should carefully consider the needs of their clients and their ability to provide uncompromised treatments through this medium. Given that the use of technology to provide treatment is evolving as quickly as the technology itself, state laws and regulations and ethical guidelines from professional organizations have not kept pace. International guidelines are nonexistent. Family therapists considering service delivery through the Internet or using other technology should keep abreast of the laws and regulations governing the practice of family therapy in both the state in which they are licensed and the state in which the client resides before entering into an agreement to provide treatment. Therapists should also carefully consider the limitations of using technology to deliver services and receive proper training prior to doing so.

Globalization

Globalization is a broad force influencing the future of family therapy and encouraging family therapists to become more competent in dealing with cultural diversity, economic disparities, and gender (Keeling & Piercy, 2007). In 2007, *The Lancet,* a British medical journal, published a series of papers on the need for mental health services in countries that previously had none. The World Bank defines these countries by their GDP (gross domestic product) and they are categorized as low- or middle-income countries. At present, initiatives are occurring around the world to create, deliver, and pay for mental health services in places that previously had no services. Family therapists are also working to deliver services in the global community (Crane, 2013; Patel et al., 2007, 2013; Patel & Saxena, 2014; Patterson, Edwards, & Vakili, 2017; Prince et al., 2007; Saxena, Thornicroft, Knapp, & Whiteford, 2007; Underhill, 2007).

The globalization of family therapy raises important issues. In different societies gender roles, views about alternative family forms, and the very definition of *family* often differ from American norms. For example, in many countries, when clients speak about family, they mean extended family, not the nuclear family. Furthermore, mental health services to treat disorders such as depression or ADHD have been nonexistent in many countries. In addition, many cultural practices "denote recurrent, locality-specific patterns of aberrant behavior . . . that may or may not be linked to a particular DSM diagnostic category" (American Psychiatric Association, 2000, p. 898). In other words, the boundaries between cultural differences and mental disorders are not always clear. Increasing globalization means that the impact of culture on mental health services is becoming more important.

In general, family therapists outside the United States work in countries with developed economies. While there are AAMFT-approved supervisors in many countries outside the United States, the majority live in Europe or Hong Kong. Professional organizations such as the International Family Therapy Association (*www.ifta-familytherapy.*

org), the European Family Therapy Association (*www.europeanfamilytherapy.eu*), and Asia's regional family-based professional organization, the Consortium of Institutes on Family in the Asian Region (*www.cifa-net.org*), are building their own communities of family therapy professionals. In addition, many regions have created their own family therapy journals such as the *Australia and New Zealand Journal of Family Therapy* (*www.anzjft.com*) or the *Journal of Family Therapy* in the United Kingdom (*www.aft.org.uk*).

In addition to developing awareness about gender, economic disparities, and cultural diversity in their home country, family therapists can expand to a global focus on families and their struggles. Becoming bilingual, using the Internet for teaching or supervision, cross-cultural teaching exchanges, and reading international literature about families and their struggles are all ways to become aware of global issues in family therapy.

There are numerous globalization efforts in family therapy. A family therapy training program in Hong Kong conducts live group supervision with a training program in Taiwan using video conferencing. Japanese colleagues translate a popular English-language family therapy text into Japanese. Colleagues from the International Family Therapy Association set up a voluntary program to send well-known therapists to clinics in countries with developing economies. Colleagues from Australia, Israel, and other countries publish their research in American journals. A university takes a group of family therapy students to a family therapy conference in Asia. Family therapy programs in the United States discuss the possibilities of creating joint training programs and offering joint degrees with family therapy clinics in Asia and Europe. Discussions about an international credential in family therapy occur between different stakeholders.

In the coming years, more countries will develop family therapy programs and create their own unique training programs and models. Family therapists of the future will have to tease out the universal characteristics of families and simultaneously identify regional differences. The impact of factors such as race, gender, culture, and class on family members' mental health will become even more complex. With the complexities of globalization come new intellectual challenges that can make a career as a family therapist even more interesting.

Genetics and Neuroscience

Some of the most exciting work for family therapists is taking place in disciplines that are traditionally associated with biology and other natural sciences. Research in genetics and neuroscience is providing new understanding of vexing problems. As with other mental health disciplines, family therapists have had to focus on observable signs and reported symptoms when they assess their clients' problems. This has meant that clients often do not receive treatment until problems are entrenched. Family therapists, like other health providers, focus on treatment, not prevention. Focusing on treatment alone can be frustrating because many family therapists have strong backgrounds in human development and recognize the powerful influence of family interaction. Is it possible for family therapists to intervene earlier, before problems and illnesses have caused disability and suffering?

Recent advances in neuroscience and genetics point to underlying biology as a powerful source of human suffering. However, the same research suggests that biology is not destiny. In fact, for many (but not all) mental illnesses, one's genetics are only part of the etiology. A Stanford professor of biology and neurology resolves the age-old nature-versus-nurture argument by stating:

> Genes don't cause behaviors. Sometimes they influence them. . . . Genes influence behavior, environment influences behavior, and genes and environment interact. . . . The effects of a gene on an organism will usually vary with changes in the environment, and the effects of environment will vary with changes in the genetic makeup of the organism. (Sapolsky, 2005, p. 30)

Research in neuroscience has also begun to illuminate our understanding of mental disorders. For example, neuroscience research has pointed out that the brain is more malleable than scientists once thought. The plasticity of the brain and the fact that adult brains produce new neurons provide hope that changing the environment (such as creating a supportive, loving family environment) can influence family members' individual biology. Neuroscientists explore the influence of epigenetic factors, or the way the environment shapes gene expression. Some of the most interesting research about environment shaping biology, based on attachment theory, is called interpersonal neurobiology (Schore, 2003a, 2003b, 2005; Siegal, 1999, 2007). In a nutshell, this research suggests that a person's brain is wired for optimal development when the person receives love and nurture from a warm caretaker.

As discussed in Chapter 9, research from genetics and neuroscience is also changing our views of mental disorders. Many of the DSM disorders are probably several disorders that have been clumped together based on signs and symptoms. In general, new research tells us that mental disorders are genetic disorders (affected by the environment or "epigenetic influences"), brain disorders, and developmental disorders (Insel, 2014). In essence, even if there is a genetic proclivity for an illness, the emergence of symptoms may or may not occur as a person ages. Sapolsky (2017) identifies the numerous influences that determine behavior.

Other findings have suggested that early interventions might create important changes in human development. In animal studies, baby rats who were licked and groomed by their mothers (attachment behaviors) developed a stronger capacity to deal with stress as adults, and scientists demonstrated the neuropathways between attachment behaviors and stress regulation mechanisms in the brain (Insel & Quirion, 2005). Stated more simply, research indicates that "the neurons that fire together, wire together" (Hebb, 1949). Similar questions are being raised about the impact of families on children's emerging mental illnesses. For example, in research on bipolar disorder in children, "kindling theory" suggests that the first manic episode is more likely to be associated with major stressors than are later episodes, which implies that stress might change and reinforce pathways inside the central nervous system so that future episodes of mania will occur without an outside stimulus. In an attempt to prevent the child's brain from becoming increasingly sensitized and perhaps prevent the first manic episode, researchers are exploring whether family therapy can fortify a child against a genetic proclivity for bipolar disorder (Egan, 2008). Family therapists do not need to wait until research in genetics and neuroscience have explicitly explained the pathways of the interaction between biology and the environment. Instead, we can begin applying our current understanding of the family's impact on mental health by helping families create supportive, nurturing environments that minimize stress and negativity.

Much research in neuroscience and genetics is only emerging. However, as experts in family interaction and family development, family therapists will have exciting opportunities in the future. While some mental illnesses will remain intractable to psychosocial interventions, many other mental health problems can be ameliorated by creating healthy families, especially families that support and nurture their younger members. In this way, family therapists might become agents of prevention, not treatment. In a healthcare culture focused on cost-effective interventions, influencing children and adolescents in the context of their families makes sense—especially given the research suggesting that most mental health problems begin in childhood and adolescence. The chance to contribute to an understanding of how healthy family life contributes to healthy children is just one of the pluses of work as a family therapist (Patterson & Vakili, 2014).

BENEFITS AND LIABILITIES OF BEING A THERAPIST

The work of being a therapist can be profoundly meaningful. The reward for the therapist is to share in the client's learning and increased understanding. Virginia Satir (1967) saw this connection with the client as the greatest gift she could offer. Opportunities for self-growth and lifelong learning are also available to the therapist. The profession understands that if therapists are to take care of others, they also need to take care of themselves.

Probably the biggest concern that most therapists face in maintaining effectiveness in their work is burnout. Burnout involves three dimensions: emotional exhaustion, depersonalization, and reduced personal accomplishment (Maslach, 1993). Emotional exhaustion is the feeling of being fatigued and depleted. This can result in a lack of compassion. Depersonalization is a negative or cynical attitude associated with thoughts like "I am not sure therapy works or is helpful." These feelings of boredom, self-doubt, and a negative self-evaluation can occur by consistently identifying with and being in the presence of other people's pain and torment.

Thus, it is normal to experience these sensations at times—particularly for one to doubt the effectiveness of therapy. The process is often ambiguous with many variables that cannot be controlled. The client's motivation will vary significantly and many outside factors, which can be biological, psychological, and/or social, will influence the therapeutic outcome. Knowing this can be helpful, but self-doubt can creep in at unexpected times and create tension and anxiety for the therapist. Assistance from colleagues or supervisors is often the best remedy to managing one's anxiety.

THE PERSONAL AND PROFESSIONAL JOURNEY OF BEING A THERAPIST

One of the questions we ask our graduating master's-level students is where they see themselves in 5 years. Some respond with the hopes of a good job, some want to be in a doctoral program, and almost all want the opportunity to do therapy. The profession offers increasing possibilities in the public and private sectors. Jobs can be found doing clinical work, management, consulting, teaching, and working as an administrator.

Many therapists work in several settings. It is not unusual for a therapist to have a part-time job in an agency, school, or institution and to have a part-time private practice. Teaching and consulting can be instrumental in providing challenging opportunities for professional colleagueship and exposure to current ideas in the field. Most therapists enjoy diversity in their work and have considerable freedom in establishing their workload and schedule. Exposure to clients with various life experiences and diverse backgrounds can add richness to the therapist's life.

At graduation, we also ask our students to think about their lives and how they would like to balance their personal and professional goals. We share some of the goals that we've had over the years and then we ask them what they wish they'd known when they started their training. Here are some issues they mention:

> "I didn't realize how much of my own struggles with my family would be brought up in graduate school. I wish I would have started my own personal therapy sooner."

> "Graduate school in family therapy and clinical training took more of an emotional toll on my life than my general undergraduate education did."

> "Having a positive work environment is worth everything. I would be willing to take a lower-paying job to be in a setting where I feel valued and supported."

> "I realized that there is no point in doing this work if you don't love it because you'll be a therapist for a long time. In addition, I realize that being a therapist is a lifestyle, not just a job, because I'm working with humans whose needs don't stop when it is five o'clock."

> "Money and salary matters. When I started graduate school, I never thought about my future income. Now, as I face paying off student loans and supporting a family, I care a great deal about finding a job with a good salary."

> "Taking time for self-care and not making my clients my whole life is important. At first, I felt so overwhelmed by my clients' needs that I wouldn't take out time for myself. Eventually I realized that I had to have a break from my clients and my work if I was going to last in this profession."

> "Ultimately, my relationships with my own family and friends are the most important parts of my life. When I first started, I inadvertently ignored them because I was so focused on my clients' needs. As time passed, I realized that I wouldn't be happy if I didn't stay close to the people I love."

One of the unique aspects of being a therapist is the merging of one's personal and professional life. Therapists need to be aware of their personal boundaries and clear about how their personal lives can affect their work. In addition, most therapists readily acknowledge that their professional work influences the choices they make in their personal lives.

CONCLUSION

"I rarely hear my therapist colleagues complain that their lives lack meaning. Life as a therapist is a life of service to others" (Yalom, 2002, p. 256). The profession offers the therapist a consistent opportunity to learn from others, self-reflect, and be a part of life-changing experiences. Most therapists rely heavily upon their intuition. Trusting one's own sense of things, as well as helping others make sense of their experiences, is a constant creative challenge. For many therapists, the interplay between a life of service and meaning plus the constant challenge of responding creatively to new problems makes any stresses of work as a therapist well worth the effort.

Screening Instruments

MOOD DISORDERS

Beck Depression Inventory
Patient Health Questionnaire (PHQ-9)
Mood Disorder Questionnaire (MDQ)
Altman Self-Rating Mania Scale (ASRM)
Mood and Feelings Questionnaire (MFQ)
Zung Self-Rating Depression Scale (SDS)
Hamilton Rating Scale for Depression
Depression and Anxiety in Youth Scale (DAYS)
Child Depression Inventory (CDI)
Healthy Living Questionnaire
Suicidal Ideation Questionnaire (SIQ)
Suicide Behaviors Questionnaire—Revised (SBQ-R)

ANXIETY DISORDERS

Generalized Anxiety Disorder 7-Item Scale (GAD-7)
Hamilton Anxiety Rating Scale (HAM-A)
Liebowitz Social Anxiety Scale—Child and Adolescent Version
Social Phobia and Anxiety Inventory for Children (SPAI-C)
Panic Disorder Severity Scale (PDSS)
Children's Yale–Brown Obsessive Compulsive Scale (CY-BOCS)
Yale–Brown Obsessive Compulsive Scale (YBOCS)

IMPULSE CONTROL DISORDERS

Vanderbilt Parent Rating Scale
Vanderbilt Teacher Rating Scale

ADHD Rating Scale
Conners' Rating Scales—Revised (CRS-R)
Conduct Disorder Scale (CDS)
Adjustment Scales for Children and Adolescents (ASCA)

ADDICTIVE BEHAVIORS

Video Game Functional Assessment—Revised (VGFA-R)
Young Internet Addiction Test (IAT)
Compulsive Internet Use Scale
Generalized Problematic Internet Use Scale–2
Internet Sex Screening Test (ISST)
Cyber-Pornography Use Inventory (CPUI)
Sexual Addiction Screening Test—Revised (SAST-R)
Hypersexual Behavior Inventory
Compulsive Sexual Behavior Inventory
Child Pornography Use Inventory (CPUI)
Focal Adult Gambling Screener (FLAGS)
CAGE Assessment for Alcohol Abuse
Michigan Alcoholism Screening Test (MAST)
Alcohol Use Disorders Identification Test (AUDIT)
CRAFFT for Alcohol and Drug Screening
Opioid Risk Tool

EATING DISORDERS

Eating Disorder Diagnostic Scale (EDDS)
Sick, Control, One, Fat, Food Screening Tool (SCOFF)

TRAUMA

Impact of Event Scale—Revised (IES-R)
Los Angeles Symptom Checklist (LASC)
The Post-Traumatic Stress Disorder Checklist—Civilian Version (PCL-C)
Trauma Symptom Inventory (TSI)
The Trauma History Questionnaire (THQ)

PSYCHOSIS

Prodromal Questionnaire—Brief Version (PQ-B)
Schizophrenia Test and Early Psychosis Indicator (STEPI)
Structured Interview for Prodromal Syndromes (SIPS)
Scale of Prodromal Symptoms (SOPS)

FAMILY MEASURES

Ages and Stages Questionnaires, Third Edition (ASQ-3)
Parents' Evaluation of Developmental Status
Pediatric Symptoms Checklist
McMaster Family Assessment Device (FAD)
Family Assessment Measure—Version III (FAM-III)
Family Environment Scale (FES)
Circumplex Model Family Adaptability and Cohesion Evaluation Scales
    (FACES)
Family Relations Scale (FRS)
Systemic Therapy Inventory of Change (STIC)

COUPLE MEASURES

Couples Satisfaction Index (CSI)
Dyadic Adjustment Scale (DAS)
Marital Satisfaction Inventory—Revised (MSI-R)
Marital Status Inventory (MSI)
Parenting Alliance Measure (PAM)
Parent Relationship Questionnaire (PRQ)
Parenting Satisfaction Scale (PSS)
Parenting Stress Index (PSI)
Parent Relationship Inventory (PRI)
Revised Conflict Tactics Scale (CTS2)

SOMATIZATION

Patient Health Questionnaire (PHQ-15)
Screening for Somatoform Symptoms (SOMS-7)

PERSONALITY DISORDERS

The Borderline Evaluation of Severity over Time (BEST)

SPIRITUALITY

FACIT Spiritual Well-Being Scale

References

Achenbach, T. (2008). Assessment, diagnosis, nosology, and taxonomy of child and adolescent psychopathology. In M. Hersen & A. M. Gross (Eds.), *Handbook of clinical psychology: Vol. 2. Children and adolescents* (pp. 429–457). Hoboken, NJ: Wiley.

Adler, L. D., Slootsky, V., Griffith, J. L., & Khin Khin, E. (2016). Teaching the fundamentals of the Risk Assessment Interview to clinicians. *Psychiatric Annals, 46*(5), 293–297.

Ahrons, C. R. (1994). *The good divorce.* New York: HarperCollins.

Ahrons, C. R. (2007). Family ties after divorce: Long-term implications for children. *Family Process, 46,* 53–65.

Ahrons, C. R., & Rodgers, R. H. (1987). *Divorced families: A multidisciplinary view.* New York: Norton.

Alexander, J. F., Holtzworth-Munroe, A., & Jameson, P. (1994). The process and outcome of marital and family therapy: Research review and evaluation. In A. Bergin & A. Garfield (Eds.), *Handbook of psychotherapy and behavior change* (pp. 595–630). New York: Wiley.

Alexander, J. F., & Sexton, T. L. (2002). Functional family therapy: A model for treating high risk, acting out youth. In F. W. Kaslow (Ed.), *Comprehensive handbook of psychotherapy: Vol. 4. Integrative/eclectic* (pp. 111–132). New York: Wiley.

American Psychiatric Association. (2000). *Diagnostic and statistical manual of mental disorders* (4th ed., text rev.). Washington, DC: Author.

American Psychiatric Association. (2013). *Diagnostic and statistical manual of mental disorders* (5th ed.). Arlington, VA: Author.

Amstadter, A. (2008). Emotion regulation and anxiety disorders. *Journal of Anxiety Disorders, 22*(2), 211–221.

Anandarajah, G., & Hight, E. (2001). Spirituality and medical practice: Using the HOPE questions as a practice tool for spiritual assessment. *American Family Physician, 63,* 81–89.

Anderson, C. M. (2003). The diversity, strength, and challenges of single-parent households. In F. Walsh (Ed.), *Normal family processes* (3rd ed., pp. 121–152). New York: Guilford Press.

Anderson, C. M., & Stewart, S. (1983). *Mastering resistance: A practical guide to family therapy.* New York: Guilford Press.

Arean, P. A., Perri, M. G., Nezu, A. M., Schein, R. L., Christopher, F., & Joseph, T. X. (1993). Comparative effectiveness of social problem-solving therapy and reminiscence therapy as treatments for depression in older adults. *Journal of Consulting and Clinical Psychology, 61,* 1003–1010.

Arean, P. A., Raue, P., Mackin, R. S., Kanellopoulos, D., McCulloch, C., & Alexopoulos, G. S. (2010). Problem-solving therapy and supportive therapy in older adults with major depression and executive dysfunction. *American Journal of Psychiatry, 167,* 1391–1398.

Arkowitz, H., Westra, H. A., Miller, W. R., & Rollnick, R. (Eds.). (2008). *Motivational interviewing in the treatment of psychological problems.* New York: Guilford Press.

Ayers, C. R., Sorrell, J. T., Thorp, S. R., & Wetherell, J. L. (2007). Evidence-based psychological treatments for late-life anxiety. *Psychological Aging, 22,* 8–17.

Ayers, M. M., & Haddock, S. A. (2009). Therapists' approaches in working with heterosexual couples struggling with male partners' online sexual behavior. *Sexual Addiction and Compulsivity, 16,* 55–78.

Baldwin, S. A., Wampold, B. E., & Imel, Z. E. (2007). Untangling the alliance–outcome correlation: Exploring the relative importance of therapist and patient variability in the alliance. *Journal of Consulting and Clinical Psychology, 75,* 842–852.

Bandler, R., & Grinder, J. (1982). *Reframing.* Moab, UT: Real People Press.

Barrett, M. S., Chua, W., Crits-Christoph, P., Gibbons, M. B., & Thompson, D. (2008). Early withdrawal from mental health treatment: Implications for psychotherapy practice. *Psychotherapy: Theory, Research, Practice, Training, 45,* 247–267.

Baruchin, A. (2008, May 22). Nature, nurture and attention deficit. *New York Times.* Retrieved from *health.nytimes.com/ref/health/healthguide/esn-adhd-expert.html.*

Baucom, D. H., Hahlweg, K., & Kuschel, A. (2003). Are waiting-list control groups needed in future marital therapy outcome research? *Behavior Therapy, 34,* 179–188.

Beach, S., & Gupta, M. (2005). Understanding and treating depression in couples. *Journal of Family Psychotherapy, 16*(3), 69–83.

Beach, S., & Gupta, M. (2006). Directive and nondirective spousal support: Differential effects? *Journal of Marital and Family Therapy, 32*(4), 465–477.

Beach, S., & Jones, D. (2002). Marital and family therapy for depression in adults. In I. H. Gotlib & C. L. Hammen (Eds.), *Handbook of depression* (pp. 422–440). New York: Guilford Press.

Beach, S. R. H., Wambold, M., Kaslow, N., Hegman, R., First, M., Underwood, L., et al. (2006). *Relational process and DSM-V.* Washington, DC: American Psychiatric Association.

Beach, S. R. H., & Whisman, M. A. (2012). Affective disorders. *Journal of Marital Family Therapy, 38*(1), 201–219.

Beaton, J., Dienhart, A., Schmidt, J., & Turner, J. (2009). Clinical practices of Canadian couple/marital/family therapists. *Journal of Marital and Family Therapy, 35*(2), 193–203.

Becker, D., & & Liddle, H. A. (2001). Family therapy with unmarried African American mothers and their adolescents. *Family Process, 40,* 413–427.

Beekman, A. T., Copeland, J. R., & Prince, M. J. (1999). Review of community prevalence of depression in later life. *British Journal of Psychiatry, 174,* 307–311.

Beidel, D. C., & Turner, S. M. (2007). *Shy children, phobic adults: Nature and treatment of social anxiety disorder* (2nd ed.). Washington, DC: American Psychological Association.

Belmaker, R. H., & Agam, G. (2008). Major depressive disorder. *New England Journal of Medicine, 358*(1), 55–68.

Belous, C. K., Timm, T. M., Chee, G., & Whitehead, M. R. (2012). Revisiting the sexual genogram. *American Journal of Family Therapy, 40,* 281–296.

Belsky, J., & Kelly, J. (1994). *The transition to parenthood: How a first child changes a marriage and why some couples grow closer and others apart.* New York: Dell.

Berg, B., & Rosenblum, N. (1977). Fathers in family therapy: A survey of family therapists. *Journal of Marriage and Family Counseling, 3,* 85–91.

Berger, D., & Berger, L., (1991). *We heard the angels of madness.* New York: Morrow.

Bergin, A. (1991). Values and religious issues in psychotherapy and mental health. *American Psychologist, 46*(4), 394–403.

Beutler, L. E., Harwood, T. M., Michelson, A., Song, X., & Holman, J. (2011). Resistance/reactance level. *Journal of Clinical Psychology: In Session, 67,* 133–142.

Bischoff, R. J., & Barton, M. (2002). The pathway toward clinical self confidence. *American Journal of Family Therapy, 30,* 231–242.

Bischoff, R. J., Barton, M., Thober, J., & Hawley, R. (2002). Events and experiences impacting the development of clinical self confidence: A study of the first year of client contact. *Journal of Marital and Family Therapy, 28,* 371–382.

Bischoff, R. J., Hollist, C., Smith, C., & Flack, P. (2004). Addressing the mental health needs of the rural underserved: Findings from a multiple case study of a behavioral telehealth project. *Contemporary Family Therapy, 26,* 179–198.

Blow, A. J., & Hartnett, K. (2005). Infidelity in committed relationships: II. A substantive review. *Journal of Marital and Family Therapy, 31,* 217–234.

Borum, R., & Reddy, M. (2001). Assessing violence risk in Tarasoff situations: A fact-based model of inquiry. *Behavioral Sciences and the Law, 19,* 375–385.

Boss, P. (1999). *Ambiguous loss: Learning to live with unresolved grief.* Cambridge, MA: Harvard University Press.

Bowlby, J. (1980). *Attachment and loss.* New York: Basic Books.

Bray, J., & Kelly, J. (1998). *Stepfamilies: Love, marriage, and parenting in the first decade.* New York: Broadway Books.

Bridle, C., Spanjers, K., Patel, S., Atherton, N. M., & Lamb, S. E. (2012). Effect of exercise on depression severity in older people: Systematic review and meta-analysis of randomised controlled trials. *British Journal of Psychiatry, 201,* 180–185.

Brown, E. M. (1991). *Patterns of infidelity and their treatment.* New York: Brunner/Mazel.

Brown, F. H. (1989). The impact of death and serious illness on the family life cycle. In B. Carter & M. McGoldrick (Eds.), *The changing family life cycle: A framework for family therapy* (2nd ed., pp. 457–482). New York: Allyn & Bacon.

Brown, M. T., & Bussell, J. K. (2011). Medication adherence: WHO cares? *Mayo Clinic Proceedings, 86*(4), 304–331.

Brubacher, L., & Lee, A. (2012, Fall). Emotion is more than a feeling: The elements of emotion in action. *The EFT Community News, 15th Issue.* Retrieved September 5, 2016, from *www.iceeft.com/nlissue15.pdf.*

Bryant, C., Jackson, H., & Ames, D. (2008). The prevalence of anxiety in older adults: Methodological issues and a review of the literature. *Journal of Affective Disorders, 109,* 233–250.

Buck, J., & Jolles, I. (1966). *House–Tree–Person.* Los Angeles: Western Psychological Services.

Bulloch, A., & Paten, S. (2009). Non-adherence with psychotropic medication in the general population. *Social Psychiatry and Psychiatric Epidemiology, 45,* 47–56.

Cacioppo, J. T., & Patrick, B. (2008). *Loneliness: Human nature and the need for social connection.* New York: Norton.

Carey, B. (2006, December 22). Parenting as therapy for child's mental disorders. *New York Times.* Retrieved from *www.nytimes.com/2006/12/22/health/22KIDS.html.*

Carter, E. M., & McGoldrick, M. (Eds.). (1989). *The changing family life cycle: A framework for family therapy* (3rd ed., pp. 457–482). New York: Allyn & Bacon.

Castle, D., Kulkarni, J., & Abel, K. M. (Eds.). (2006). *Mood and anxiety disorders in women.* New York: Cambridge University Press.

Centers for Disease Control and Prevention. (2006). Homicides and suicides— National Violent Death Reporting System, United States, 2003–2004. *Mortality and Morbidity Weekly Report, 55*(26), 721.

Chapman, G. D. (2015). *The five love languages: The secret to love that lasts.* Chicago: Northfield.

Chenail, R. J., St. George, S., Wulff, D., Duffy, M., Scott, K. W., & Tomm, K. (2012). Clients' relational conceptions of conjoint couples and family therapy quality: A grounded formal theory. *Journal of Marital and Family Therapy, 38,* 241–264.

Chochinov, H. M., Hack, T., Hassard T., Kristjanson, L. J., McClement, S., & Harlos, M. (2005). Dignity therapy: A novel psychotherapeutic intervention for patients near the end of life. *Journal of Clinical Oncology, 23,* 5520–5525.

Christensen, A., Dimidjian, S., & Martell, C. R. (2015). Integrative behavioral couple therapy. In A. S. Gurman, J. L. Lebow, & D. K. Synder (Eds.), *Clinical handbook of couple therapy* (5th ed., pp. 61–94). New York: Guilford Press.

Chu, C., Klein, K. M., Buchman-Schmitt, J. M., Hom, M. A., Hagan, C. R., & Joiner, T. E. (2015). Routinized assessment of suicide risk in clinical practice: An empirically informed update. *Journal of Clinical Psychology, 71*(12), 1186–1200.

Clarkin, J. F., & Glick, I. (1992). *A manual for psychoeducational marital intervention of bipolar disorder.* New York: Cornell Medical Center.

Cohen, S. (2004). Social relationships and health. *American Psychologist, 59*(8), 676–684.

Combrinck-Graham, L. (1985). A developmental model for family systems. *Family Process, 24,* 139–150.

Connell, J. (1995, December 6). Bridging gap between faith and medicine. *San Diego Union–Tribune,* p. D-1.

Conners, C. K. (1997). *Conners' Rating Scale—Revised technical manual.* North Tonawanda, NY: MultiHealth Systems.

Cooper, A. (1998). Sexuality and the Internet: Surfing into the new millennium. *Cyber-psychology and Behavior, 1*(2), 181–187.

Cordova, J. V., & Gee, C. B. (2001). Couples therapy for depression: Using healthy relationships to treat depression. In S. R. H. Beach (Ed.), *Marital and family processes in depression: A scientific foundation for clinical practice* (pp. 185–204). Washington, DC: American Psychological Association.

Costello, J. E., Mustillo, S., Erkanli, A., Keeler, G., & Angold, A. (2003). Prevalence and development of psychiatric disorders in childhood and adolescence. *Archives of General Psychiatry, 60*(8), 837–844.

Crane, D. R. (2013). Editor's introduction to the special issue on international developments in family therapy. *Contemporary Family Therapy, 35,* 177–178.

Crane, D., Newfield, N., & Armstrong, D. (1984). Predicting divorce at marital therapy intake: Wives' distress and the Marital Status Inventory. *Journal of Marital and Family Therapy, 10*(3), 305–312.

Craske, M., & Zoellner, L. (1995). Anxiety disorders: The role of marital therapy. In N. S. Jacobson & A. S. Gurman (Eds.), *Clinical handbook of couple therapy* (pp. 394–410). New York: Guilford Press.

Dadds, M. (1995). *Families, children and the development of dysfunction.* Thousand Oaks, CA: Sage.

Dattilio, F. M., Piercy, F. P., & Davis, S. D. (2014). The divide between "evidenced-based" approaches and practitioners of traditional theories of family therapy. *Journal of Marital and Family Therapy, 40,* 5–16.

Davis, J. L., & Petretic-Jackson, P. A. (2000). The impact of child sexual abuse on adult interpersonal functioning: A review and synthesis of the empirical literature. *Aggression and Violent Behavior, 5,* 291–328.

DeFife, J. A., & Hilsenroth, M. J. (2011). Starting off on the right foot: Common factor elements in early psychotherapy process. *Journal of Psychotherapy Integration, 21*(2), 172–191.

Dell'Osso, B., Marazziti, D., Hollander, E., & Altamura, A. (2007). Traditional and newer impulse control disorders: A clinical update. *Clinical Neuropsychiatry: Journal of Treatment Evaluation, 4*(1), 30–38.

Denton, W., & Burwell, S. (2006). Systemic couple intervention for depression in women. *Journal of Systemic Therapies, 25*(3), 43–57.

Denton, W., Patterson, J., & Van Meir, E. (1997). Use of the DSM in marriage and family therapy programs: Current practices and attitudes. *Journal of Marital and Family Therapy, 23*(1), 81–86.

Desmond, J. (1993, October). *The physician–patient relationship.* Paper presented at the meeting Managed Care: An Approach for the Physician, San Diego County Medical Society, San Diego, CA.

Dilsaver, S. C. (1990). The Mental Status Examination. *American Family Physician, 41*(5), 1489–1497.

Doherty, W. J., Harris, S. M., & Wilde, J. L. (2015). Discernment counseling for "mixed-agenda" couples. *Journal of Marital and Family Therapy, 42,* 246–255.

Doherty, W. J., & Simmons, D. (1996). Clinical practice of marriage and family therapists: A national survey. *Journal of Marital and Family Therapy, 22,* 9–25.

Dube, P., Kurt, K., Bair, M. J., Theobald, D., & Williams, L. S. (2010). The P4 Screener: Evaluation of a brief measure for assessing potential suicide risk in 2 randomized effectiveness trials of primary care and oncology patients. *Primary Care Companion to the Journal of Clinical Psychiatry, 12*(6).

Duncan, B. L., & Miller, S. D. (2008). *The Outcome and Session Rating Scales: The revised administration and scoring manual, including the Child Outcome Rating Scale.* Chicago: Institute for the Study of Therapeutic Change.

Duncan, G. J., Dowsett, C. J., Claessens, A., Magnuson, K., Huston, A. C., Klebanov, P., et al. (2007). School readiness and later achievement. *Developmental Psychology, 43*(6), 1428–1446.

Dutra, L., Stathopoulou, G., Basden, S. L., Leyro, T. M., Powers, M. B., & Otto, M. W. (2008). A meta-analytic review of psychosocial interventions for substance use disorders. *American Journal of Psychiatry, 165*(2), 179–187.

Duvall, E. (1955). *Family development.* New York: Lippincott.

Edwards, G. (1986). *Current issues in clinical psychology.* New York: Springer.

Edwards, J., Johnson, D., & Booth, A. (1987). Coming apart: A prognostic instrument of marital breakup. *Journal of Applied Family and Child Studies, 36*(2), 168–170.

Edwards, M., & Steinglass, P. (1995). Family therapy treatment outcomes for alcoholism. *Journal of Marital and Family Therapy, 21*(4), 475–509.

Edwards, T. M., & Patterson, J. (2012). The daily events and emotions of master's-level family therapy trainees in off-campus practicum sites. *Journal of Marital and Family Therapy, 38,* 688–696.

Edwards, T. M., Patterson, J., Scherger, J., & Vakili, S. (2013). Policy and practice: A primer on the past, present, and future of healthcare reform in the United States. In J. Hodgson, A. Lamson, T. Mendenhall, & R. Crane (Eds.), *Medical family therapy: Advanced applications* (pp. 343–356). New York: Springer.

Egan, J. (2008, September 14). The bipolar puzzle: What does it mean to be a manic depressive child? *New York Times.* Retrieved from *www.nytimes. com/2008/09/14/magazine/14bipolar-t.html.*

Engel, G. L. (1977). The need for a new medical model: A challenge for bio-medicine. *Science, 196,* 535–544.

Essex, M., Kraemer, H., Armstrong, J., Boyce, W., Goldsmith, H., Goldsmith, H., et al. (2006). Exploring risk factors for the emergence of children's mental health problems. *Archives of General Psychiatry, 63*(11), 1246–1256.

Estrada, A., & Pinsof, W. (1995). The effectiveness of family therapies for selected behavioral disorders of childhood. *Journal of Marital and Family Therapy, 4,* 403–440.

Etkin, A., & Wager, T. (2007). Functional neuroimaging of anxiety: A meta-analysis of emotional processing in PTSD, social anxiety disorder, and specific phobia. *American Journal of Psychiatry, 164*(10), 1476–1488.

Everett, C. A., & Volgy, S. S. (1991). Treating divorce in family-therapy practice. In A. S. Gurman & D. P. Kniskern (Eds.), *Handbook of family therapy* (Vol. 2, pp. 508–524). New York: Brunner/Mazel.

Ewing, J. A. (1984). Detecting alcoholism: The CAGE Questionnaire. *Journal of the American Medical Association, 252,* 1905–1907.

Fals-Stewart, W., Kashdan, T., O'Farrell, T., & Birchler, G. (2002). Behavioral couples therapy for drug abusing patients: Effects on partner violence. *Journal of Substance Abuse Treatment, 22,* 87–96.

Fals-Stewart, W., O'Farrell, T., Birchler, G. R., Cordova, J., & Kelley, M. L. (2005). Behavioral couples therapy for alcoholism and drug abuse: Where we've been, where we are, and where we're going. *Journal of Cognitive Therapy, 19*(2), 225–246.

Felitti, V., Anda, R., Nordenberg, D., Williamson, D., Spitz, A., Edwards, V., et al. (1998). Relationship of childhood abuse and household dysfunction to many of the leading causes of death in adults: The Adverse Childhood Experiences (ACE) Study. *American Journal of Preventive Medicine, 14,* 248–258.

Fingerman, K., Miller, L., & Seidel, A. (2009). Functions families serve in old age. In S. H. Qualls & S. H. Zarit (Eds.), *Aging families and caregiving* (pp. 19–43). Hoboken, NJ: Wiley.

Finkelhor, D., Hotaling, G., Lewis, I. A., & Smith, C. (1990). Sexual abuse in a national survey of adult men and women: Prevalence, characteristics and risk-factors. *Child Abuse, 14,* 19–28.

Fisch, R., Weakland, J. H., & Segal, L. (1985). *The tactics of change: Doing therapy briefly.* San Francisco: Jossey-Bass.

Fitchett, G. (1993). *Spiritual assessment in pastoral care: A guide to selected resources.* Decatur, GA: Journal of Pastoral Care Publications.

Forsman, A. K., Nordmyr, J., & Wahlbeck, K. (2011). Psychosocial interventions for the promotion of mental health and the prevention of depression among older adults. *Health Promotion International, 26,* 85–107.

Frances, A. (2013). *Essentials of psychiatric diagnosis: Responding to the challenge of DSM-5* (rev ed.). New York: Guilford Press.

Fredman, S. J., Baucom, D. H., Boeding, S. E., & Miklowitz, D. J. (2015). Relatives' emotional involvement moderates the effects of family therapy for bipolar disorder. *Journal of Consulting and Clinical Psychology, 83*(1), 81–91.

Friedman, H., Rohrbaugh, M., & Krakauer, S (1988). The time-line genogram: Highlighting temporal aspects of family relationships. *Family Process, 27,* 293–303.

Funk, J. L., & Rogge, R. D. (2007). Testing the ruler with item response theory: Increasing precision of measurement of relationship satisfaction with the Couples Satisfaction Index. *Journal of Family Psychology, 21,* 572–583.

Ganong, L., Coleman, M., Fine, M., & Martin, P. (1999). Stepparents' affinity-seeking and affinity-maintaining strategies with stepchildren. *Journal of Family Issues, 20,* 299–327.

Garbarino, J., & Stott, F. (1989). *What children can tell us: Eliciting, interpreting, and evaluating information from children.* San Francisco: Jossey-Bass.

Gawande, A. (2014). *Being mortal.* New York: Metropolitan Books.

Gilbody, S., Bower, P., Fletcher, J., Richards, D., & Sutton, A. J. (2006). Collaborative care for depression: A cumulative meta-analysis and review of longer-term outcomes. *Archives of Internal Medicine, 166,* 2314–2321.

Givens, J., Datto, C. J., Ruckdeschel, K., Knott, K., Zubritsky, C., Oslin, D. W., et al. (2006). Older patients' aversion to antidepressants: A qualitative study. *Journal of General Internal Medicine, 21,* 146–151.

Glied, S., & Frank, R. (2008). Shuffling toward parity—bringing mental health care under the umbrella. *New England Journal of Medicine, 359,* 113–115.

Goldner, V. (1985). Feminism and family therapy. *Family Process, 24,* 31–47.

Gordon, K. C., Khaddouma, A., Baucom, D. H., & Snyder, D. K. (2015). Couple therapy and the treatment of affairs. In A. S. Gurman, J. L. Lebow, & D. K. Synder (Eds.), *Clinical handbook of couple therapy* (5th ed., pp. 412–444). New York: Guilford Press

Gotlib, I., & Beach, S. (1995). A marital/family discord model of depression: Implications for therapeutic intervention. In N. S. Jacobson & A. S. Gurman (Eds.), *Clinical handbook of couple therapy* (pp. 411–436). New York: Guilford Press.

Gottman, J. M. (1994). *What predicts divorce?* Hillsdale, NJ: Erlbaum.

Gottman, J. M. (1999). *The marriage clinic.* New York: Norton.

Gottman, J. M., & Gottman, J. S. (2015). Gottman couple therapy. In A. S. Gurman, J. L. Lebow, & D. K. Synder (Eds.), *Clinical handbook of couple therapy* (5th ed., pp. 129–157). New York: Guilford Press.

Gottman, J. M., & Notarius, C. I. (2000). Decade review: Observing marital interaction. *Journal of Marriage and the Family, 62,* 927–947.

Gould, J. W., & Martindale, D. A. (2007). *The art and science of child custody evaluations.* New York: Guilford Press.

Gould, R. L., Coulson, M. C., & Howard, R. J. (2012a). Cognitive behavioral therapy for depression in older people: A meta-analysis and meta-regression of randomized controlled trials. *Journal of the American Geriatrics Society, 60,* 1817–1830.

Gould, R. L., Coulson, M. C., & Howard, R. J. (2012b). Efficacy of cognitive behavioral therapy for anxiety disorders in older people: A meta-analysis and meta-regression of randomized controlled trials. *Journal of the American Geriatrics Society, 60,* 218–229.

Grant, J. (2008). *Impulse control disorders: A clinician's guide to understanding and treating behavioral addictions.* New York: Norton.

Granvold, D. K. (1983). Structured separation for marital treatment and decision-making. *Journal of Marital and Family Therapy, 9,* 403–412.

Green, R.-J., & Mitchell, V. (2015). Gay, lesbian, and bisexual issues in couple therapy. In A. S. Gurman, J. L. Lebow, & D. K. Synder (Eds.), *Clinical handbook of couple therapy* (5th ed., pp. 489–511). New York: Guilford Press.

Greene, K., & Bogo, M. (2002). The different faces of intimate violence: Implications for assessment and treatment. *Journal of Marital and Family Therapy, 28,* 455–466.

Griffith, J. L. (2013). Existential inquiry: Psychotherapy for crises of demoralization. *European Journal of Psychiatry, 27,* 42–47.

Griffith, J. L., & Griffith, M. E. (1994). *The body speaks: Therapeutic dialogues for mind–body problems.* New York: Basic Books.

Griffiths, M. D. (2012). Internet sex addiction: A review of empirical research. *Addiction Research and Theory, 20,* 111–124.

Groopman, J. (2007). *How doctors think.* Boston: Houghton Mifflin.

Gross, J. J. (Ed.). (2007). *Handbook of emotion regulation.* New York: Guilford Press.

Grunebaum, H. (1988). What if family therapy were a kind of psychotherapy?: A reading of the handbook of psychology and behavioral change. *Journal of Marital and Family Therapy, 14*(2), 195–199.

Gupta, M., Coyne, J. D., & Beach, S. R. H. (2003). Couples treatment for major depression: Critique of the literature and suggestions for some different directions. *Journal of Family Therapy, 25,* 317–346.

Haldane, D. (2006). MoodGym. *Occupational Medicine, 56*(8), 586. Retrieved from *https://moodgym.anu.edu.au.*

Hardy, K. (2011). *Integrative family therapy* [streaming video file]. Mill Valley, CA: Psychotherapy.net.

Hebb, D. O. (1949). *The organization of behavior: A neuropsychological theory.* Mahwah, NJ: Erlbaum.

Herek, G. M. (2008). Hate crimes and stigma-related experiences among sexual minority adults in the United States: Prevalence estimates from a national probability sample. *Journal of Interpersonal Violence, 24,* 54–74.

Hertlein, K. M., & Piercy, F. P. (2012). Essential elements of Internet infidelity treatment. *Journal of Marital and Family Therapy, 38*(1), 257–270.

Hetherington, E. M., & Stanley-Hagan, M. (2002). Parenting in divorced and remarried families. In M. Bornstein (Ed.), *Handbook of parenting* (2nd ed., pp. 287–316). Mahwah, NJ: Erlbaum.

Hill, C. E., Sullivan, C., Knox, S., & Schlosser, L. Z. (2007). Becoming psychotherapists: Experiences of novice trainees in a beginning graduate class. *Psychotherapy: Theory, Research, Practice, Training, 44*, 434–449.

Hirschfeld, R., & Russell, J. (1997). Assessment and treatment of suicidal patients. *New England Journal of Medicine, 337*(13), 910–915.

Hodge, D. R (2005). Spiritual assessment in marital and family therapy: A methodological framework for selecting from among six qualitative assessment tools. *Journal of Marital and Family Therapy, 31*(4), 341–356.

Hodgson, J. L., Lamson, A. L., & Kolobova, I. (2016). A biopsychosocial-spiritual assessment in brief or extended couple therapy formats. In G. R. Weeks, S. T. Fife, & C. M. Peterson (Eds.), *Techniques for the couple therapist: Essential interventions from the experts* (pp. 213–217). New York: Routledge/Taylor & Francis Group.

Hof, L., & Berman, E. (1986). The sexual genogram. *Journal of Marital and Family Therapy, 12*, 39–47.

Hoffman, L. (1981). *Foundations of family therapy.* New York: Basic Books.

Hofstra, M., Van der Ende, J., & Verhulst, F. (2000, July). Continuity and change of psychopathology from childhood into adulthood: A 14-year follow-up study. *Journal of the American Academy of Child and Adolescent Psychiatry, 39*(7), 850–858.

Hunsley, J., & Mash, E. (2005). Developing guidelines for the evidence-based assessment of adult disorders. *Psychological Assessment, 17*, 251–255.

Imber-Black, E. (1988). *Families and larger systems: A family therapist's guide through the labyrinth.* New York: Guilford Press.

Insel, T. R. (2014, August 21). *UCSD Department of Psychiatry Research Colloquium.* U.C. San Diego Health Sciences, San Diego, CA.

Insel, T. R., & Quirion, R. (2005). Psychiatry as a clinical neuroscience discipline. *Journal of the American Medical Association, 294*(17), 2221–2224.

Iveniuk, J., & Schumm, L. P. (2016, August). *Relationships with family members, but not friends, decrease likelihood of death.* Paper presented at the 111th annual meeting of the American Sociological Association, Seattle, WA.

Jacobs, B. J. (2016). *Meditations for caregivers: Practical, emotional, and spiritual support for you and your family.* Boston: Da Capo Press.

Jacobson, N. S., & Gurman, A. S. (Eds.). (1995). *Clinical handbook of couple therapy.* New York: Guilford Press.

James, K., & McIntyre, D. (1983). The reproduction of families: The social role of the family. *Journal of Marital and Family Therapy, 9*, 119–129.

Jensen, F. E., & Nutt, A. E. (2015). *The teenage brain: A neuroscientists survival guide to raising adolescents and young adults.* New York: HarperCollins.

Johnson, S. M. (2004). *The practice of emotionally focused couple therapy: Creating connection.* New York: Brunner-Routledge.

Johnson, S. M. (2015). Emotionally focused couple therapy. In A. S. Gurman, J. L. Lebow, & D. K. Snyder (Eds.), *Clinical handbook of couple therapy* (5th ed., pp. 97–128). New York: Guilford Press.

Kamel Boulos, M. N. (2012). Xbox 360 Kinect exergames for health. *Games Health Journal, 1*, 326–330.

Karel, M. J., Gatz, M., & Smyer, M. A. (2012). Aging and mental health in the decade ahead: What psychologists need to know. *American Psychologist, 67,* 184–198.

Kase, L., & Ledley, D. R. (2007). *Anxiety disorders.* Hoboken, NJ: Wiley.

Kaslow, F. (2000). Families experiencing divorce. In W. C. Nichols, M. A. Pace-Nichols, D. S. Becvar, & A. Y. Napier (Eds.), *Handbook of family development and intervention* (pp. 341–368). New York: Wiley.

Kaslow, N. J., Broth, M. R., Smith, C. O., & Collins, M. H. (2012). Family-based interventions for child and adolescent disorders. *Journal of Marital and Family Therapy, 38,* 82–100.

Keeling, M. L., & Piercy, F. P. (2007). A careful balance: Multinational perspectives on culture, gender, and power in marriage and family therapy practice. *Journal of Marital and Family Therapy, 33*(4), 443–463.

Keitner, G., Ryan, C., Miller, I., & Kohn, R. (1993). The role of the family in major depressive illness. *Psychiatric Annals, 23*(9), 500–507.

Kerr, M. E., & Bowen, M. (1988). *Family evaluation.* New York: Norton.

Kessler, R. C., Adler, L., Barkley, R., Biederman, J., Conners, C. K., Demler, O., et al. (2006). The prevalence and correlates of adult ADHD in the United States: Results from the National Comorbidity Survey Replication. *Archives of General Psychiatry, 163*(4), 716–722.

Kessler, R. C., Angermeyer, M., Anthony, J. C., De Graaf, R., Demyttenaere, K., Gasquet, I., et al. (2007). Lifetime prevalence and age-of-onset distributions of mental disorders in the World Health Organization's World Mental Health Survey Initiative. *World Psychiatry, 6*(3), 168–176.

Kessler, R. C., Berglund, P., Demler, O., Jin, R., Merikangas, K. R., & Walters, E. E. (2005). Lifetime prevalence and age-of-onset distributions of DSM-IV disorders in the National Comorbidity Survey Replication. *Archives of General Psychiatry, 62*(6), 593–602.

Kessler, R. C., Chiu, W. T., Demler, O., & Walters, E. E. (2005, June). Prevalence, severity, and comorbidity of twelve-month DSM-IV disorders in the National Comorbidity Survey Replication (NCS-R). *Archives of General Psychiatry, 62*(6), 617–627.

Kessler, R. C., Eaton, W., Wittchen, H., & Zhao, S. (1994). DSM-III-R: Generalized anxiety disorder in the National Comorbidity Survey. *Archives of General Psychiatry, 51*(5), 355–364.

Kitchens, J. M. (1994). Does this patient have an alcohol problem? *Journal of the American Medical Association, 272*(22), 1782–1787.

Knox, S., Adrians, N., Everson, E., Hess, S., Hill, C., & Crook-Lyon, R. (2011). Clients' perspectives on therapy termination. *Psychotherapy Research, 21,* 154–167.

Kung, W. W. (2000). The intertwined relationship between depression and marital distress: Elements of marital therapy conducive to effective treatment outcome. *Journal of Marital and Family Therapy, 26,* 51–63.

Lambert, M. J. (1992), Psychotherapy outcome research: Implications for integrative and eclectic therapists. In J. C. Norcross & M. R. Goldfried (Eds.), *Handbook of psychotherapy integration* (pp. 94–129). New York: Basic Books.

Larocca-Pitts, M. (2012). FACT, a chaplain's tool for assessing spiritual needs in an acute care setting. *Chaplaincy Today, 28*(1), 25–32. Retrieved from *www.professionalchaplains.org/files/publications/chaplaincy_today_online/volume_28_number_1/28_1laroccapitts.pdf.*

Larson, J. H., Newell, K., Topham, G., & Nichols, S. (2002). A review of three comprehensive premarital assessment questionnaires. *Journal of Marital and Family Therapy, 28,* 233–239.

Lawson, A. (1989). *Adultery: An analysis of love and betrayal.* New York: Basic Books.

Lebow, J. L. (2004). The integrative revolution in couple and family therapy. *Family Process, 36,* 1–17.

Lebow, J. L. (2015). Separation and divorce issues in couple therapy. In A. S. Gurman, J. L. Lebow, & D. K. Synder (Eds.), *Clinical handbook of couple therapy* (5th ed., pp. 445–463). New York: Guilford Press.

Lester, B. M., Conradt, E., & Marsit, C. (2016). Introduction to the special section on epigenetics. *Child Development, 87*(1), 29–37.

Liddle, H. A., & Dakof, G. (1995). Efficacy of family therapy for drug abuse: Promising but not definitive. *Journal of Marital and Family Therapy, 21*(4), 511–543.

Lindblad-Goldberg, M. (1989). Successful minority single-parent families. In L. Combrinck-Graham (Ed.), *Children in family contexts* (pp. 116–134). New York: Guilford Press.

Linn-Walton, R., & Pardasani, M. (2014). Dislikable clients or countertransference: A clinician's perspective. *The Clinical Supervisor, 33,* 100–121.

Livingston, S., & Bowen, L. (2006). Treating divorce families in family therapy: A literature review. In C. A. Everett & R. E. Lee (Eds.), *When marriages fail: Systemic family therapy interventions and issues* (pp. 3–20). New York: Haworth Press.

Loyer-Carlson, V. L. (2016). RELATE Assessment. In J. J. Ponzetti Jr. (Ed.), *Evidence-based approaches to relationship and marriage education* (pp. 148–162). New York: Routledge.

Lozano, R., Naghavi, M., Foreman, K., Lim, S., Shibuya, K., Aboyans, V., et al. (2012). Global and regional mortality from 235 causes of death for 20 age groups in 1990 and 2010: A systematic analysis for the Global Burden of Disease Study 2010. *The Lancet, 380,* 2095–2128.

MacFarlane, M. (2003). Systemic treatment of depression: An integrative approach. *Journal of Family Psychotherapy, 14*(1), 43–61.

Maltz, W., & Maltz, L. (2010). *The porn trap: The essential guide to overcoming problems caused by pornography.* New York: HarperCollins.

Margulies, S. (2007). *Working with divorcing spouses: How to help clients navigate the emotional and legal minefield.* New York: Guilford Press.

Markman, H. J., Stanley, S. M., & Blumberg, S. L. (2010). *Fighting for your marriage: A deluxe revised edition of the classic best seller for enhancing marriage and preventing divorce.* San Francisco: Jossey-Bass.

Mash, E., & Hunsley, J. (2005). Evidence-based assessment of child and adolescent disorders: Issues and challenges. *Journal of Clinical Child and Adolescent Psychology, 34,* 362–379.

Maslach, C. (1993). Burnout: A multi-dimensional perspective. In W. B. Schaufeli, C. Maslach, & T. Marek (Eds.), *Professional burnout: Recent developments in theory and research* (pp. 19–32). Philadelphia: Taylor & Francis.

McClement, S., Chochinov, H. M., Hack, T., Hassard, T., Kristjanson, L. J., & Harlos, M. (2007). Dignity therapy: Family member perspectives. *Journal of Palliative Care, 10,* 1076–1082.

McCollum, E. E. (1990). Integrating structural-strategic and Bowen approaches in training beginning family therapists. *Contemporary Family Therapy, 12,* 23–34.

McFarlane, W. R., Dixon, L., Lukens, E., & Lucksted, A. (2003). Family psycho-education and schizophrenia: A review of the literature. *Journal of Marital and Family Therapy, 29,* 223–245.

McGoldrick, M., Gerson, R., & Petri, S. (2008). *Genograms: Assessment and intervention* (3rd ed.). New York: Norton.

McGoldrick, M., & Shibusawa, T. (2012). The family life cycle. In F. Walsh (Ed.), *Normal family processes: Growing diversity and complexity* (4th ed., pp. 375–398). New York: Guilford Press.

McGrath, E., Keita, G. P., Strickland, B. R., & Russon, N. F. (1990). *Women and depression: Risk factors and treatment issues.* Washington, DC: American Psychological Association.

McNeil, B. J. (2001). Hidden barriers to improvement in the quality of care. *New England Journal of Medicine, 345*(22), 1612–1620.

Mead, N., Lester, H., Chew-Graham, C., Gask, L., & Bower, P. (2010). Effects of befriending on depressive symptoms and distress: Systematic review and meta-analysis. *British Journal of Psychiatry, 196,* 96–101.

Mikesell, R. H., Lusterman, D., & McDaniel, S. H. (1995). *Integrating family therapy: Handbook of family psychology and systems theory.* Washington, DC: American Psychological Association.

Miklowitz, D. J. (2008). *Bipolar disorder: A family-focused treatment approach* (2nd ed.). New York: Guilford Press.

Miller, D. M., Rose, T., & Van Amburgh, J. A. (2016). Behavioral interviewing: Techniques to improve patients' medication adherence. *Consultant, 56*(8), 702–705.

Miller, S. D., Duncan, B. L., Brown, J., Sparks, J. A., & Claud, D. A. (2003). The Outcome Rating Scale: A preliminary study of the reliability, validity, and feasibility of a brief visual analog measure. *Journal of Brief Therapy, 2,* 91–100.

Miller, S. D., Duncan, B. L., & Hubble, M. A. (1997). *Escape from Babel: Toward a unifying language for psychotherapy practice.* New York: Norton.

Miller, S. D., Duncan, B. L., Sorrell, R., & Brown, G. S. (2005). The partners for change outcome system. *Journal of Clinical Psychology: In Session, 61,* 199–208.

Miller, S. D., & Sherrard, P. A. D. (1999). Couple communication: A system for equipping partners to talk, listen, and resolve conflicts effectively. In R. Berger & M. T. Hannah (Eds.), *Preventive approaches in couples therapy* (pp. 73–105). Philadelphia: Brunner/Mazel.

Miller, W. R., & Rollnick, S. (2013). *Motivational interviewing: Helping people change* (3rd ed.). New York: Guilford Press.

Minuchin, P., Colapinto, J., & Minuchin, S. (2006). *Working with families of the poor* (2nd ed.). New York: Guilford Press.

Minuchin, S., & Fishman, H. C. (1981). *Family therapy techniques*. Cambridge, MA: Harvard University Press.

Minuchin, S., Montalvo, B., Guerney, B. G., Rosman, B. L., & Schumer, F. (1967). *Families of the slums*. New York: Basic Books.

Mohr, D., Vella, L., Hart, S., Heckman, T., & Simon, G. (2008). The effect of telephone-administered psychotherapy on symptoms of depression and attrition: A meta-analysis. *Clinical Psychology: Science and Practice, 15*(3), 243–253.

Moltz, D. (1993). Bipolar disorder and the family: An integrative model. *Family Process, 32*(4), 409–423.

Mondor, J., Sabourin, S., Wright, J., Poitras-Wright, H., McDuff, P., & Lussier, Y. (2013). Early termination from couple therapy in a naturalistic setting: The role of therapeutic mandate and romantic attachment. *Contemporary Family Therapy, 35,* 59–73.

Montross, L., Winters, K. D., & Irwin, S. A. (2011). Dignity therapy implementation in a community-based hospice setting. *Journal of Palliative Medicine, 14,* 729–734.

Morris, T. L., & March, J. S. (Eds.). (2004). *Anxiety disorders in children and adolescents* (2nd ed.). New York: Guilford Press.

Mukherjee, S. (2016). *The gene: An intimate history*. New York: Scribners.

Napier, A. Y., & Whitaker, C. (1978). *The family crucible*. New York: Harper & Row.

National Alliance on Mental Illness. (2016). Mental health by the numbers. Retrieved from *www.nami.org/Learn-More/Mental-Health-By-the-Numbers*.

National Collaborating Centre for Mental Health. (2009). *Depression: The NICE guideline on the treatment and management of depression in adults* (Updated ed.) (National Clinical Practice Guideline 90). London: British Psychological Society and Royal College of Psychiatrists.

National Conference of Commissioners on Uniform State Laws. (1970). *Uniform Marriage and Divorce Act*. Chicago: Author. (Approved by the American Bar Association in 1974)

National Institute of Mental Health. (2005, June). Mental illness exacts heavy toll, beginning in youth. Retrieved from *www.nimh.nih.gov/news/science-news/2005/mental-illness-exacts-heavy-toll-beginning-in-youth.shtml*.

National Institute of Mental Health. (2016). Research Domain Criteria (RDoC). Retrieved from *www.nimh.nih.gov/research-priorities/rdoc/index.shtml*.

Neimeyer, R. A., & Holland, J. M. (2015). Bereavement in later life: Theory, assessment, and intervention. In P. A. Lichtenberg & B. T. Mast (Eds.), *APA handbook of clinical geropsychology: Vol. 2. Assessment, treatment, and issues of later life*. Washington, DC: American Psychological Association.

Nichols, W. C. (1988). *Marital therapy: An integrative approach*. New York: Guilford Press.

Nichols, W. C., & Everett, C. A. (1986). *Systemic family therapy*. New York: Guilford Press.

Norcross, J. C., & Guy, J. D. (2007). *Leaving it at the office: A guide to psychotherapist self-care.* New York: Guilford Press.

Northey, W. F. (2002). Characteristics and clinical practices of marriage and family therapists: A national survey. *Journal of Marital and Family Therapy, 28*(4), 487–494.

O'Brian, C., & Bruggen, P. (1985). Our personal and professional lives: Learning positive connotation and circular questions. *Family Process, 24,* 311–322.

O'Farrell, T. J., & Fals-Stewart, W. (2006). *Behavioral couples therapy for alcoholism and drug abuse.* New York: Guilford Press.

Ogrodniczuk, J. S., Joyce, A. S., & Piper, W. E. (2005). Strategies for reducing patient-initiated premature termination of psychotherapy. *Harvard Review of Psychiatry, 13*(2), 57–70.

O'Hanlon, W. (1982). Strategic pattern intervention. *Journal of Strategic and Systemic Therapies, 4,* 26–33.

Olson, A. K., & Olson, D. H. (2016). Discoveries about couples from PREPARE/ ENRICH. In J. J. Ponzetti Jr. (Ed.), *Evidence-based approaches to relationship and marriage education* (pp. 123–136). New York: Routledge.

Pallanti, S. (2006). From impulse-control disorders toward behavioral addictions. *CNS Spectrums, 11*(12), 921–922.

Paolucci, E. O., Genius, M. L., & Violato, C. (2001). A meta-analysis of the published research on the effects of child sexual abuse. *Journal of Psychology, 135*(1), 17–36.

Parkes, C. M. (1972). *Bereavement: Studies of grief in adult life.* New York: International University Press.

Pasley, K., Rhoden, L., Visher, E. B., & Visher, J. S. (1996). Successful stepfamily therapy: Clients' perspectives. *Journal of Marital and Family Therapy, 22,* 342–357.

Patel, V., Araya, R., Chatterjee, S., Chisholm, D., Cohen, A., De Silva, M., et al. (2007). Treatment and prevention of mental disorders in low-income and middle-income countries. *The Lancet, 370,* 991–1005.

Patel, V., Chisholm, D., Dua, T., Laxminarayan, R., & Medina-Mora, M. E. (Eds.). (2015). *Mental, neurological, and substance use disorders* (3rd ed.). Washington, DC: World Bank.

Patel, V., & Saxena, S. (2014). Transforming lives, enhancing communities— Innovations in global mental health. *New England Journal of Medicine, 370*(6), 498–501.

Patterson, J. E., Albala, A. A., McCahill, M. E., & Edwards, T. M. (2010). *The therapist's guide to psychopharmacology, revised edition: Working with patients, families, and physicians to optimize care.* New York: Guilford Press.

Patterson, J., Edwards, T., & Vakili, S. (in press). Global mental health: A call for increased awareness and action in marriage and family therapy. *Family Process.*

Patterson, J. E., & Magulac, M. (1994). The family therapist's guide to psychopharmacology: A graduate level course. *Journal of Marital and Family Therapy, 20*(2), 151–173.

Patterson, J. E., Miller, R., Carnes, S., & Wilson, S. (2007). Evidence-based practice for marriage and family therapists. *Journal of Marital and Family Therapy, 30,* 183–195.

Patterson, J. E., & Vakili, S. (2014). Relationships, environment, and the brain: How emerging research is changing what we know about the impact of families on human development. *Family Process, 53*(1), 22–32.

Pendagast, E., & Sherman, C. O. (1977). A guide to the genogram. *Family, 5,* 3–13.

Penn, C. D., Hernandez, S. L., & Bermudez, J. M. (1997). Using a cross-cultural perspective to understand infidelity in couples therapy. *American Journal of Family Therapy, 25,* 169–185.

Peris, T. S., & Miklowitz D. J. (2015). Parental expressed emotion and youth psychopathology: New directions for an old construct. *Child Psychiatry and Human Development, 46*(6), 863–873.

Pinsoff, W. (1995). *Integrative problem-centered therapy: A synthesis of biological, individual, and family therapy.* New York: Basic Books.

Prina, A. M., Ferri, C. P., Guerra, M., Brayne, C., & Prince, M. (2011). Prevalence of anxiety and its correlates among older adults in Latin America, India and China: Cross-cultural study. *British Journal of Psychiatry, 199,* 485–491.

Prince, M., Patel, V., Saxena, S., Maj, M., Maselko, J., Phillips, M. R., et al. (2007). No health without mental health. *The Lancet, 370,* 859–877.

Prince, S., & Jacobson, N. (1995). Couple and family therapy for depression. In E. E. Beckham & W. R. Leber (Eds.), *Handbook of depression* (2nd ed., pp. 404–424). New York: Guilford Press.

Prochaska, J., Norcross, J., & DiClemente, C. (1994). *Changing for good.* New York: Avon.

Qualls, S. H. (2000). Therapy with aging families: Rationale, opportunities, and challenges. *Aging and Mental Health, 4,* 191–199.

Qualls, S. H. (2016). Caregiving families within the long-term services and support system for older adults. *American Psychologist, 71,* 283–293.

Qualls, S. H., & Williams, A. (2013). *Caregiver family therapy: Empowering families to meet the challenges of aging.* Washington, DC: American Psychological Association.

Rainer, J. P., & Campbell, L. F. (2001). Premature termination in psychotherapy: Identification and intervention. *Journal of Psychotherapy in Independent Practice, 2*(3), 19–41.

Rappaport, L. (1970). Crisis intervention as a brief mode of treatment. In R. W. Roberts & R. H. Nee (Eds.), *Theories of social casework* (pp. 123–159). Chicago: University of Chicago Press.

Regier, D. A., Boyd, J. H., Burke, J. D., & Rae, D. A. (1988). One-month prevalence of mental disorders in the United States. *Archives of General Psychiatry, 45,* 977–986.

Reiss, D., Steinglass, P., & Howe, G. (1993). The family's organization around the illness. In R. E. Cole & D. Reiss (Eds.), *How do families cope with chronic illness?* (pp. 173–214). Hillsdale, NJ: Erlbaum.

Renk, K., & Dinger, T. M. (2002). Reasons for therapy termination in a university psychology clinic. *Journal of Clinical Psychology, 58,* 1173–1181.

Riggs, D. S., Caulfield, M. B., & Street, A. E. (2000). Risk for domestic violence: Factors associated with perpetration and victimization. *Journal of Clinical Psychology, 56,* 1289–1316.

Rogers, C. R. (1972). *On becoming a person.* Boston: Houghton Mifflin.

Rolland, J. S. (1990). Anticipatory loss: A family systems developmental framework. *Family Process, 29,* 229–244.

Rolland, J. S. (1994). *Families, illness, and disability.* New York: Basic Books.

Roos, J., & Werbart, A. (2013). Therapist and relationship factors influencing dropout from individual psychotherapy: A literature review. *Psychotherapy Research, 23,* 394–418.

Rosenberg, T. (2015, June 19). Depressed?: Try therapy without the therapist. *New York Times.* Retrieved from *http://opinionator.blogs.nytimes.com/2015/06/19/depressed-try-therapy-without-the-therapist/?_r=0.*

Rowe, C. L. (2012). Family therapy for drug abuse: Review and updates 2003–2010. *Journal of Marital and Family Therapy, 38,* 59–81.

Rowe, C. L., & Liddle, H. A. (2007). Substance abuse. *Journal of Marital and Family Therapy, 29*(1), 97–120.

Rubin, S. S. (1999). The two-track model of bereavement: Overview, retrospect and prospect. *Death Studies, 23,* 681–714.

Rumstein-McKean, O., & Hunsley, J. (2001). Interpersonal and family functioning of female survivors of childhood sexual abuse. *Clinical Psychology Review, 21,* 471–490.

Sackett, D. L., Strauss, S., Richardson, S. W., Rosenberg, W., & Haynes, B. R. (2000). *Evidence-based medicine: How to practice and teach EBM.* New York: Churchill Livingstone.

Sapolsky, R. (2005). *Monkeyluv.* New York: Scribners.

Sapolsky, R. (2017). *Behave.* New York: Penguin.

Satir, V. (1967). *Conjoint family therapy.* Palo Alto, CA: Science & Behavior Books.

Saunders, J. B., Aasland, O. G., Babor, T. F., De La Fuente, J. R., & Grant, M. (1993). Development of the Alcohol Use Disorders Identification Test (AUDIT): WHO Collaborative Project on Early Detection of Persons with Harmful Alcohol Consumption—II. *Addiction, 88,* 791–804.

Saxena, S., Thornicroft, G., Knapp, M., & Whiteford, H. (2007). Resources for mental health: Scarcity, inequity, and inefficiency. *The Lancet, 370,* 878–889.

Schore, A. (2003a). *Affect dysregulation and disorders of the self.* New York: Norton.

Schore, A. (2003b). *Affect regulation and the repair of the self.* New York: Norton.

Schore, A. (2005). Back to basics: Attachment, affect regulation, and the right brain: Linking developmental neuroscience to pediatrics. *Pediatrics in Review, 26*(6), 204–217.

Scuka, R. F. (2016). Relationship enhancement program and mastering the mysteries of love. In J. J. Ponzetti Jr. (Ed.), *Evidence-based approaches to relationship and marriage education* (pp. 165–179). New York: Routledge.

Seaburn, D., Landau-Stanton, J., & Horwitz, S. (1995). Core techniques in family therapy. In R. H. Mikesell, D. Lusterman, & S. H. McDaniel (Eds.), *Integrating family therapy: Handbook of family psychology and systems theory* (pp. 5–26). Washington, DC: American Psychological Association.

Selzer, M. L. (1971). The Michigan Alcoholism Screening Test: The quest for a new diagnostic instrument. *American Journal of Psychiatry, 127,* 1653–1658.

Serrano, J. P., Latorre, J. M., Gatz, M., & Montanes, J. (2004). Life review therapy using autobiographical retrieval practice for older adults with depressive symptomatology. *Psychology and Aging, 19,* 272–277.

Shapiro, A. F., & Gottman, J. M. (2005). Effects on marriage of a psycho-communicative–educational intervention with couples undergoing the transition to parenthood, evaluation at 1-year post intervention. *Journal of Family Communication, 5,* 1–24.

Shapiro, A. F., Gottman, J. M., & Carrere, S. (2000). The baby and the marriage: Identifying factors that buffer against decline in marital satisfaction after the first baby arrives. *Journal of Family Psychology, 14,* 345–360.

Sharf, J., Primavera, L. H., & Deiner, M. J. (2010). Dropout and therapeutic alliance: A meta-analysis of adult individual therapy. *Psychotherapy Theory, Research, Practice, Training, 47,* 637–645.

Shaw, P., Eckstrand, K., Sharp, W., Blumenthal, J., Lerch, J. P., Greenstein, D., et al. (2007). Attention-deficit/hyperactivity disorder is characterized by a delay in cortical maturation. *Proceedings of the National Academy of Sciences of the USA, 104*(49), 19649–19654.

Shea, M. T., Gibbons, R., Elkin, I., & Sotsky, S. (1995). Initial severity and differential treatment outcome in the National Institute of Mental Health Treatment of Depression of Collaborative Research Program. *Journal of Consulting and Clinical Psychology, 63*(5), 841–847.

Shields, C. G., Wynne, L. C., McDaniel, S. H., & Gawinski, B. A. (1994). The marginalization of family therapy: A historical and continuing problem. *Journal of Marital and Family Therapy, 20,* 117–138.

Shonkoff, J. P., Garner, A. S. (2012). The lifelong effects of early childhood adversity and toxic stress. *Pediatrics, 129,* 232–236.

Siegel, D. J. (1999). *The developing mind: How relationships and the brain interact to shape who we are.* New York: Guilford Press.

Siegel, D. J. (2007). *The mindful brain: Reflection and attunement in the cultivation of well-being.* New York: Norton.

Skoog, I., Nilsson, L., Palmertz, B., Andreasson, L., & Svanborg, A. (1993). A population-based study of dementia in 85-year-olds. *New England Journal of Medicine, 328,* 153–158.

Skovholt, T. M. (2010). *Becoming a therapist on the path to mastery.* Hoboken, NJ: Wiley.

Skovholt, T. M., & Rønnestad, M. H. (2003). Struggles of the novice counselor and therapist. *Journal of Career Development, 30,* 45–58.

Snyder, D. K. (1979). Multidimensional assessment of marital satisfaction. *Journal of Marriage and Family, 41*(4), 813–823.

Snyder, D. K., Castellani, A. M., & Whisman, M. A. (2006). Current status and future directions in couple therapy. *Annual Review of Psychology, 57,* 317–344.

Spanier, G. B. (1976). Measuring marital adjustment: New scales for assessing the quality of marriage and similar dyads. *Journal of Marriage and Family, 38,* 15–28.

Sprenkle, D. H., & Bischoff, R. J. (1991). Research in family therapy: Trends, issues and recommendations. In M. Nichols & R. Schwartz (Eds.), *Family therapy: Concepts and methods* (pp. 542–580). Boston: Allyn & Bacon.

Sprenkle, D. H., Davis, S. D., & Lebow, J. L. (2009). *Common factors in couple and family therapy: The overlooked foundation for effective practice.* New York: Guilford Press.

Stanton, M. D. (1992). The time line and the "why now"? question: A technique and rationale for therapy, training, organizational consultation and research. *Journal of Marital and Family Therapy, 18,* 331–343.

Steinglass, P., Bennett, L. A., Wolin, S. J., & Reiss, D. (1987). *The alcoholic family.* New York: Basic Books.

Stith, S. M., McCollum, E. E., Amanor-Boadu, Y., & Smith, D. (2012). Systemic perspectives on intimate partner violence treatment. *Journal of Marital and Family Therapy, 38*(1), 220–240.

Straus, M. A. (1979). Measuring intrafamily conflict and violence: The Conflict Tactics Scale. *Journal of Marriage and Family, 41,* 75–88.

Stroebe, M., & Shut, H. (2010). The dual process model of coping with bereavement: Rationale and description. *Death Studies, 23,* 197–224.

Strong, T. (2015). Diagnoses, relational processes, and resourceful dialogs: Tensions for families and family therapy. *Family Process, 54,* 518–532.

Sullivan, H. S. (1953). *Conceptions of modern psychiatry.* New York: Norton.

Swift, J. K., Greenberg, R. P., Whipple, J. L., & Kominiak, N. (2012). Recommendations for reducing premature termination in therapy. *Professional Psychology: Research and Practice, 43,* 379–387.

Swisher, A. K. (2010). Practice-based evidence. *Cardiopulmonary Physical Therapy Journal, 21*(2), 4.

Taggart, M. (1985). The feminist critique in epistemological perspective: Questions of context in family therapy. *Journal of Marital and Family Therapy, 11,* 113–126.

Tanyi, R. A., McKenzie, M., & Chapek, C. (2009). How family practice physicians, nurse practitioners, and physician assistants incorporate spiritual care in practice. *Journal of the American Academy of Nurse Practitioners, 21*(12), 690–697.

Taylor, R. (1990). *Distinguishing psychological from organic disorders: Screening for psychological masquerades.* New York: Springer.

Tomm, K. (1988). Interventive interviewing: Part III. *Family Process, 27*(1), 1–15.

Tonelli, L. A., Pregulman, M., & Markman, H. J. (2016). The Prevention and Relationship Education Program (PREP) for individuals and couples. In J.

J. Ponzetti Jr. (Ed.), *Evidence-based approaches to relationship and marriage education* (pp. 180–196). New York: Routledge.

Treas, J., & Giesen, D. (2000). Sexual infidelity among married and cohabiting Americans. *Journal of Marriage and Family, 62,* 48–60.

Uebelacker, L., Weishaar, M., & Miller, I. (2008). Family or relationship problems. In M. A. Whisman (Ed.), *Adapting cognitive therapy for depression: Managing complexity and comorbidity* (pp. 326–347). New York: Guilford Press.

Underhill, C. (2007). Barriers to improvement of mental health services in low-income and middle-income countries. *The Lancet, 370,* 1164–1174.

Van Der Kolk, B. A. (1997). The body keeps the score: Approaches to the psychobiology of posttraumatic stress disorder. In B. A. van der Kolk, A. C. McFarlane, & L. Weisaeth (Eds.), *Traumatic stress: The effects of overwhelming experience on mind, body and society* (pp. 214–241). New York: Guilford Press.

Vincent, G. K., & Velkoff, V. A. (2010). The next four decades: The older population in the United States: 2010 to 2050 (Current Population Report P25-1138). Retrieved from *www.census.gov/prod/2010pubs/p25-1138.pdf.*

Visher, E. B., & Visher, J. S. (1988). *Old loyalties, new ties: Therapeutic strategies with stepfamilies.* New York: Brunner/Mazel.

von Bertalanffy, L. (1968). *General system theory.* New York: Braziller.

Vossler, A. (2016). Internet infidelity 10 years on: A critical review of the literature. *Family Journal, 24,* 359–366.

Walsh, F. (2010). *Spiritual resources in family therapy* (2nd ed.). New York: Guilford Press.

Wang, P. S., Lane, M., Olfson, M., Pincus, H. A., Wells, K. B., & Kessler, R. C. (2005). Twelve month use of mental health services in the United States. *Archives of General Psychiatry, 62*(6), 629–640.

Watkins, C. E., Jr. (2012). Demoralization, therapist identity development, and persuasion and healing in psychotherapy supervision. *Journal of Psychotherapy Integration, 22,* 187–205.

Weber, T., & Levine, F. (1995). Engaging the family: An integrative approach. In R. H. Mikesell, D. Lusterman, & S. H. McDaniel (Eds.), *Integrating family therapy: Handbook of family psychology and systems theory* (pp. 45–72). Washington, DC: American Psychological Association.

Wechsler, D. (1991). *Wechsler Intelligence Scale for Children* (3rd ed.). San Antonio, TX: Psychological Corporation.

Weeks, G. R., Odell, M., & Methven, S. (2005). *If only I had known . . . : Avoiding common mistakes in couples therapy.* New York: Norton.

Weiss, R., & Cerrato, M. (1980). The Marital Status Inventory: Development of a measure of dissolution potential. *American Journal of Family Therapy, 8*(2), 80–85.

Whelton, W. J. (2004). Emotional processes in psychotherapy: Evidence across therapeutic modalities. *Clinical Psychology and Psychotherapy, 11,* 58–71.

Whisman, M. A., & Beach, S. R. H. (2015). Couple therapy and depression. In

A. S. Gurman, J. L. Lebow, & D. K. Synder (Eds.), *Clinical handbook of couple therapy* (5th ed., pp. 585–605). New York: Guilford Press.

White, M. (1988). Saying hullo again: The incorporation of the lost relationship in the resolution of grief. In *Selected Papers*. Adelaide, South Australia: Dulwich Centre.

Williams, L. M. (2016). FOCCUS and REFOCCUS: Preparing and sustaining couples for marriage. In J. J. Ponzetti Jr. (Ed.), *Evidence-based approaches to relationship and marriage education* (pp. 137–147). New York: Routledge.

Williams, L. M., & Day, A. (2007). Strategies for dealing with clients we dislike. *American Journal of Family Therapy, 35,* 83–92.

Williams, L. M., Edwards, T. M., Patterson, J., & Chamow, L. (2011). *Essential assessment skills for couple and family therapists.* New York: Guilford Press.

Williams, L. M., & Jimenez, M. (2012). Treating the overfunctioning and underfunctioning couple. *American Journal of Family Therapy, 40,* 141–151.

Williams, L. M., Patterson, J., & Edwards, T. M. (2014). *Clinician's guide to research methods in family therapy: Foundations of evidence-based practice.* New York: Guilford Press.

Williams, L. M., Patterson, J., & Miller, R. B. (2006). Panning for gold: A clinician's guide to using research. *Journal of Marital and Family Therapy, 32,* 17–32.

Williams, L. M., & Winter, H. (2009). Guidelines for an effective transfer of cases: The needs of the transfer triad. *American Journal of Family Therapy, 37,* 146–158.

Wolff, J. L., & Kasper, J. D. (2006). Caregivers of frail elders: Updating a national profile. *The Gerontologist, 46,* 344–356.

Woodside, M., Oberman, A. H., Cole, K. G., & Carruth, E. K. (2007). Learning to be a counselor: A prepracticum point of view. *Counselor Education and Supervision, 47,* 14–28.

World Health Organization. (2010). *mhGAP intervention guide for mental, neurological and substance use disorders in non-specialized health settings.* Geneva, Switzerland: Author.

Yalom, I. D. (2002). *The gift of therapy: An open letter to a new generation of therapists and their patients.* New York: HarperCollins.

Zarit, S. H., & Heid, A. R. (2015). Assessment and treatment of family caregivers. In P. A. Lichtenberg & B. T. Mast (Eds.), *APA handbook of clinical geropsychology: Vol. 2. Assessment, treatment, and issues of later life* (pp. 521–552). Washington, DC: American Psychological Association.

Zitzman, S. T., & Butler, M. H. (2005). Attachment, addiction, and recovery: Conjoint marital therapy for recovery from a sexual addiction. *Sexual Addiction and Compulsivity, 12,* 311–337.

Zuckerman, E. L., & Kolmes, K. (2017). *The paper office for the digital age: Forms, guidelines, and resources to make your practice work ethically, legally, and profitably.* New York: Guilford Press.

Index

Note. *f* or *t* following a page number indicates a figure or a table.

Abuse. *See* Child abuse; Domestic
    violence; Violence/abuse
ACTION acronym, 58
Addictive behaviors, screening
    instruments for, 294
ADHD. *See* Attention-deficit/
    hyperactivity disorder
    (ADHD)
Administrative issues, 27–32
Adolescents
    brain development in, 145
    family therapy with, 142–147
    technology focus of, 145–146
    treatment of, 146–147
    See also Child/adolescent therapy
Adult disorders, APA treatment
    classification for, 84–85
Adverse Childhood Experience
    (ACE) study, 208–209
Agency, mobilizing, 121–122
Agoraphobia, 224
Alcohol Use Disorders Identification
    Test (AUDIT), 59, 61*f*
Alcoholism
    characteristics of, 228
    suicide risk and, 49*t*

Alcoholism/drug abuse, 226–231
    clinical guidelines for treatment,
        230–231
    clinical research on, 227–228
    controversies over, 226–227
    impacts of, 227
    interventions for, 227–231
Alzheimer's Association, 170*t*
American Academy of Child and
    Adolescent Psychiatry, practice
    guidelines of, 85
American Association for Marriage
    and Family Therapy (AAMFT),
    20, 286
American Psychiatric Association,
    practice guidelines for adults,
    85
American Psychological Association,
    website of, 84–85
Anger management, referrals for, 192
Antidepressants, primer on, 96*t*
Anxiety/anxiety disorders, 222–226
    assessment with psychiatric
        screening instruments, 214
    of beginning therapists, 2
    brain changes and, 223

Anxiety/anxiety disorders *(cont.)*
  in children, 225
  clinical guidelines for treatment
      of, 225–226
  cure rate for, 222
  drugs for, 96*t*
  of family, 12–14
  managing, 4–6
  in older adults/caregivers, 160–161
  prevalence, age at onset,
      proportion seeking help, 215*t*
  screening instruments for, 293
  during sessions, 123
Appointments, missed, 80, 245–247
Assessment guidelines
  for biological and neurological
      factors, 60, 62–64
  for clinical priorities, 43–44
  in initial stage, 45–58
    for attempted solutions, 46–47
    for crisis and stressful life
        events, 47
    for presenting problems, 45–46
    for larger systems, 74–76
    outline for, 44*t*
    for potential issues of harm, 47–58
      duty-to-warn issues and, 57–58
      substance abuse, 58–60, 61*t*
      suicide, 48, 49*t*–51*t*, 51–53
      violence and abuse, 53–57
    for psychological issues, 64–66
      affect, behavior, cognition, 64–65
      meaning for client, 65–66
    for social factors, 66–71
      in couple system, 70–71
      in family system, 66–69
    for social systems outside family,
        73–74
    for spiritual issues, 72–73
Assessment tools, 17. *See also*
    Screening instruments
Attachment, brain development and,
    128–129
Attention-deficit/hyperactivity
    disorder (ADHD), 231–233
  adult, 232
  research on, 128–129

B

Beginning therapist
  academic versus therapeutic
      competence of, 2
  burnout and, 9–11
  challenges of, 1–11
  developmental stages of, 6–9
  feelings of, 4
  and future of family therapy,
      276–277
  and the jitters, 4
  See also Therapist
Behaviors
  normalizing, 109
  reframing, 109–110
Benefits Check Up, 170*t*
Benzodiazepines, primer on, 96*t*
Biological/neurological factors
  assessing for, 60, 62–64
  symptoms of, 62
Biopsychosocial (BPS) model, 3,
    82–83
  neglect of biological component
      of, 91
Biopsychosocial systems
    assessment, in treatment
    plan, 88–89
Bipolar depression, 218
Bipolar disorder
  drugs for, 96*t*–97*t*
  symptoms of, 219
Blame, moving away from, 186
Body Keeps the Score, The (Van Der
    Kolk), 223
Boundaries, establishing, 10
Brain changes, anxiety disorders
    and, 225
Brain development, attachment and,
    128–129
Brain disorders, mental illness and,
    208
Bupropion, primer on, 94*t*
Burnout, beginning therapist and,
    9–11
Business issues, addressing, 15–16
Buspirone, primer on, 96*t*

C

CAGE questionnaire, 60
Cancellations, dealing with, 245–247
Caregiver Action Network, 172*t*
Caregiver Family Therapy (CFT),
    169*t*
Caregivers
    of older adults, anxiety and
        depression in, 160–161
    resources for, 172*t*–173*t*
Case conceptualization, learning,
    7–8
Change
    versus acceptance, 241–242
    clarifying client and therapist
        goals for, 238
    client ambivalence about,
        236–238
    key factors in, 115
    motivation for, 38–39
Child abuse, 54–57
    neglect as, 55
    reporting of, 55
    sexual, 55–56
    See also Violence/abuse
Child Behavior Checklist, 128
Child custody, evaluation for,
    151–152
Child/adolescent disorders
    APA treatment classification for,
        85
    common, 127–128
    practice guidelines of, 85
Child/adolescent therapy, 125–156
    assessment in, 126–128
    emerging resources for, 128–130
    family life cycle and, 130,
        131*t*–132*t*, 132–148. *See also*
        Family life cycle
    family system and, 126–127
    neglect family issues in, 279
    and variations in family
        development, 149–156
Childhood
    diagnostic complications of, 126
    disorders of, 64
Children
    anxiety disorders in, 225
    couple relationship and, 71
    couple system and, 70
    parental divorce therapy and,
        199–200
    parental monitoring of, 69
    in single-parent families, 153–154
Circular questions, 107–108
Client
    confronting, 110–111
    expectations and anxieties of,
        12–14
    gifts from, 267
    identified patient as, 45–46
    initial contact with, 14–16
    joining with, 25–27
    motivation of, 37–40
    obsessing about, 9
    providing support for, 110
    and relationships outside therapy,
        267–268
    and release of information, 46
    therapist dislike of, 249–251
    therapy goals of, 33–35
    understanding ambivalence of,
        236–238
Client expectations
    about personal issues, 33–36
    about therapy process, 36–37
Client-focused feedback, 100
Clinical hypotheses. *See* Hypotheses
Clinical work, obsessing about, 9
Cognitive-behavioral therapy (CBT)
    for anxiety disorders, 224
    primer on, 95*t*
Collaborative care, older adults and,
    159
Collusion, 248–249
Communication
    establishing guidelines for, 80
    family, 68
Communication skills
    in couple therapy, 189–190
    teaching during premarital
        counseling, 201–202
Communion, mobilizing, 121–122

Conceptual map, theory and
  research and, 81–86
Conduct disorder, 231–232
Confidence
  developmental perspective and, 4
  managing, 4–6
Conflict, parental, 150–151
Conflict resolution skills
  of couples, 71
  teaching during premarital
    counseling, 201–202
Confronting, 110–111
Connection, developing with client,
  25–27
Conners' Rating Scales, 128
Consultations, medication, 90–93
Control issues, 244
  assessing, 70–71
Counseling
  discernment, 183
  premarital, 200–202
  See also Family therapy; Therapy
Counseling skills, 105–114
  confronting, 110–111
  crisis intervention, 112–114
  leading, 111–112
  normalizing, 109
  offering psychoeducational
    information, 114
  pacing, 111–112
  providing support, 110
  reframing, 109–110
  specific to systemic/relational
    therapist, 114–122
    and common factors in couple/
      family therapy, 114–115
    genogram development,
      116–117, 118f, 119–120
    identifying/interrupting negative
      interactional patterns,
      115–116
    inviting absent family members
      to sessions, 116
    mobilizing hope, agency,
      communion, 121–122
    timeline development, 120–121

using questions, 107–109
using/not using self-disclosure,
  105–107
Countertransference
  and stuckness in therapy,
    242–245
  and therapist dislike of client,
    249–250
Couple system
  assessing, 70–71
  joining with, 177–181, 178f
Couple therapy, 176–206
  and empathy for each partner,
    177–178
  key factors in, 114–115
  key principles in, 177–191
    building commitment to
      therapy, 181–183
    identifying and altering vicious
      cycles, 183–186
    identifying and managing
      individual psychopathology,
      187–188
    joining with couple system,
      177–181, 178f
    managing emotions, 188–191
    moving away from blame, 186
    strengthening cohesion and
      caring, 187
  limits of, 205
  special topics in, 191–205
    divorce therapy, 199–200
    domestic violence, 191–193
    gay and lesbian couples,
      202–205
    infidelity, 193–194
    pornography, 194–197
    premarital counseling,
      200–202
    sexual difficulties, 197–198
    structured separations,
      198–199
  therapist as translator in,
    180–181
  and working with couple as unit,
    179–180

Couples
   evaluating for domestic violence,
      53
   screening instruments for, 295
   with young children, 134–138
Credibility, therapist, 40–42
Crisis, assessing for, 15, 47
Crisis intervention, 112–114
   goals for, 113
   infidelity and, 194
Crisis orientation, 80
Cross-cultural assessment, 75–76
Cultural issues, 12–13
   assessment, 75–76
   therapist's learning posture and,
      104–105
Cycling without Age, 171*t*

D

DALY (disability adjusted life year),
      209
Decision making, assessing, 70–71
Denial, client, 38–39
Depressed persons
   family response to, 219–220
   guidelines for working with,
      221–222
   spouse of, 220–221
Depression, 217–222
   assessment with psychiatric
      screening instruments, 214
   bipolar, 218
   case example of, 92
   common syndromes involving,
      217–218
   drugs for, 94*t*–95*t*, 96*t*–97*t*
   general health and, 209
   marital quality and, 221
   in older adults/caregivers,
      160–161
   prevalence of, 218
   risk factors for, 218–219
Developing treatment plan. *See*
   Treatment plan

Diagnoses
   individual, in family context,
      212–217
   for substance abuse, 226–227
*Diagnostic and Statistical Manual
   of Mental Disorders* (DSM),
      64–65
   anxiety disorders in, 223
   impulse control/
      neurodevelopmental
      disorders in, 231
   limitations of, 212–213
   NIMH alternative to, 208
   in treatment plan, 89
Discernment counseling, 183
Divorce
   in families with adolescents, 142
   in families with young children,
      134–135
   family development and, 149–151
   mediation and, 151–152
   structured separation and,
      198–199
Divorce therapy, 199–200
Domestic violence
   assessing for, 53
   couple therapy and, 191–193
   versus patriarchal terrorism, 54
   therapist beliefs and reactions to,
      192–193
   types of, 53–54
   See also Child abuse; Violence/
      abuse
"Do-something syndrome," 103
Duty-to-warn issues, 57–58
Dysthymia, 218

E

Eating disorders, screening
      instruments for, 294
Elder abuse/neglect, 56
Electroconvulsive therapy (ECT), 95*t*
Emotion management, in couple
      therapy, 188–191

Emotional Survival Guide for
Caregivers, 172t–173t
Empathy, communicating, 103–104
Epigenetics, 208
Evidence-based treatments (EBTs),
84–86
concerns about, 283
in future of family therapy,
282–283
for older adults, 169t
Exergaming with Xbox Kinect, 171t

F

Families of origin, premarital
counseling and, 202
Family(ies)
alcoholic, 228
of depressed persons, 219–220
establishing rapport with, 15
expectations and anxieties of,
12–14
genogram of, 116–117, 118f,
119–120
hidden agendas/overt/covert rules
in, 225
identified patient in, 45–46
influence on course of mental
illness, 210–211
initial contact with, 14–16
of members with mental illness,
207–234. See also Mental
illness
screening instruments for, 295
shared responsibility in, 137
single-parent, 152–154
substance abuse and, 227–228
technology focus in, 145–146
transitioning, 147–148
Family Caregiver Alliance, 172t
Family Crucible, The (Napier &
Whitaker), 79
Family development
divorce and, 149–151
mediation and child custody
evaluation, 151–152

single-parent families and,
152–154
stepfamilies and, 154–156
variations in, 149–156
Family life cycle, 130–148,
131t–132t
adolescents in, 142–147
assessment of, 69
criticism and alternatives, 130
school-age children in, 138–142
stages of, 131t–132t
tasks by stages of, 132–133
themes by stages of, 133–134
young children in, 134–138
Family members, absent, inviting to
sessions, 116
Family structure, 67
Family system, social assessment of,
66–69
Family therapy
absent family members and,
247–248
with adolescents, 142–147
for alcoholism/drug abuse,
228–230
assessing appropriateness of, 3
choosing participants for, 17,
20–21, 79–80
client expectations for, 33–37
collusion in, 248–249
and cost-effectiveness versus
quality, 279
determining who participates in,
36–37
developing time line in, 120–121
extended family and, 138
feminist, 74
future of, 275–292
getting unstuck in. *See* Getting
unstuck in therapy; Stuckness
in therapy
integrating with individual
therapy, 213
key factors in, 114–115
launching children, parents in
transition, 147–148
pacing, 111–112

and previously attempted
    solutions, 46–47
research on difficult cases, 256–
    258, 259*t*–260*t*, 260–261
school system and, 138–142
with school-age children, 138–142
and social systems outside family, 74
space considerations, 136–137
termination of. *See* Termination
theoretical models of, 81–83
and transference of case, 269–270
transference versus
    countertransference in, 243
vicious cycle pattern in, 183–186
with young children, 134–138
Family therapy theory, integration
    with individual diagnosis and
    treatment, 3
Family violence. *See* Child abuse;
    Domestic violence; Violence/
    abuse
Family-based interventions, reviews
    of, 85–86
Fears/worries, child's versus adult's,
    224
Feedback, client-focused, 100
Feelings, therapist, 4
Feminist family therapy, 74
Fierce with Age, 171*t*
5As, for using research/literature,
    257–258, 260–261
Friendship Line, 171*t*
Future of family therapy, 275–292
    for children/adolescents, 279
    emerging treatment trends in,
        282–289
        evidence-based treatments,
            282–283
        in genetics and neuroscience,
            287–289
        globalization and, 286–287
        technology-related, 283–286
    healthcare reform in, 277–282,
        277*f*
    payment models in, 280–281
    and personal/professional journey
        of therapist, 290–292

pertinent issues for beginning
    clinicians, 276–277
team approach and, 279–280
and therapist benefits/liabilities,
    290
treatment authorization in,
    280–281

G

Gay/lesbian couples, counseling of,
    202–205
Gender issues, 135
Gender socialization, 74–75
General systems theory, 82
Genetic disorders, mental illness
    and, 208
Genetics
    child/adolescent problems and,
        129–130
    and future of family therapy,
        287–289
    in mental disorders, 288–289
    and response to psychotropic
        medications, 210
Genograms, 67, 87, 88*f*
    developing, 116–117, 118*f*, 119–120
    in premarital counseling, 202
Getting unstuck in therapy, 235–261.
    See also Stuckness in therapy
    by matching directness level to
        client, 239
    supervision resources and,
        254–256
    using research and literature,
        256–261, 259*t*–260*t*
    using self-supervision questions,
        256, 257*t*
Gifts, client, 267
Globalization, and future of family
    therapy, 286–287
Go Wish card game, 169*t*
Grieving
    support during, 169*t*, 172*t*
    therapy for, 174
Group norms, assumptions about, 76

H

Harm, assessing potential for, 47–53
Harvard Center on the Developing
    Child, 209
Healthcare agencies, and stuckness
    in therapy, 251–254
Healthcare reform, and future of
    family therapy, 277–282,
    277*f*
Heredity, child/adolescent problems
    and, 129–130
Hidden agendas, 225
Hope, mobilizing, 121–122
HOPE assessment tool, 72–73
Human development, early
    interventions and, 289
Hypotheses
    developing, 46
    family structure as source for, 67
    forming, 21–22
    in treatment plan, 89

I

Identified patient (IP), 45–46
Illness, suicide risk and, 49*t*
Impulse control disorders, 127,
    231–234
    screening instruments for,
    293–294
Individual diagnoses
    common, 215–217, 215*t*
    in family context, 212–217
Infants/toddlers, family therapy with,
    134–138
Infidelity, couple therapy and,
    193–194
Information, release of, 46
Initial contact, suggestions for,
    14–16
Initial interview, 24–42
    assessing and building motivation,
    37–40
    defining client expectations in,
    33–37

developing connection with client,
    25–32
establishing credibility in, 40–42
period preceding. *See* Preinterview
    issues
stages of, 24–25
Intake forms, 16–17, 18*f*, 19*f*
Interactional patterns, negative,
    identifying and interrupting,
    115–116
International Family Therapy
    Association, 286–287
Internet
    in future of family therapy,
    283–286
    infidelity and, 193
    pornography and, 194
Interventions
    choosing, 123
    content versus process of, 122–123
    early, human development and,
    289
    increasing sophistication in,
    122–123
    pacing, 111–112
    paradoxical, 239
    rushing, 102–105
    in termination process, 266–267
    therapist reluctance to implement,
    239–240
    See also Family therapy
Intimate terrorism. *See* Patriarchal
    terrorism

J

JOIMAT mnemonic, 63
Joining
    with client, 25–27
    with couple system, 177–181, 178*f*
*Journal of Marital and Family
    Therapy*
    recommended articles from, 128
    reviews of family-based
    interventions, 85–86
Journals, international, 286–287

L

Legal issues
  avoiding, 13
  with suspected violence/abuse,
    56–57
LGBT individuals, discrimination
  against, 203
Limit setting, 10
Lineal questions, 107
Listening, in preinterview session, 15
Literature review, 5As for evaluating,
  257–258, 260–261
Lithium, for bipolar disorder, 97t
Loneliness, as predictor of decline,
  213
Love languages, teaching, 202

M

Mania, drug treatment for, 96t
Manic-depressive disorder. See
  Bipolar disorder
Marital adjustment, assessing, 70
Marital evaluation, 182–183
Marital problems, suicide risk and,
  49t
Marital separations, structured,
  198–199
Marital therapy, for anxiety
  disorders, 224
Meaning, assessing for, 65–66
Mediation, and divorce and child
  custody, 151–152
Medication consultations, 90–93
Medication management, 3
Medications
  for ADHD/impulse control
    disorders, 233
  attitudes toward, 90–91
  cautious use of, 90–91
  factors in choosing, 91–92
  for mental illness, 210
Mental health agencies, and
  stuckness in therapy, 251–254
Mental health services, in U. S., 278

Mental illness, 207–234
  alcoholism and drug abuse,
    226–231
  anxiety, 222–226
  biological role in, 3, 92–93
  common, 215–217, 215t
  in couple therapy, 187–188
  depression, 217–222
  environmental factors and,
    207–209
  environmental risks for, 129–130
  family influence on course of,
    210–211
  family support and, 213–214
  genetic transmission of, 210
  impulse disorders/
    neurodevelopmental
    disorders, 231–234
  individual diagnosis in family
    context, 212–217
  individual/family concepts and,
    208–211
  neuroscience research and,
    288–289
  overall health and, 209
  prevalence, age at onset,
    proportion seeking help, 215t
  prevalence of, 212
  prevention of, 208–209
  Research Domain Criteria (RDoC)
    and, 208
  research on, 209–210
  suicide risk and, 49t
  and syndromes versus everyday
    problems, 212–213
  See also Alcoholism/drug
    abuse; Anxiety/anxiety
    disorders; Depression;
    Impulse control disorders/
    neurodevelopmental
    disorders
Mental status exam (MSE), 62–63
Meta-emotions, in couple therapy,
  190–191
Michigan Alcoholism Screening Test
  (MAST), 59
Mirtazapine, primer on, 94t

Monoamine oxidase inhibitors (MAOIs), primer on, 94t–95t
Mood disorders
  prevalence, age at onset, proportion seeking help, 215t
  questions for identifying, 217
  screening instruments for, 293
Motivation
  assessing and building, 37–40
  factors affecting, 38
  therapist versus client, 39
Motivational interviewing, 38
Music therapy, in end of life care, 169t

N

Narrative therapy, for anxiety disorders, 224
National Hospice and Palliative Care Organization, 172t
National Institute of Mental Health (NIMH), research of, 208
National Institute on Aging, 170t
Nefazodone, primer on, 94t
Neurodevelopmental disorders, 127, 231–234
Neurological factors. See Biological/ neurological factors
Neuropsychiatric testing, 63–64
Neuropsychological evaluations, for children/adolescents, 129
Neuroscience, and future of family therapy, 287–289
Normalizing, 109
No-shows, dealing with, 245–247

O

Obsessive–compulsive disorder, 223. See also Anxiety/anxiety disorders
Older adults, 157–175
  aerobic exercise for, 162
  ageism and, 158
  anticipatory loss and, 167
  anxiety and depression in, 160–161
  assessment and treatment of, 158–165
  barriers to treatment of, 158–159
  client resources for, 170t–171t
  cognitive-behavioral therapy for, 162
  collaborative care and, 159
  death of, family grief and, 168, 174–175
  enhancing social contacts of, 161
  family caregiving for, 165–175
    at end of life, 167–168
    resources for, 168
  family/caregiver resources and, 172t–173t
  illness and losses and, 162–163
  life review therapy and, 162
  percentage of world population, 158
  physical decline and disability in, 163–165
  and referrals to therapy, 159–160
  therapist resources for, 169t–170t
  therapy options for, 160–161
Oppositional defiant disorder, 231–232
Outcome Rating Scale (ORS), 100

P

Panic disorder, 224
Paper Office for the Digital Age, The, 17
Paradoxical interventions, 239
Parental conflict, 150–151
Parent–child dyads, assessing, 68
Parents
  custodial versus noncustodial, 150
  involvement of, 139–140
  midlife concerns of, 142–144
Partners for Change Outcome Management System (PCOMS), 100

Patriarchal terrorism, 53, 192
versus common couple violence, 54
Perpetrators, male, therapy considerations, 54
Personality disorders, screening instruments for, 295
Porn addiction, treating, 196–197
Pornography, couple therapy and, 194–197
Positive Aging Newsletter, 171*t*
Posttraumatic stress disorder (PTSD), management versus cure of, 223
Practice-based evidence, 99–100
Preinterview issues, 12–23, 17, 20–21
determining who participates in therapy, 17, 20–21
family expectations/anxieties, 12–14
initial contact with family, 14–16
initial hypothesizing, 21–22
necessary information/intake form, 16–17, 18*f*–19*f*
Premarital counseling, 200–202
Premarital inventories, 200–201
Presenting problem
exploring, 45–46
in treatment plan, 88
Prevention and Relationship Enhancement Program (PREP), 189–190
Priorities, setting, 81. *See also* Treatment focus
Problems, prioritizing, 81
Problems/goals/interventions, in treatment plan, 89–90
Propranolol, primer on, 96*t*
Psychiatrist, referrals to, 216
Psychoeducational information, offering, 114
Psychological ABCs, 64–65
Psychological assessment, 64–66
Psychological testing, indications and contraindications for, 93, 98
Psychological testing consultations, 93, 98–99

Psychopathology, individual, in couple therapy, 187–188
Psychosis
hallmark signs of, 216
screening instruments for, 294
Psychotherapist, referrals to, 214
Psychotherapy, primer on, 95*t*
Psychotic disorders, 216
drugs for, 97*t*–98*t*
Psychotropic drug primer, 94*t*–98*t*
Psychotropic medications
attitudes toward, 90–91
for children/adolescents, 129
lack of therapist training in, 91
for mental illness, 210

Q

Questions, types of, 107–109

R

Racial/ethnic issues, 75–76
Referrals
to psychiatrist, 216
to psychotherapist, 214
Reflexive questions, 108–109
Reframing, 109–110
Relational ambiguity, in gay and lesbian relationships, 203
Relationship evaluation, 182–183
Relationship separations, structured, 198–199
Relationships
developing with client, 25–27
family, 67–69
as motivation for therapy, 13–14
See also Therapist–client relationship
Religion, as factor in therapy, 72–73
Research
on ADHD, 128–129
on alcoholism/drug abuse, 227–228
on difficult cases, 256–258, 259*t*–260*t*, 260–261

Research *(cont.)*
  5As for evaluating, 257–258,
    260–261
  on mental illness, 209–210
  neuroscience, 288–289
  online, 284–285
  questions for evaluating, 259*t*–260*t*
  on trauma, 223
Research Domain Criteria (RDoC),
    208
Resistance, client, 236–238
Respecting Choices, 170*t*

S

Safety issues
  duty-to-warn and, 57–58
  during therapy with young
    children, 137
Same-sex couples, counseling of,
    202–205
School system, family therapy and,
    138–142
School-age children, family therapy
    with, 138–142
Scope-of-practice issues, 15
Screening instruments, 293–295
  for addictive behaviors, 294
  for anxiety disorders, 293
  couple measures, 295
  for depression/anxiety, 214
  for eating disorders, 294
  family measures, 295
  for impulse control disorders,
    293–294
  for mood disorders, 293
  for personality disorders, 295
  for psychosis, 294
  for somatization, 295
  for spirituality, 295
  for trauma, 294
Secrets, handling, 248–249
Selective serotonin reuptake
    inhibitors (SSRIs), primer on,
    94*t*

Self-care, therapist, 11
Self-disclosure, using/nonusing,
    105–107
Self-doubts, dealing with, 11
Self-reports, for assessing meaning,
    66
Self-supervision, questions for, 256,
    257*t*
Serotonin and norepinephrine
    reuptake inhibitors (SNRIs),
    primer on, 94*t*
Sexual abuse, of children, 55–56
Sexual difficulties, couple therapy
    and, 197–198
Sexual history, 197
Sexuality, in therapist–client
    relationship, 244–245
Single-parent families, 152–154
Skill acquisition, 7
Social assessment, 66–71
  of family system, 66–69
Social systems, outside family,
    assessing, 73–74
Solutions, attempted, 46–47
Somatic symptom disorder, 216–217
Somatization, screening instruments
    for, 295
Somatization disorders, 216
"Speaker–listener" technique, 190
Spiritual assessment, 72–73, 295
Spouses, in treatment of anxiety
    disorders, 224
Stepfamilies, 154–156
Strategic questions, 108
Strengths, focusing on, 2
Stress
  and child's developing brain, 209
  therapist, 9–11
Stressful life events, assessing for, 47
Structural family therapy, for anxiety
    disorders, 224
Structure, establishing, 79–80
Stuckness in therapy
  agency contributions to, 251–254
  and ambivalence about change,
    236–238

and cancellations and no-shows, 245–247

change versus acceptance and, 241–242

countertransference and, 242–245

and difficulty getting family members to therapy, 247–248

secrets and, 248–249

and therapist dislike of client, 249–251

and therapist lack of conceptual clarity, 240–241

and therapist reluctance to intervene, 239–240

and therapist–client agenda/timing mismatch, 238

See also Getting unstuck in therapy

Substance abuse

assessing for, 58–60

developmental view of, 228

overlooking, 59

prevalence, age at onset, proportion seeking help, 215*t*

See also Alcoholism/drug abuse

Substance Abuse and Mental Health Services Administration (SAMSHA), 60

Suicidal ideation, discussing with family, 52–53

Suicide

assessing potential for, 48, 49*t*–51*t*, 51–53

demographics of, 48, 49*t*–50*t*

misconceptions about, 48

prevention of, 52

warning signs of, 50*t*–51*t*

Supervision

role in getting unstuck in therapy, 254–256

self-, questions for, 256, 257*t*

Support, providing, 110

Support network

importance of, 10–11

outside family, 73–74

Systems theory, 82

T

Talk therapies, complementary approaches to, 3

Tarasoff v. Regents of the University of California, 56–58

Technology

in future of family therapy, 283–286

impacts on families, 145–146

Teenage Brain: A Neuroscientist's Survival Guide to Raising Adolescents and Young Adults, The (Jensen & Nutt), 145

Termination, 262–274

client, 271–274

client disagreement about, 264–265

goals of, 265

mutual, 263–268

as process, 265–266

role of, 263

special issues in, 267–268

therapeutic interventions in, 266–267

therapist, 269–271

timing of, 264–265

and transference of case, 269–270

Terrorism, patriarchal, 53, 192

Testing

psychological, 93, 98

See also Screening instruments

Theoretical models

integrating into therapy, 81–84

role of, 83–84

Therapist

beliefs and reactions to domestic violence, 192–193

benefits and liabilities of, 290

comfort with gay/lesbian couples, 203–204

countertransference and, 242–245

credibility of, 40–42

directness of, matching to client, 239

Therapist *(cont.)*
  and dislike for client, 249–251
  and "do-something" syndrome,
    103
  and fears for personal safety, 53
  goals of, versus client goals,
    35–36
  intentions for self-disclosure,
    106–107
  and lack of conceptual clarity,
    240–241
  motivation of, 39
  personal and professional journey
    of, 290–292
  and reluctance to intervene,
    239–240
  staying current with individual
    diagnoses, 214
  support role of, 110
  terminations initiated by, 269–271
Therapist development, stages of,
  6–9
Therapist-as-self, exploring, 8–9
Therapist–client relationship
  agenda and timing mismatch in,
    238
  continuing after termination,
    267–268
  control issues in, 244
  as most critical variable, 102–103
  self-disclosure in, 105–107
  sexuality in, 244–245
  therapeutic nature of, 5
  transference/countertransference
    in, 243
Therapy. *See* Family therapy;
    Treatment focus; Treatment
    plan
Therapy effectiveness, evaluating,
  99–100
Time line, developing, 120–121
Time-outs, in couple therapy, 189,
  192
Transcranial magnetic stimulation
  (TMS), 95*t*

Transference, by client, 243
Trauma
  research on, 223
  screening instruments for, 294
Trauma and stressor disorders,
  223
Trazodone, primer on, 94*t*
Treatment effectiveness, evaluating,
  99–100
Treatment focus, 78–86
  conceptual map in, 81–86
  obstacles to, 79–81
Treatment plan, components of,
  86–99, 87*t*
  biopsychosocial systems
    assessment, 88–89
  clinical hypotheses, 89
  DSM diagnosis, 89
  genogram, 87, 88*f*
  medication consultations, 90–93,
    94*t*–98*t*
  presenting problem, 88
  problems/goals/interventions,
    89–90
  psychological testing
    consultations, 93, 98–99
Tricyclic antidepressants (TCAs),
  primer on, 94*t*
Trust, communicating, 104

U

United States, mental health
    controversies in, 278

V

Vicious cycles
  identifying and altering,
    183–186
  mental illness and, 188
Video conferencing, in future of
    family therapy, 285

Video games, problems with, 146
Vilazodone, primer on, 94*t*
Violence/abuse
   ACTION for assessment of, 58
   assessing for, 53–57
   against elders, 56
   See also Child abuse; Domestic
      violence
Vortioxetine, primer on, 94*t*

W

Wechsler Intelligence Scale for
   Children, 3rd edition, 128
Well Spouse Association, 172*t*
World Health Organization (WHO)
   mental health care pyramid of,
      277–278, 277*f*
   mental health program of, 209

Made in the USA
Columbia, SC
12 October 2023

24354099R00189